Level 3

PRACTICAL GRAMMAR

John Hughes and Ceri Jones

HEINLE
CENGAGE Learning

Australia • Brazil • Japan • Korea • Mexico • Singapore • Spain • United Kingdom • United States

Practical Grammar Level 3
John Hughes and Ceri Jones
Series devised by David Riley

Publisher: Jason Mann

Commissioning Editor: Carol Goodwright

Development Editor: Louisa Essenhigh

Consultants: Phillip Kerr, Mary Rigby

Senior Marketing Manager:
Ruth McAleavey

Senior Content Project Editor: Natalie Griffith

Manufacturing Team Lead: Paul Herbert

Art Editor: Emma Whyte

Cover Designer: Adam Renvoize

Text Designer: Rouli Manias

Compositor: MPS Limited, A Macmillan Company

Audio: James Richardson

Dedication

The original concept for the *Practical Grammar* series was David Riley's. David was a well-known and highly respected ELT author, teacher and publisher. He died before the Practical Grammar books were completed but the memory of David inspired everyone working on the project.

ISBN: 978-1-4240-1807-9 [with answers]
ISBN: 978-1-4240-1806-2 [without answers]

Heinle ELT, Cengage Learning EMEA
Cheriton House
North Way
Andover
Hampshire
SP10 5BE
United Kingdom

Cengage Learning is a leading provider of customised learning solutions with office locations around the globe, including Singapore, the United Kingdom, Australia, Mexico, Brazil and Japan. Locate our local office at: **international.cengage.com/region**

Cengage Learning products are represented in Canada by Nelson Education, Ltd.

Visit Heinle online at **elt.heinle.com**
Visit our corporate website at **cengage.com**

Printed in China
1 2 3 4 5 6 7 8 9 10 – 14 13 12 11 10

Contents

Contents

Contents

Introduction

Welcome to *Practical Grammar* Level 3. This is the third in a series of grammar books for students of English. Level 3 introduces grammar to students at intermediate to upper-intermediate level. It aims to:

- teach all the key grammar at intermediate – upper-intermediate level.
- improve accuracy with grammar.
- help students use grammar in real-life situations, including conversations.

Organisation of the book

Practical Grammar Level 3 has 100 units and is organised into blocks of five units. Each block is made up of four main units focusing on one area of grammar and a review unit. After every ten units, there is a progress test at the back of the book to check understanding. You'll also find extra useful information in the appendices (pages 232–245) and an index (pages 277–284) for quick reference. A key feature of the book is the CDs which you can use to listen to the conversations in the book and improve your pronunciation of grammar items.

Using *Practical Grammar* Level 3

Practical Grammar Level 3 is ideal for use as self study or in the classroom with a teacher. Some students may want to begin at unit 1 and work through the units in order. Other students may prefer to choose specific areas of grammar from the contents pages and index, and focus on those areas first. (Use the contents or the index to do this.) If you want to use *Practical Grammar* Level 3 as a supplementary study book with your classroom course, you can also select particular units to match the lessons.

Grammar in real contexts

The rules of grammar are important but it's also important to see the grammar being used in a real-life situation. For this reason, each unit introduces the grammar through a short conversation or text. After the presentation of the grammar, there are exercises that practise the new language in authentic contexts with recordings on the CDs to hear the language in use.

Study at home (to the student)

This book helps you understand English grammar. Here are some ideas for using *Practical Grammar* Level 3:

- Study the grammar regularly. For example, complete one unit every day. Read the introductory conversation or text and study the presentation of the grammar. Then complete the exercises and listen to the CDs.
- Complete the review unit and check you understand the grammar by doing the progress tests (pages 212–231).
- Study with a friend. Do the units together and read some of the conversations aloud.
- If you find some of the grammar in a unit especially difficult, it's a good idea to repeat the unit.

- Remember that grammar isn't the only part of English. If you find new words in *Practical Grammar* Level 3, check them in your dictionary and write them down.

- Use the online component my*pg* at **myelt.heinle.com**. The activities allow you to continue working with all the grammar in new contexts. There is a gradebook where you can build up a picture of your progress.

In the classroom (to the teacher)

Students can use *Practical Grammar* Level 3 for self study but you can also use it in class. It is aimed at students at intermediate and upper-intermediate levels.

If you are using a course book, *Practical Grammar* Level 3 will be a useful supplementary grammar book as it reflects the order of the grammar often taught on many courses.

Ask students to read the conversation or text at the beginning of the unit. If there is a conversation, you could ask two students to read it aloud to the class. Then read through the presentation of the grammar and deal with any questions the students might have.

As students work through the exercises, monitor their progress and help out with any questions they have. Students could also work in pairs or small groups for some exercises and compare their answers. In some units, the final exercise asks students to personalise the grammar and write their own sentences. Afterwards, ask some students to read theirs aloud or to compare with a partner.

If you have done the first four units of a section in class, you could set the review unit for homework. However, the review unit also includes help with pronunciation and listening linked to the grammar, so sometimes you might want to work on these as a class.

The progress tests (pages 212–231) check students' progress after every ten units. You can use these in class to monitor how much students have learnt. If students have particular difficulties with certain parts of the test, you will be able to see if they need to work on any of the units again.

Also note that for further practice you can use the online component my*pg*. This component has a Content Management System, which allows you to set specific exercises to be completed in a set time. When students 'submit' the exercises, their scores appear in the gradebook, allowing you to see how each student is progressing.

There are two CDs at the back of the book. They contain all the listening and pronunciation activities. Use them to help students hear the grammar in use and also for revision of the forms.

Overview of *Practical Grammar* Level 3

The units

Every unit is made up of two pages and has a similar format so it's easy to follow.

Title

The title tells you the main grammar area. Some units also have subtitles to give extra information.

Context

Practical Grammar teaches you how to use grammar in real situations. Each unit starts with a conversation or a short text to show the grammar in context. Read this first.

Presentation

The presentation explains the rules of the grammar and has information on the form, meaning and use of the grammar with example sentences. Use the presentation to help you complete the exercises.

Tip

This gives you extra information about the grammar in real situations.

Review units

At the end of every block of four units, there is a review unit.

Grammar

This section gives extra practice of all the grammar in the four units. It's also a good way to check progress.

Grammar in context

It's important to be able to recognise and use grammar in real situations, so this section provides practice with the grammar from all four units in an authentic context.

Pronunciation

It's important to know the rules of grammar but you also need to be able to say the grammatical forms correctly. *Practical Grammar* includes a pronunciation practice section with recordings.

Listen again

A key feature of *Practical Grammar* is the listening practice. Listening is a great way to learn a new language. Here you listen again to one of the recordings from the four units and become more confident with the grammar in context.

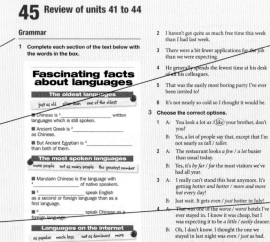

Exercises

Exercises

1 Write the words in the correct order to make sentences.

1 home when I'll get you I call.
I'll call you when I get home.

2 my work I until won't finished I've come out.

3 Sue I'll next time her I speak to see.

4 the dinner you cooked I'll get home have by the time.

5 text the station us they'll get to before.

6 I a chance as soon as get I'll to the boss speak.

7 the dishes do the football I'll after finished has.

8 be once I the exams won't finish so busy.

2 **2.12** Choose the correct form of the verbs. Then listen and check.

A: Have you spoken to Tim yet?
B: No, sorry, I forgot. I ¹*call* / *'ll call* him as soon as I ²*'ve finished* / *'ll have finished* this email.
A: No, don't worry. I ³*see* / *'ll see* him this afternoon when he ⁴*comes* / *'ll come* to get his stuff.
A: Come on! The shops ⁵*are* / *'ll be* closed by the time we ⁶*get* / *'ll get* there if you ⁷*don't* / *won't* hurry up a bit!
B: OK, I'm coming. Don't panic, we ⁸*'re* / *'ll be* there in plenty of time.
A: I ⁹*get* / *'ll get* your dinner ready for you for when you ¹⁰*arrive* / *'ll arrive*.
B: No thanks, Mum. We ¹¹*'ve had* / *'ll have had* something to eat before we ¹²*leave* / *'ll leave*.

3 Complete the sentences using *if* or *when*. In two sentences, both answers are possible.

1 We won't go to the beach this afternoon .... it rains.
2 We'll tell you all about it .... we see you.
3 .... you get there before me, you'll have to ask the neighbour for the key.
4 What are we going to do .... the train's late?
5 It's been a long day. We're going to be exhausted .... we get home.
6 .... you don't get a good night's sleep, you'll be exhausted in the morning.
7 .... you've finished your dinner, you can watch some TV.
8 What are you going to do .... you grow up?

4 Complete these sentences so that they are true for you.

1 When I finish this exercise, I'm going to ....
2 If I've got enough time later today, I'll ....
3 I'll .... when I've finished ....
4 I won't .... until I ....
5 I'll be happy with my English when ....

127

Exercises

Every unit gives lots of practice with the grammar. Always start with exercise 1 because it helps with learning the form of the grammar. Later exercises help you to understand its meaning.

Listening

A really useful feature in *Practical Grammar* is the recordings. Most units include a listening exercise so you can listen to the completed exercise and hear the grammar in a real situation.

Grammar in context

5 Choose the correct options to complete the text below.

MARCH ISSUE

Health tip of the week: slow down, lose weight!

The faster you eat, ¹*the more* / *more* you eat, so if you want to lose weight, you'd better start slowing down. Medical researchers in Athens have found that the more slowly you eat, ²*the more time* / *the less time* your stomach has to produce natural hormones that tell you that you're full. As a result, you don't feel as hungry and you eat ³*least* / *less*. A group of volunteers were asked to eat 300ml of ice cream, some faster and others much ⁴*slowly* / *more slowly*. Their blood was tested before and after eating, and then

at intervals to measure the levels of hormones. Those volunteers who ate ⁵*the faster* / *the fastest* had the lowest levels of hormones in their blood, which meant that they felt twice ⁶*hungrier* / *as hungry* as the volunteers who had eaten their ice cream at half the pace. They ⁷*felt like* / *felt as* they could still eat more, while the slower eaters felt that they'd eaten ⁸*more* enough / *more* than enough. So, the lesson is, eat ⁹*slower* / *as slowly as you can*, enjoy what you're eating and lose weight at the same time!

Eat slowly, say experts.

Pronunciation: *as ... as ...* weak form

6 **1.48** Listen to the first two sentences with *as ... as ...*. Notice the pronunciation of *as* and the stress on the main content words.

    /əz/   /əz/
1 The children were as good as gold.

    /əz/   /əz/
2 This is definitely not as easy as I thought.

Now listen to the other sentences and underline the stressed words.

3 I'll get it done as soon as I possibly can.
4 Her hair was as white as snow.
5 The concert wasn't nearly as good as last time.
6 Watch out for him! He's as cunning as a fox.
7 There's no hurry. Take as much time as you want.
8 There weren't quite as many people as we'd expected.

Listen again and repeat the sentences.
Remember to stress the main content words.

Listen again

7 **1.49** Listen to three short conversations and answer the questions.

Conversation 1: Why doesn't Nick like his new job?

Conversation 2: Why does Sue tell the driver to slow down?

101

Progress tests

After every ten units, there is a progress test (see pages 212–231).

Appendices

These have more useful information on spelling and punctuation. There are also summaries of the key grammar areas, including verb forms and phrasal verbs (see pages 232–245).

Index

Use the index to find items of grammar quickly and help with terminology (see pages 277–284).

my*pg*

This online component provides extra practice of all the language covered in the book through a wide range of exercise types.

1 Present simple
Adverbs and expressions of frequency

He shoots!

It says here that the average human walks 150,000 km in a lifetime. That's four times round the Earth. I don't believe it! You never walk anywhere.

I'm not average.

I agree.

It's a typical Saturday afternoon in the Smith house. Suddenly, Mrs Smith interrupts Mr Smith's favourite pastime …

Presentation

Common uses

You use the present simple to talk about:

- facts (things that are generally or currently true): *The average human **walks** over 150,000 km in a lifetime.*

- habits, routines and regularly repeated events: *I **walk** to work every day. You never **walk** anywhere.*

- states, thoughts and feelings: *I **don't believe** it!*

See Unit 3: Stative verbs

Other uses

You often use the present simple:

- with performative verbs (these are verbs which describe the action you are performing, e.g. *apologise, promise, refuse*): *I **agree**. / I **disagree**.*

- to tell stories, jokes and anecdotes: *It's a typical Saturday afternoon in the Smith house. Suddenly, Mrs Smith **interrupts** Mr Smith's favourite pastime …*

- to describe the plot of a book or film and to review them: *The film **begins** in a jungle in Borneo. Daniel Craig **plays** a hunter …*

- to commentate on sporting or special events: *He **runs** to the penalty spot and he **shoots**!*

*The President **walks** to the Queen and the two heads of state meet for the first time.*

- to give instructions, demonstrations or directions: *You **mix** the eggs, milk and butter in a bowl …*

See page 233: Spelling rules

Adverbs and expressions of frequency

You often use adverbs and expressions of frequency with the present simple: *You **never walk** anywhere.*

Adverbs of frequency (*always, frequently, normally, often, regularly, occasionally, sometimes, rarely, hardly ever, seldom, never*) normally come before the main verb but after the verb *to be*:

*You **never walk** anywhere.* (don't say *You ~~walk never~~ anywhere.*)

*I'm **often** at home on Saturdays.* (don't say *I ~~often am~~ at home on Saturdays.*)

Expressions of frequency such as *once a week, every Monday, twice an hour* can come at the beginning or the end of the sentence: *I walk to work **once a week**. **Once a week**, I walk to work.*

Exercises

1 Complete the article using the verbs in the box in the present simple.

> brush   carry   eat   have   love   ~~make~~   spend   watch

WOWMAG! WOWMAG! WOWMAG! WOWMAG! WOWMAG! WOWMAG! WOWMAG!

Are you average?
The average human ...

- ★ [1] _makes_ 1,140 telephone calls every year.
- ★ [2] _____ a minimum of two hours of TV every day.
- ★ often [3] _____ more than three dreams a night.
- ★ female [4] _____ three kilos of lipstick in her bag over a lifetime.
- ★ [5] _____ two weeks of their life waiting for a traffic light to turn green.
- ★ normally [6] _____ their teeth with a blue toothbrush.
- ★ [7] _____ eight spiders in their lifetime while they're asleep.
- ★ [8] _____ reading useless facts!

2 🔊 1.02 Read parts of different TV programmes. Write the words in brackets in the present simple. Then listen and check.

Comedy show

There [1] _____ (be) this man and he [2] _____ (go) to his doctor and [3] _____ (ask): 'Doctor, Doctor. Why [4] _____ (everyone/call) me a liar?' The doctor [5] _____ (look) at him and [6] _____ (reply): 'I [7] _____ (not/believe) you.'

Sports programme

It [8] _____ (not/look) good for the opponents of the two Williams sisters. Surely, it [9] _____ (not/be) possible to survive match point against the powerful serve of Venus. She [10] _____ (study) the ball and then she [11] _____ (serve). It's all over! The two sisters [12] _____ (celebrate) an easy victory.

Cookery show

[13] _____ (you/ have) problems with your kitchen knives? Perhaps they [14] _____ (not/cut) the way you want. Well now you [15] _____ (not/need) to worry. The new 'Goliath' [16] _____ (slice) through any type of meat every time.

3 Write the words in the correct order to make sentences.

1 I long once holiday take a a year.

2 late you are always why?

3 isn't always sunny it here.

4 he times practises the piano three a week.

5 canoeing every they weekend do go?

6 misses from work rarely a day Robert.

4 Complete each sentence in your own words using the present simple.

1 Once a week, I _____ .

2 I don't believe _____ .

3 My favourite film begins _____ .

4 To get to my house from the station, you _____ .

2 Present continuous
Comparison with present simple

Presentation

Use the present continuous:

- to talk about temporary events and actions in progress at the moment of speaking:
  *The bus **is coming**!*

- to talk about repeated events over a specific period of time (around now but not necessarily at the moment of speaking):
  *The buses **aren't stopping** at the station this week.*

- to talk about trends and changing situations:
  *Public transport **is getting** really expensive!*

- with *always* to emphasise the frequency of a habitual action (and sometimes to express annoyance):
  *They're **always digging** up these roads.*

- to describe background events in a story when the present simple describes the main events:
  *A woman **is waiting** for her bus when a young man turns to her and asks…*

See Unit 58: Present continuous for future reference

Time expressions

We often use the present continuous tense with time expressions such as: *now, at the moment, currently, today, this week, nowadays,* etc.

See page 233: Spelling rules

See page 235: Summary of present continuous

Present simple or present continuous?

Present simple	Present continuous
Facts/things that are generally true: *The bus stops at the train station.*	Happening now: *The bus is coming!*
Routines: *The bus comes every day.*	Regularly repeated events over a period of time (around now): *The buses aren't stopping at the station this week.*
Regular change: *Public transport gets more expensive every year.*	Changing situation: *Public transport is getting more expensive.*
With *always* meaning 'every time': *They always dig up the road in the summer.*	With *always* meaning 'all the time': *They're always digging up the road in the summer.*
The main events in a story: *… a young man turns to her and asks …*	To describe the background events in the story: *A woman is waiting for her bus when …*

Exercises

1 Look at the pictures. Complete the descriptions of the people using the present continuous. Use the negative form where necessary.

1 Lots of people ___are looking for___ (look for) work these days.

2 He _____ (study) for his English exam.

3 The price of things _____ (always/go up).

4 They _____ (always/work) late.

2 🔊 **1.03** Choose the correct options. Then listen and check.

A: What [1]*do you watch / are you watching*?

B: A really good film about a scientist. One day he [2]*works / 's working* with insects when he suddenly [3]*discovers / is discovering* he can make them bigger.

A: Sounds great. [4]*Is it / Is it being* nearly over?

B: I don't know. Why?

A: Manchester United [5]*play / are playing* Barcelona. Can I change channels?

B: No, you can't. You [6]*always watch / 're always watching* the football. It's so boring! I [7]*never watch / 'm never watching* anything I like.

A: But you [8]*enjoy / 're enjoying* football.

B: That's not true. When you aren't here, [9]*I don't watch / I'm not watching* it.

3 Make sentences with the words. Use the present simple or the present continuous.

1 They / currently / develop
   ___They are currently developing___ a new type of medicine for the flu.

2 The postman / deliver / our letters
   _____ once a day.

3 You / always / talk
   _____ during the movie. It's so annoying!

4 This room / be / always / cold
   _____ .

5 Why / my course fees / go up
   _____ again this term?

6 It's night time and the wind / blow
   _____ when there's a loud scream in the air ...

3 Stative verbs
With the present simple and present continuous

Normally, he isn't well behaved.   **But today he's being very well behaved.**

Presentation

There are two types of main verbs: *dynamic* and *stative*.

Dynamic verbs

You use dynamic verbs to talk about actions or events. You can use them to talk about facts/routines and actions that are in progress:

*I **talk** to my students individually once a term.* (= routine)

*Sorry, I**'m talking** to a student right now. Can we talk later?* (= action in progress)

Stative verbs

You use ***stative verbs*** to talk about states. These include talking about existence (*be, exist*), beliefs and opinions (*know, think, understand*) and possession (*have got, belong*):

*I**'m** from England.* (= existence)

*I **know** what you mean.* (= belief)

*I**'ve got** one brother and two sisters.* (= possession)

Some stative verbs are only used in the present simple and *not* in the present continuous:

*Ask me. I **know** the answer!* (don't say *Ask me. I'm knowing the answer!*)

*Speak more slowly. I **don't understand** English very well.* (don't say *Speak more slowly. I'm not understanding English very well.*)

*You **seem distracted** today.* (don't say *You're seeming distracted today.*)

*This house **belongs** to my grandmother.* (don't say *This house is belonging to my grandmother.*)

*I **don't believe** you!* (don't say *I'm not believing you!*)

*I'm sorry but I **don't agree** with you.* (don't say *I'm sorry but I'm not agreeing with you.*)

You can use some stative verbs in both the present simple and the present continuous:

* in the present simple the verb describes a general state or situation:

   *Normally, he **isn't** well behaved.* (= generally true)

   *What **do you think** about the situation?* (= general opinion)

* in the present continuous the verb describes a temporary state or new situation:

   *He**'s being** very well behaved today.* (= temporary situation)

   *I'm not sure. I**'m thinking** about it.* (= in progress)

Changes in meaning

The meaning of some verbs can change because they can be both stative and dynamic, e.g. *have*:

Stative: *I **have** a shower.* (= I own a shower.)

Dynamic: *I**'m having** a shower.* (= I'm taking a shower at the moment.) *I **have** a shower every morning.* (= I take a shower every morning.)

Other verbs that can change their meaning include: *come, love, appear, see* and *weigh*.

See page 241: Dynamic / Stative verbs

TIP The rules for using dynamic and stative verbs with the present simple or present continuous are also true for other tenses in the simple or continuous forms.

Exercises

1 Complete the sentences with A or B.

1	I see my colleagues ___B___	**A**	at the moment.
2	I'm seeing my colleagues ___A___	**B**	twice a week.
3	I'm weighing _____	**A**	the package.
4	I weigh _____	**B**	too much!
5	Jill and John come from _____	**A**	Canada via the USA.
6	Jill and John are coming from _____	**B**	Canada – Ottowa to be exact.
7	I think _____	**A**	about it.
8	One moment. I'm thinking _____	**B**	we should go.
9	Mandy is being clever _____	**A**	by saving all the money from her new job.
10	Mandy is clever _____	**B**	and always gets good grades.

2 ⏺**1.04** **Read this conversation. Find five more mistakes in the tourist's English. Then listen and check.**

Tourist: Hello. I'm trying to find Trafalgar Square but I ~~'m not knowing~~ *don't know* the way. Can you help me?

Local person: Sure. It's easy from here. Go straight on and turn left at the large bookshop on the corner.

Tourist: Sorry, I'm not understanding you. I'm not speaking English very well. Are you meaning straight up this road?

Local person: That's right.

Tourist: Thanks very much. Sorry for my English.

Local person: No, it's very good.

Tourist: Thank you, but I'm not believing you. I'm being in England for a month, so I hope it gets better.

Local person: I'm sure it will.

3 Choose the correct form of the verbs.

1. I *believe* / *'m believing* you might be right about this answer.
2. Give it back. It *belongs* / *'s belonging* to me.
3. I *love* / *'m loving* my new school. It's much better than my old one.
4. I'm sorry but I *don't agree* / *'m not agreeing* with you. I think you're wrong.
5. The Queen *owns* / *is owning* most of the land around here.
6. I *see* / *'m seeing* what you mean.
7. Matthew *sees* / *is seeing* someone about a new job. I hope he gets it.
8. A: Why are your neighbours *being* so difficult about your plans to add a new floor to your house?
   B: I *have* / *'m having* no idea. Jealousy, probably.

4 Write sentences that are true for you using both forms of the verbs.

1. I love _____ . I'm loving _____ .
2. I have _____ . I'm having _____ .
3. I think _____ . I'm thinking _____ .

4 Present perfect simple and present perfect continuous 1
For actions and situations in progress in the present

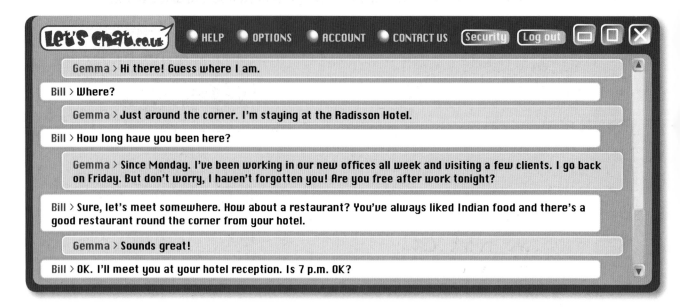

Presentation

You can use both the present perfect simple and the present perfect continuous to talk about an action, event or situation that started in the past and continues in the present:

I've been here since Monday. (I'm still here.)

I've been visiting clients all week. (I started on Monday and I'm still visiting clients.)

See page 235: Summary of present perfect

Present perfect simple or present perfect continuous?

You can use the present perfect simple or the present perfect continuous when you talk about general facts which are long term:

I've worked for this company all my life.

I've been working for this company all my life.

(Don't say *I work for this company all my life* or *I'm working for this company all my life*.)

You can use both forms with verbs such as *live, work, teach*.

You also use the present perfect simple with stative verbs: *How long have you been here?*

You use the present perfect continuous to talk about:

- something temporary: *I've been working in our new offices all week.*

- repeated actions: *I've been visiting clients every day.*

You usually use dynamic verbs in the present perfect continuous when talking about an action, or series of repeated actions, that is still in progress: *I've been talking to clients.*

how long, for / since

You often use the present perfect with *how long, for* and *since*. Use *for* to talk about a **period of time.** Use *since* with the **point in time** and **when it started**:

A: *How long **have** you **been** here?*

B: *For about an hour.*

A: *How long **have** you **been working** here?*

B: *Since I left school.*

See Unit 7: Present perfect simple and present perfect continuous 2

Exercises

1 **Write sentences about the pictures. Use the present perfect simple and *since* or *for*.**

1 They / be / in this traffic jam / hours
   They have been in this traffic jam for hours.

3 They / be married / 1957

2 I / have toothache / three hours

4 We / support / this team / we were children

2 **Rewrite these sentences using the present perfect continuous and *since* or *for*. Use the verb in brackets.**

1 We live in France. We moved here a month ago.
   We 've been living in France for a month . (live)

2 My uncle smokes. He began when he was a child.
   My uncle . (smoke)

3 Switch the TV off! You started watching it three hours ago.
   Switch the TV off! You . (watch)

4 How far is it to the campsite? We left home at nine this morning!
   How far is it to the campsite? We . (drive)

5 Jane's playing it again! She was practising the same piece of music yesterday.
   Jane . (practise)

3 **Write the verbs in brackets in the present perfect simple or present perfect continuous. Use the present perfect continuous where possible.**

1 Sorry, I didn't call you back. I 've been working (work) long hours every day this week.

2 Wow! I (not/see) you for ages. You look great!

3 How long (you/be) here?

4 How long (wait) for me?

5 I'm surprised you haven't seen them. They (stay) at the same hotel as you.

6 Sandra (want) to become a doctor since she was a child.

7 Frank (talk) about the new girl in his class ever since she arrived.

8 In my life, I (always/spend) too much time on unimportant things.

5 Review of units 1 to 4

Grammar

1 Tick the correct sentence, A or B.

1 A Does anyone here drives a red car?
   B Does anyone here drive a red car? ✓

2 A I live in this town for 20 years.
   B I've lived in this town for 20 years.

3 A That building's been there since the 1950s.
   B That building's been there for the 1950s.

4 A Come quick! They're showing our street on the news!
   B Come quick! They show our street on the news!

5 A He seems to be telling the truth.
   B He's seeming to be telling the truth.

6 A I work here all my life, but today is my last day.
   B I've worked here all my life, but today is my last day.

7 A I have my lunch with me.
   B I'm having my lunch with me.

8 A Every hour, the bell opposite my hotel room rings.
   B Every hour, the bell opposite my hotel room is ringing.

9 A For the last few days, I'm waking up with a headache.
   B For the last few days, I've been waking up with a headache.

10 A How long have you known about her illness?
   B How long have you been knowing about her illness?

2 Read the questions and the responses. Complete each question with the words in brackets. Change the verb form where necessary.

1 _____ for this company? (always/you/work)
   Yes, I have.

2 _____ for this company? (always/you/work)
   Yes, I do, but I also have other clients, too.

3 _____ for me? (he/wait)
   Yes, for ages!

4 _____ about something? (you/think)
   Yes, but it isn't important. I'll tell you about it later.

5 What _____ ? (you/think)
   We agree. It's a good idea.

6 _____ ? (Leila/eat/seafood)
   Yes, always. Even when she was a child.

7 What _____ ? (she/weigh)
   Some vegetables.

8 How much _____ ? (he/weigh)
   About 80 kilos.

3 Complete the text with the words in the box.

> all week   always (x2)   at the moment
> for a few years   nowadays
> three times a day

I've [1] _____ enjoyed travelling and learning languages, but I'm living back at home [2] _____ , with my parents. However, I've been reading a book [3] _____ about national stereotypes. I don't [4] _____ agree with everything the writer says but it's very interesting. For example, in chapter one he says that the English drink tea at least [5] _____ . The author obviously hasn't been out with any English people [6] _____ . Maybe it was true in the past, but [7] _____ the English are drinking more coffee than ever.

4 Choose the correct options. In some cases, both verb forms are possible.

Language from the Stone Age

Everyone ¹*agree* / *agrees* that language is ²*always changing* / *changing always*. For example, words often disappear after a few years and new ones – especially among teenagers and young adults – ³*are appearing* / *have appeared* all the time. But speakers of English ⁴*are using* / *have been using* certain words ⁵*for* / *since* tens of thousands of years. That's what researchers at the University of Reading now ⁶*believe* / *are believing*.

Dr Mark Pagel, who is leading the research at the University of Reading, ⁷*thinks* / *is thinking* that words including 'I', 'we' and 'two' ⁸*are* / *have been* with us ⁹*for* / *since* the Stone Age. Over the last few months, his team ¹⁰*is comparing* / *has been comparing* modern and ancient languages using computers and the results show that humans ¹¹*have said* / *have been saying* some words for the last 15,000 to 20,000 years.

Since these findings, Dr Pagel ¹²*is also studying* / *has also been studying* how quickly words change or disappear. For example, numbers and pronouns ¹³*don't often change* / *aren't often changing* because we use them extremely often. However, less frequently used words ¹⁴*evolve* / *are evolving* more quickly and are also likely to die out very quickly.

Pronunciation: contracted forms

5 🔊 **1.05** We often use contracted forms when we speak, but we can also use full forms for emphasis. Listen and tick the form you hear.

1 I don't believe you!
  I do not believe you! ✓

2 He doesn't live here any more.
  He does not live here any more.

3 Wait! Caroline's coming, too.
  Wait! Caroline is coming, too.

4 The trains aren't stopping here.
  The trains are not stopping here.

5 I'm not going and that's final!
  I am not going and that is final!

6 You've been studying for hours.
  You have been studying for hours.

7 A: Have you been eating these chocolates?
  B: No I haven't.
    No, I have not.

Listen again and repeat the sentences.

Listen again

6 🔊 **1.06** Listen. What is the speaker doing in each programme? Tick A or B.

1 Programme 1: A telling a story
             B telling a joke

2 Programme 2: A reviewing a show
             B commentating on an event

3 Programme 3: A demonstrating a product
             B giving instructions

7 Which verb form did the speaker use? The present simple or the present continuous?

6 Past simple and present perfect simple
Finished actions in the past

> I saw the most incredible documentary on TV last night. It was brilliant. Did you see it too?

> Do you mean the one about Antarctica? I didn't see it last night, but I've seen it before. It's great, isn't it?

I've seen so many incredible things on this trip. Things that very few people have ever seen before.

Presentation

Past simple

You use the past simple to talk about finished actions and events in the past when there is a clear reference to a specific time in the past or when the past time reference is clearly implied or understood:

*I saw a great film **last night**.*

Did you see it too? (It is clear in the context that the question refers to *last night*.)

The past simple is often used with a past time expression such as *yesterday, last week, three years ago.*

Present perfect

You can use the present perfect simple to talk about finished actions and events in the past when there is **no time reference**, or when it's not important, or we don't know exactly when the action happened:

I've seen it before. (It is not important to know exactly when.)

Common expressions that refer to periods of time which continue to the present include: *so far, up to now, over/during the last three years.*

Some time expressions can refer to both a period of time that has finished and a period of time that continues in the present: *this morning, today, this week, this month.*

Have you talked** to Simon **this morning? (It is still morning.)

Did you talk** to Simon **this morning? (It is the afternoon, the morning has finished.)

ever / never

Use *ever/never* to talk and ask about life experiences when the person is still alive:

*Have you **ever** been to the South Pole?* (ever = at any time during your life so far)

*I've **never** been to Asia.* (never = at no time during my life so far)

If the person is dead, we use the past simple.

*Charles Darwin never **went** to the North Pole.*

(not) ... yet

Use *(not) ... yet* to emphasise that an action or event has not happened at any time up to the present moment:

*I **haven't** seen the film **yet**.*

Use *yet ...?* to ask if an action or event has happened before the present moment in time:

*Have you seen John **yet**? Has John arrived **yet**?*

already

Use *already* to emphasise the fact that an action has happened before the present moment in time:

*They've **already** gone home.*

You can use ***already*** in questions to express your surprise at the fact that something happened sooner than expected.

*Have you **already** finished? Have you finished **already**?*

See page 235: Summary of past simple and present perfect simple

Exercises

1 Read about Simon Reeve. Circle the correct form of the verbs.

Simon Reeve is an author and TV presenter. Several of his books and TV programmes [1]*won / (have won)* international awards. He [2]*made / has made* a series of fascinating travel documentaries for the BBC. He [3]*travelled / has travelled* to the four corners of the earth. In 2006 he [4]*circled / has circled* the earth following the Equator. In 2008 he [5]*did / has done* the same again, but this time following the tropic of Capricorn. He [6]*visited / has visited* some of the most dangerous places on earth. He [7]*also went / has also been* to places no other foreign visitor [8]*ever visited / has ever visited*. His taste for travel first [9]*developed / has developed* when he and his family [10]*drove / have driven* across Europe on their summer holidays.

2 Write questions using the present perfect simple or past simple.

1 _____Has_____ he _ever won_ (ever/win) any international awards? – Yes, several.

2 Which tropic _____ he _____ (follow) in 2008? – The tropic of Capricorn.

3 Where else _____ he _____ (visit)? – Some very dangerous places.

4 How many countries _____ he _____ (visit)? – Too many to count!

5 When _____ he first _____ (develop) a taste for travelling? – During his summer holidays as a child.

3 🔊**1.07 Complete the interview using the present perfect simple or past simple of the verbs in brackets. Then listen and check.**

A: What's the most exciting thing you [1]_have ever done_ (ever/do)?

B: I [2]_____ (do) so many exciting things. Perhaps the most exciting was when I [3]_____ (climb) to the top of Kilimanjaro. I [4]_____ (climb) a lot of mountains, but Kilimanjaro was definitely the best. When I [5]_____ (reach) the top, I just [6]_____ (want) to shout. It's amazing standing on a snow-capped mountain looking down over sun-baked Africa.

A: What [7]_____ (be) the worst moment of your last trip?

B: When I [8]_____ (catch) malaria. I [9]_____ (never/feel) so ill.

A: Is there anywhere you [10]_____ (not/visit)?

B: I [11]_____ (never/be) to the Arctic Circle. I'd love to visit the North Pole. I [12]_____ (never/see) the midnight sun or the Northern Lights. I'd love to do that some day.

4 🔊**1.08 Add *already, ever* or *yet* to the dialogues. Add only one word per dialogue. Then listen and check.**

1 A: Has John arrived ^yet^? I need to see him.

   B: No, he hasn't. He phoned to say he'd be late today.

2 A: Have you been on a cruise?

   B: No, but my parents are going on one at the end of the month. They're really excited about it.

3 A: Is there anything I can do to help?

   B: No, I've cooked dinner. We just need to heat it up when the others get back.

4 A: Shall I throw out this old magazine?

   B: No, please don't. I haven't read it.

5 A: Do you mind if I change the channel? Or are you watching the film?

   B: No, turn over. I've seen this film twice!

7 Present perfect simple and present perfect continuous 2
Recent events, news stories and present/future results of past events, *just*

A: Have you seen this article about that fire in the stadium?

B: Oh, yeah, we've just been talking about that. What does the newspaper say about it?

A: Well, it seems that the police have been looking at the evidence again and they've taken the manager in for questioning.

B: Really? They've questioned him three or four times already, haven't they?

A: Yes. But this time it looks more serious. They've closed the stadium. There'll be no match on Saturday.

Presentation

You can use both the present perfect simple and the present perfect continuous to talk about:

- recent past events and news stories:

  The police **have reopened** the case about the fire in the football stadium.

  We've just **been talking** about the fire at the stadium.

- a past event or action that has a present or future result:

  The police **have closed** the stadium. (Result: there'll be no match on Saturday.)

  They've **been looking** at the evidence again. (Result: they've closed the stadium.)

Use the present perfect simple to talk about a single, complete action: *They've **taken** the manager in for questioning.*

Use the present perfect continuous to talk about an action, or series of actions, that was in progress in the recent past but is no longer happening: *The kids **have been playing** football.* (They are not playing football now.)

You don't usually use stative verbs in the present perfect continuous.

Say *I've known the manager for several years.* (don't say *I've been knowing the manager for several years.*)

See Unit 3: Stative verbs in the continuous

See page 235: Summary of present perfect simple and present perfect continuous

just

Use *just* to show that an action took place, or was in progress, recently. Use the present perfect simple to talk about a single, finished action: *I've **just finished**.*

Use the present perfect continuous to talk about an action that was in progress until recently: *I've **just been talking** to your mum on the phone.*

Quantity and duration

Use the present perfect simple to talk about a specific number of times you have done something in the past or the number of things you have produced or made:

*She's **been** to Paris three times in the last year.*

*He's **written** five books.*

*He's **had** several different jobs.*

TIP You often use the present perfect simple with expressions of quantity: *three books, four times, several jobs.*

Use the present perfect continuous to emphasise the duration of an action, or series of actions, in progress recently (we don't always know if the action is complete):

*The police **have been questioning** the manager all morning.*

*I've **been working** at the computer all morning.*

*I've **been having** some strange dreams recently.*

TIP You often use the present perfect continuous with expressions of time such as *all morning, this week, over the last few months.*

Exercises

1 **Look at the pictures and write sentences in the present perfect continuous.**

1   They / play / garden
    They have been playing in the garden.

2   She / chop / onions

3   What / you / do?

4   you / hit / sister?

2 **Choose the correct form of the verbs.**

1   A: Why isn't Sam here?
    B: His car's *broken* / *been breaking* down.

2   A: Why is the office such a mess?
    B: We've *looked* / *been looking* for something.

3   A: What's the smell?
    B: I've *cooked* / *been cooking*.

4   A: Are you going to buy a cake for Dad?
    B: No, Sue's *baked* / *been baking* one already.

5   A: I need a cup of tea. I'm exhausted! I've *helped* / *been helping* Sue all day.
    B: Here you are. Put your feet up and relax.

6   A: Have you *finished* / *been finishing*?
    B: Yes, we have. We can take it easy now.

3 **Look at the verbs in bold. Which should *not* be in the present perfect continuous? Where necessary, write the verbs in the present perfect simple.**

1   **I've been working** hard all morning. I'm taking a break. ✓

2   **I've been writing** ten pages of the report.
    I've written

3   **They've been playing** really well all season.

4   **They've been winning** the last ten matches.

5   **He's been making** more than ten films in his short career.

6   **He's just been finishing** filming a new documentary.

4 **🎧 1.09 Complete the conversation using the present perfect simple or present perfect continuous form of the verbs in brackets. Then listen and check.**

A: ¹_____ (you/hear) the news? Bill ²_____ (just/resign).

B: No! You're kidding! Why?

A: Well, he ³_____ (not get on) with the boss recently.

B: Yes, I noticed they ⁴_____ (argue) quite a lot recently.

A: Yes, they ⁵_____ (have) two really big arguments in the last week. And he ⁶_____ (decide) that enough is enough. He ⁷_____ (quit) his job. He ⁸_____ (already/start) looking for a new one.

B: Well, good luck to him, I say.

8 Past simple, past continuous and past perfect simple

When I arrived, the party had already started and everyone was laughing and talking.

As I walked in, they all stopped talking and looked at me.

Presentation

Past simple

Use the past simple to talk about the sequence of the main events in a story:

*When I **arrived**, they all **stopped** and **looked** at me.*

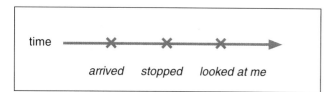

Past continuous

Use the past continuous with the past simple to explain that two actions happened at the same time. The action in the past continuous was in progress at the time the action in the past simple happened:

*When I **arrived**, everyone **was laughing**.*

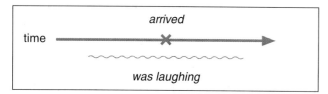

The past simple action may interrupt the longer past continuous action:

*Everybody **was laughing** and **talking** when the door burst open. Suddenly they all **stopped** talking and **turned** around to look at the door.*

You don't usually use stative verbs in the past continuous.

Say *I **knew** the waiter very well.* (don't say *I was knowing the waiter very well.*)

See Unit 3: Stative verbs in the continuous

Past perfect simple

You use the past perfect simple to show that something happened before the main event:

*When I arrived, the party **had** already **finished**.*

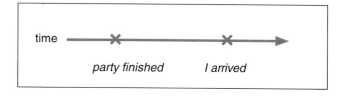

If you use the past simple, it shows that one action happened after the other:

*When the police **arrived**, the party **finished**.*

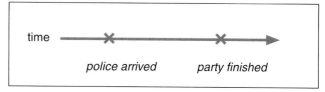

See page 235: Summary of past simple, past continuous and past perfect simple

26

Exercises

1 Put 1–8 in the correct order to complete the story.

I'd been …

1 been years since I'd last seen my twin brother. _____

2 walked over to me. It was Tom. He _____

3 got to the restaurant, I thought he hadn't _____

4 looked so much older than when I'd last _____

5 arrived yet. Then a man with a long beard _____

6 seen him. I was so happy. It'd _____

7 seen him for more than ten years. When I first _____

8 looking forward to seeing Tom again. I hadn't   1

2 Circle the correct form of the verbs.

1   He ¹*had climbed /(was climbing)* a tree when the accident ²*was happening / happened*. He ³*had come / was coming* down when he ⁴*was falling / fell* and ⁵*was breaking / broke* his leg.

2   We ⁶*had been / were* incredibly late. The party ⁷*had finished / finished* by the time we ⁸*had got / got* there. The music ⁹*had stopped / was stopping* and all the guests ¹⁰*got / were getting* ready to go. We ¹¹*had explained / explained* that our car ¹²*had broken / was breaking* down. Steff ¹³*had already put / already put* her coat on, but she ¹⁴*was inviting / invited* us to have a drink in a nearby bar.

3   I had just got into bed when I ¹⁵*heard / was hearing* a loud noise. I ¹⁶*had run / ran* to the window to see what ¹⁷*was happening / happened*. A dog ¹⁸*had knocked / was knocking* over our rubbish bin. It ¹⁹*was eating / ate* the food that ²⁰*had fallen / was falling* on to the pavement.

3 🎧 1.10 Complete the dialogue using the past simple, past continuous, or past perfect simple. Then listen and check.

A: ¹ ____Did____ you ____hear____ (hear) about the party last night?

B: No, what party?

A: The one at Hugh's house. You remember, the one for his girlfriend's 30th birthday.

B: Oh yes, I remember. So, what ² _____ (happen)?

A: Well, everyone ³ _____ (have) a great time. There was a band and a disco …

B: Sounds just like Hugh!

A: Yeah, but while the band ⁴ _____ (play), some thieves ⁵ _____ (break) into the house.

B: No! Really?

A: Yes! Hugh ⁶ _____ (not find out) till a few hours after it had happened. Everybody ⁷ _____ (already/leave).

B: What ⁸ _____ they _____ (take)?

A: Everything: the TV, the hi-fi, the computer …

B: Oh, no! Poor Hugh!

9 Past perfect simple and past perfect continuous

He'd been working hard all his life. He'd had a lot of different jobs. He'd worked as a truck driver, a builder and a car mechanic, but now it was time to retire. He'd always wanted to travel, so he'd bought himself a motorbike and now he and his dog were going to travel around the world!

Presentation

Past perfect continuous

Use the past perfect continuous to talk about an action that was in progress before a given time in the past:

He **had been working** hard all his life, but now it was time to retire.

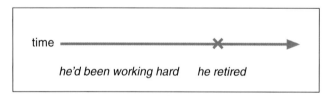

time ———————————✕————————➤

he'd been working hard   he retired

It is possible that the action (working hard) finished before he retired, or at that point in time. It is also possible that it continued: he had been working hard all his life, and he had no intention of stopping, even after he'd retired.

To form the past perfect continuous use:
had + been + verb + -ing

Affirmative and negative

I/You/He/She/It/ We/They	'd/had/ hadn't	been	working hard.

Questions and answers

Had	I/you/he/she/it/ we/they	been	working hard?

Yes,	I/you/he/she/it/we/they	had.
No,		hadn't.

Past perfect continuous or past perfect simple?

Use the past perfect simple to talk about:

* single, complete events: *He'd worked as a truck driver. He'd bought a bike.*

* repeated actions when we give the number of times the action is repeated: *He'd done a lot of different jobs in his lifetime.*

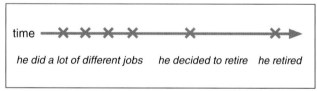

time ——✕—✕—✕—✕————✕————————✕—➤

he did a lot of different jobs   he decided to retire   he retired

Use the past perfect continuous to talk about how long an action, or series of actions, was in progress:

*He **had been working** hard all his life.*

*He'd **been riding** his bike for five hours without stopping.*

You don't usually use stative verbs in the past perfect continuous.

Say *I had known him for years.* (don't say *I had been knowing him for years.*)

See Unit 3: Stative verbs in the continuous

See page 235: Summary of past perfect simple and past perfect continuous

Exercises

1 Look at the pictures and complete the sentences using the past perfect continuous of the verbs in the box.

> cry   not listen   not live   work

1 She was exhausted. She _had been working_ all night.

3 The baby _____ all night. It was six o'clock and he hadn't had any sleep.

2 He had no idea what the answer was. He _____ to the teacher.

4 She _____ there very long, but she already felt totally at home.

2 Look at the pictures in exercise 1 and complete the questions using the past perfect continuous.

1 How long _____ ? All night.

2 _____ to the teacher? No, he hadn't.

3 What _____ all night? Crying!

4 How long _____ there? Not very long.

3 Choose the correct form of the verbs to complete the story.

1 He'd never ⟨fallen⟩ / been falling in love before. She was his first love.

2 They'd gone / been going out together for a couple of months.

3 Then she'd started / been starting making excuses so as not to see him.

4 She'd met / been meeting another man at a party a few weeks earlier.

5 She'd seen / been seeing him for a few weeks.

6 He hadn't realised / been realising what was happening.

7 Then one day, he'd seen / been seeing the two of them walking down the street hand in hand.

8 And he understood that she'd found / been finding a new boyfriend.

4 (🔊 1.11) Complete the text using the past perfect simple or past perfect continuous form of the verbs in brackets. Then listen and check.

We ¹_____ (work) for the same company for a couple of months. I ²_____ (see) her in the distance and I ³_____ (notice) how attractive she was, but we ⁴_____ (never/speak). Then, while we ⁵_____ (do) a training course together, we finally got to know each other. We ⁶_____ (have) a drink with the other people on the course at the end of the first day, and we ⁷_____ (all/talk) about how difficult it was. I ⁸_____ (not notice) that she was standing just behind me. I laughed at one of the jokes, stepped back and spilt her drink down her dress! I ⁹_____ (never/feel) so embarrassed in my life. But she was really nice about it. I bought her another drink and we got talking. She told me she ¹⁰_____ (just/buy) a house on my street and that she ¹¹_____ (spend) her weekends painting and decorating. I offered to help her. That's how it all started!

10 Review of units 6 to 9

Grammar

1 Choose the best response or ending.

1 Why did he run away?
   a Because he'd seen a ghost. ✓
   b Because he was seeing a ghost.

2 Are they still working on the house?
   a No, they aren't. They've just finished.
   b No, they aren't. They've just been finishing.

3 What happened when they heard the news?
   a They had decided to have a party.
   b They decided to have a party.

4 He's just rung and …
   a he's coming here now.
   b he came here.

5 I've lost my mobile phone …
   a and I don't know where it is.
   b then I bought a new one.

6 Where had they been all that time?
   a They'd been playing golf.
   b They'd played golf.

2 Choose the correct form of the verbs.

Collect cool

In the past, collecting ¹was / had been a hobby for rich people. Kings and queens ²sent / were sending explorers to find new objects in strange new countries. Since those times, people from all types of background ³collected / have collected every kind of object from the normal (stamps and coins) to the weird (lunchboxes and toilet paper).

Mike Bryant ⁴collected / has been collecting antique bottles for years. Bryant ⁵has built / has been building an extra room above his garage to keep all the bottles.

Another collector, Pat Sonnenberg, has also ⁶created / been creating a special room in the house for her collection of 350 lunchboxes. She ⁷started / has started collecting lunchboxes because she ⁸didn't have / hasn't had one for school when she was a child.

3 Complete the story using the past simple, past continuous, past perfect or past perfect continuous. Sometimes more than one form is possible.

It was 8 o'clock and at last I was ready. I ¹_____ (spend) hours deciding what to wear. This was a special occasion and I ²_____ (want) to look my best. I ³_____ (walk) to the bus stop when a friend ⁴_____ (pass) me in his car. He ⁵_____ (drive) into town. He ⁶_____ (offer) to give me a lift. We ⁷_____ (stop) the car opposite the restaurant. I could see the people inside. They ⁸_____ (already/start) eating. As I waited on the pavement, a huge lorry ⁹_____ (drive) straight through a big puddle of water. My dress was covered in mud. I ¹⁰_____ (look) a real mess. All the customers in the restaurant ¹¹_____ (laugh) at me. I ¹²_____ (never/feel) so embarrassed in my whole life.

4 Complete the sentences with the words in the box.

all weekend   already   for years and years
just   last year   never   when   yet

1 A: Have you seen the Grand Canyon _____?
   B: No. We're going there tomorrow.

2 A: My children have _____ tried sushi.
   B: I think they should. They'll love it.

3 I was working in the office _____ I heard a loud bang.

4 Hello. I've _____ left you a message on your phone. Did you get it?

5 I've been working on this project _____. I can't wait to hand it in tomorrow morning!

6 They'd been arguing about the same old things _____, ever since they got married.

7 It was very late when she got home. Her husband had _____ gone to bed and was sound asleep.

8 We didn't have a holiday _____ and I don't know if we'll get one this year either.

Grammar in context

5 Choose the correct option to complete the text below.

The strange story of a tree in the night...

Do you believe in ghosts? I ¹*thought / 've been thinking* about this question a lot recently. I ²*'d never met / 've never met* a ghost, but a friend of mine has. And her story has made me think again about my answer to the question.

It ³*had been / was* a dark, foggy night – as it often is, of course, in all good ghost stories – and my friend ⁴*was driving / drove* home along a quiet country road. Suddenly, a large white shadow ⁵*was flying / flew* across the road in front of her car. My friend slowed down and ⁶*had been looking / looked* behind her in her mirror. But there was nothing there. The strange white shadow ⁷*had disappeared / was disappearing*. She drove on a bit further, when the shadow ⁸*was appearing / appeared* again. This time it flew straight at her windscreen and blocked her view. She stopped the car. And at that very moment she heard a loud crashing sound just in front of her. She looked up. There, in the middle of the road, ⁹*was being / was* a huge tree. It ¹⁰*had been falling / had fallen* down into the middle of the road. My friend was shaking with shock. Had the strange white shadow ¹¹*been trying / tried* to warn her of the danger? ¹²*It had saved / Had it saved* her life?

Pronunciation: *had* and *was*

6 🔊**1.12** The auxiliary verbs *had* and *was* are often unstressed in affirmative sentences, but they are stressed in negative sentences, short answers and to add emphasis. Listen to these short dialogues. Are the verbs in bold *a) stressed* or *b) unstressed*?

1 A: ¹**Was** he working when you phoned?
   B: Yes, he ²**was**. But his wife ³**wasn't**. She ⁴**was** at home.

2 A: So, ⁵**had** he seen her or not?
   B: Yes, ⁶he **had**. But she ⁷**hadn't** seen him.

3 A: She ⁸**hadn't** finished the report yesterday.
   B: Yes, she ⁹**had**! I read it.

Listen again and repeat the sentences.

Listen again

7 🔊**1.13** Listen and correct the mistakes in the sentences.

1 They'd been working for the same company for a couple of ~~years~~. *months*

2 They'd been working on a project together when they first got to know each other.

3 They'd been having lunch with the other people on the course.

4 They'd been talking about how easy it was.

5 She'd been standing just in front of him.

6 She stood on his foot and spilt his drink.

7 She had just bought a car.

8 She had been spending her weekends gardening.

11 Time linkers 1

Sequencing: *after*, *when*, *as soon as*, *once*, *before*, *until*, *by the time*

DAY 3:
Camping in the rain

When we got to the campsite, we put our tent up and unpacked our bags. Once everything was ready, we walked down to the nearest village. There was only one bar. It sold bread and cheese and fruit and served big bowls of hot soup. We bought some fruit for the morning, before sitting down to eat our soup. As soon as we sat down, it started to rain — and rain and rain! After eating, we played a game of cards and waited until the rain had finally stopped. By the time we got back to the campsite, the sky had cleared with not a cloud in sight. But when we got to our tent, we couldn't believe our eyes. It was completely flooded! We spent the night in the reception block!

Presentation

Use time conjunctions such as *after*, *when* and *before* to connect two sentences and explain how they are related by time:

We got to the campsite. We put our tent up. → *We put our tent up **when** we got to the campsite.*

When the time clause is at the beginning of the sentence, you need a comma between it and the main clause:
When we got to the campsite, *we put the tent up.*

See Unit 58: Future time clauses

after, when, as soon as, once

Use *after*, *when*, *as soon as* and *once* to introduce the first action to happen in a series of actions:

***After/When/As soon as/Once** we got to the campsite, we put up the tent.*

action 1 = arrive   action 2 = put up the tent

You usually use the past simple with *when*: *When we **arrived** at the campsite …*

With *after*, *as soon as* and *once*, you can also use the past perfect: *After/As soon as/Once **we'd arrived** …*

See Units 8 and 9: Past simple and past perfect simple

before, until, by the time

Use *before*, *until* and *by the time* to introduce the second action in a series of actions:

*We bought some fruit **before we sat down to eat.***

action 1 = buy fruit   action 2 = sit down

Until shows that the first action stops <u>just before</u> the second action starts:

*We waited **until** the rain stopped/had stopped.*

You do not normally use *until* at the beginning of a sentence.

By the time shows that the first action takes place at an unspecified time before the second action:

*The sky had cleared **by the time** we'd got back to the campsite.* (We don't know exactly when the sky cleared.)

You normally use the past simple with *before*. You can use either the past simple or the past perfect with *until* and *by the time*: *We waited until it **stopped/had stopped** raining. By the time we **got** there/**had got** there, it had stopped raining.*

after / before + -ing

You can also form time phrases using *after* or *before* followed by verb + *-ing*:

After we ate … → ***After eating**, …*

Only use the *-ing* form when the subject of the verb is the same for both phrases:

After <u>we</u> had eaten, <u>we</u> played cards. (The subject is the same.) → *After eating, we played cards.*

After <u>we</u> had eaten, <u>the barman</u> invited us to a game of cards. (The *-ing* form is not possible without changing the meaning.)

Exercises

1 Add the conjunctions in brackets to the sentences.

1 _When_
   ∧ I got home, the first thing I did was have a quick shower. (when)

2 I checked my emails I started making some food. (before)

3 I'd seen that there were no messages for me, I started preparing supper. (once)

4 I waited the pasta had cooked, then I switched on the TV. (until)

5 I had finished watching the news, I started writing my blog. (as soon as)

2 Combine the two sentences using the time linker in brackets.

1 We checked the train times carefully. We left for the concert. (before)
   We checked the train times carefully before we left for the concert. / Before we left for the concert, we checked the train times carefully.

2 It was getting late. Our train arrived at the station. (by the time)

3 We got off the train. We ran to the bus stop. (as soon as)

4 We were on the bus. We texted the others to tell them we were on our way. (once)

5 We finally got there. We found out that the concert had been cancelled. (when)

3 Rewrite the clauses in bold using the *-ing* form where possible.

1 **Before she left the house,** she closed all the windows and switched off all the lights.
   Before leaving the house, ...

2 **After they left,** we cleaned the house and prepared for our next guests.
   -ing form not possible

3 **After we'd left our bags at the hostel,** we decided to take a walk around the city centre.

4 **Before he plays an important match,** he always checks that he's got his lucky socks.

5 **After the storm had finished,** the streets were covered in water and fallen trees.

6 **Before she left home and moved into her own flat,** she shared a bedroom with her sister.

4 Complete these sentences so that they are true for you.

1 As soon as I got home yesterday, _____ .

2 When the alarm rang this morning, _____ .

3 I always _____ before going to bed.

4 I usually _____ after doing sport.

33

12 Time linkers 2
Actions that happen at the same time: *when*, *while* and *as*

NEWS.COM | SIGN UP | SIGN IN | SITE MAP

NEWS

SEARCH

THIS PAGE IS UPDATED EVERY TEN MINUTES

TODAY'S TOP STORIES

▶ **PRESIDENT TRAVELS TO CHINA**

▶ **SNOW CAUSES CHAOS IN MID WEST**

▶ **OSCAR ROUND-UP**

OSCAR ROUND-UP

When collecting his prize, he turned to the waiting crowd and lifted the award up high for everyone to see. While the crowd cheered, a voice shouted out, 'Who are you going to dedicate it to?' As he thought about his answer, a large smile spread across his face. 'To my mother, of course!' he replied.

▶ SEE FULL PHOTO GALLERY

Presentation

Use the time conjunctions *when, while* and *as* to connect two sentences and show that the two actions happen at the same time:

I was walking down the street. I saw the strangest thing.

*I saw the strangest thing happen **when/while/as** I was walking down the street.*

You need a comma after the time clause when it is at the beginning of the sentence:

***When/While/As** I was walking down the street, I saw the strangest thing.*

when

Use *when* (and not *as* or *while*) to talk about:

- a short action that happened at the same time as a longer action. Use the past simple for the short action: *We were eating supper **when it started to rain.***

while

You usually use *while* (although *when* is also possible) to talk about:

- two long actions that happened at the same time. Use the past continuous for both actions: ***While** he **was putting** the tent up, the others **were unpacking** the car.*

as

Use *as* to talk about:

- two short actions that happened at the same time. Use the past simple for both actions: *As I **opened** the door, I **heard** a noise.*

See Unit 8: Past simple and past continuous

when/while + -ing

You can also form time phrases with *when/while* + verb + *-ing*. Use *when* for a short action, and use *when* or *while* for a long action:

***When receiving the award**, he smiled and shook her hand.* (= at the moment when he received the award)

***When/While answering questions from the press**, he took time to think carefully about his answers.* (= during the whole time)

You often use clauses with *when* + *-ing*:

- to introduce a set of instructions: ***When speaking in public**, always remember to speak slowly and clearly.*
- to talk about habits: ***When talking to the camera**, he always looked at his feet.*

Use clauses with *while* + *-ing* to talk about two long actions that are in progress at the same time. Use *while* with either of the actions:

*He looked around nervously for support **while answering the questions**.*

*He answered the questions **while looking around nervously** for support.*

Exercises

1 The use of *while* is incorrect in four of the sentences below. Replace the incorrect examples of *while* with *when*.

1   ~~While~~ I got up this morning, Elena and Hans were preparing breakfast. _____ ✗ When

2   Hans was making the coffee, while Elena fried the eggs. _____ ✓

3   I was really surprised while I saw all the food. _____

4   We talked about our plans while we ate breakfast. _____

5   While Hans and I were clearing the table, Elena was checking the weather on the internet. _____

6   While checking the weather, she came across an interesting news story. _____

7   The roof of the town hall was damaged while it was struck by lightning last night. _____

8   While we heard this, we decided we had to go into town to see it. _____

2 Cross out the incorrect conjunctions. In one sentence all three conjunctions are possible.

1   *As/When/~~While~~* I arrived home, I heard a strange noise.

2   *As/When/While* I was walking up the stairs, I heard it again.

3   *As/When/While* I put my hand out to open the door to the bedroom, it slowly opened by itself.

4   *As/When/While* I jumped back in horror, a dark shadow crept out of the room.

5   I was about to scream *as/when/while* I saw that it was only the cat!

6   The cat turned and looked at me *as/when/while* I quietly laughed to myself.

3 Combine the two sentences using the conjunction in brackets and the verb + *-ing*.

1   You are giving a presentation to a room full of people. Always speak slowly and clearly. (when)
    When giving a presentation to a room full of people, always speak slowly and clearly.

2   You are crossing the road. Remember to look both ways. (when)

3   You are waiting for the pasta to cook. You can prepare the sauce. (while)

4   He looked very uncomfortable. He answered the questions from the press. (when)

5   She looked distractedly through the window at the rain. She listened to my questions. (while)

6   You are driving the car. Don't use your mobile phone. (while)

13 Past habits: *used to* and *would*

We used to live in the centre of a large city. We used to go out every night. We'd go out to eat or we'd go to the cinema, or the theatre or to exhibitions. Then we had kids and moved to the country.

Now our lives are very different.

Presentation

used to

Use *used to* to talk about past habits, and situations or states:

*We **used to** go out every night.* (habit)

*We **used to** live in the city.* (situation)

*We **used to** be city people.* (state)

You only use *used to* to talk about past habits. Use the present simple and *usually* (or other adverbs of frequency) to talk about habits in the present:

*We **don't usually** go out at the weekend.* (don't say *I don't use to go out at the weekend.*)

You can also use the past simple to talk about past habits:

*We **went** out every night.*

*We **used** to go out every night.*

+	We used to live in the city.
−	She didn't use to like the country.
?	Did you use to go out every night?
Yes/No	Yes, we did. / No, we didn't.

TIP Be careful with the question and negative forms: there is no *-d* on *use to*:

*Did you **use to** have pets when you were in school?* (don't say *Did you ~~used~~ to ...?*)

*I didn't **use to** like dogs when I was younger.* (don't say *I didn't ~~used~~ to ...*)

would

You can also use *would/wouldn't* to talk about past habits: *We'd go out to eat.*

You use *would* to talk about actions but not to talk about states or situations: *We'd go to exhibitions.* (don't say ~~We'd live~~ *in the city.*)

Don't use *used to* or *would* to talk about:

- a single past action: *I ~~used to/would go~~ to a great exhibition yesterday.*

  We went to a great exhibition yesterday.

- how long an action lasted: *I ~~used to live~~ in the city for three years.*

  I lived in the city for three years.

- the number of times an action was repeated in total: *We ~~used to/would visit~~ the museum at least a hundred times.*

  We visited the museum at least a hundred times.

Exercises

1 Complete the conversation using the correct form of *used to* and short answers.

A: ¹ _____ (you live) in the country when you were a kid?

B: Yes, we ² _____ . I loved it! We ³ _____ (have) cats and dogs, and even a couple of chickens!

A: ⁴ _____ (you/eat) their eggs?

B: Yes, we ⁵ _____ (have to) collect the eggs every morning. We ⁶ _____ (take) it in turns. My sister ⁷ _____ (not like) looking after the chickens very much. She ⁸ _____ (be) scared they'd peck her.

2 Rewrite the sentences using *used to* where possible.

1 I went to belly-dancing classes when I was at school.

   I used to go to belly-dancing classes when I was at school.

2 I started my first classes when I was eight.

3 We took part in competitions.

4 I loved performing in front of an audience.

5 I continued dancing for almost six years.

6 Then I lost interest and I took up basketball instead.

7 I played in the school team and we trained every day of the week.

8 We were pretty good and we won three local championships.

3 🔊 1.14 Look at the verbs in bold. Replace *used to* with *would/wouldn't* where possible. Then listen and check.

I ¹**used to** love chocolate. I ²**used to** eat it all day long. Some days I ³**didn't use to** eat anything else, until one day I developed an allergy to it – and now I can't eat it anymore!

I ⁴**used to** be scared of the dark. I ⁵**used to** refuse to go into a dark room on my own. My little sister ⁶**used to** hold my hand!

I ⁷**didn't use** to do any sport at all. I ⁸**used to** think I was fit and healthy enough without it. I ⁹**used to** spend all day at my desk and I ¹⁰**never used to** ever get any exercise. But then I broke my leg and I had to follow an intensive exercise programme. I actually enjoyed it and I've kept doing sport ever since.

1	—	4		7		9	
2	would	5		8		10	
3		6					

4 Complete the text so that it is true for you or someone you know.

When _____ was a kid, _____ used to _____ . _____ would always _____ and _____ would never _____ .

14 *be used to* and *get used to*

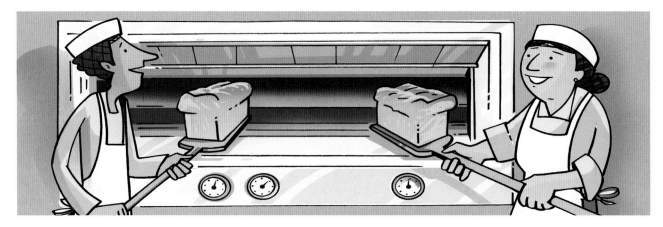

A: How do you feel about your new job? Are you getting used to the new routine?

B: Getting up so early in the morning is still a bit difficult. I used to work in a bar and the hours were very different. I was used to staying in bed late in the morning, and having a long, slow breakfast.

A: Did you prefer working in the evenings, then?

B: No, not at all. I love finishing at midday. Give me another couple of weeks and I'm sure I'll be used to getting up at four o'clock!

Presentation

You can use *used to* as an adjective:

*I'm **used to** working at night.* (= I'm accustomed to working at night.)

be used to

Use *be used to* to explain that someone is familiar with a situation or a routine:

*I'm **used to** staying in bed late.*

Don't use *be used to* in the continuous:
~~*I'm being used to* working late at night.~~

get used to

Use *get used to* in the present continuous to explain that someone is in the process of becoming familiar with a situation:

*I'm **getting used to** working early in the morning.*

Use the past simple to show that the process is complete:

*I quickly **got used to** the new routine.*

used to (verb) and *be/get used to* (verb + adjective)

When you use *used to* as a verb, it is followed by the infinitive:

*I **used to** work nights.*

You can only use *used to* as a verb to talk about the past.

Use *be/get used to* with a noun or with verb + *-ing*:

*I'm used to **early mornings**.* (noun)

*I'm getting used to **working** early in the morning.* (verb + *-ing*)

You can use *be/get used to* to talk about the past, present or future:

past: *I **was/got used to** getting up late.*

present: *I'm/I'm **getting used to** working in the morning.*

future: *I'll **be/get used to** getting up at four o'clock.*

See page 235: Summary of *be used to*

Exercises

1 Choose the correct options.

I grew up in the city, so ¹*(I'm)/ I'm getting* used to noise and traffic. It's taking me some time to ²*be / get* used to the peace and quiet out here in the country!

Our daughter is almost a year old now. ³*I'm slowly / I'm slowly getting* used to life as a parent. I quickly ⁴*was / got* used to the sleepless nights and the toys all over the house. And I know I'll have to ⁵*be / get* used to being called 'Daddy' pretty soon, too, now that Rosie's started talking.

2 Complete the sentences with the correct form of *be* or *get*.

1 He _____ used to travelling on the train to work every day. He'd been doing it for years and always took a book with him.

2 They soon _____ used to the new routine and really enjoyed the change.

3 Moving to a new town can be quite stressful, but I'm sure I _____ used to it pretty quickly.

4 At the beginning, I _____ (not) used to working nights and I found it very difficult to adapt.

5 She had always lived alone and _____ used to having the house to herself, so she didn't like having visitors to stay.

6 We _____ (not) used to all this noise and we're finding it very difficult to sleep at night.

3 🔊1.15 Complete the dialogue with the correct form of *used to*, *be used to* and *get used to*. Then listen and check.

A: So, what ¹ _____ you _____ do before you became a teacher?

B: I ² _____ work as a banker in the City, in London.

A: Why did you decide to become a teacher?

B: My working life ³ _____ be very stressful. I ⁴ _____ working ten or twelve hours a day and under a lot of pressure. It was very tiring and I decided it was time for a change.

A: Was it difficult to ⁵ _____ your new lifestyle?

B: Well, I ⁶ _____ earning a lot more money, so it took me a bit of time to ⁷ _____ living on a teacher's salary! And I ⁸ _____ (not) working with kids, but now I'm slowly ⁹ _____ the role of teacher and I'm loving every minute of it – well, almost!

A: And what about your new working routine?

B: I ¹⁰ _____ the shorter working hours and the longer holidays very quickly! I only ¹¹ _____ take ten or fifteen days' holiday a year when I was a banker. Now I have six weeks' holiday in the summer alone. That's great!

4 Complete these sentences so that they are true for you.

1 I'm used to _____ at work/school/university.

2 I'm still not used to _____ .

3 I'm slowly getting used to _____ .

15 Review of units 11 to 14

Grammar

1 Correct the mistake in each sentence.

1 I checked my diary before ~~call~~ *calling* Tom to arrange a time to meet next week.

2 I didn't used to do a lot of sport when I was younger.

3 I was really surprised while I opened the door and saw Matt standing there with an enormous suitcase at his feet.

4 I use to visit my grandparents every weekend, if possible.

5 My grandparents would live in an old house by the sea.

6 He wasn't used to have so many people in the house.

7 We were really late, and by the time we got there, the film already started.

8 I used to go to the gym three times last week.

9 Before starting, making sure your work surface is clean.

2 Write the words in the correct order.

1 after you did he What left do ?
What did you do after he left?

2 new you Are your routine used getting to ?

3 did What do you to use ?

4 leaving remember you What before to do must ?

5 she in What doing came were you when ?

6 Are working you with used to animals ?

7 do you long winter nights What use did to on those ?

8 the restaurant after Where they go did leaving ?

3 Match the questions in exercise 2 with the answers below.

1 No, this is the first time for me.   6

2 We found someone else to take his place.

3 I used to work as a sports instructor.

4 Turn out all the lights and lock all the windows.

5 They caught a taxi and went home.

6 Yes, I am, thanks.

7 We'd sit around the fire and tell stories, of course!

8 Nothing special. Just watching TV.

4 Choose the correct options.

1 A: Did you stay long last night?
   B: I stayed [1]*before / until* the class had finished and I went straight home.

2 A: [2]*Did / Would* you live in the city when you were kids?
   B: No, we [3]*used to / would* live in a really small village in the country.
   A: Really?
   B: Yeah, it was so small it [4]*didn't even use to / wouldn't even* have a shop.

3 A: Wow! It's really cold here. But I suppose you [5]*get / 're* used to it after a while.
   B: Yes, it's difficult at first, but I [6]*'m / get* used to it now and I hardly notice.

4 Make sure the oven is heated to 220° [7]*before / as* placing the cake in the oven. [8]*After / While* the cake is cooking, prepare the chocolate topping.

5 [9]*When / Once* climbing alone, make sure that someone knows where you're going and when you plan to be back.

6 A: Did you see Dan at the office?
   B: No, he'd already finished work [10]*by the time / as soon as* we got there.

Grammar in context

5 Complete the stories on the website. Use one word only in each gap. Contracted forms count as one word.

Chitchat.com

Unanswered questions | New questions | Help | SEARCH

Enter question or phrase here: >> **I used to like going to school …** **Go**

I loved my primary school. I was so happy there, I ¹_____ run to school every morning. I wanted to be a teacher myself ²_____ I grew up, or so I used ³_____ say.

When I was younger, I ⁴_____ to love school. I had a lot of friends and we'd do all kinds of fun things. But I moved to secondary school ⁵_____ I was 11 and things changed. It took me a long time to ⁶_____ used to being in such a huge building and having to do so much homework. ⁷_____ the time I got used to it, it was too late. The fun had gone. Now I can't wait to leave!

I used to hate school – especially sports. I ⁸_____ do anything to try and get out of doing sports. Once I painted red spots all over my face and ⁹_____ I got to school, I went to the teacher and told her I was feeling ill. I thought she'd send me straight home. As ¹⁰_____ as she saw me, she grabbed some soap and water and tried to wash them off. Unfortunately she couldn't – I'd used a permanent marker!

Pronunciation: *used to*

6 🎧 **1.16** Listen to the dialogues. Notice the pronunciation of the words in bold and answer questions 1 and 2.

1 Is the 's' in 'use' and 'used' pronounced as an /s/ or a /z/?

2 Can you hear the final 'd' on *used to*?

A: Did you **use to** enjoy school?

B: No, I didn't! I **used to** hate it! I didn't **use to** want to go and I **used to** make all kinds of excuses to try and stay at home!

A: Did you **use** computers in your last school?

B: Yes, for forms and records and things, but we never **used** them in class.

Listen again and repeat the sentences.

Listen again

7 🎧 **1.17** Listen and answer the questions.

1 What did he use to do for a living?

2 Why did he change his job?

3 What are the main differences between his past job and his new job?

4 Did he find it difficult to adjust to his new lifestyle? Why/Why not?

5 What does he like about his new working routine?

16 Questions 1
Review of common question forms

Can I ask you a question?

Have the police been to your home?

Do they want to interview your wife?

What have they been looking for?

Who telephoned the newspapers?

Which secretary spoke to journalists?

How long has the Prime Minister known?

Presentation

Yes/No questions

To ask questions requiring the answer 'yes' or 'no', you use an auxiliary verb (e.g. *be, do, have, can*) followed by the subject:

Are you going to resign?

Have the police been to your home?

Do they want to interview your wife?

Can I ask you a question?

Subject and object questions

You can ask questions about the subject or the object of a verb using *what, who, which, whose, how much* and *how many*.

    subject   object

The journalists asked a lot of difficult questions.

A subject question asks about the subject of the verb:

Who asked the questions? *The journalists.*

An object question asks about the object of the verb:

What did the journalists ask? *A lot of difficult questions.*

Subject questions

In subject questions, the question word or expression (*who, what, how many journalists*) is the subject of the verb. The verb follows the question word and there is no other pronoun.

Say ***How many journalists** came to interview the minister?* (don't say *How many journalists ~~they~~ came to interview the minister?*)

You do not normally use the auxiliary verbs *do, does* or *did* in subject questions. (don't say *How many journalists ~~did come~~ to interview the minister?*)

Object questions

In an object question you need a question word, an auxiliary verb and a subject. The auxiliary verb comes before the subject. Use the auxiliary verbs *do, does, did* with the present simple and the past simple:

*What **did the journalists** ask?*

*How much **did the Prime Minister** know?*

Question expressions

As well as single question words such as *what, when, who, where, which, how*, you can also use multi-word expressions such as *what time, what sort, what type, what kind, how much, how many, how well, how big*:

***What time** are you giving the press conference?*

***What sort/type/kind** of career do you want?*

***How much** does the Prime Minister know?*

Questions with *like*

Use questions with *What … like?* to ask for a description:

What's he like? (kind and friendly)

What does she look like? (short and blonde with glasses)

Questions with prepositions

In everyday speech, you put prepositions at the end of the question:

*What were they looking **for**?*

With questions about time, you don't need the preposition *at*.

What time are you giving a press conference ~~at~~?

See page 237: Summary of statements questions, short answers and short responses

Exercises

1 Write the missing auxiliary verbs in these *yes/no* questions.

1 _Am_ I late for the press conference?

2 _____ the Prime Minister going to make a statement?

3 _____ that journalist telephoned yet?

4 _____ he think no one cares?

5 _____ you get a photograph of his wife yesterday?

6 _____ he already left the house by the time you arrived?

2 Complete the subject and object questions about this news report.

Politician resigns

■ THE MINISTER for Education, Gordon Fortescue, met the Prime Minister this morning at ten o'clock. Mr Fortescue spent 30 minutes with his ex-boss and then walked from 10 Downing Street. He told the waiting newspaper reporters that he had resigned and immediately returned to his home to be with his family. Fortescue is married and has three children.

Later in the day, the Prime Minister's Press Secretary made an official statement, saying that the Prime Minister understood the reason Mr Fortescue gave for leaving, which was that he couldn't continue as a politician while the police were investigating his private life.

1 Which minister _____ the Prime Minister this morning? The Minister for Education.

2 What time _____ the Prime Minister? At ten o'clock.

3 How long _____ with his ex-boss? Thirty minutes.

4 What _____ the waiting newspaper reporters? That he had resigned.

5 Where _____ immediately? To his home.

6 How many _____ ? Three.

7 Who _____ an official statement? The Prime Minister's Press Secretary.

8 What reason _____ for leaving? That he couldn't continue as a politician while the police were investigating his private life.

3 ⏵1.18 Complete the telephone conversation. Write one word in each gap. One gap does not need a word. Then listen and check.

Customer: Hello. I'm calling about your camping equipment.

Supplier: Sure. What exactly are you looking [1] _____ ?

Customer: I need a tent.

Supplier: What [2] _____ of tent?

Customer: I've seen one called 'The Bonnington Mountain Tent'. What's it [3] _____ ? How [4] _____ people can sleep in it?

Supplier: It's for two people.

Customer: I see. And [5] _____ I use it in any season?

Supplier: It depends on the weather. What time of year are you planning to use it [6] _____ ?

17 Questions 2
Negative questions, indirect ways of asking questions and statements as questions

What type of boss do you work for? Tick one.

Type 1: My boss always needs it now!
'Haven't you finished it yet? Hurry up!' ☐

Type 2: My boss needs it today.
'Sorry, but can I ask you if you've finished it yet?' ☐

Type 3: My boss needs it sometime this week (or next).
'You haven't finished it? No problem.' ☐

Presentation

Negative questions

You can ask questions using the negative form of the verb:

Haven't you finished it yet?

When you use negative questions in spoken English, you normally use contracted forms. Full forms are less common:

Haven't they called you back? (more common)

Have they not called you back? (less common)

You often use negative questions to:

- show surprise or annoyance: *Haven't you finished it yet? You've been working on that report for hours.*
- suggest something: *Why don't you work late tonight?*
- request something (often impolite or expecting a negative response): *Can't I finish it later?*
- check information or something you think is probably true: *Isn't the deadline for this report next Friday?*
- exclaim something: *Don't you work long hours!*

When you use negative question forms for exclamations, you use an exclamation mark (!) not a question mark (?).

Indirect ways of asking questions

You can use certain expressions to make questions less direct. They often make the questions more polite or more tentative:

Have you finished it yet? → *Can I ask you if you've finished it yet?* (more polite and less direct)

Common expressions to ask a question indirectly:
Can/Could I ask you if …? Can/Could you/anyone tell me …? Do you know/remember/think …? Do you have any idea …? I don't know/'d like to know … I wonder/ was wondering …

After the expression, the word order is the same as an affirmative sentence (subject before the verb):

*I was wondering if **you've finished it yet**.* (not *I was wondering if ~~have you~~ finished it yet.*)

With *yes/no* questions, use *if/whether*:

*Can I ask you **if/whether** you've finished it yet?*

With object questions, do not use an auxiliary verb (*do, does, did*) in the present simple or past simple:

*Do you have any idea what time **she wants** the report?* (not *Do you have any idea what time ~~does she want~~ the report?*)

Statements as questions

You can make an affirmative sentence into a question by using rising intonation at the end. This type of question often shows surprise or checks information:

You haven't finished it? [↗] What have you been doing?
(= This has taken longer than I expected.)

A: *The office is open on Saturday? [↗]* (= I'm fairly certain, but I want to check.)

B: *That's right, but only until midday.*

See page 237: Summary of statements, questions, short answers and short responses

Exercises

1 **Put these words in the correct order to make questions or statements.**

1 done he a hasn't good job
  Hasn't he done a good job ?

2 come you I with can't
  ?

3 they take a break soon won't
  ?

4 they how expensive know don't this is
  ?

5 Phillip me can you tell where is
  ?

6 you think will like Marilyn do our idea
  ?

7 know mistakes how I made so many I don't
  .

8 idea you have are coming do any how many people
  ?

2 **Match a statement as a question (1–6) to the questions (A–F).**

1 You've left your job? _____
2 They've changed the password? _____
3 It's this afternoon? _____
4 Your car's broken down again? _____
5 No one's replied to our invitations? _____
6 The boss is on holiday? _____

A What is it now?
B So who's in charge?
C What will you do instead?
D Do you think they all received one?
E Wasn't it in the garage only last week?
F Why did I need to get up so early then?

3 **Read the first sentence or question. Rewrite each to ask the question indirectly, or form a negative question, or make a statement as a question.**

1 Have you talked to your boss about the problem? It would be a good idea to.
  Why _____ about the problem?

2 Is it OK if I take the rest of the day off?
  Can't _____ of the day off?

3 I thought today's lesson was cancelled.
  Isn't _____ cancelled?

4 How much are potatoes this week?
  I'd like to know _____ this week?

5 Aren't they coming? Why not?
  They _____ ? Why not?

6 I need you to help me move these books.
  Could you _____ these books, please?

7 How long has Gabriel been playing that computer game?
  Do you have any idea _____ that computer game?

8 Do you spell his surname C-H-U-I?
  You _____ ?

18 Question tags

Jim:	It's Lisa, isn't it?
Lisa:	Yes, Lisa Rogers. Have we met before?
Jim:	Once, but it was a long time ago. I'm Jim Smythe. I work for KMC.
Lisa:	You don't work with León Alvarez, do you?
Jim:	That's right.
Lisa:	Oh, I remember now. You were at that meeting with León in Barcelona, weren't you?
Jim:	Yes, about two years ago. There was that wonderful reception, wasn't there?
Lisa:	Yes! Well it's nice to meet you again. Anyway, what do you think of the conference? It's been interesting, hasn't it?

Presentation

Use question tags for asking for information, or for checking and confirming information. They are used in informal speech at the end of affirmative or negative sentences:

*It's Lisa, **isn't it?***

*There was a meeting, **wasn't there?***

Do not use them after questions:

Is it Lisa, isn't it?

Was there a meeting, wasn't there?

Always use contracted forms in the tag.

Don't say: *It's Lisa, is not it?*

When the main verb is affirmative, the tag question is negative:

    +   −

*It's been an interesting conference, **hasn't it?***

When the main verb is negative, the tag question is affirmative:

    −   +

*You don't work with León Alvarez, **do you?***

When the subject is a pronoun, repeat the pronoun:

*It's Lisa, isn't **it?***

When the subject is a noun, use an appropriate pronoun:

*The conference has been interesting, hasn't **it?***

Punctuation

When you write question tags, put a comma between the main sentence and the tag: *It's Lisa, isn't it?*

For the following verbs or verb forms, use the auxiliary (given in brackets) in the question tag.

Verb or verb form + (auxiliary)	Examples
to be (is, are, was, were)	It's Lisa, *isn't it?* I'm late, *aren't I?** (*With I am ..., don't say I'm late, am not I?) You were at that meeting with León in Barcelona, *weren't* you? There was that wonderful reception, *wasn't* there?
Present simple (do/does)	You work for KMC, *don't* you? You don't know my colleague, *do* you?
Past simple (did)	He went to the conference, *didn't* he? They didn't enjoy the presentation, *did* they?
Perfect and continuous (the same auxiliary verb)	The conference has been interesting, *hasn't* it? You aren't listening to me, *are* you?
Modal verbs (the same modal auxiliary verb)	I should leave now, *shouldn't* I? I couldn't buy you a drink, *could* I?
Imperative (will/won't)	Send me your contact details, *won't* you? Don't forget to call me, *will* you?
Let's (shall)	Let's go out for dinner again sometime, *shall* we? Let's not spend too long discussing this, *shall* we?

See page 237: Summary of statements, questions, short answers and short responses

Exercises

1 (8 **1.19**) **Write the question tags in the conversation. Then listen and check.**

> are you   didn't you   do you   haven't we   isn't it   shall we   shouldn't I
> wasn't it   weren't you   will you   won't you

A: We've met before, [1] _____ ?

B: Sorry, you'll have to remind me.

A: You were on a training course with me in Bristol, [2] _____ ?

B: Yes! That was a long time ago, [3] _____ ? I remember now. You aren't Malcolm,
     [4] _____ ?

A: That's right. Malcolm Savage.

B: Peter Franks. Nice to meet you again. It's funny how you meet people again at these events,
     [5] _____ ?

A: Well, it's a small world. You worked for Haversham Plastics then, [6] _____ ?

B: Yes. I still do. You don't do any business with us, [7] _____ ?

A: No, I'm afraid not. But I have a colleague here who works in your industry. In fact he's looking for
     a supplier.

B: I should meet him, [8] _____ ?

A: Yes, but I can't see him at the moment. Never mind. You'll be here later, [9] _____ ?

B: Actually I have to go in a minute.

A: OK. Well, let's keep in touch about this, [10] _____ ? Here's my card with my phone number.
     Don't forget to call me, [11] _____ ?

B: No, I won't. Thanks. It was nice meeting you again.

2 **Write the missing question tags.**

1   You're Marie, _____ ?

2   It's my turn to pay, _____ ?

3   They don't work here, _____ ?

4   She likes sugar in her tea, _____ ?

5   When I lived here, there was a tree here,
    _____ ?

6   They've closed the post office, _____ ?

7   I'm in your group, _____ ?

8   I couldn't borrow a pen, _____ ?

9   He'd already asked her to marry him before,
    _____ ?

10 Sheila's going to be angry about the mess,
    _____ ?

11 Don't forget to give this package to your mother,
    _____ ?

12 All you children must work harder,
    _____ ?

13 Let's take a taxi home, _____ ?

14 It's been a lovely day, _____ ?

3 **Think of someone you know who you haven't seen for a long time. Imagine you meet again. Write questions using these tags.**

1   _____ , aren't you?

2   _____ , don't you?

3   _____ , haven't you?

4   _____ , didn't you?

19 Short answers and responses
Yes, I am./No, I'm not. So do I./Neither do I. Do you?/Don't you?

A: Do you ever buy celebrity magazines?
B: No, I don't.
A: Neither do I. I hate all those lies they print about people.
B: So do I. Did you see what they said about Brad last week?
A: No, I didn't.
B: He's leaving her.
A: Is he?
B: But I don't believe it.

A: Don't you?
B: No, I don't. And do you know why? She'll leave him first.
A: Will she?
B: I'm sure of it. Anyway we'll find out in next week's edition.
A: I thought you said you never read them?
B: No, I said I never *buy* them!

Presentation

Short *yes/no* answers

You can answer a question with just 'yes' or 'no' but it can sound unnatural, abrupt and possibly impolite:

A: *Do you ever read celebrity magazines?*

B: *No.*

When you add a pronoun and an auxiliary verb, a short answer can sound more natural:

A: *Do you ever buy celebrity magazines?*

B: *No, **I don't.***

TIP You can also add extra information after the short answer. This helps the conversation: *Neither do I.* ***I hate all those lies they print about people.***

Use the auxiliary verb from the question in your answer:

Are you ...? *Yes, **I am.**/No, **I'm not.***
Has it ...? *Yes, **it has.**/No, **it hasn't.***
Did we ...? *Yes, **we did.**/No, **we didn't.***
Would you ...? *Yes, **I would.**/No, **I wouldn't.***

Do not use contracted forms in *Yes* answers.

Say *Yes, **I am.*** (don't say ~~Yes, I'm.~~)

*Yes, **I have.*** (don't say ~~Yes, I've.~~)

When writing, put a comma after *yes* or *no*: *Yes, I am.*

Short responses

Use *so do I, neither do I, so am I, neither am I, so have I, neither have I,* etc. to show agreement with the speaker or to say that it is also true for you or someone else.

Affirmative responses

I hate all those lies they print about people. ***So do I.*** (= Me too. I also hate them.)

I'm interested in celebrities. ***So am I.***

Paolo eats at this restaurant. ***So does Pilar.***

Negative responses

I never buy them. ***Neither do I.*** (= I don't buy them either.)

She hasn't got a boyfriend. ***Neither has Anna.***

Short questions

You can respond to a statement with a short question. This shows the other person that you are listening and interested. It can also show surprise:

A: *He's leaving her.*

B: ***Is he?***

If the statement is affirmative, the short question is in the affirmative:

A: *She'll leave him first.*

B: ***Will she?***

If the statement is negative, the short question is in the negative:

A: *I don't believe it.*

B: ***Don't you?***

TIP Using short questions helps a conversation to continue more naturally.

See page 237: Summary of statements, questions, short answers and short responses

Exercises

1 Match the questions and statements (1–10) to the responses (A–J).

1 Are you interested in hearing about Hugh and Penelope? ___D___

2 Was it all true? _____

3 Have you read this month's copy? _____

4 He's in today's newspaper. _____

5 Did he leave her again? _____

6 Will they get back together? _____

7 Would you like to hear some gossip? _____

8 I don't like any of his films. _____

9 I'd love to meet him. _____

10 They told me you had a new girlfriend. _____

A No, he didn't.

B Yes, I would.

C Did they?

D Yes, I am.

E Neither do I.

F So is she.

G Would you?

H No, I haven't.

I No, it wasn't.

J No, they won't.

2 🔊 1.20 Write the missing verbs in these conversations. Then listen and check.

Conversation 1

A: Did you watch the news last night?

B: Yes, I ¹ _did_ . Why?

A: Was there anything on about our town?

B: No, there ² _____ . Was there supposed to be?

A: I thought there'd be something on about that local scandal at the town council.

B: Is there a scandal?

A: Yes, there ³ _____ ! Haven't you heard about it?

B: No, I ⁴ _____ . Tell me!

Conversation 2

C: I'm exhausted!

D: So ⁵ _____ I.

C: Why are you exhausted? You haven't been working all day.

D: Neither ⁶ _____ you.

C: Yes, I have. I was outside in the garden. I wasn't sitting staring at a computer all day.

D: Neither ⁷ _____ I. I was helping Mum and Dad set up their new computer.

C: Well, it's the same thing! Anyway you don't have to be so sensitive about it.

D: Well, neither ⁸ _____ you!

Conversation 3

E: What's the matter with Angie?

F: She won't come out of her room.

E: ⁹ _____ she? Why not?

F: Some problem with her boyfriend. Maybe she'd come out if you spoke to her.

E: ¹⁰ _____ she? I doubt it. She never tells me anything.

F: ¹¹ _____ she? I thought you two were very close.

E: We were until she found a new boyfriend. I told her not to get involved with him.

F: ¹² _____ you? Well, it sounds like you were right!

3 Write questions or statements for B's responses.

A: _____

B: No, I haven't. Tell me about it.

A: _____

B: So did Lisa.

A: _____

B: Were they? I didn't know that.

20 Review of units 16 to 19

Grammar

1 Write in the missing verbs.

1 A: Why _did_ you buy this one?

  B: It was in the sale.

2 You need a new coat. Why _____ you buy yourself one?

3 _____ it a long way? I thought it would be quicker than this.

4 _____ you tell me if this is the right way for the post office?

5 You've got a cat, _____ you?

6 A: I'd love to be able to play the piano.

  B: _____ you? Me too.

7 A: I didn't know we had a test today.

  B: Neither _____ anyone else in the class.

8 Let's stop and take a break, _____ we?

2 Delete the extra word in the questions and conversations.

1 Who ~~did~~ came to your party?

2 What time does everyone arrive at?

3 Haven't not you seen them for a while?

4 Do you have any idea where do they live?

5 Is your daughter is getting married to him? I don't believe it!

6 I wonder whether do that man over there can give us directions.

7 A: I love steak and chips!
  B: Do you love?

8 They weren't very happy about something, were not they?

3 Rewrite the question in bold in three other ways.

Are you going to tell her?

1 You are going to tell her, _aren't you?_

2 Can I ask you if _____ to tell her?

3 Aren't _____ to tell her?

Hasn't Rachel finished her course?

4 Rachel's finished her course, _____?

5 Has _____ her course?

6 Do you know if _____ her course?

Could you help me move this wardrobe?

7 You couldn't help me move this wardrobe, _____?

8 I wonder if _____ this wardrobe?

9 Couldn't _____ this wardrobe?

Does he look like you?

10 He looks _____?

11 He doesn't _____?

12 I'd like to know if _____.

4 Write a statement or question for the responses using the words in brackets.

1 (what / like) _____
  Quite short, but he's good looking.

2 (when / happen) _____
  At about three in the morning.

3 (do / know / if) _____
  Yes, it is. It's going to rain this afternoon.

4 (you / Maria / aren't) _____
  Yes, I am. Have we met before?

5 (type / car / drive) _____
  I think she drives a Mercedes.

6 (can't / give / report / tomorrow) _____
  No, you can't! If you give me it tomorrow, it'll be too late.

7 (my daughter / eat / any kind of vegetable) _____

  Neither does my son. He also refuses to eat any kind of fruit.

8 (buy / new hat) _____
  So have I. This is mine. Let's see yours.

Grammar in context

5 🎧 **1.21 Read an extract from a short story called *The man with the twisted lip*. Complete the questions in the text with the words in brackets. Then listen and check.**

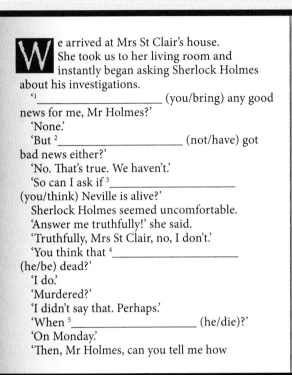

We arrived at Mrs St Clair's house. She took us to her living room and instantly began asking Sherlock Holmes about his investigations.

'¹_____ (you/bring) any good news for me, Mr Holmes?'

'None.'

'But ²_____ (not/have) got bad news either?'

'No. That's true. We haven't.'

'So can I ask if ³_____ (you/think) Neville is alive?'

Sherlock Holmes seemed uncomfortable.

'Answer me truthfully!' she said.

'Truthfully, Mrs St Clair, no, I don't.'

'You think that ⁴_____ (he/be) dead?'

'I do.'

'Murdered?'

'I didn't say that. Perhaps.'

'When ⁵_____ (he/die)?'

'On Monday.'

'Then, Mr Holmes, can you tell me how

⁶_____ (I receive) a letter from him today?'

'⁷_____ (do/you)?' Sherlock Holmes jumped from his chair.

She passed him the letter and there was silence for a few minutes as Holmes studied the writing. Finally, he spoke, 'And you're certain it's your husband's handwriting, ⁸_____ (be)?'

'I am. He must be alive, Mr Holmes.'

Pronunciation: intonation in question tags

6 🎧 **1.22 The intonation on question tags rises when the speaker is unsure and falls when the speaker is sure. Listen to these sentences and tick the intonation you hear.**

1 We've met before, haven't we? ↑ ✓ ↓

2 That was a long time ago, wasn't it? ↑ ↓ ✓

3 You aren't Michael's colleague, are you? ↓ ↑

4 You don't do any business with us, do you? ↑ ↓

5 You will be here later, won't you? ↑ ↓

6 Let's keep in touch about this, shall we? ↑ ↓

7 Don't forget to call me, will you? ↑ ↓

8 We weren't at school together, were we? ↑ ↓

Listen again and repeat the sentences.

Listen again

7 🎧 **1.23 Listen to the intonation in this conversation at a conference. Are these sentences true or false? Circle the correct answer.**

1 The two men haven't met before.   True / False

2 Both men recognised each other straight away.   True / False

3 Malcolm doesn't do business with Peter's company.   True / False

4 Peter can stay late to meet someone.   True / False

5 Malcolm suggests they stay in touch.   True / False

6 Peter will forget to call him back.   True / False

21 Pronouns

Personal, possessive, reflexive and reciprocal pronouns and *one/ones*

Man:	Excuse me, that's mine.
Woman:	But I bought it in London.
Twins:	Actually, it's ours.
Woman:	Well, whose is that one?
Twins:	It's also ours. We gave each other those bags for our birthdays.
Man:	How do you know those are yours? There's no difference between them!
Twins:	Of course we know which ones are ours – we packed them ourselves!

Presentation

Use pronouns to substitute for a noun:

Subject pronouns (*I, you, he, she, it, we, you, they*): *He bought it in London.*

Object pronouns (*me, you, him, her, it, us, you, them*): *He bought **it** in London.*

Possessive pronouns (*mine, yours, his, hers, its, ours, yours, theirs*): *It's **mine**. (= my case)*

Reflexive pronouns

Use reflexive pronouns:

- when the subject and object are the same: *I hurt **myself** with this knife.*

- to emphasise that the subject did something alone (without anyone else): *We packed them **ourselves**.*

Reflexive pronouns come after:

- the verb: *I **hurt** myself.*

- the direct object: *We packed **them** ourselves.*

English doesn't use reflexive pronouns as much as some other languages. You normally use reflexive pronouns to emphasise the verb/action. For example:

He got up at six. (= normal everyday activity)

*He got **himself** up this morning.* (= not typical. Someone else normally gets him up.)

Reciprocal pronouns

You use *each other* or *one another* to say that each person or thing does the same to the other person or thing:

*We bought **each other** those bags for our birthdays.*
(= One twin gave her sister a case and the other twin did the same.)

TIP Notice the difference between these sentences:
They bought each other those bags. (= bought the bag for another person)
They bought themselves bags. (= didn't buy the bag for another person)

one/ones as a pronoun

You can use *one/ones* as pronouns:

*This silver case is mine. = This **one** is mine.*

*These silver cases are ours. = These **ones** are ours.*

You often use *one/ones*:

- with *this, that, these,* and *those*: *this one is mine, these ones are ours*

- with adjectives: *the metal one*

- in questions with *Which ...?*: *Which one is yours?*

- with articles (*the, a/an*): *It's the one over there ..., it's a metal one*

Note that you cannot use *a/an + one* without an adjective. (don't say *It's a one.*)

Exercises

1 **Rewrite the sentences. Replace the words in bold with personal or possessive pronouns.**

1 Joanna doesn't like **Nigel**.
   She doesn't like him.

2 **Their homework** is easier than **our homework**.

3 Is there any difference between **the bags**?

4 **Mandy and Alena** worked with **Greg and Bettina** in Budapest.

2 **Look at the pairs of sentences (A and B). One sentence is incorrect. Cross out the unnecessary reflexive or reciprocal pronoun.**

1 A: My son dressed himself for the first time today! ✓
   B: Every day, I get dressed ~~myself~~ and then go to work. ✗

2 A: I won't be here tomorrow, so you need to get yourself dinner.
   B: I won't be here tomorrow, so go out yourself for dinner.

3 A: That painting's wonderful. Did they paint it themselves?
   B: That painting's wonderful. Did they paint themselves it?

4 A: Let's save money this Christmas and just buy each other something small.
   B: Let's save money this Christmas and just buy yourselves something small.

5 A: Patrick always hurts themselves when he plays outside with other children.
   B: Patrick always hurts himself when he plays outside with other children.

3 **⏸1.24 Underline the correct pronouns in these conversations. Then listen and check.**

A: I'm calling again about the cases I lost on the bus from Glasgow yesterday.

B: Which ¹one / ones were those?

A: There was a metal ²one / ones and two blue ³one / ones.

B: Sorry, but I don't know anything about it.

A: But don't you have my report form? I filled ⁴one / ones in yesterday.

4 **Write the missing pronoun.**

1 A: Who broke this vase?
   B: Well, it wasn't _____ . I've only just arrived.

2 What's the matter with _____ ? You look terrible!

3 We want to hear your plans, so tell _____ everything.

4 That book's _____ . Can you pass it to me?

5 This coat looks a bit like Sally's. Is it _____ ?

6 A: Did you make this cake _____ ?
   B: No, I bought it.

7 If you don't like the way I'm doing it, you can do it _____ !

8 Which _____ is yours? The blue or the grey bag?

22 Countability and plural nouns

Barman:	Would you like to order any drinks?
Guest:	Yes, please. What is a Pussyfoot?
Barman:	It's a type of cocktail.
Guest:	What's in it?
Barman:	It's mainly orange juice with some sparkling water and a tablespoon of lemon juice and two tablespoons of lime juice. You add an egg and shake it. Then you serve it with ice and a slice of orange.

Presentation

Nouns can be countable, uncountable or both.

Countable nouns have a singular and a plural form: *a drink, drinks; an egg, eggs*

Uncountable nouns only have a singular form (*advice, advices, furniture, furnitures, milk, milks*) and use a singular verb: *Orange juice **is** a drink.*

Countable and uncountable nouns

Some nouns are both countable and uncountable, but the meaning changes:

There's some pizza left. (= part of a pizza)

*There are **some pizzas** in the oven.* (= more than one whole pizza)

*The job interview was **an interesting experience**.* (= a specific experience)

Experience is more important than qualifications for this job. (= knowledge or skills in general)

*Keep your seatbelts fastened at all **times**.* (= on all occasions)

*There isn't much **time** left!* (= the general concept of time)

Do you drink coffee? (= coffee in general)

I'd like a coffee, please. (The speaker misses out 'cup of' as in *I'd like a cup of coffee, please.* This is also true for many type of drinks: *an orange juice, a water*, etc.)

Only plural or only singular

Some nouns are only plural (they have no singular form) and need a plural verb. They include: *glasses (for your eyes), goods, jeans, savings, scissors, stairs, trousers.*

*The **goods** are at the warehouse.*

*Are these your **glasses**? (not Is this your glasses?)*

Some nouns are only singular (they have no plural form) and need a singular verb. They include: *news, politics, economics, mathematics.*

*Mathematics **is** my favourite subject.*

*The news **isn't** good I'm afraid.*

Singular or plural

Nouns that describe **groups of people** (*band, class, family, government, staff, team*) can take a **singular or plural** verb.

*Our family **is/are** coming to our house for Christmas.*

When we think of the group as being made up of many individuals, each acting separately, we use a plural form:

*The government **are** currently discussing the proposal.* (= the various members of the government)

When acting as a united group, we use a singular form:

*The government **is** ready to cut taxes.* (= the government acting as one body)

Police and *people* are always followed by a **plural** verb.

*The police **have arrested** a man for the murder.*

*The people **are waiting** for information about the delay.*

We say **police officer** to refer to an individual member of the police force.

Two police officers appeared before the court.

Noun phrases using *a ... of*

You can modify countable and uncountable nouns with expressions such as *a kind of, a sort of, a type of, a bit of, a piece of, a lot of*:

*A bowler is **a kind of** hat.*

*A penguin is **a type of** bird.*

*I need **a bit of** time.*

TIP Often a specific expression collocates with a specific noun: *a loaf of bread, a slice of lemon, a glass of water, a tin of beans.*

Exercises

1 **Seven sentences have one incorrect word (*X*). Three sentences are correct (✓). Cross out the incorrect words and write them correctly.**

1 How much ~~baggages~~ have you got with you?
   baggage

2 That's a nice watch. _____ ✓

3 A lot of snows fell last night.
   _____

4 My glasses needs mending.
   _____

5 Goggles must be worn at all time.
   _____

6 DVDs are really cheap at this shop.
   _____

7 Would you like some drink?
   _____

8 Sorry, I don't have any gossips for you today.
   _____

9 Have you got an information about the castle?
   _____

10 Three coffees, please. _____

2 **Match the expressions on the left to the nouns on the right. Then write the phrases beneath the pictures.**

| a type of | a loaf of | a piece of | lemon | cards | soup |
| a tin of | a pack of | a slice of | bread | cake | insect |

1 *a slice of lemon*

2 _____

3 _____

4 _____

5 _____

6 _____

3 **Underline the correct verb form, singular or plural, in italics. In one sentence, both forms are possible.**

1 Be careful. These stairs *is / are* very steep.

2 A pinch of salt *help / helps* the taste.

3 Your advice *is / are* always very helpful.

4 How well *do / does* your trousers fit?

5 Your scissors *cut / cuts* really well.

6 My team *isn't / aren't* very good. They lose every match.

7 The police *haven't / hasn't* arrested anyone yet.

4 **Read the pairs of sentences and match them to the correct responses (A or B).**

1 I'd like an orange juice, please. *B*

2 I'd like a carton of orange juice, please. *A*

A Sorry, we've sold out. We're waiting for a delivery.

B With ice?

3 I've baked the cakes. _____

4 There's some cake left. _____

A Let's try one.

B OK. I'll have some with my tea.

5 Do I have to wear a safety helmet? _____

6 Shall I wear this as well? Does it go with my necklace? _____

A Yes, at all times.

B Yes, but hurry up. We haven't got much time.

23 Articles 1
Indefinite and definite articles, zero article, *some*

JRR Tolkein was a professor at Oxford University. He wrote a children's book called The Hobbit *in 1937. Since then, the book has been translated into more than 30 languages and sold millions of copies worldwide. The book begins at the home of a hobbit called Bilbo Baggins …*

Chapter 1

In a hole in the ground there lived a hobbit.

Presentation

Indefinite article *a/an*

Use the indefinite article *a/an*:

- to talk about one person or one thing in a general way (and it doesn't matter which one):
  *She lived in **a house** in Manchester.*

- to talk about something or someone for the first time (we don't know which one):
  *In **a hole** in the ground …*

- to say that a person or thing is one of many:
  *He was **a professor** at Oxford University.* (There is more than one professor.)

Definite article *the*

Use the definite article *the*:

- to talk about a specific person or thing:
  *JRR Tolkien was **the author** of* The Hobbit.

- to add a description of the specific thing or person:
  ***The hole** had a round door.*

- to refer back to the same thing or person:

  The hole had a round door. The door opened on to a hall.

- to say that a person or thing is the only one in that context:
  … by the entrance (the entrance to the house; there is only one entrance)

Zero article

Use no article to talk about:

- people or things in a general way:

  *The hobbit was fond of **visitors**.*

  ***Houses** in England often have gardens.*

some

Note that *some* isn't an article but it can replace *a/an* or the *zero article* when you talk about plural countable nouns, or uncountable nouns.

*There's **a chair** in the hall.* → *There are **some chairs** in the hall.*

*There's **furniture** in the hall.* → *There's **some furniture** in the hall.*

We often use *some* to say *a number of …* rather than talking about people/things in general:

I like books about fantasy. (= all books)

*I like **some** books about fantasy.* (= a number of books, but not all)

Exercises

1   Read the text. One of the options in italics (1–6) is not possible. Underline it.

Last weekend we visited ¹*a / the / Ø* castle near my home. It has ²*an / some / Ø* ancient statues at the entrance. The main door opens on to ³*an / some / the* entrance hall and the first painting you see is a portrait of ⁴*a / Ø / the* previous owner. All the rooms have ⁵*a / some / Ø* beautiful furniture. The disappointing thing was that I wanted ⁶*Ø / an / some* information about its history but no one there seemed to know anything about it.

2   🔊1.25 Read this description of a room from a play called *A Doll's House*. Complete it using *a*, *an* or *the*. Then listen and check.

> ## ACT I Scene 1
>
> The audience sees ¹_____ comfortable room. At the back of ²_____ stage, there are two doors. There is ³_____ piano between ⁴_____ two doors. One door leads to ⁵_____ entrance-hall and ⁶_____ other door, which is partly open, leads to a study. We can see part of a desk in ⁷_____ study. On the left-hand wall of the main room, there is ⁸_____ window and there are two armchairs near it. On the right-hand side, there is another window and, in front of it, ⁹_____ stove and ¹⁰_____ rocking-chair. There's ¹¹_____ small table between ¹²_____ stove and ¹³_____ rocking-chair. There are pictures on ¹⁴_____ walls and a small bookcase with some books. A fire burns in ¹⁵_____ stove.

3   Read the sets of three sentences. Write one indefinite article, one definite article and one zero article (Ø) in A, B and C.

1   A   Henrik Ibsen was _____ author of the play *A Doll's House*.
    B   Henrik Ibsen was _____ playwright from Norway.
    C   Henrik wrote _____ plays in the 19ᵗʰ century.

2   A   I like watching _____ comedy shows on TV.
    B   There's _____ episode of that new TV show on this evening.
    C   Have you seen _____ new detective show on Channel 5? It's great!

3   A   We have _____ accommodation for 30 guests.
    B   Here are your keys. _____ room is on the second floor.
    C   Do you have _____ room for two, please?

4   A   They live in _____ house in the centre of Rome.
    B   Some people still live in _____ houses made of straw.
    C   They live in _____ same house that Shakespeare once lived in.

5   A   Would you like _____ piece of chocolate?
    B   In my opinion _____ chocolate they make in Mexico is the best in the world.
    C   I'm very fond of _____ chocolate.

Benjamin Franklin

Benjamin Franklin is famous as one of the Founding Fathers of the United States of America, but did you also know that ...?

- His inventions included the lightning rod, the Franklin Stove, the Glass Armonica (a type of musical instrument), as well as bifocals and swim fins!
- He set up the first public library and the first team of firefighters in Philadelphia.
- He believed that hard work, education and community spirit were the most important values for a society.
- He played the violin, the harp and the guitar. He also played chess and spoke Italian and French.
- He was the US Ambassador to France during the Revolutionary War and had a home near the River Seine.

Presentation

the

Use *the* with:

- *play* + musical instrument: *play the violin, the harp and the guitar*
- the name of (a specific) invention: *the lightning rod, the Franklin Stove*
- an adjective to talk about a group of people: *the rich, the guilty*
- professional bodies: *the police, the army, the media*
- words about the weather and climate: *the wind, the rain*
- deserts: *the Gobi, the Sahara*
- rivers: *the Amazon, the Seine*
- mountain ranges: *the Alps, the Himalayas*
- oceans and seas: *the Pacific, the Mediterranean*
- groups of countries or states: *the USA, the European Union*
- countries whose names are plural: *the Philippines, the Maldives*
- countries whose names include a political label: *the United Kingdom, the People's Republic of China*
- some buildings: *the White House, the Eiffel Tower*
- periods of time and history: *the holidays, the weekend, the sixties, the 18ᵗʰ century, the Enlightenment*
- geographical regions: *the Americas, the north, the coast, the mountains, the countryside, the world*
- superlatives: *the best, the most important*
- titles: *the President, the Revolutionary War*
- newspapers: *The Pennsylvania Gazette, The Times*
- some common expressions: *go to the theatre/bank/cinema/gym/shops/city centre*

No article

You use no article with:

- meals as part of a routine: *What do you have for breakfast?*
- *play* + sports/games: *play tennis, play chess*
- *by* + transport: *by car, by taxi, by train*
- possessive *'s*: *Sally's house, Franklin's invention*
- towns and cities: *Paris, Boston*
- most countries: *France, New Zealand, South Africa*
- continents: *Asia, Africa, Europe, Antarctica*
- lakes and mountains: *Lake Geneva, Mount Everest*
- days of the week, months and years: *Monday, Tuesday, January, February, 1991, 2001*
- languages: *Italian, Japanese*
- school subjects: *Geography, History, Art*
- magazines: *Vogue, Hello!*
- some common expressions: *to/at/from school/university/college/church/work; to/in(to)/out of hospital/prison; on holiday*

Exercises

1 **🔊1.26** **Complete the text with _the_ or no article (Ø). Then listen and check.**

Hedy Lamarr
Actress and inventor

Hedy Lamarr was an Austrian actress born in ¹_____ Vienna who went on to become one of ²_____ most famous Hollywood actresses of ³_____ 20th century. Her real name was Hedwig Eva Maria Kiesler. Her mother was a pianist and influenced her daughter's artistic skills as she studied ⁴_____ ballet and soon became an actress. She became well known in ⁵_____ European films and was called '⁶_____most beautiful woman in ⁷_____ Europe'. In 1933, she married Fritz Mandal, but she left him ⁸_____ four years later. She went to ⁹_____ London and met Louis B. Mayer, a film producer. He changed her name to Hedy Lamarr and she went to ¹⁰_____ Hollywood. Nowadays, Lamarr is well known for her many films from ¹¹_____ forties and fifties. However, she was also very intelligent and invented ¹²_____ secret communications system in ¹³_____ 1942 which could change radio frequencies and protect radio messages. At the time, the technology was too advanced to help ¹⁴_____ US Army in World War II, but since then it has been used by ¹⁵_____ modern military and the mobile phone industry.

2 **Cross out _the_ in sentences 1–11 where it's not needed.**

1 What time do you normally eat ~~the~~ lunch.

2 *The Times of India* is the country's most widely-read English newspaper. ✓

3 Have you finished with your copy of the *Newsweek?* Can I read it?

4 The United Nations' headquarters is in the New York.

5 Let's leave the car and go by the bus for a change.

6 Are you going to the gym later?

7 What can we do about the poor in our society?

8 My uncle is in the hospital with a broken leg.

9 The Italian Renaissance was famous for painters like Michelangelo and Leonardo da Vinci.

10 My favourite subject has always been the Geography.

11 They say you can float and read a newspaper on the Dead Sea.

3 **Complete these sentences in your own words. Use _the_ or no article in your answers.**

1 The most famous place to visit in my country is _____ .

2 I can play _____ .

3 The invention of _____ was probably the most important of the last century.

4 My country is part of the continent of _____ .

5 In my country, everyone has to study _____ in school.

6 My favourite meal of the day is _____ .

25 Review of units 21 to 24

Grammar

1 Match the two halves of the sentences (1–10 and A–J).

1. There's a _D_   A is yours?
2. I wrote it _____   B is cheaper here.
3. These ones _____   C some keys here.
4. Help each _____   D giant hole in the road.
5. Food _____   E other with this exercise.
6. Goods _____   F are ours.
7. This _____   G any keys here.
8. There are _____   H are cheaper here.
9. There aren't _____   I myself.
10. Which one _____   J one is hers.

2 One word is missing from each sentence. Complete the sentences using the words in the box.

> a   he   hers   itself   of   the   two
> us   yourself

1. There's ᵃ good film on TV tonight.

2. Where did you find it? Julia had a ring just like that one, so I think it might be.

3. Give a piece of your chocolate!

4. This machine is automatic, so you don't need to switch it off. It switches off.

5. Ladies and gentlemen, please stand up for President.

6. I always like a bit sugar in my tea.

7. Can I have apple juices, please?

8. Don't hurt with that knife!

9. If argues with you, then argue back!

3 Cross out one word in each sentence so the sentence is still correct (though the meaning might change).

1. I'll have ~~an~~ orange, please.
2. Is this one his?
3. Sandra likes her flowers.
4. The breakfast was disgusting!
5. There's some cheese in the fridge.
6. That one is yours.

4 Match the names to the places. Add *the* where necessary.

> Dubai   Gobi Desert   Lake Balaton   Moon
> Mount Kilimanjaro   Taj Mahal

1 _____

2 _____

3 _____

4 _____

5 _____

6 _____

Grammar in context

5 🔊**1.27** **Read part of a play. Complete the text with the words A, B or C. Then listen and check.**

Jamieson enters the hotel. He is carrying a package. Menning is at reception.

Jamieson Good afternoon. Do you have a guest staying with ¹_____ called Ms Green?

Menning Yes, we do.

Jamieson Good. She asked me to deliver ²_____.

Menning I can give it to ³_____.

Jamieson Actually, she specifically requested that I deliver it ⁴_____ – in person.

Menning As you like. But I know she's gone out. You'll have to wait.

Jamieson Does the hotel have a car park? ⁵_____ car is parked illegally out the front.

Menning Sorry, we don't. You might want to move it. ⁶_____ police often drive up this street.

Jamieson Damn!

Menning Honestly, I can give her ⁷_____. It'll be perfectly safe.

Jamieson I suppose so.

Jamieson reluctantly hands Menning the package and runs out the main doors. Menning places the package below reception. At the same time, Ms Green comes out of the lift.

Green Hello. Did ⁸_____ man come looking for me? He has black hair and he would have a package for me.

Menning I haven't seen him. But you do have ⁹_____.

Menning hands her some letters.

Green Thanks. If he comes, tell him I'm at the bar, will you? It's important that we see ¹⁰_____.

Menning Of course.

Green exits and Menning hurriedly opens the package. He pulls out a large wad of notes.

1	A you	B your	C yours	6	A A	B The	C Ø
2	A this	B that	C one	7	A them	B that	C those
3	A she	B her	C hers	8	A a	B the	C Ø
4	A itself	B herself	C myself	9	A this	B these	C those
5	A Me	B My	C Mine	10	A ourselves	B each other	C himself

Pronunciation: vowel sounds

6 🔊**1.28** **Listen to the vowel sounds in these words. Put them in the correct column.**

bit mine I she type me each
him piece his it my we

/ɪ/	/iː/	/aɪ/

Listen again and repeat the words.

Listen again

7 🔊**1.29** **Listen to a biography of Hedy Lamarr. Write the missing words in these statements. Be careful to use the correct article.**

1 Hedy Lamarr was _____ actress.

2 She became _____ most famous actresses in Hollywood.

3 Her mother was _____.

4 She was called _____ in Europe.

5 After her first marriage, she went to _____ and met Louis B. Mayer.

6 She invented _____.

7 Nowadays it's used by _____ and the mobile phone industry.

26 *some, any, no, none, some-, any-, no-*

The problems people have with their computers

When you work for Computer Support, customers telephone with some crazy problems. Here are some of the best!

'This side of the CD works, but there isn't anything on the other side …'

'Does any of this software need a computer?'

'I'd like some stamps so I can send emails.'

'The screen says "press any key" but I can't see the ANY KEY button.'

'There's nowhere to insert the disc. Is it anywhere near the cup holder?'

'If I log in as me, how does the computer know it isn't someone else?'

Presentation

Use *some, any* and *no* with plural and uncountable nouns.

some and *any*

Some refers to a part of a group or thing, but not all of it. You can use *some*:

- in affirmative sentences: *I'd like **some** stamps.* (= an unspecified number); *I'd like **some** cake.* (= part of, but not all of it)

- to make requests and offers: *Can I have **some** help? Would you like **some** help?* (an unspecified amount)

- with a negative verb to exclude part of a group or thing: ***Some** computers aren't as reliable as others.* (an unspecified number of computers, but not all)

Any can refer to a part, all or none of a group or thing. You can use *any*:

- in affirmative sentences when the quantity is not important: *Tell me if there are **any** problems with your computer.* (all problems, no matter how many or what kind of problem it is)

- in questions, with plural or uncountable nouns: *Do you have **any** stamps? How we got **any** butter?*

- in affirmative sentences, often with a singular noun, when *any* means 'it doesn't matter which': *Press **any** key.*

- with negative sentences and questions: *There aren't **any** stamps.* (none)

You can use *some* and *any* without a noun when the meaning is clear: *Have you got **any** stamps? Yes, there are **some** in my purse. / Sorry, I haven't got **any**.*

You can also use *some* and *any* with *of*. The verb with *some/any of* + plural noun is plural: ***Some of** the computers **are** very old.* The verb with *some/any of* + uncountable noun is singular: ***Does any of** the software need updating?*

no and *none*

Use *no* and *none* with an affirmative verb in both questions and statements. The meaning is similar to *not any* but *no/none* is slightly more emphatic:

*Are there **no** stamps? There are **none**.* (don't say *There ~~aren't~~ no stamps/none.*)

Do not use *no* without a noun or with *of*. Say *There are **none** left.* (don't say *There are ~~no~~ left.*) Say ***None of** the computers work.* (don't say *~~No~~ of the computers work.*)

Do not use *none* with a noun: *Are there ~~none~~ stamps left? No, there are none ~~stamps~~.*

> **TIP** *none of* + plural noun can take a plural verb or singular verb: *None of the computers work.* ✓ *None of the computers works.* ✓

some-, any-, no-

You can add *-one, -body, -where, -thing* to *some-, any-, no-* to talk in general about people, places and things: *How does the computer know it isn't **someone** else? There isn't **anything** on the other side. There's **nowhere** to put a disc.*

When one of these words is the subject of a sentence, the verb is in the singular form: ***Someone is** on the phone.*

You can also use these words before an adjective: *This computer is too slow. I'd like **something** faster.*

Exercises

1 ⏵1.30 **Write *some, any, no* or *none* in this conversation. Then listen and check.**

A: Computer Support. Briony speaking.

B: Hello, I need ¹_____ help with my new computer. There are ²_____ pictures on the screen. It's completely blank.

A: OK. I'm going to ask you ³_____ questions first. What sort of computer is it?

B: A white one.

A: What's the serial number on your computer?

B: I can't see ⁴_____ numbers.

A: There should be ⁵_____ small letters and numbers on the left side of the screen. Are there ⁶_____ on it?

B: Oh yes! They're very small. VFN-FF2303.

A: And when you bought the computer, did you put ⁷_____ new software on it?

B: No, ⁸_____. Perhaps that's why the screen is black.

A: Black? Have you switched it on?

B: Switched it on?

2 **All the sentences below contain a mistake. Correct the sentences by changing or crossing out one word in each.**

              any
1 We don't have ~~some~~ copies of Mafia Maze II.

2 I've got any blank discs. I'll give you them.

3 There aren't no lessons today.

4 No, there are none lessons today.

5 Some of people prefer this kind of mouse.

6 Do no of these machines work properly?

3 **Complete the conversations with words beginning with *some-, any-* or *no-*. More than one word is possible in some sentences.**

1 A: Who's the person at the door?

   B: It's _____ about the plumbing. He's here to fix it.

2 A: Did you go away at the weekend?

   B: No, we didn't go _____. I was so bored!

3 A: Did you call that number?

   B: Yes, but _____ answered.

4 A: Is there _____ interesting on TV?

   B: Yes, there's a programme about polar bears.

5 A: What's the matter with your computer?

   B: I don't know. _____ isn't working properly.

6 A: This car is very popular with families.

   B: I don't like it. Do you have _____ more sporty?

4 **Describe the room you are in by completing these sentences.**

1 It has got some _____ , but there aren't any _____ .

2 Also, there are no _____ .

3 None of the _____ are new, but some of the _____ are.

4 My _____ are somewhere in the room, but I can't see them at the moment.

The Rules of Chess Boxing

If you already know all the rules of chess and boxing, then the rules of Chess boxing are simple:

1 Both opponents are required to box and play chess over eleven rounds. All contests start with a round of chess which is followed by a round of boxing.

2 Every round of chess is four minutes long and every round of boxing lasts three. There is a one-minute pause between each of the rounds to put the gloves on or take them off.

3 Each contestant can win either by checkmate or by a knockout. If neither person wins, the referee makes the final decision based on the number of punches in the ring and pieces left on the board.

Presentation

all, every, each

Use *all, every* and *each* to talk generally about people or things.

Use *all/all the/all of the* + plural and uncountable nouns to talk about **three** or more people or things: *All contests/All the contests/All of the contests start with a round of chess.*

Use *every* + singular noun to talk about **three** or more people or things: *Every round of boxing lasts three minutes.*

You can also use *every* with *-where, -thing, -one, -body*: *Everyone who chess-boxes is physically and mentally strong.*

Use *each* + singular noun to talk about **two** or more people or things: *Each contestant can win by checkmate or by a knockout.*

You can say *each of the* without any change of meaning but with a plural noun: *Each of the contestants can win …* (don't say *Each of contestants can win …* or *Each of the contestant can win …*)

all, each or every?

There is a slight difference in meaning between *all* and *each/every*. You use *all* to refer to the group as a whole: *All rounds of boxing last three minutes.* You use *each/ every* to refer to the individual parts of the group: *Every/Each round of boxing lasts three minutes.*

You can only use *every* when it refers to **three or more.** You can always use *each* because it refers to **two or more**: *Every round …* (11 rounds), *Each contestant …* (two contestants)

Use *all* + plural noun with a plural verb: *All the contests start with a round of chess.* Use *all* +

uncountable noun with a singular verb: *All the money goes to charity.*

Use *every* (and compounds of *every*) and *each* with a singular verb: *Every match ends in checkmate or a knockout. Everybody takes it very seriously.*

You can use *each of* + plural countable noun with either a plural or a singular verb: *Each of the contestants have/ has a personal coach.*

both, either, neither

You use *both/both of the* + plural noun to say the same thing about two people or things: *Both opponents/Both of the opponents are required to box and play chess.*

Either/neither is followed by a singular noun: *either contestant, neither contestant*

Use *neither* to express a negative meaning: *If neither person wins, the referee makes the final decision.*

Use *either … or* to say that there are two possible options: *A contestant can win either by checkmate or by a knockout.*

You can use *not … either* instead of *neither*: *The fighter didn't win either match. = The fighter won neither match.*

Use *both/neither/either of …* with pronouns or *the* + noun: *Both of them play chess. Neither of us know(s) how to box. Either of the contestants could win.*

Use *neither … nor* to talk about two people or things in a negative sentence: *Neither he nor his brother play chess.* (= neither of the brothers play chess)

TIP With *both*, the verb is plural: *Both of them know how to box.* With *either* and *neither*, the verb can be singular or plural: *Neither of us know(s) how to box. Do/Does either of you know how to box?*

Exercises

1 Underline the correct option. Both answers are possible in one sentence.

1 *All / Every* player on our team wants to play in the World Cup.

2 *Every / Each* performer appears in front of three judges.

3 *Every / Each of the* players wears a helmet in ice hockey.

4 *All / Both* halves in a football match are 45 minutes long.

5 This is a close match. *Both / Either* competitor could win.

6 A: Do you ever watch golf or bowls?

   B: No, I'm not interested in *either / neither*.

2 Look at the verbs in these sentences. Tick the correct verbs and change the incorrect verbs.

1 Each person on the team has a number. ✓

2 Each of them ~~are~~ *is* allowed five shots at the goal.

3 All of the information were helpful.

4 All the managers were at the meeting.

5 Every athlete need a medical inspection before the event.

6 Both answers are correct.

7 Either contestant is a potential world champion.

8 Neither of us have played this game before.

3 🔊 1.31 Choose the correct options to complete the article. Then listen and check.

The Rules of Football-Tennis

THE COURT
[1]*All / Each / Every* football-tennis matches are played on a court.
[2]*All / Every / Both* court must be the same size as a standard doubles tennis court. The court is divided into two halves by the net.

THE TEAMS
[3]*Each / All / Both* team has a total of five players, with three players on the court. [4]*Each / Both / Neither* team is allowed to make more than two substitutions per game, but they can make more over the whole match.

THE MATCH
[5]*Either / Every / All* match is decided over three games or when [6]*either / every / all* of the teams has won two games. The winner of [7]*neither / each / both* game must score 15 points. There is a three-minute break between [8]*all / both / every* game.

OTHER RULES
A team can pass the ball three times but then has to kick or head it over the net. [9]*Neither / Either / Both* the player's hand nor arm can touch the ball.

4 Complete these sentences about sport so that they are true for you.

1 In my country, all children learn to play either _____ or _____ at school.

2 All my friends like watching _____ .

3 I'm not interested in either _____ or _____ .

28 lots, much, many, little, few

lots of, a lot of, how much/many, not much/many, a little/few, too much/many, too little/few

The world has water for everyone but...

■ HOW MANY COUNTRIES WILL HAVE A serious water shortage by the end of the 21st century? Few experts are in any doubt about the answer to this question: 'Too many.' Even by 2025, the World Resources Institute predicts that 3 billion people in 48 countries will have too little water for their everyday needs. However, a few experts say there could be water for everyone on one condition – that more of us recognise its real value. John Briscoe, senior water advisor to the World Bank, says that if we don't pay much money for it, 'as with anything else, people will waste it.'

Presentation

You use *lots of* (or *a lot of*), *much*, *many*, *a little* and *a few* to talk about quantities:

	Uncountable nouns	Plural nouns
Questions	*How much ...?*	*How many ...?*
Large quantities	*lots of / a lot of*	*lots of / a lot of, many*
Small quantities	*(a) little, not much*	*(a) few, not many*

lots of / a lot of

Use *lots of* or *a lot of* to talk about large quantities. *Lots of* is less formal than *a lot of*:

Lots of experts agree. = *A lot of experts agree.*

Do not use *of* when there is no noun, for example, in short answers:

How many people believe this? Say ***A lot***. (don't say *A lot ~~of~~*.)

much / many

You usually use *much/many* in:

- questions: ***How many*** *countries are affected?* ***How much*** *water do they have?*

- negative statements to talk about small quantities: *People* ***don't*** *pay* ***much*** *money for water.* ***Not many*** *countries have a lot of water.*

You can also use *not much* and *not many* in short answers: *How many countries will have a lot of water?* ***Not many.***

You don't normally use *much* in affirmative statements. You normally use *a lot/lots*. Say *We've got* ***a lot of*** *juice in the fridge.* (don't say *We've got ~~much~~ juice in the fridge.*)

You can use *many* in affirmative statements which are more formal (and often written): ***Many*** *people agree on the solution* (formal). ***A lot of*** *people waste water* (everyday).

little / a little / few / a few

You use *little/a little* and *few/a few* to talk about small quantities in affirmative statements. *A little* and *a few* have a positive meaning. *Little* and *few* have a negative meaning:

There's ***a little*** *water left in the jug.* ☺

There's ***little*** *water left in the jug.* ☹

A ***few*** *experts believe there is no water shortage.* ☺

Few *experts believe there is no water shortage.* ☹

> **TIP** *not much/not many* have a similar meaning to *very little/very few*:
> *There* **isn't much** *time.* = *There's* ***very little*** *time.*

too many / too much / too few / too little

Use *too much/too many* to talk about **more** than you want or need: ***Too much*** *water is wasted.* ***Too many*** *countries will have a water shortage. You've got* ***too much*** *food on your plate. Put some back.*

Use *too little/too few* to talk about **less** than you want or need: ***Too little*** *sleep can be very bad for you.* ***Too few*** *senior jobs in the world of finance go to women.*

> **TIP** *too* often has a negative meaning.

See Unit 37: Modifying adjectives and adverbs

Exercises

1 **Complete the pairs of sentences using the words in bold.**

little / a little

1 I've got _____ sympathy with anyone who breaks the law! They should go to prison!

2 I've got _____ time, so tell me what's on your mind.

much / many

3 How _____ people visit your blog?

4 How _____ time do you spend online?

lot / lots

5 A _____ of people their age also go to nightclubs.

6 They go to _____ of nightclubs.

too many / a lot of

7 _____ people take courses throughout their lives to improve their qualifications.

8 _____ people are looking for the same job as me. It's really annoying!

few / not much

9 There are _____ wild animals left in this part of the world.

10 _____ money is given to protecting animals in this part of the world.

2 **Look at the pictures. Use the words in the box to complete the sentences.**

| a few   a lot of   lots   not many   too   too many   too much |

1 _____ people came to watch the fireworks.

2 The roads have _____ cars but _____ cyclists.

3 _____ for me, please!

4 There are _____ few signposts round here.

5 _____ people came but not very many.

6 That's _____ for me.

3 **There is one word missing in each sentence or conversation. Write it in.**

1 I think there's ᵃ little cheese left. Would you like some?

2 Count how questions you answered correctly.

3 There are many people here. I only invited ten. Who are the other fifteen?

4 A lot new mobile technology comes out every week.

5 There are only a possibilities left to us. Which should we choose?

6 A: Do you like her new album?   B: I like lot of the songs but not all of them.

29 enough, plenty of, most, a large number of, a large amount of, a great deal of, several

Presentation

Use *enough, plenty of, most, a large amount of, a great deal of, a number of* and *several* to talk about quantities without giving a specific amount:

with uncountable nouns	with plural countable nouns	with both
a large amount of a great deal of	a large number of several	enough plenty of most

enough

Use *enough* to say you have the correct or sufficient quantity: *We've got **enough** money to pay for this.*

Use *not enough* to say you have less than you want or need: *Some people **don't** have **enough** time to relax.*

TIP *Not enough has a similar meaning to too little and too few. See Unit 28. We haven't got enough schools where we live. = We've got too few schools where we live.*

plenty of

Use *plenty of* to talk about large quantities or to say there is/are more than enough: *We've got **plenty of** hospitals in our area.*

most

Use *most* or *most of the* to talk about the largest quantity or number compared to any other: ***Most** people in Denmark are satisfied with life **most of the** time.*

With pronouns, use *most of* without *the*. Say ***most of** them.* (don't say *most of the them.*)

a large number of / a large amount of / a great deal of

Use *a large number* of with plural nouns only: ***A large number of people** mentioned money.*

Use *a large amount of/a great deal of* with uncountable nouns only: ***A large amount of/A great deal of time** is spent at work.*

These expressions mean the same as *lots of/a lot of* but they are normally used in formal or written texts.

several

You use *several* to talk about three or more things or people: *People gave **several** reasons for their answers.*

You can also use *several of the*: ***Several of the** people in the survey mentioned that education was important.*

With pronouns, use *several of*, not *several of the*: ***Several of them** mentioned education.*

You can use *a large amount, a great deal, enough, plenty, several* without nouns when the meaning is clear: *Do you have enough schools where you live? Yes, we have **enough/plenty/several.***

Do not use *of* in this case. Say *Yes, we have **plenty**.* (don't say *Yes, we have plenty of.*)

Exercises

1 **Match the two halves of the sentences.**

1 Several _B_
2 Most of _____
3 Plenty _____
4 At number four, people in Sweden have a large _____
5 Ireland had enough _____
6 Financial security explains a large _____

A of people in the Netherlands enjoy life.
B other northern European countries also appear in the top five.
C the Finns seems very happy.
D happiness to be in the top five.
E number of these results.
F amount of time for relaxation.

2 **Underline the correct options. Both options are possible in one sentence.**

1 *Several / Most* of the voters wanted the current Prime Minister to continue leading the country. Only about five percent voted for his opponent.

2 That's *enough / isn't enough*! Otherwise, I'll never eat everything on my plate!

3 A: Do you have any sugar?
    B: Yes, there's *plenty / several* in that packet.

4 *A large amount of / A great deal of* electricity is wasted every year.

5 We've seen *several / a large amount of* pictures of his girlfriend but we've never met her.

6 *A great deal of / A large number of* people have visited our company's website since we launched it last month.

7 We asked over 200 people if a good job was the most important factor in their life, and *a large amount of / most of* them answered 'Yes'.

3 **Complete sentences 1–6 using the words in the box.**

| ~~enough~~ great deal large number most not enough plenty |

1 We have twelve chairs and eleven people, so we have _____enough_____ chairs for everyone.

2 Geoff now says he wants a hamburger too, but I only bought five, so I'm afraid there are _____ .

3 It's seven o'clock and the film doesn't start until nine, so we have _____ of time.

4 There are 30 people in my class and _____ of them really enjoy learning English. Only two people don't enjoy it.

5 When you have a car, you spend a _____ of time in traffic jams!

6 A _____ of schools have closed for the day because of the snow.

4 **Complete the sentences about the results from a survey of 100 people using the words from the box. There is more than one possibility in some sentences. You may need to add *a* or *of*.**

| large number most plenty several |

What is most important for happiness?

_____ people answered that family and the community were most important.
However, _____ people also believe money is important for happiness.
_____ people said that access to healthcare was important.
_____ people also said that good schools were important.

30 Review of units 26 to 29

Grammar

1 Tick the correct response to 1–8.

1 Have you got any change?
   A   No, none. ✓
   B   No, any of it.

2 Shall we leave?
   A   Yes, anywhere is better than here.
   B   Yes, somewhere is better than here.

3 Which sport do you play? Basketball or baseball?
   A   All.
   B   Both.

4 How many of your friends do you want to invite to your party?
   A   All of them.
   B   Every of them.

5 How much time did you spend on your school project this term?
   A   A great deal.
   B   A large number.

6 How much cheese would you like on your pizza?
   A   Much!
   B   Lots!

7 Is that enough?
   A   Yes, that's several.
   B   Yes, that's plenty.

8 We only have two days to read the whole of this book. That isn't enough time.
   A   I agree. It's little.
   B   I agree. It's too little.

2 Correct the mistake in each sentence.

1 We have ~~none~~ *no* milk in the fridge.

2 A: Do you like that group's songs?
   B: Yes. Some of.

3 Let's change channels. Anything are better than this.

4 Are you going nowhere this weekend?

5 All of products in our shop are handmade.

6 I didn't win neither match. I never want to play again!

7 There was a large number local people at the town council meeting.

8 Few people have volunteered to help, so that's good. We need as many as possible.

3 Complete the second sentence so it has a similar meaning to the first. Use between two and five words, including the word in bold.

1 There aren't any new emails in your inbox.
   no   There _are no new emails_ in your inbox.

2 Are there none left?
   any _____ left?

3 I don't think all their products are very well made.
   some _____ are not very well made.

4 My team didn't win either match.
   neither My team _____ .

5 Each of the contestants had to run 20 kilometres.
   every _____ to run 20 kilometres.

6 We've got more than enough food to share with you.
   plenty We've got _____ to share with you.

7 Lots of people are now concerned about climate change.
   many _____ now concerned about climate change.

8 There aren't many parks in our town.
   few There _____ in our town.

9 Most people give very little thought to their future.
   much Most people _____ to their future.

10 We've got too little time to plan a big party.
   enough We _____ to plan a big party.

4 Underline the correct options in italics. In some sentences, both options are possible.

HOLIDAYS

ARE YOU TIRED OF SHARING THE BEACH WITH ¹*ALL / EVERY* THOSE OTHER HOLIDAYMAKERS?

Do you fancy going ²*somewhere / something* different this year?

We have ³*lots / a lot* of holiday rentals on the coast of Mallorca.

⁴*Each / Every* apartment comes with its own balcony with great views of the pool.

Call now for our free brochure.

DIETING

You probably think you've tried ⁵*all / every* diet there is, but you still haven't lost ⁶*some / any* weight. But FastDiet is like ⁷*no / any* other diet. It was created by qualified nutritionists, so you never feel like you've eaten ⁸*enough / too much* food and you only eat ⁹*enough / little* of the right kinds of food.

FastDiet
The safest way to lose wight and stay slim for life

EARN EXTRA MONEY

■ ¹⁰*Most / A large number* of people have either full-time jobs or busy lives, but often they've still got too ¹¹*few / little* money at the end of the week to afford the things they want. Now you can earn ¹²*a great deal / plenty* of extra money by logging on to www.homeemployee.com. Homeemployee puts you in contact with ¹³*lots of / a great deal of* employers who will pay you to work from home. So don't waste those ¹⁴*few / little* extra hours doing nothing when you could be making ¹⁵*some / any* extra cash. Log on to www.homeemployee.com now!

Pronunciation: linking

5 🔊 1.32 **Words ending in a consonant sound followed by a word starting with a vowel sound often sound like one word. Speakers link the words. Listen to these sentences and decide which words are linked.**

1 We don't have any left.
2 Would he like some of these?
3 I don't like chicken either.
4 A large amount goes down the drain.
5 Not enough people pay for water.
6 We could save lots of time.
7 I'll take a few, please.
8 Most of my friends live here.

Listen again and repeat the sentences.

Listen again

6 🔊 1.33 **Listen to the rules of a sport. Change words in the rules to make them correct.**

1 ~~Plenty of~~ All football-tennis matches are played on a court.

2 A lot of courts must be the same size as a standard doubles tennis court.

3 Either team is allowed to make more than two substitutions per game.

4 Every match is decided over three games or when both teams have won two games.

5 The winner of each game must score a few points.

6 There is a three-minute break between some games.

7 Every player's hand or arm can touch the ball.

31 Adjectives 1
Position and order of adjectives, *the* + adjective

Presentation

Adjectives are used to describe people, things and abstract ideas. They are used:

- before a noun: *the next **big** thing, **cool** gift ideas*

- after a copula verb (a verb that introduces a description of the subject, e.g. *appear, be, get, feel, look, taste*): *getting **old** is **optional**; the lanterns look **beautiful***

Most adjectives can be used in both positions:
*A **wonderful** gift* (adjective + noun)
*That gift looks **wonderful*** (copula verb + adjective)

A few adjectives can only be used before a noun:

Say *It's the **only** choice.* (don't say *The choice is ~~only~~.*)

TIP Other adjectives only used before a noun include: *chief, entire, former, future, main* and *principal*.

Some adjectives can only be used after a copula verb:

Say *You're **alone**.* (don't say ~~You're an alone person.~~)

TIP Other adjectives only used after a copula verb include: *afraid, ashamed, asleep, awake, glad, ill, well*.

Order of adjectives

Before a noun: opinion adjectives (e.g. *wonderful, delicious*) always come before adjectives that describe facts (e.g. *big, Belgian*): ***delicious Belgian** chocolate*. When you use more than one 'fact' adjective, they usually follow this order:

size/shape, quality (e.g. *warm, soft*), age, colour, origin/nationality, material, type (e.g. *winter, movie*), e.g.: *enormous white paper lanterns; classic French movie posters*

You can also use a noun to describe a noun: *a paper lantern, a chocolate pizza, a movie poster*.

There is no rule for the order of adjectives after a copula verb, although some common groupings always follow the same order, e.g.: *tall, dark and handsome; short and sweet; safe and sound*.

Using *and*

Before the noun use *and* between two adjectives which describe the same quality or feature (e.g. material). Say *a paper and cloth lantern* (don't say ~~a paper, cloth lantern~~).

The word order is often based on convention: e.g. *black and white* (not ~~white and black~~).

Other pairs of adjectives which are always used in the same order include: *hot and cold, bright and sunny, weird and wonderful*.

After a copula verb, add *and* between the last two adjectives. With three or more adjectives, use a comma between the other adjectives: *Gifts that are inspirational, quirky, bizarre **and** fun*.

the + adjective

You can sometimes use *the* + *adjective* to talk about a group of people: *the young, the romantic, the French, the British*.

Do not use *a/an* + *adjective* to talk about one person or thing. Say *a young person* (don't say ~~a young~~).
Say *a French woman* (don't say ~~a French~~).

Note: some nationality adjectives are also nouns: *an American movie, the Americans; a German producer, the Germans*

See Units 23 and 24: *the* and no article

Exercises

1 Use the adjectives to complete the pairs of sentences.

1 asleep/sleepy

   a The _____ dog lay in the hot sun.

   b The baby was _____ in the pram.

2 important/main

   a The _____ problem was how to get the box in the car.

   b It's _____ to get there before the shops close.

3 good/well

   a He had very _____ health for a man his age.

   b She wasn't feeling very _____ .

4 complete/entire

   a I spent the _____ night staring at the ceiling.

   b When he asked me to marry him, my happiness was _____ .

2 ⊙ 1.34 Add the adjectives in brackets to the sentences. Write them in the correct order. Then listen and check.

1 No more boring moments with this _____ game. (*desktop magnetic tiny*)

2 Try our _____ snow (*amazing instant new*). It even works indoors!

3 A _____ blanket (*cotton huge warm*) – with sleeves! Perfect for those _____ nights (*winter cold long*).

4 Make your own _____ ice cream (*Italian home-made delicious*) with this _____ gadget. (*plastic clever little*)

3 Add *and* to the sentences below where necessary.

1 My brother collects black white movie posters.

2 That joke was silly childish!

3 I love all these weird wonderful gadgets.

4 Why aren't all male Hollywood film stars tall, dark handsome?

5 They serve great Asian Western food.

6 I love strawberry chocolate cheesecake.

4 Choose the correct answers.

1 Our gifts appeal to everyone, *the young and the old / the youngs and the olds*.

2 The TV advert shows *a young / a young person* playing with the latest gadgets.

3 *British / The British* spend more money on ice cream than any other nationality.

4 I met a really interesting *Spanish girl / Spanish* at a party last week.

5 *The Italian / The Italians* love strong, dark coffee.

6 *The super rich / Super rich* spend millions on personalised, luxury gifts.

5 Write sentences describing two of your possessions using at least two adjectives.

1 I drive an old, grey delivery van.

2 _____

3 _____

32 Adjectives 2

-ing and *-ed* participles as adjectives, adjectives + dependent prepositions, adjectives + *to* infinitive

aries March 21 – April 20

You have a passionate, caring nature, but sometimes you like to be alone and you are often jealous of your privacy. Some people think you are cold and reserved. This is not true, although you don't like talking about your feelings to people you don't know very well. You're a doer not a talker. You're happy when you're active and working with your hands. You get irritated with boring, repetitive household chores. You're not very good at sitting still at a desk. You get bored with paperwork and you often find it difficult to concentrate on administrative tasks.

Presentation

Present and past participles as adjectives

You can use the present participle (*-ing*) and past participle (*-ed*) of some verbs as adjectives: *you get **irritated** with household chores; household chores are **irritating**.*

-ing adjectives describe a characteristic of a person or thing. They are often used before a noun: ***boring** household chores; a **caring** nature.*

-ed adjectives describe a person's emotional or physical state. They are often used with copula verbs: *some people think you are **reserved**; I'm really **tired** today.*

Past participle adjectives and dependent prepositions

-ed adjectives are often followed by dependent prepositions (i.e. these adjectives are always used with the same preposition):

* *about: excited about, worried about*
* *in: interested in, involved in*
* *of: frightened of, scared of, terrified of, tired of*
* *with: bored with, pleased with, satisfied with*

You use prepositions when you want to explain the relationship between the adjective and an object, person or situation. The preposition is followed by a noun or gerund: *You get bored **with paperwork** (noun). I'm tired **of working** (gerund) on this.*

The dependent preposition comes at the end of a sentence or question when the object, person or situation it refers to has already been mentioned:

*This is <u>the present</u> I was so pleased **with**.*

*<u>Who</u> are you so angry **with**?*

Other adjectives with dependent prepositions

Other adjectives also have dependent prepositions: *you're often **jealous of** your privacy*

* *about: angry about, anxious about, passionate about*
* *at: good at, bad at*
* *in: successful in, lucky in*
* *of: afraid of, fond of, proud of*
* *on: dependent on, fair on, hard on, keen on*
* *to: accustomed to, close to, friendly to, kind to*
* *with: angry with, happy with, honest with*

Some adjectives have more than one dependent preposition, e.g.

* *angry: I'm angry **with** you.* (the person who had made me angry)

  *I'm angry **about** working overtime.* (the specific situation)

* *honest: He wasn't honest **with** me.* (the person)

  *He wasn't honest **about** the money.* (what he lied about)

Adjectives + *to* + infinitive

You can use *to* + infinitive following an adjective used after a copula verb. The adjective describes the infinitive.

*You sometimes find it difficult to **concentrate on paperwork**.*
(= Concentrating on paperwork is difficult for you.)

Common adjectives which can be followed by *to* + infinitive include: *difficult, easy, free, glad, good, hard, likely, lucky, nice, pleased, proud, ready, sorry.*

Exercises

1 🔊 **1.35** **Choose the correct options. Then listen and check.**

TAURUS   **April 21 – May 21**

If you're getting ¹*tiring / tired* of the day-to-day routine, don't sit at home feeling ²*depressing / depressed*. Plan a special treat for yourself! Try an ³*exciting / excited* new sport or buy a ticket to see something ⁴*interesting / interested* at the theatre. Remember, keep active and your life won't seem so ⁵*boring / bored*!

GEMINI   **May 22 – June 22**

Not ⁶*satisfying / satisfied* with the way things are going at work at the moment? These are ⁷*worrying / worried* times for everyone, but don't sit brooding at your desk. Talk to your boss about the situation. You may be ⁸*surprising / surprised* by how understanding she can be!

2 **Cross out the unnecessary dependent preposition in three more of the sentences.**

1 He always gets bored ~~with~~ in class.

2 She had a happy, satisfied with look on her face.

3 I'm terrified of spiders!

4 What are you so pleased about?

5 Why are you angry with?

6 There's nothing to be worried about.

7 That's the woman he got irritated with.

8 I always find it difficult to deal with worried about parents.

3 **Each sentence has one mistake in it. Find the mistakes and correct them.**

1 The boss gets really angry ~~about~~ *with* us when we're late for work.

2 I don't think you've been completely honest with what happened yesterday.

3 Philip is very interested of maritime history.

4 Soraya is really good on cooking.

5 He isn't accustomed in working on his own.

6 I'd be really happy to looking after your dog for you.

4 **Complete these sentences so that they are true for you.**

1 I'm tired of ....

2 I got really angry with .... because ....

3 I sometimes find it difficult to ....

33 Adverbs 1: -ly adverbs
Adverbs of manner, comment adverbs

She quietly picked up the gun. She turned to face him and spoke remarkably calmly.

'Luckily, you knew Matthews was the murderer,' she said. She held the murder weapon firmly in her hand, 'And you led me straight to him.'

'Apparently I did,' he answered slowly, as he looked at the newly dead body of Matthews, lying on the floor beside him.

'But does that mean I'm next?' he thought to himself.

Presentation

You can add -ly to a number of adjectives to form adverbs: *bad → badly, loud → loudly, sudden → suddenly*

Sometimes you need to make changes to the spelling: *true → truly, full → fully, happy → happily, terrible → terribly, realistic → realistically.*

See page 233: Spelling rules

-ly adverbs with verbs

Adverbs of manner describe how something is done, or how something happens: *He answered slowly. She quietly picked up the gun.*

Adverbs of manner can come in three positions in a sentence or clause:

* They usually come **after the verb** they describe. If the verb has an object, the adverb comes after the verb + object: *She spoke calmly. She held the gun firmly.*

* They can also come in the middle of the sentence, **between the subject and the main verb**: *She calmly spoke to the man in the chair. She quietly picked up the gun.*
  When there is an auxiliary verb, the adverb comes after the auxiliary and before the main verb: *She had quietly picked up the gun.*

* They can also come **at the beginning of the sentence**: *Calmly, she spoke to the man in the chair. Quietly, she picked up the gun.*

You don't normally use adverbs of manner between the subject and the verb, or at the beginning of the sentence, when no other additional information is given after the verb (e.g. an object, a prepositional phrase).

Say *She spoke calmly.* (don't say *She calmly spoke. Calmly she spoke.*)

See Unit 37: Word order

-ly adverbs with adjectives and adverbs

You can use -ly adverbs to add information about, or comment on, an adjective or another adverb. The -ly adverb always comes before the adjective or adverb.

*Her voice was **remarkably** calm. He was **incredibly** relieved. He moved **surprisingly** quickly.*

-ly adverbs commenting on a clause or sentence

You can use an -ly adverb to comment on a whole sentence or clause. These adverbs usually come:

* at the **beginning** of the sentence or clause: *Luckily, he knew Matthews was the murderer.*

* or at the **end** of the sentence or clause: *He knew Matthews was the murderer, luckily.*

Use commas to separate the comment adverb from the rest of the sentence.

Change of position and meaning

The meaning of the sentence sometimes changes when the position of the adverb changes. This happens when the focus of the adverb changes.

Slowly, we realised that he had taken all our money. (*Slowly* refers to the whole sentence.)

*We realised that he had **slowly** taken all our money.* (*Slowly* refers to the way he took the money.)

Exercises

1 **Add *-ly* in the gaps. Sometimes you will need to make some changes to the spelling.**

He looked at her critical ¹_____ . She looked true ²_____ awful and he was sure she was going to sing horrible ³_____ . But lucky ⁴_____ , when she opened her mouth, he was amazed. She sang beautiful ⁵_____ and she immediate ⁶_____ won everyone's hearts. When she finished, the crowd stood on their feet and clapped enthusiastic ⁷_____ .

2 **The adverbs in five of the sentences below are in the wrong position. Move them to a better position. Sometimes there is more than one correct position.**

1 I was sitting comfortably on the sofa.
    ✓

2 I heard a loud suddenly noise from outside.
    I suddenly heard a loud noise from outside.

3 I went quickly to the door.

4 I looked up and carefully down the street.

5 Then I stepped out slowly and cautiously extremely.

6 The street outside was silent completely.

7 There was nothing or nobody there, apparently.

8 So I closed quietly the door and went back to the TV.

3 **Change the position of the adverbs so that the sentence has a different meaning.**

1 a Honestly, I can't speak to him.
  b *I can't speak to him honestly.*

2 a I don't think he'll have the courage to tell her personally.
  b _____

3 a Normally, I can't work if there's music on.
  b _____

4 a He laughed happily when he heard the joke.
  b _____

5 a We quickly realised that he couldn't walk.
  b _____

6 a I said something incredibly stupid.
  b _____

4 **Match the explanations below to either *a* or *b* in 1–6 in exercise 3.**

1 I find it difficult to tell him the truth.
    b

2 He'll probably get someone else to tell her.

3 I find I work more slowly with music on.

4 I was worried that he might think it was offensive. _____

5 So we all slowed down to his walking pace.

6 I don't normally say anything stupid.

34 Adverbs 2: adverbs of place and time
Word order

> Is that Raúl Gómez, the football player, over there?

> Yes, it is. We often see him in the neighbourhood.

> I didn't know he lived locally.

> Yes, he's just bought a house in the next street. He moved there last week. Sometimes we see him playing football in the park.

> Wow! I'll have to come with you next time!

Presentation

Adverbs of place

Adverbs of place explain *where* something is or happens:

*Is that Raúl Gómez **over there**? He lives **nearby**.*

Prepositional phrases (preposition + noun phrase), also called adverbial phrases, can also describe where something is or happens: *He's bought a house **in the next street**. They play football **in the park**.*

Position of adverbs of place

Adverbs of place usually come *after the verb* (and object if there is one): *We live **here**. We play football **in the park**.*

Adverbs of time

Adverbs (and adverbial phrases) of time tell us *when*, or *how often*, something happens:

*We **often** see him in the neighbourhood. He moved there **last week**.*

Position of adverbs of time

Adverbs of time can come in three different positions in the sentence:

- at the beginning: ***Recently,** we saw him in the park.*
- between the subject and the verb: *We **recently** saw him in the park.*
- after the verb (and object if there is one): *We saw him in the park **recently**.*

TIP The following adverbs can be used in all three positions: *now, recently, usually, sometimes, occasionally, often, soon, still* and *already*.

Often, soon, still and *already* are less frequent at the beginning of the sentence.

Some adverbs are only used after the verb, e.g. *yet, early, lat   I haven't seen him play **yet**.*

Other adverbs can only be used between the subject and the verb, e.g. *always, never, just* (= very recently): *I've **just** seen him.* (don't say *~~Just~~ I've seen him* or *I've seen him ~~just~~*.)

Some adverbs cannot be used between the subject and the verb, e.g. *today, tomorrow, yesterday, nowadays:* **Yesterday**, *I saw him in the supermarket.* (don't say *I ~~yesterday~~ saw him in the supermarket.*)

Adverbial phrases such as *last year, now and then, three days ago, at night* do not usually go between the subject and the verb. (don't say *They ~~last week~~ moved into their new house.*)

Word order with auxiliaries

Adverbs used in the middle of a sentence come after the subject (and the auxiliary verb if there is one) and before the other verbs:

*He **always** shops here. He **doesn't always** shop here. He **hasn't always** shopped here.*

They come after the verb *to be* in the present simple or past simple: *He's **always** late for class.*

Adverbs of certainty (e.g. *possibly, probably, certainly*) also go between the subject and the verb. They come after an affirmative auxiliary, but before a negative one: *He'll **probably** be there tonight. He **probably won't** be there tonight.*

Position of adverbs of place and time together

Adverbs of place usually come before adverbs of time when both are being used after the verb: *We saw them **here** (place) **last night** (time).*

TIP Never use an adverb between a verb and its object: *They are playing ~~tonight~~ football.*

Exercises

1 Write the words in the correct order to make sentences.

1 at lives the end the street he of .
   He lives at the end of the street.

2 school to nearby children go the .

....

3 there parked car over is my .

....

4 here live you near do ?

....

5 parents locally both work my of .

....

6 area parks there are in the any ?

....

7 working ten years abroad spent she .

....

8 door outside the my shoes left I .

....

2 In which position can the adverbs in brackets *not* be used?

1 [1] He [2] bought a new car [3]. (last week)
   position number 2

2 They [1] play [2] football in the park [3]. (often)

....

3 I [1] have to get up [2] tomorrow. (early)

....

4 He's [1] got into his car [2]. (just)

....

5 They [1] have [2] lived here. (always)

....

6 [1] We're [2] going to the football match [3]. (tomorrow)

....

7 I [1] get up [2] at 6.30 [3]. (every morning)

....

8 Sorry, I [1] haven't [2] finished the book [3]. (yet)

....

3 ⏺**1.36** **Write the adverbs in the conversations. Then listen and check.**

| already   just   soon   still   yet |

Conversation 1

A: Why aren't Tom and Luke here [1] .... ?

B: Tom's [2] .... called. He says Luke is [3] .... looking for his football boots.

A: What?! But the other team are [4] .... on the field. We have to start now!

B: We'll have to play with nine players and hope they both get here [5] ....

| ago   already   here   now |

Conversation 2

C: Hurry up Luke! We need to go [6] .... , this minute! The rest of the team were there ages [7] ....

D: OK. Call Dan and tell him we'll be late.

C: He [8] .... knows! I've called him twice. Maybe they're in your bedroom?

D: Good idea. I'll have a look … You're right! They're [9] ....

4 Look at each pair of sentences. Tick the correct sentence. In one pair of sentences, both are correct.

1 A That famous actor locally lives. ✗
  B That famous actor lives locally. ✓

2 A Have you been to see yet your tutor?
  B Have you been to see your tutor yet?

3 A An old lady used to live long ago in the house.
  B An old lady used to live in the house long ago.

4 A You were seen walking last night here.
  B You were seen walking here last night.

5 A Everyone else has just arrived.
  B Everyone else has arrived just.

6 A Elaine is currently visiting friends.
  B Currently, Elaine is visiting friends.

35 Review of units 31 to 34

Grammar

1 **There is a mistake in each of the sentences below. Find the mistakes and correct them.**

1 He was ~~an alone~~ *a lonely* old man, with no family and few friends.

2 Now that they had dealt with the problem main, the rest seemed quite easy.

3 She looked great in a white and black jacket over long, black, leather boots.

4 The poor are getting poorer, and rich are getting richer.

5 They were really exciting by the news.

6 I always find it difficult to saying sorry.

7 I must get tomorrow an appointment with the dentist.

8 Can you please come now here!

2 **Choose the correct options.**

1 <u>*That was our chief concern.*</u> / *That concern was chief.*

2 In the end they chose the *red Italian small* / *small red Italian* sports car.

3 During flu epidemics, *the old and the sick* / *old and sick* are always the first to suffer.

4 It was definitely the most *terrified* / *terrifying* thing I had ever done.

5 It was easy *seeing* / *to see* how he had made the mistake.

6 He turned *slowly his head* / *his head slowly* and looked her in the eye.

7 She ate *quickly her food* / *her food quickly* in order to leave the table.

8 It was *an incredible truly* / *a truly incredible* sight. I could hardly believe my eyes.

9 It moved *remarkably quickly* / *quickly remarkably*, considering its size.

10 I've *worked always* / *always worked* here.

3 **Complete the second sentence so that it has the same meaning as the first. Use the words in bold. Do not use more than five words.**

1 The baby had gone to sleep and the house was quiet.

asleep The baby was asleep and the house was quiet.

2 She spoke with a quiet voice.

quietly She _____ .

3 He was the only person in the house.

alone He _____ in the house.

4 He wants to leave his job it seems.

apparently He _____ leave his job.

5 Studying in the evening can be difficult when you've been working all day.

to It's _____ in the evening when you've been working all day.

6 He was very careful when he moved the painting.

carefully. He moved _____ .

4 **Complete the text using the words in the box.**

> accidentally   alone   at the beginning   busily
> finally   happily   quietly   soon   that night
> whole

One Christmas, the McCallister family
¹ *accidentally* _____ leave their eight-year-old son at home ² _____ over Christmas. As they are ³ _____ preparing to go the airport, their son, Kevin is ⁴ _____ sleeping upstairs. When he ⁵ _____ wakes up, he realises that his family have left without him and he has the ⁶ _____ house to himself.
⁷ _____ , he loves the freedom. He eats all the junk food he wants, and ⁸ _____ watches his favourite programmes on TV. But he ⁹ _____ discovers that two thieves are planning to enter his house ¹⁰ _____ . That's when the fun starts, as Kevin cleverly prepares a series of traps that are sure to catch the thieves.

Grammar in context

5 Write the words in italics in the correct order.

AllyoueverwantedtoknowaboutmoviesI.com

Home | Log In | Message Boards | Today's Posts | Links | Archive | Sign Up | Contact Us | DVD Store | TV and Music

Ask your questions here! **Q** What's a tagline?

A tagline is a [1]*phrase short memorable* that sums up the [2]*tone or atmosphere basic* of a movie. [3]*hilarious totally Some are*, others [4]*serious are deadly*. The best taglines [5]*become successfully have* part of popular culture:

[6]*afraid Be. very Be afraid.*

Just when you thought [7]*safe was go to it back in the water ...*

A [8]*long ago time in a galaxy far, far away ...*

Five [9]*reasons stay good single to.*

1 .... 2 .... 3 ....
4 .... 5 .... 6 ....
7 .... 8 .... 9 ....

Pronunciation: syllables in adverbs

6 Read these adverbs. Which have a) two syllables? b) three syllables? c) four syllables?

apparently _4_	naturally __	remarkably __
beautifully __	normally __	slowly __
carefully __	quickly __	terribly __
completely __	really __	truly __
extremely __	recently __	

7 (1.37) Listen and mark the stress on each adverb, then match them to the stress patterns below.

1 ●● *quickly* ....

2 ●●● ....
....

3 ●●● ....

4 ●●●● ....

Listen again and repeat the words.

Listen again

8 (1.38) Listen and tick the adjectives you hear.

1 tiring
  tired

2 depressing
  depressed

3 exciting
  excited

4 interesting
  interested

5 boring
  bored

6 satisfying
  satisfied

7 worrying
  worried

8 surprising
  surprised

36 Adjectives or adverbs?

Dad: How was your maths test? Was it hard?

Son: No, I did it really quickly.

Dad: Really? You haven't been studying much lately.

Son: Yeah, I know, but it was easy.

Presentation

You use **adjectives** to describe **nouns**. They come before the noun or after a copula verb (e.g. *appear, be, become, get, feel, seem, sound, look, taste, smell*):

*It was an **easy** test.*

*The test was **easy.***

You use **adverbs** to describe **verbs**, **adjectives** or other **adverbs**:

*He did it **quickly.***

*It was **really** easy.*

*He did it **reasonably** well.*

Some words can be used as both adjectives and adverbs, e.g. *clean, daily, deep, early, far, fast, free, high, hourly, late, loud, hard, weekly, well, yearly*:

*The test was **hard.*** (adjective: it describes the test)

*He works **hard.*** (adverb: it describes the way he works)

*You don't look **well.*** (adjective: well = in good health)

*She plays the piano **well.*** (adverb: it describes how she plays the piano)

*They have **weekly** tests.* (adjective: it describes the tests)

*They do maths tests **weekly.*** (adverb: it describes how often they do the tests)

*I hate **early** mornings.* (adjective: it describes the mornings)

*I hate getting up **early.*** (adverb: it describes when I get up)

hardly and *lately*

The adverbs *late* and *hard* have a different meaning from the adverbs *lately* and *hardly. Lately* means *recently. Hardly* means *almost not/almost never.*

*I worked **late** last night.* (*late* refers to the time when I was working.)

*I've been doing a lot of work **lately.*** (*lately* = recently)

*He worked **hard** for his exam.* (*hard* describes the way he worked.)

*He **hardly** did any work for his exam.* (*hardly any work* = almost no work)

Notice the position of *hardly.* It can come before the verb: *We **hardly** see you anymore.* Or before *any* + noun: *He did **hardly** any work.*

Exercises

1 (♪ 1.39) Choose the correct options. Then listen and check.

The father looked ¹*close /* *closely* at his son. Was he being ²*honest / honestly*? Or was he just giving his usual, ³*easy / easily* answer? His son stared back at him ⁴*defiant / defiantly*. He knew his ⁵*terrible / terribly* test mark was going to get him into trouble. He knew his father was going to get really ⁶*angry / angrily*. But still he stared at his father. His father sighed ⁷*quiet / quietly*. With a ⁸*tired / tiredly* look on his face, he took the test paper from his son's hand. The boy waited ⁹*anxious / anxiously* for the ¹⁰*inevitable / inevitably* explosion. Nothing came. The father looked ¹¹*sad / sadly* at his son, shook his head and walked ¹²*slow / slowly* away.

2 Decide whether the words in bold are adjectives or adverbs.

1 The nurses make **hourly** checks on their patients all through the night. _adjective_

2 The church bells are rung **hourly,** day and night, filling the square with noise. ____

3 We hadn't walked **far** when we came to a gate. ____

4 The figure was very **far** away; we couldn't really see it properly. ____

5 She talks so **fast** I can't understand a word she says! ____

6 He loves **fast** cars and beautiful women. ____

7 My mum says I play my music too **loud**. ____

8 They all jumped when they heard the **loud** bang behind them. ____

9 They all looked really **friendly**. ____

10 He said goodbye to us with a **friendly** wave. ____

3 Look at the pictures and the captions. Add -ly in the gaps where necessary.

1 He ran quick ____ after his ball.

2 She was very tired ____ after walking for such a long ____ time.

3 Atlantic Star is in the lead followed close ____ by Kaboura.

4 *Who's Who* is published annual ____ .

4 Complete the sentences using the words in bold.

late/lately

1 Did you stay up ____ last night? You look tired.

2 You've been working very long hours ____ . You deserve a rest.

3 We haven't seen a lot of you ____ . Have you been away?

4 We had a ____ lunch and then we went to the cinema.

hard/hardly

5 This bread is very ____ . How old is it?

6 You've ____ touched your food. Aren't you hungry?

7 It's a ____ decision. I really don't know what to do.

8 We had ____ arrived when it started raining really heavily.

37 Modifying adjectives and adverbs
Gradable and non-gradable adjectives, adverbs of degree

Presentation

modifying gradable adjectives

Adjectives can be gradable or non-gradable. Gradable adjectives describe a feature that can be strong or weak. Adverbs of degree such as *very, extremely, really* make the adjective stronger. Adverbs such as *not very* and *quite* make it weaker: *a **very** nice day,* **not a very** *nice day,* **quite** *a nice day.*

Most adverbs of degree come immediately before the adjective: *It was a **very** hot day; the sun was **extremely** hot.*

quite, not very, rather

Quite and *not* in *not very* come before *a/an*: *It was **quite** a nice day. It wasn't a **very** nice day.* (don't say *It was a quite nice day. It was a not very nice day.*)

Rather can come either before or after *a/an*: *rather a nice day / a **rather** nice day.*

Use *rather* to suggest that you are surprised: *It was **rather** a nice day* (= I didn't expect a nice day), or to express a negative opinion: *It's **rather** cold* (= I don't like the cold).

too and enough

Use *too* to criticise and say there is more than is necessary of a quality: *It was **too** big. He moved **too** slowly.* Use *enough* to say that the thing or action has the correct amount of a quality: *It was big **enough**. He moved quickly **enough**.*

Enough comes **after** the adjective but **before** a noun: *(not) big **enough**; (not) **enough** money.*

modifying non-gradable adjectives

Non-gradable adjectives describe a quality that is extreme or absolute. They cannot be made stronger or weaker. Examples include: *amazed, convinced, delicious, delighted, exhausted, freezing, starving, unbearable.*

Do not use adverbs such as *very, fairly, too* or *enough* with non-gradable adjectives. You cannot say: *~~very~~ delicious, ~~too~~ freezing.*

But you can use adverbs such as *absolutely, really, totally* or *utterly* to emphasise the quality of the adjective: *We're **absolutely delighted** you came. I'm **completely exhausted**. It was **really delicious**.*

You can use *quite* and *really* with both gradable and non-gradable adjectives. *Quite* used with a non-gradable adjective means *totally*. The meaning of *really* does not change.

*It was **quite** tasty.* (= a little bit, not very)

*It was **quite** delicious.* (= totally). (This use is more common in British English.)

modifying adverbs

You can also use adverbs of degree to modify other adverbs:

*He rode his bike **really quickly**. The customer spoke to me **extremely rudely**.*

gradable only	non-gradable only	both gradable and non-gradable
extremely, fairly, rather, very, too, enough, pretty	absolutely, completely, totally, utterly	quite*, really (* the meaning changes)

TIP Certain non-gradable adjectives collocate more frequently with certain adverbs. For example *absolutely freezing* is far more common than *utterly freezing*. You can check the collocations in a good dictionary.

Exercises

1 Add the adverbs in brackets to the sentences.

1 I've been working ^too^ hard recently so I'm going to take a rest! (too)

2 His boss said he hadn't been working hard and gave him the sack! (enough)

3 Their relationship has always been strained. (very)

4 She was a domineering woman. (quite)

5 He was a quiet man, who never had much to say. (rather)

6 When he heard the news, he got angry. (pretty)

2 (1.40) **Match the adverbs to sentences *A* and *B*. Use each adverb once only. Then listen and check.**

1 totally / very

A: This is _____ tasty. How did you make it?

B: Wow! This is _____ delicious. You didn't make it yourself, did you?

2 n't very / utterly

A: I was _____ unconvinced by his explanation.

B: I was _____ sure I was making the right decision.

3 absolutely / rather

A: It's _____ hot today, don't you think?

B: Hot? It's _____ boiling!

4 completely / extremely

A: They had been walking for ten hours and were _____ exhausted.

B: They were _____ tired and went straight to bed.

5 pretty / absolutely

A: I hadn't eaten all day and I was _____ starving when I got home.

B: I'd only had a couple of biscuits for breakfast and I was _____ hungry by the time I got to work.

3 Rewrite the sentences with a similar meaning, using the words in bold.

1 He was walking too slowly.

enough He _wasn't walking quickly enough._

2 It was a fairly mild day.

quite It _____

3 It had taken them quite a long time to find the house.

pretty It _____

4 It wasn't warm enough to go swimming.

cold _____

5 Rather a long time had passed since we last saw them.

fairly _____

6 She wasn't speaking loudly enough.

too _____

4 Add adverbs of degree to the sentences below to make them true for you.

1 I study hard. _I study quite hard. / I don't study very hard. / I study extremely hard._

2 My hometown is small and quiet. _____

3 My neighbours are friendly. _____

4 I speak English well. _____

38 Focus adverbs
alone, only, just, also, as well, too, even

A: Today's lesson was really difficult!

B: Yes. Even Melissa didn't understand it.

A: And I can't believe how much homework he's given us.

B: It's only two exercises.

A: But remember that we've also got the work from yesterday. I'm only halfway through that. I haven't got time to do today's work as well!

B: True. I'd forgotten we have that too. Well, we'll just have to work really late tonight!

Presentation

Focus adverbs emphasise a particular piece of information:

Only Ali knew what he was talking about.

We've got to do yesterday's homework as well.

alone, only, just

Use *alone*, *only* and *just* to focus on a particular element or feature to the exclusion of others:

He could only play the guitar. (He couldn't play the piano.)

He alone could play the guitar. (Nobody else could play the guitar.)

Just and *only* can be used to focus on nouns, verbs and adjectives. They come before the noun, verb or adjective they are focusing on:

He's just / only joking.

Just / Only Jim's coming tonight.

Alone can only be used with nouns. It comes after the noun:

Jim alone was coming tonight. (no one else)

When *alone* is used after a verb, it has a different meaning.

Jim was coming alone tonight. (= He was on his own, no one else was coming with him.)

also, as well, too

Use *also*, *as well* and *too* to emphasise an additional element or feature in a sentence. *Also* comes before most verbs, but after the verb *to be*, or at the beginning of a sentence.

He also writes his own songs. He's also a song writer. Also, he writes his own songs.

As well and *too* come after the verb (and object if there is one):

He writes his own songs, too. He writes his own songs as well.

You can use *too* and *as well* with nouns and pronouns in short answers: *Me too. John as well.*

even

Use *even* to show that you think something is unusual or surprising. You can use *even* to focus on verbs and nouns. *Even* comes before the element it is focusing on:

He even writes his own songs. (in addition to playing the guitar and singing)

Even John couldn't do it! (= This is surprising as John can usually do everything!)

Changes in meaning

Sometimes the meaning of a sentence can change when you change the position of the adverb:

Even Sally doesn't understand the question. (= It's surprising that Sally doesn't understand because she's clever.)

Sally doesn't even understand the question. (= Sally doesn't understand the question, let alone the answer.)

Only Dawn eats meat. (= Nobody else eats meat.)

Dawn eats only meat. (= She doesn't eat anything else.)

Just Nigel took the exam. (= Nigel took the exam on his own.)

Nigel just sat in on the classes. (= But he didn't take the final exam.)

Kim alone cycles to work. (= Only Kim cycles to work.)

Kim cycles to work alone. (= Kim cycles on her own.)

Exercises

1   Read the article and underline the correct adverb.

OCTOBER ISSUE

Art appreciation

■ Research is being carried out to find out whether it's ¹*only / even* humans who can appreciate and produce art, or whether animals can do it ²*too / just*. Both elephants and chimpanzees have been trained to produce paintings such as the one in the photo, but are these really works of art or ³*alone / just* random shapes and lines? Elephants and chimpanzees can see a range of colour, but animals who are completely colour-blind, such as seals, have ⁴*also / only* been trained to paint. The 'artwork' they produce ⁵*even /alone* looks similar to pictures painted by elephants. However, since they do not see in colour, surely we have to deduce that these paintings can ⁶*too / only* be random strokes, however much we would like to believe otherwise.

2   Put the adverb in brackets in the correct position in the sentence. In some sentences there is more than one possibility.

1   I bought some new shirts and I ˄ also bought a cool pair of shoes. (also)

2   Jeremy doesn't know the answer and he's the cleverest kid in the class. (even)

3   I think it's Richard coming tonight. Everyone else is too busy. (just)

4   My teacher thinks local history is really interesting. My father thinks it is interesting. (as well)

5   She wanted to come but she couldn't. (too)

6   I'm asking you to do the dishes. I'm not asking you to do anything else. (only)

7   Sue finished the race in time. All the others took too long. (alone)

8   I have to finish this last exercise and then I can come out. (just)

3   Rewrite the first sentence using the adverb in bold.

1   Did you also meet the rest of the band?

   too Did you _meet the rest of the band, too_ ?

2   Steffi was the only person who passed the exam.

   alone Steffi _____ .

3   We like Bollywood movies as well.

   also We _____ .

4   My parents don't listen to anything except classical music.

   only My parents _____ .

5   I want to be left in peace, that's all.

   just I _____ .

6   He does most of the housework, including the cooking.

   even He _____ .

39 *so, such*

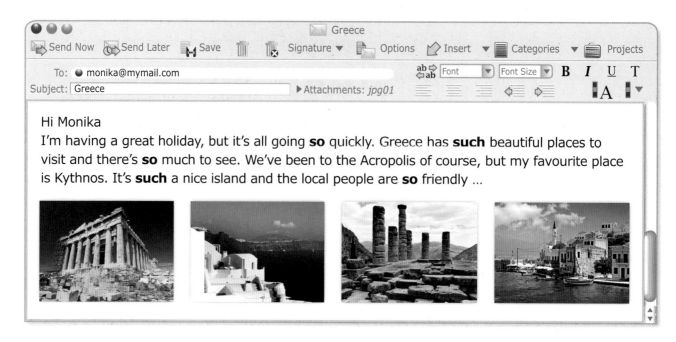

In the email (screenshot):

Hi Monika

I'm having a great holiday, but it's all going **so** quickly. Greece has **such** beautiful places to visit and there's **so** much to see. We've been to the Acropolis of course, but my favourite place is Kythnos. It's **such** a nice island and the local people are **so** friendly …

Presentation

You use *so* and *such* to add emphasis to an adjective, adverb or noun.

so

Use *so* before:

* an adjective without a noun:

  *The local people were **so nice** and **welcoming**.*

* an adverb:

  *The holiday is going **so quickly**.*

* *much, many:*

  *There's **so much** to see in Greece.*

* *few:*

  *There are **so few** people here. (= It's too quiet.)*

* *little:*

  *There's **so little** space here. (= It's too small.)*

> **TIP** *Little* can be an adjective or a quantifier.
>   *This flat is so little!* (adjective)
>   *We have so little space.* (quantifier)

such

Use *such* before:

* an adjective + noun:

  *Greece has **such beautiful places**.*

  *Kythnos is **such a nice island**. (don't say Kythnos is ~~a such nice~~ island.)*

* a noun without an adjective:

  *The Acropolis is beautiful. I've never seen **such a place**.*

We often use *so* and *such* to show cause and effect between two clauses:

←----- cause clause -----→	that	←- effect clause -→
The party was so good	*that*	*we stayed longer.*
It was such a good party	*that*	*we stayed longer.*

Say: *She's so nice. (don't say She's ~~so a nice person~~.)*

Say: *She's such a nice person. (don't say She's a ~~such nice~~ person.)*

> **TIP** *Such* always comes before the article *a/an*.

Exercises

1 Underline the correct option, *so* or *such*.

> ○○○ ⌄ Re: Greece
>
> **From:** Monika   **Subject:** Re: Greece
>
> Hi Hewlett
> I'm ¹*so / such* glad you're having ²*so / such* a good time in Greece. We're all ³*so / such* jealous of you here at work. You chose the right time for a holiday. There have been ⁴*so / such* few people here this week – and we've had ⁵*so / such* a lot of extra work to do. Anyway, I can't wait to see you. You'll have ⁶*so / such* a good tan, I expect!

2 🔊1.41 Write *so* or *such* in the conversation. Then listen and check.

A: Thank you for ¹_____ a lovely evening.

B: I'm ²_____ glad that you enjoyed it.

A: And you went to ³_____ much effort. How long did it take you to prepare everything?

B: Not ⁴_____ a long time.

A: But there were ⁵_____ many dishes! But then I'm ⁶_____ an awful cook.

3 Look at pictures 1–4. Write what each person is saying. Use the words and add *so* or *such*.

1   Why / she / drive / slowly?

2   I don't know why there / few people

3   India / beautiful country.

4   There's / much / do

4 Rewrite the first sentence using the words in the second sentence and *so* or *such*.

1   That was such a nice idea of yours.
    That idea of yours was _____ so nice.

2   Question three is so difficult.
    Three is _____ such a difficult _____ question.

3   The book I'm reading is so strange.
    I'm reading _____ book.

4   Don't be such an impatient person!
    Don't _____ impatient!

5   That new boy in our class is so handsome!
    There's someone new in our class. He's _____ boy.

6   We had such a wonderful holiday.
    Our holiday was _____

7   Have you ever met anyone so rude?
    Have you ever met _____ person?

40 Review of units 36 to 39

Grammar

1 Write the words in the correct order.

1 finish worked he to job the hard
   <u>He worked hard to finish the job</u>

2 strong you coffee for the enough is
   _____?

3 lately holiday you have on been
   _____?

4 eat something like would to you too
   _____?

5 quietly moved he so nobody sound that a heard
   _____.

6 mistake that clever she's make much to too
   _____.

7 birthday forgot even he his mother's
   _____

8 game as that played well I've
   _____.

9 hair such a my mess today is
   _____.

10 your so has useful work been
   _____.

2 Underline and correct the mistakes in 1–6.

1 John only is staying. Everyone else is leaving.
   <u>Only John . . .</u>

2 On this diet you only meat eat and no carbohydrates.

3 This necklace is such beautiful. Where did you buy it?

4 That's so a good idea!

5 He had got up lately that morning and was in no hurry to leave the house.

6 It was a quite good idea, but I knew it'd never work.

3 Complete the conversation with the words in the box. You will not need to use all the words.

> alone also as well even hard hardly
> just late lately only

A: What are you doing here so ¹_____?
   Your classes ended hours ago!

B: Yes, but I ²_____ had to finish this last piece of homework.

A: What are you doing? Your German assignment?

B: It's really ³_____. And I have to study all this new vocabulary ⁴_____!

A: Let's see. That's ⁵_____ new! We studied that last year. Don't you remember? You know that already. ⁶_____ I know it – and you know I've got a terrible memory!

B: Oh yes, you're right! Great! Listen, leave me ⁷_____ for ten minutes so I can finish. Then we can go and get a coffee or something.

A: OK, but ⁸_____ ten minutes, no more!

B: See you outside in ten minutes.

4 Rewrite the sentences keeping the same meaning, but using the words in bold.

1 He laughed very loudly.
   loud <u>His laugh was very loud.</u>

2 The flat wasn't big enough for the four of them.
   small _____

3 The party was quite successful.
   it _____

4 I've been going to bed at three o'clock in the morning these last few weeks.
   lately _____

5 We were extremely hungry when we got home.
   absolutely _____

6 She was delighted with her present.
   very _____

7 He spoke too quickly.
   enough _____

8 He looked at her with a happy smile on his face.
   smiled _____

Grammar in context

5 Complete the text using the words in the box. Note that some words are used more than once.

> also hard just late only so such too

RIGHT NOW.co.uk

SEARCH

Home News | World News | Business | Money | Travel | Sports | Entertainment | TV | Culture | Careers | Health | Comment

WORLD NEWS

Preventing global warming:
Is it already too [1]_____?

When you ask this question, [2]_____ much depends on who you ask. There are people who don't believe it really exists. There are others who say that even if it's true that the world is getting warmer, it's [3]_____ part of the natural cycle and we can all look forward to enjoying warmer summers and shorter winters [4]_____.

But it's [5]_____ to argue with the evidence nowadays when [6]_____ many scientists accept it as a fact. [7]_____ last week, another report from a team of experts said that there is [8]_____ a large amount of greenhouse gas in the atmosphere already that it will take at least another century for it all to clear.

Tim Barnett, a senior scientist at the Scripps Institution of Oceanography in California, [9]_____ believes that it's already [10]_____ late to stop the temperature rising. Even if the world suddenly stops producing greenhouse gases today, temperatures will still rise by one degree by 2050.

Pronunciation: stressing words in sentences

6 🔊 **1.42** We often stress particular words in sentences for emphasis. Notice the stressed words in sentences 1 and 2 and then underline the stressed words in 3–8.

1 Thank you. It's <u>really</u> beautiful.
2 Rosa's <u>so</u> lucky! She met Johnny Depp and she <u>even</u> got his autograph!
3 Can I come, too?
4 That's such a good point you made.
5 Snowboarding is so much fun.
6 I'll only go if Ray isn't going.
7 Jon alone knows the secret.
8 I'm sorry, it's just too big.

Listen again and repeat the sentences.

Listen again

7 🔊 **1.43** Listen and decide: does the adjective describe the father or the son?

1	dishonest	son
2	defiant	
3	angry	
4	quiet	
5	tired	
6	anxious	
7	sad	

41 Comparatives and superlatives 1
Adjectives and adverbs

TODAY'S TOP QUESTION: I want to study a foreign language. What's the easiest language to learn?

AND THE TOP FIVE ANSWERS:

The simple answer to this question is whichever language is closest to your own. So, for example, if you're a Spanish speaker, Italian is easier than German.

It's not English! English is one of the hardest ones.

The easiest language to learn is the one that you are most motivated to learn. The less motivated you are, the more difficult it is.

I totally agree :) and once you've got the basics, find a friend who speaks the language. You'll learn more quickly if you're having fun!

Don't forget, once you know two or three other languages, it just gets easier and easier!

Presentation

You use comparative and superlative forms to make comparisons: *Italian is **easier** than German. The **easiest** language is the one you're **most motivated** to learn.*

Comparative forms are used to compare two things or people. They are used to:

- say that one has more or less of a quality than the other: *Spanish is **easier** than Portuguese.*

- show how a situation has changed: *I find it **more difficult** to study now* (than I did in the past).

- describe a change that is in progress: *It's getting **more difficult** as I get older.*

Use the **superlative** to say that one thing or person has more or less of a certain quality than all the others in the same group: *Spanish is **the easiest** European language.*

Comparative and superlative forms can be used in different ways to say the same thing: *Spanish is **the easiest** language to learn. Spanish is **easier** than any other language.*

To form comparative adjectives and adverbs, we use -*er, more* or *less*: *easy → easier; motivated → more motivated; efficient → less efficient.*

To form superlative adjectives and adverbs, we use -*est, most* or *least*: *easy → easiest; motivated → most motivated; efficient → least efficient.*

See page 233: Spelling rules

Some adjectives and adverbs are irregular. For example *good/well → better → best; bad/badly → worse → worst; far → further/farther → furthest/farthest.*

Use the preposition *than* with comparative forms to link the two objects, people or situations that you are comparing: *Italian is easier **than** German. Speaking it is more difficult **than** reading it.*

You usually use *the* before a superlative adjective: ***The** easiest language to learn. **The most** beautiful language in the world.*

Expressions with comparative forms

You can repeat the comparative using *and* to emphasise a process of change: *It's getting easier **and** easier. She worked less **and** less enthusiastically.*

You can use two comparative expressions with *the* to explain how one thing changes in relation to another:

***The older** you are, **the harder** it is.* (= As you get older, it gets more difficult.)

***The more confident** you feel, **the better** you learn.*

Expressions with superlative forms

You often use superlative expressions with:

- *one/some of the …*: ***one of the** hardest languages; **some of the** easiest languages*

- *the second/third, etc. … is …*: ***the second** easiest language is Italian*

- *the most … ever …*: ***the most** beautiful language I've **ever** heard.*

Exercises

1

🔊 1.44 **Write the comparative or superlative form of the words in brackets. Then listen and check.**

1. A: How's the new job going? Is it any ¹_____ (good) than the last one?

   B: No! It's ²_____ (bad) if anything! It's probably the ³_____ (boring) job I've ever had! And the hours are ⁴_____ (long) than my other job, too. Changing jobs was the ⁵_____ (bad) decision I've ever made!

   A: Well, if it's so bad, why don't you quit?

   B: Because the wages are ⁶_____ (high) and I need the extra money!

2. A: I think maybe you should drive a little ⁷_____ (slowly).

   B: Why? Do you think I'm going too fast?

   A: Well you're certainly going ⁸_____ (fast) than anyone else on the road! But ⁹_____ (importantly), there's a police car over there, and they're going to stop you for speeding!

2 Complete the second sentence so that it has a similar meaning to the first sentence. Use the words in bold and use no more than four words in each gap.

1. This one's cheaper, but it's not very reliable.

   expensive   This one's _____, but it's not very reliable.

2. This is the best model in the range in terms of reliability.

   reliable   This model is _____ in the range.

3. Their new delivery service isn't very efficient compared to the old one.

   less   Their new delivery service _____ the old one.

4. This car is certainly not the most comfortable car I've ever driven!

   least   This car is probably _____ car I've ever driven!

5. Sam has been attending more classes this term.

   frequently   Sam has been missing classes _____ this term.

6. Their business has been improving over the last year.

   successfully   Their business has been performing _____ over the last year.

3 Complete the expressions using the words in the box.

| biggest difficult happier happiest harder least less (x2) longer |

1. It's getting more and more _____ to find a good job. There are none advertised in the newspaper.
2. The _____ you wait, the _____ it gets. So start learning a new language today!
3. The _____ enthusiastic students always have the _____ problems.
4. I've never felt _____ than I do now. I have everything I could possibly want in life.
5. It was one of the _____ days of her life. She had always wanted to be a mother.
6. She has been working _____ and _____ enthusiastically over the last year.

4 Write your own answers to the questions below. Use comparative and superlative structures.

1. What do you think is the easiest language to learn? Why? _____
2. Do you think English is a difficult language? _____
3. What do you think is the most difficult thing about learning a language? _____
4. What do you think is the best way to learn a language? _____

Ask Annie!

Got a problem at work? Need advice about a difficult decision? Annie has helped more people than any other online advice service.

End of the line?

■ My job's getting me down more and more every day! I spend more time at the office than I do at home and I have less and less time to spend with my family and friends. Of all the people I know, I'm the one who works the most hours and I'm also the one who has the fewest holidays! And now my boss has asked me to work on Saturdays as well! I'm already doing more than I want to, but if I say no, I'll lose my job. What should I do?

Brad

■ *Try talking to your boss. Maybe you can negotiate to work fewer hours during the week? Or get more holidays to make up for the extra work? If your boss won't listen to sense, then you need to decide what matters most to you, your job or your personal life.*
Good luck!

Annie

Presentation

Comparative and superlative structures with nouns

You can form comparative and superlative expressions using nouns:

*I spend **more time** at the office than I do at home.*

*I have **less time** to spend with my friends.*

*I'm the one who works **the most hours**.*

*I'm also the one who has **the fewest holidays**.*

Use *more, less* and *fewer* to form comparative structures.

Use *most, least* and *fewest* to form superlative structures.

	uncountable	countable
+	more/most + noun more time, the most money*	more/most + noun more hours, the most holidays*
−	less/least + noun less time, the least money	fewer/fewest + noun fewer people, the fewest things

*You must always use *the* with *most* + noun if you want to express a superlative meaning.

***The most people** who can fit in the room is 200. (most =* the largest number possible)

***Most people** live in flats. (most =* the majority of)

more, most, less, least as adverbs

More, most, less and *least* can also be used as adverbs. They come after the verb (and the object if there is one):

*My job is getting me down **more and more**.*

*These days, I care about my family **more and more**.*

*I'm working **more** than I want to.*

*The thing that matters **most** is my family.*

*The thing I care about **least** is the money.*

*When I'm tired, I work **less**.*

Expressions

The following comparative and superlative expressions can be used with nouns and as adverbs:

- ***more and more / less and less**: I spend **more and more** time at work. I have **less and less** time to spend with my family. I worry **more and more** about my job.*

- ***The more … the less …**: **The more** time I spend at work, **the less** time I spend with my family. **The more** I work, **the less** I play.*

- ***The most / least / fewest … possible**: The company employs **the fewest** people possible. I spend **the least** time possible at the office.*

See page 233: Spelling rules

Exercises

1 (1.45) **Choose the correct options. Then listen and check.**

A new survey shows that teenagers spend ¹*few / least /* (*more*) time watching TV than most adults. In fact, of all the age groups covered in the survey, teenagers spend the ²*fewer / less / most* hours in front of a TV screen. But, in contrast, they spend ³*fewer / fewest / less* time on the internet. They are, in fact, one of the groups that spends the ⁴*fewest / least / less* hours on the internet. This may be because adults have ⁵*least / more / most* access to the internet than teenagers. Teenagers have ⁶*less / fewer / fewest* opportunities to go online because they spend most of the day either at school or in after-school activities. They also spend ⁷*fewer / least / less* time playing video games than most people think. The people who play the ⁸*less / more / most* video games are in the 21–30 age group.

2 **Add *more, most, less* or *least* to the sentences below.**

1 I'm enjoying my dance classes _____ this year than I did last year. They're really good.
2 The thing I like _____ about them is the teacher. She's great!
3 She makes us work _____ than the old teacher did. The old teacher was a bit lazy.
4 She shouts _____ as well! The old teacher was forever shouting at us!
5 He spent most of the lesson sitting down in front of the class, telling us what to do. He spent the _____ possible time actually dancing.
6 The new teacher explains things _____ and shows us the steps herself, instead of just talking.
7 And I suppose that the thing that matters _____ is that I'm getting really fit and having fun at the same time.

3 **Correct the mistakes in the sentences below.**

1 He's spending ~~fewer and fewer~~ *less and less* time with his family.

2 She's studying less or less and I'm really worried she'll fail her exams.

3 They told the less people possible, but the story still got into the newspapers.

4 The more I get to know him, less I like him.

5 The more I try, the most mistakes I make.

6 He really made the fewest effort possible to make us feel at home.

7 The few options you have, the easier it is to make a decision.

8 They're making most and most money, but they have no time to spend it.

4 **Complete these sentences so that they are true for you.**

1 I spend _____ time _____ than _____ .
2 I spend _____ money on _____ than on _____ .
3 The thing I like _____ about studying English is _____ .
4 The one thing that matters _____ in life is _____ .

43 Modifying comparatives and superlatives

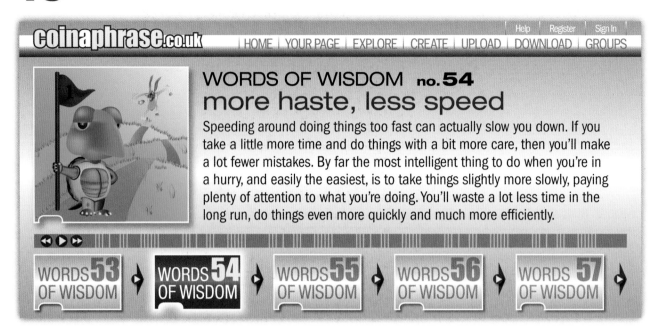

WORDS OF WISDOM no.54
more haste, less speed

Speeding around doing things too fast can actually slow you down. If you take a little more time and do things with a bit more care, then you'll make a lot fewer mistakes. By far the most intelligent thing to do when you're in a hurry, and easily the easiest, is to take things slightly more slowly, paying plenty of attention to what you're doing. You'll waste a lot less time in the long run, do things even more quickly and much more efficiently.

WORDS **53** OF WISDOM ▶ WORDS **54** OF WISDOM ▶ WORDS **55** OF WISDOM ▶ WORDS **56** OF WISDOM ▶ WORDS **57** OF WISDOM

Presentation

Modifying comparative expressions

You use modifiers such as *a bit, a little, a little bit, slightly, much, a lot* in comparisons to show the degree of difference between the two things being compared:

- small difference: *this holiday is **a bit** cheaper; it works **slightly** better*
- big difference: *you can book **much** more cheaply online*

With plural countable nouns, for small differences use *a few more* or *slightly more*. Say ***a few more** hours* (don't say ~~a bit~~ or ~~a little more~~ *hours*).

With plural countable nouns, for big differences use *many more* or *a lot more*. Say ***many more** hours* (don't say ~~much more~~ *hours*).

even

We can use *even* to add emphasis to a comparative expression:

***even less** fun*

***even more** cheaply than before*

***even fewer** people than we'd expected*

We use the same forms for adjectives, adverbs and uncountable nouns:

small differences		big differences	
a bit	cheaper	much	cheaper
a little	more	a lot	more
slightly	carefully	far	carefully
	more time	considerably	more time

Modifying superlative expressions

We can use modifiers such as *easily* and *by far* with superlative expressions to say that something has much more of a particular quality than all the other things it is being compared to:

- *easily: this is **easily the most exciting** (= much more exciting than anything else)*

  *This is **easily the most time** we've spent away from home.*
- *by far: this is **by far the best** (= much better than anything else)*

  *This is **by far the most interesting** place we've visited during this holiday.*

Exercises

1 (1.46) **Add the modifiers in brackets to the sentences. Then listen and check.**

1 A: He always does his work *far* more quickly than anyone else. (far)

  B: Yes, but he also makes more mistakes. (a lot)

2 A: What's the quickest way to get to the centre from here?

  B: The train is probably the quickest, but the bus isn't bad either. It takes more time, but it costs less. (a little / a lot)

3 A: That was the best film I've seen this year. Better than the original. (easily / even)

  B: Really? You think so? I thought the original was better. (much)

4 A: Well, there were more people there tonight than I'd expected. (a few)

  B: Yes, there were definitely more tonight than last week. (a lot)

2 **Choose the best word(s) from the brackets to replace the words in bold.**

1 I got **a few** *slightly* more birthday presents than last year. (*slightly / a bit*)

2 It took me **much** more time to do the homework this week than usual. (*far / many*)

3 He was **easily** the most attractive man in the room. (*by far / far*)

4 The time passed **a lot** more quickly than we'd expected. (*easily / far*)

5 She had **much** more support from her parents than I ever did. (*a bit / a lot*)

6 There are **far** more job opportunities in a large town. (*many / much*)

3 **Look at the information about three cities in Spain and answer the questions using comparative and superlative structures. Use modifiers where possible.**

		Founded in	Population	Average temperatures	Number of visitors per year
	Cádiz	3,000 BC	160,000	Summer 24° Winter 12°	400,000
	Madrid	9th century AD	3 million	Summer 30° Winter 5°	7 million
	Santiago de Compostela	5th century AD	94,000	Summer 18° Winter 8°	3.5 million

1 Which city is the oldest?

  Cádiz is the by far oldest. It's much, much older than both Madrid and Santiago de Compostela.

2 Which is the largest in terms of population?

3 Which has the best climate?

4 Which city is the most popular with tourists?

5 Which city would you prefer to visit? Why?

44 as ... as ...

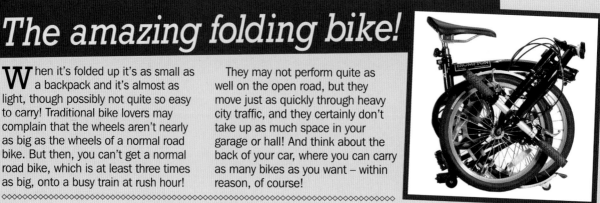

The amazing folding bike!

When it's folded up it's as small as a backpack and it's almost as light, though possibly not quite so easy to carry! Traditional bike lovers may complain that the wheels aren't nearly as big as the wheels of a normal road bike. But then, you can't get a normal road bike, which is at least three times as big, onto a busy train at rush hour!

They may not perform quite as well on the open road, but they move just as quickly through heavy city traffic, and they certainly don't take up as much space in your garage or hall! And think about the back of your car, where you can carry as many bikes as you want – within reason, of course!

Presentation

Use *as ... as ...* to compare two things and say that they are *similar*:

*It's **as small as** a normal backpack.* (= A backpack is small. The bike, when it is folded up, is equally small.)

Use *not as ... as ...* to compare two things and say that they are *different,* and that one possesses *less* of a certain quality or ability than the other:

*The wheels **aren't as big as** the wheels of a normal road bike.* (= The wheels are smaller than the wheels of a normal road bike.)

TIP You can also use *not so ... as ...* The meaning is the same. *It's not so easy to carry as a normal bike.*

Use *(not) as ... as ...* with adjectives and adverbs:

*It's **as small as** a backpack.*

*It's moves **as quickly as** a normal bike.*

Use *(not) as much/many ... as ...* with nouns:

*It doesn't take up **as much space as** a normal bike.*

The second *as* can be followed by a noun phrase or a clause:

*not as big **as a normal bike*** (noun phrase)

*not as heavy **as you think*** (clause)

You can drop the second *as* and the following noun phrase or clause if the comparison is clear from the context:

*It's as small as a normal backpack though it's **not so easy to carry*** (~~as a normal backpack~~).

Modifying *as ... as ...*

We can modify expressions using *(not) as ... as ...* to show the degree of similarity or difference:

- small differences: use *almost/nearly/not quite as ... as ...*:
  *This one is **not quite as** exciting as that one.*

- big differences: *use twice/three times (etc.)/not nearly as ... as ...*:
  *This one is **twice as expensive as** that one.*
  *This one is **not nearly as attractive as** that one.*

You can use *just* to emphasise that one thing is equal to another:

*They move **just** as quickly as other bikes in heavy traffic.* (= There is no difference between them.)

like and *as*

You use the preposition *like* in expressions that compare two things and say that they are similar in some way:
*He runs **like** the wind. She looks **like** you. It sounds **like** a dream come true.*

You use the preposition *as* to explain the jobs and functions of people and things:

*She works **as** a TV actor. You can use this box **as** a seat.*

You also use the preposition *as* with the adjective *same*:
*He looks just the **same as** you.* (= He looks just like you.)

Exercises

1 (1.47) **Complete the expressions using the words in the box. Then listen and check.**

easy	fit	good	new	quickly

1 A: Hi, my car's broken down! Can you come and pick me up?
   B: Yes, sure, I'll come as ¹_____ as I can. Where are you?

2 A: Hey, you sound out of breath! What have you been doing?
   B: The lift's broken. I came up the stairs. I'm obviously not as _____ as I used to be!

3 A: Oh dear, this isn't going to be as _____ as I thought. Can I give it to you tomorrow?
   B: Yes, sure. Take all the time you want.

4 A: Does your dog bite?
   B: No! He's as _____ as gold! He'd never hurt a fly.

5 A: There you are. I've mended the hole in your trousers.
   B: Thanks. Hey, you've done a great job. They're as good as _____ .

2 **Complete the second sentence so that it has the same meaning as the first. Use structures with *as … as …***

1 It's easier than it looks.
   It's not _____as difficult as_____ it looks.

2 Yoga is more relaxing than pilates.
   Pilates is _____ as yoga.

3 Pilates is much more dynamic than yoga.
   Yoga is _____ nearly _____ as pilates.

4 More people do yoga than pilates.
   Not _____ people do pilates as do yoga.

5 Both exercise types are equally good for improving tone and balance.
   Both exercise types are _____ as _____ for improving tone and balance.

6 There are a lot more variations of yoga than pilates.
   There _____ nearly _____ of pilates as there are of yoga.

3 **Complete the sentences using *as* or *like*.**

1 It's the same height _____ a normal bike, and _____ a normal bike, it can be used on cycle lanes but not on pavements.

2 Is that a new bike you've got? It's just _____ mine! Except that it's not quite _____ big.

3 What's your new flat _____? Is it in more or less the same area _____ before?

4 It's not quite _____ close to the station, but it's twice _____ big. It feels _____ a palace after that tiny flat we used to live in!

4 **Complete these sentences so they are true for you.**

1 I'm not nearly/just as _____ my father.

2 I'm not nearly/just as _____ my mother.

3 I'm more or less as _____ .

4 Everybody says I look just/a bit like _____ .

45 Review of units 41 to 44

Grammar

1 Complete each section of the text below with the words in the box.

Fascinating facts about languages

The oldest languages

| just as old | older than | one of the oldest |

■ Chinese is ¹_____ written languages which is still spoken.

■ Ancient Greek is ²_____ as Chinese.

■ But Ancient Egyptian is ³_____ than both of them.

The most spoken languages

| more people | not as many people | the greatest number |

■ Mandarin Chinese is the language with ⁴_____ of native speakers.

■ ⁵_____ speak English as a second or foreign language than as a first language.

■ ⁶_____ speak Chinese as a foreign language.

Languages on the internet

| as popular | much less | not as dominant | more |

■ English is ⁷_____ as it used to be on the internet. The number of websites in other languages has grown dramatically over the last ten years.

■ Chinese is now almost ⁸_____ as English on the web.

■ Spanish is used ⁹_____ than Japanese but ¹⁰_____ than English.

2 Correct the mistakes in the sentences below. There is one mistake in each sentence.

1 There are ~~by far~~ *far* more students in our class this year than last year.

2 I haven't got quite as much free time this week than I had last week.

3 There were a bit fewer applications for the job than we were expecting.

4 He generally spends the fewest time at his desk of all his colleagues.

5 That was the easily most boring party I've ever been invited to!

6 It's not nearly so cold so I thought it would be.

3 Choose the correct options.

1 A: You look a lot *as /(like)* your brother, don't you?
  B: Yes, a lot of people say that, except that I'm not nearly as *tall / taller*.

2 A: The restaurant looks *a few / a lot* busier than usual today.
  B: Yes, it's *by far / far* the most visitors we've had all year.

3 A: I really can't stand this heat anymore. It's getting *hotter and hotter / more and more hot* every day!
  B: Just wait. It gets *even / just* hotter in July!

4 A: That was one of the *worse / worst* hotels I've ever stayed in. I know it was cheap, but I was expecting it to be *a little / easily* cleaner.
  B: Oh, I don't know. I thought the one we stayed in last night was *even / just* as bad.

4 Complete the second sentence so that it has the same meaning as the first. Use the words in bold. Use no more than five words.

1 My room is much colder than yours.
  warm My room isn't *as warm as* yours.

2 I spend more money on food than on clothes.
  less I spend _____ than on food.

3 Mike was much happier in his old job.
  nearly Mike isn't _____ in his new job.

4 My previous office was half the size of this one.
  big This office is _____ my previous one.

Grammar in context

5 Choose the correct options to complete the text below.

Health tip of the week: slow down, lose weight!

Eat slowly, say experts.

The faster you eat, ¹*the more / more* you eat, so if you want to lose weight, you'd better start slowing down. Medical researchers in Athens have found that the more slowly you eat, ²*the more time / the less time* your stomach has to produce natural hormones that tell you that you're full. As a result, you don't feel as hungry and you eat ³*least / less*. A group of volunteers were asked to eat 300ml of ice cream, some faster and others much ⁴*slowly / more slowly*. Their blood was tested before and after eating, and then at intervals to measure the levels of hormones. Those volunteers who ate ⁵*the faster / the fastest* had the lowest levels of hormones in their blood, which meant that they felt twice ⁶*hungrier / as hungry as* the volunteers who had eaten their ice cream at half the pace. They ⁷*felt like / felt as* they could still eat more, while the slower eaters felt that they'd eaten ⁸*more enough / more than enough*. So, the lesson is, eat ⁹*slower / as slowly as* you can, enjoy what you're eating and lose weight at the same time!

Pronunciation: *as ... as ...* weak form

6 🔊 **1.48** Listen to the first two sentences with *as ... as ....* Notice the pronunciation of *as* and the stress on the main content words.

        /əz/   /əz/

1 The children were as good as gold.

               /əz/   /əz/

2 This is definitely not as easy as I thought.

Now listen to the other sentences and underline the stressed words.

3 I'll get it done as soon as I possibly can.

4 Her hair was as white as snow.

5 The concert wasn't nearly as good as last time.

6 Watch out for him! He's as cunning as a fox.

7 There's no hurry. Take as much time as you want.

8 There weren't quite as many people as we'd expected.

Listen again and repeat the sentences. Remember to stress the main content words.

Listen again

7 🔊 **1.49** Listen to three short conversations and answer the questions.

Conversation 1: Why doesn't Nick like his new job?

_____

Conversation 2: Why does Sue tell the driver to slow down?

46 Prepositions of time 1
in, on, at

Lessons in management:
Effective meetings

1 Start on time.

2 Keep within a time limit.

3 At the end, check everyone knows the date of the next meeting.

Presentation

in, on, at (as prepositions of time)

in	• periods of time: *in the evening, in my lunch break, in the summer, in the 20th century*
	• points at the end of a period of time: *in five minutes, in an hour, in three weeks, in a year*
on	• days: *on Monday, on Saturdays, on Christmas Day, on Monday afternoon, on her birthday*
	• dates: *on July 4th*
at	• a point in time: *at 3 o'clock, at midday*
	• holiday periods: *at the weekend, at New Year*

in the night / at night

You say *in the night* for something that happened on a particular night: *I received a call **in the night** from my colleague in China.*

You say *at night* for something that happens regularly: *I often have conference calls **at night** with my colleagues in China.*

in time / on time

Use *in time* to say something happened early enough (not too late) before a point in time: *We finished **in time** to catch the last train home.* (= I wasn't too late to catch the last train home.)

Use *on time* to say that something happened at (or possibly before) a previously planned time. It was punctual and not late: *Always arrive **on time** for a meeting.* (= Never arrive late for a meeting.)

in / within

Use *in/within* to emphasise that there is a time limit: *He'll be here **in** three hours.* (= He'll arrive at the end of the three-hour period.)

*He'll be here **within** three hours.* (= He'll arrive at some point before the three-hour period ends.)

in the end / at the end

Use *in the end* to talk about the final result of something or what finally happened: *It lasted such a long time that **in the end** I feel asleep.*

Use *at the end* to talk about the time when something ended: ***At the end** of the meeting, we talked about the time and date of the next meeting.* (don't say *In the end of the meeting*)

*The next meeting is **at the end** of the month.* (don't say *in the end of the month*)

No preposition

You do not use *in, on* or *at* with:

- *tomorrow / yesterday:*
  I didn't see you ~~on~~ yesterday.
  Are you coming ~~on~~ tomorrow?

- *last / next / every / each* + noun:
  We'll meet ~~in~~ next month.
  The office meeting is ~~on~~ every Monday.

- You do not normally use the preposition with questions about time:
  What time is the meeting (at)?
  What day did you meet him (on)?

See page 244: Common prepositions and their meanings

Exercises

1 Complete each pair of sentences with the words in bold.

1 in / on   A He works _____ Mondays and Thursdays.
            B He works _____ the evenings.

2 in / at   A Let's meet _____ five o'clock.
            B Let's meet _____ an hour.

3 on / at   A I'll be at home _____ New Year's Day.
            B I'm going away _____ New Year.

4 in the night / at night   A The wind blew down a tree _____ but fortunately it missed the house!
            B When I sleep at my grandmother's house, I always hear strange noises _____ .

5 in time / on time   A I was late home last night but I arrived _____ to watch the second half of the match on TV.
            B She never starts her meetings _____ . It's so annoying!

6 in the end / at the end   A We drove round and round Paris for about half an hour. _____ , we asked someone for directions.
            B I always cry _____ of this film because they never see each other again.

2 ⏱1.50 Cross out any prepositions in this conversation where possible or necessary. Then listen and check.

A: Our next meeting will be ~~on~~ next month.

B: What date is that on?

A: The twenty-fifth.

B: Sorry, but I'm on holiday in that week.

A: OK. On what day are you back?

B: The following on Monday.

A: Right. We'll have it on the first.

B: What time are we meeting at?

A: The same at time as normal.

3 Rewrite the first sentence using the words in bold.

1 I hope he applies for the job before the deadline.
   in time   I hope he applies _for the job in time._

2 We meet on Mondays.
   every   We _____ .

3 I couldn't sleep for ages. Finally, I took some sleeping pills and fell asleep.
   end   I couldn't sleep for ages. _____ I took some sleeping pills and fell asleep.

4 You must answer ten questions. You have five minutes only.
   within   You must answer ten questions _____ .

5 My uncle is a security guard so he often works nights.
   night   My uncle is a security guard so he often works _____ .

6 She's coming to visit this Friday.
   on   She's coming to visit _____ .

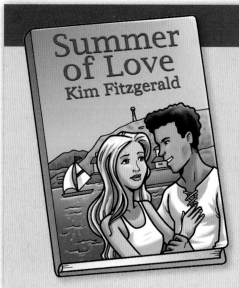

Summer of Love

Summer of Love
Kim Fitzgerald

When Rachel Knightly stays at her aunt's Italian villa for the summer, she isn't looking for romance. That is until one warm afternoon on the beach when she meets her aunt's stepson – Roberto. By the evening, she's fallen hopelessly in love.

Then, during one terrible night, she is woken by the voices of Roberto and her aunt. It is after midnight. As she opens the door she overhears their conversation and a terrible family secret ...

One critic said: 'From the moment I began reading to the moment I closed the book, I lived every day of Rachel's summer. *Summer of Love* is like no other book I've ever read – before or since!'

Rate this book

Presentation

for, in, during, from ... to, between

These prepositions are used with a period of time but there are differences in meaning.

for

For refers to the length of the period and shows how long something lasted: *Rachel Knightly stays at her aunt's Italian villa for the summer.*

in, during

In or *during* describes a shorter period of time within a longer period: *We visited my grandparents in the school holidays.* (= The visit took place at some time within the period of the school holidays, not the entire holiday.)

from ... to, between

Use *from ... to ...* to describe the length of the period of time by stating the starting and ending points: *I read the book from two o'clock to three o'clock.* (= I read for an hour.)

Use *between* to say that an action happened at some point in a period of time: *What time was Rachel woken up? Sometime between two and three o'clock.* (= We don't know exactly what time.)

See page 244: Common prepositions and their meanings

by, until (till), before

Use *by, until* and *before* when talking about the end point of a period of time. Use *by* to talk about an action/event that is completed at some point before or possibly at a point in time: *By the evening, she's fallen hopelessly in love.*

Use *until* to describe an action/event that will continue from the time of speaking to precisely the point in time: *She stays on the beach until (till) five o'clock.*

TIP You use *till* when speaking informally.

Use *before* to describe an action/event that is completed at some time previous to the time given: *I always read a book before I go to bed.*

after, since

Use *after* and *since* when talking about the starting point in a period of time. Use *after* to describe an action/event that happened at some time later than the point in time: *She woke up after midnight.*

Use *since* to refer to the time at which an action (which continues to the present) started: *She hasn't been able to sleep since midnight.* (= She is still awake.)

See also Unit 4: *for / since*

Exercises

1 Match sentences 1–8 with A and B.

1 I stayed with my friend in Warsaw for a short time during the summer. ___A___

2 I stayed with my friend in Warsaw for the summer. ___B___

   A I was there for two days.

   B So I had lots of time to learn Polish!

3 How long has Julia been here? _____

4 When did Julia arrive? _____

   A After three o'clock.

   B Since three o'clock.

5 I can be at work by five. _____

6 I can be at work until five. _____

   A Really? Can't you stay any later?

   B Really? Can't you get here any earlier?

7 How long are you working at the restaurant?
   _____

8 When are you leaving the restaurant this evening? _____

   A In two hours.

   B For four hours.

2 Underline the correct preposition.

🐾 Animal facts

1 Sharks have been on the earth *since / until* the dinosaur age.

2 A snail can sleep *for / during* three years.

3 *For / During* her lifetime, a cow gives nearly 200,000 glasses of milk.

4 A caterpillar becomes a butterfly *since / after* two weeks.

5 *During / From* the age of one to seven years, a lobster will only grow to weigh half a kilo.

6 The average fly lives *between / since* two and three weeks.

3 🎧 **1.51 Complete part of a famous story with a preposition A, B or C. Then listen and check.**

¹_____ sunset, all the guests had arrived along with the King, Queen and the Prince. The dancing began. ²_____ the evening, many young single ladies tried to attract the attention of the Prince. But ³_____ the beginning of the ball, he had shown no interest in anything or anybody.

However, ⁴_____ some time, a new, unexpected guest arrived at the ball. The Queen whispered to the King, 'Who is the girl in the white dress and glass slippers? She's beautiful.' ⁵_____ that moment, the Prince hadn't moved from his seat, but instantly, he invited the guest to dance and could not be separated from her ⁶_____ the rest of the evening.

But suddenly, just ⁷_____ midnight, the mysterious visitor began to run from the castle with no explanation. The Prince followed her as the castle bell began striking twelve. But outside, there was no sign of her – except a glass slipper.

1	A	By	B	From	C To
2	A	Before	B	After	C During
3	A	for	B	since	C between
4	A	during	B	after	C since
5	A	By	B	In	C Until
6	A	for	B	to	C before
7	A	to	B	in	C before

Presentation

in, on, at

Use *in* to say that the person/object is inside something or surrounded by something:

*Fourteen people are **in** the telephone box.* (= They're inside the telephone box.)

Common uses:

- towns, countries, continents, general locations: *in Oxford, in France, in Africa, in the countryside, in the city, in a line*
- printed material: *in the newspaper/book/magazine, in the photograph/picture*

Use *on* to say that the person/object is situated on or attached to something:

*He's **on** the wing of an aeroplane.*

*He has a parachute **on** his back.* (= The parachute is attached to his back.)

Common uses:

- technology: *on the phone, on the TV, on the internet, on the screen*
- other: *on an island, on the coast, on the second floor, on holiday*

Use *at* to say that someone or something is:

- next to or very near an object, but not in or on it: *at the table, at the bar*
- located at a certain point: *at the corner, at the end of the road, at work, at home*

Common uses:

- events and special occasions: *at a party, at a meeting*
- addresses and points of a journey: *at 23 Waldorf Street, at the traffic lights, at the bus stop*

in or on?

When you talk about types of transport, use *in* if you can only sit in the transport: *in a taxi, in a car.*

Use *on* if you can stand or sit in the transport: *on the bus, on the midday train, on a boat*

Use *on* when you talk about a point on a route: *The castle is **on** the road from York to Lincoln.* (= It's somewhere between York and Lincoln.)

Use *in* for something that is physically part of the route: *There's a bend **in** the river. There's a bump **in** the road.*

in or at?

You use *in* for things that happen inside a building: *Let's meet **in** the cinema.* (= not outside)

You can use *at* for inside or just outside a building: *Let's meet **at** the cinema.* (= inside or outside)

See also Unit 24: Articles 2

Use *in* to talk about membership: *in the Boy Scouts, in a political party*

Use *at* to talk about special events: *at a festival, at the Olympics*

See page 244: Common prepositions and their meanings

Exercises

1 Complete these world records with *in, on* or *at*.

More world records

- Nico Surings ran the fastest 100 metres [1]_____ ice.
- 201 members of the Indian army stood [2]_____ ten motorcycles and travelled 129 metres.
- The largest number of people [3]_____ a tea party was 32,681 participants, in India.
- Ashrita Furman of New York walked the longest distance (130.3 km) with a milk bottle [4]_____ his head.
- The smallest cinema is in Italy. 63 people can sit [5]_____ it.
- 2,129 pizzas were put [6]_____ a line [7]_____ the Tamburino Restaurant [8]_____ the United Kingdom on 29th June 2008.

2 Complete the sentences with the words in the box. You will also need to add a preposition to each one.

a wedding   an island   home   the newspaper   the phone   the photograph   the queue

1 She's been _____ for hours and I need to call someone.

2 A: Are you _____ for tickets?
B: Yes, I'm the last person.

3 Did you read about this man who lives by himself _____ in the Pacific Ocean?

4 A: Are the football results _____ ?
B: Yes, they're on the back page.

5 A: I can't see you _____ .
B: I'm standing at the back.

6 I'm going to be _____ on Saturday. I'm a friend of the bride.

7 With computers, lots of people work _____ nowadays, but I still prefer going to the office.

3a Complete the sentences with *in* or *on*.

1 I'm _____ a train to London now.
2 Only five people can sit _____ the taxi.
3 There are a lot of holes _____ this old road, so drive carefully.
4 There's a garage _____ this road, so let's stop for petrol.

3b Complete the sentences with *in* or *at*.

1 My grandmother is _____ hospital. She needs an operation.
2 My mother is _____ the hospital, visiting my grandmother.
3 At school, which class are you _____ ? Class 3A or 3B?
4 I'll see you _____ school tomorrow. Outside the main gates.
5 The bus stops _____ Amsterdam.
6 The bus stopped _____ Amsterdam bus station before continuing to Brussels.
7 This letter has come to the wrong house. It's for the people _____ 26 Brooks Lane.

3c Complete the sentences with *on* or *at*.

1 The next train is arriving _____ platform 2A.
2 This is the wrong platform. We need to wait _____ platform 2A.
3 I'm going _____ holiday for two weeks!
4 Why are you _____ work? Today is a public holiday.

49 Prepositions of place 2

on top of, on, next to, near, by, between, among, opposite, in front of, above, over, below, under

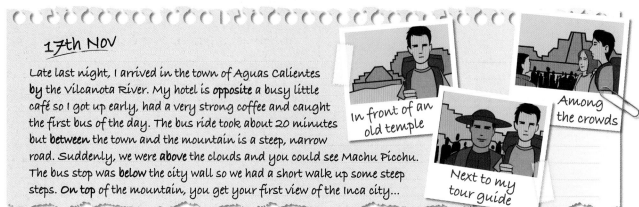

17th Nov

Late last night, I arrived in the town of Aguas Calientes **by** the Vilcanota River. My hotel is **opposite** a busy little café so I got up early, had a very strong coffee and caught the first bus of the day. The bus ride took about 20 minutes but **between** the town and the mountain is a steep, narrow road. Suddenly, we were **above** the clouds and you could see Machu Picchu. The bus stop was **below** the city wall so we had a short walk up some steep steps. **On top** of the mountain, you get your first view of the Inca city...

In front of an old temple

Among the crowds

Next to my tour guide

Presentation

on top of, on

On top of refers to the highest point of a high place, or the surface of a high place or object: *on top of the mountain* (at the highest point); *on top of the wardrobe* (on the flat, top surface)

He's on the mountain. (= somewhere on the mountain but not necessarily at the highest point)

next to, near, by

Use *next to* when there is little or no space between the two objects: *I was standing next to my tour guide.*

Use *near* to say that one object is close to or in the same area as another object: *... near the top of the mountain.*

By can have the same meaning as *next to* or *near*: *The town is by a river.*

between, among

Use *between* to describe the position of one object/person in relation to two other objects: *I was standing between my tour guide and a friend.*

Use *among* to describe the position of one object/person in relation to more than two other objects: *John was among the crowd.*

opposite, in front of

Use *opposite* to describe one object/person being on the other side of a space from another. Often there is something between the two objects: *The café is opposite the hotel.*

Use *in front of* to describe an object/person you can see when looking forwards. The opposite of *in front of* is *behind*: *I'm standing in front of my hotel.*

above, over

You use *above* and *over* to say one object is at a higher point than another object but the two objects are not in contact: *The clouds are above/over the town.*

Use *above* (but not *over*) to show that something is at a higher position but not in a direct line. Say *The bus is above the clouds.* (don't say *The bus is over the clouds.*)

Use *over* (but not *above*) to say that something is covering something else: *a mosquito net over my bed*

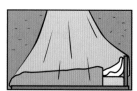

Over can also show that something crosses another object: *a bridge over the river*

below, under

Below shows that something is in a lower position, but not physically underneath: *The bus stop was below the city wall.*

Under shows that the position is directly lower: *An ancient tomb is buried under the city.*

Common expressions with *above* or *below* (but not with *over* and *under*) include *above/below sea level*, *above/below average*, *above/below room temperature*.

See page 244: Common prepositions and their meanings

Exercises

1 Complete the pairs of sentences with the words in bold.

on / on top of

1 The box is _____on_____ the floor. Pick it up.

2 He keeps all his money in a box _____ his wardrobe.

next to / near

3 My aunt lives _____ us. Her house is about five minutes away.

4 Mickey! Don't sit _____ James. You two always fight. Sit over there.

between / among

5 There's a nice café _____ this shop and the next one.

6 All six of you were in the house at the time of the murder, so someone _____ you must have seen something.

opposite / in front of

7 Stand _____ the gates and I'll take a photograph of you with the castle.

8 My block is _____ the bus stop, so when you get off the bus, just cross the road and it's flat number three.

2 Underline the correct preposition. In some sentences both prepositions are possible.

1 The lid _on / on top of_ this jar is the wrong one.

2 In 1953, Edmund Hillary and Sherpa Tensing became the first people ever to stand _on / on top of_ Mount Everest.

3 I can't find the car! I'm sure I parked it somewhere _near / by_ the pharmacy.

4 Do you want to sit _next to / by_ me?

5 A: Do you live _next to / near_ each other?

B: Not quite. There are two other houses between us.

6 I'd like Uncle Ray to sit _between / among_ the twins so they don't argue.

7 Look closely into the forest. There's a deer _between / among_ the trees.

8 I can't see the screen because this person's head is _in front of / opposite_ me!

9 At the beginning of a boxing match, the referee makes the two fighters stand _opposite / in front of_ each other and shake hands.

10 Look out of the window. We're _above / over_ New York City.

11 Put this _above / over_ your head. It'll keep you warm.

12 Your son is _above / over_ average in most of his subjects at school, but he could still do better.

13 That's disgusting! Someone stuck chewing gum _under / below_ this table.

14 I think he keeps his gold _below / under_ a floorboard in his bedroom.

15 Sometimes, Venice is 1.5 metres _below / under_ sea level.

3 Complete this description so that it is true for you.

At home, I have a _____ next to the television.

There's a _____ above the basin.

The _____ is opposite the _____.

Among all the objects in my house, my favourite is _____.

50 Review of units 46 to 49

Grammar

1 Write *in, on* or *at*.

1	_____ the summer	7	_____ five minutes
2	_____ Friday night	8	_____ the weekend
3	_____ night	9	_____ the computer screen
4	_____ September 1st		
5	_____ Independence Day	10	_____ the seaside
		11	_____ 23 King Street
6	_____ 1999	12	_____ the phone

2 There are mistakes in the prepositions in six more of the sentences below. Find the mistakes and correct them.

1 Did you hear the thunder in the night? ✓

2 Lots of people shop here ~~in~~ *on* Saturdays.

3 I'd like to take some time off on New Year, please.

4 The winning team needs to score the most goals within 90 minutes.

5 The train to Scotland is never in time. It's always late.

6 In the end of the performance, the audience stood and applauded.

7 The package is arriving on tomorrow.

8 Let's stop at this service station for some petrol.

9 My parents are in a cruise liner somewhere in the Bahamas.

10 What crime is he at prison for?

3 Underline the correct options to give the second sentence the same meaning as the first. In some sentences, both options are possible.

1 We stayed from two to four.
   We stayed *for* / *during* two hours.

2 No one has lived here since 1995.
   Someone lived here *before* / *after* 1995.

3 We can't stay any later than three o'clock.
   We have to leave *by* / *before* three o'clock.

4 The tunnels are below where we're standing.
   We're standing *above* / *over* the tunnels.

5 It's twelve o'clock now, so I'll pick you up in four hours.
   I'll pick you up *between now and four o'clock* / *after four o'clock*.

6 In Marrakesh, it's easy to get lost in the maze of streets.
   In Marrakesh, it's easy to get lost *between* / *among* the maze of streets.

7 As we climbed the mountain, we could look down on the clouds.
   As we climbed the mountain, we were *above* / *over* the clouds.

8 There's a caterpillar stuck to the other side of this leaf.
   There's a caterpillar *under* / *below* this leaf.

9 Pick up all your clothes off the floor!
   All your clothes are *on* / *on top of* the floor. Pick them up!

4 Complete the sentences with the pairs of prepositions in the box.

> at + in   ~~from + to~~   in + among   in + in
> on + over   on top of + until   opposite + by

1 Every day, they play their music _____ *from* _____ morning _____ *to* _____ night!

2 She's studying music _____ a college _____ Manchester.

3 Let's meet _____ the bridge _____ the River Seine.

4 Hide her present _____ the wardrobe _____ her birthday.

5 _____ the spring you might see a few flowers _____ all the weeds.

6 _____ the night the vampire comes for the heroine, but _____ the end he dies because the sun rises.

7 Can you stand _____ me and _____ Nigel.

Grammar in context

5 🔘**1.52** Read part of a book called *Around the World in Eighty Days*. Underline the correct preposition. In one answer, both prepositions are possible.

Phileas Fogg called out to his servant, 'Passepartout! We are going round the world.'

Passepartout was astonished, 'Round the world!'

'¹*In / During* eighty days,' added Mr Fogg. 'We'll take no luggage. We'll buy our clothes ²*on / in* the way. The train for Paris leaves ³*in / at* exactly half an hour.'

⁴*Over / Within* ten minutes, Passepartout had locked up the house and returned to his master ⁵*at / on* the front door. Mr Fogg had a small bag ⁶*on / by* his side and passed it to Passepartout. 'Take good care of this bag. There are twenty thousand pounds ⁷*in / among* it.'

Soon they were ⁸*in / on* a cab and ⁹*on / in* the road to Charing Cross. As the cab stopped ¹⁰*in front of / opposite* the railway station, the clock ¹¹*above / over* the entrance said twenty-five minutes to nine. The two men ran across the road and into the station.

Meanwhile, the five gentlemen who had made the bet with Mr Fogg stood waiting ¹²*between / among* crowds of people and their luggage ¹³*on / on top of* the platform.

'Well, gentlemen,' Mr Fogg said. 'I'm off.'

'And you haven't forgotten when you must be ¹⁴*in / at* London again?' asked one of the men.

'I have ¹⁵*until / before* Saturday, the 21st of December, 1872, ¹⁶*on / at* a quarter to nine ¹⁷*in / on* the evening. Goodbye gentlemen.'

¹⁸*By / Until* eight forty-five, Phileas Fogg and his servant were sitting ¹⁹*in / on* the train to Paris as it slowly moved out of the station.

(**Glossary:** *cab*   a taxi in the late 18ᵗʰ century, pulled by horses)

Pronunciation: linking

6 🔘**1.53** Words ending in a consonant sound followed by a word starting with a vowel sound often sound like one word. Listen to these sentences and decide which words are linked. See the first two examples.

1   It's ‿in five minutes.
2   Mr Jacobs ‿lives ‿on top ‿of the hill.
3   They're waiting on the platform.
4   What's that light among the trees?
5   We'll see Paul at the weekend.
6   Don't stand in front of me.
7   Dark clouds were over the city.
8   We didn't stop working until after nine.

Listen again and repeat the sentences.

Listen again

7 🔘**1.54** Listen to a story. Are the statements true (T) or false (F)?

1	All the guests arrived before sunset.	T / F
2	Young, single ladies tried to attract the attention of the Prince for part of the evening.	T / F
3	At the same moment that the new guest arrived, the Prince moved from his seat.	T / F
4	At midnight, the mysterious visitor began to run from the castle.	T / F
5	The Prince followed her after the castle bell had struck twelve.	T / F

51 Prepositions of movement
to, towards, at, in, into, on, onto, out of, out, over, across

He burst through the door, marched across the enormous hall, past the smiling receptionist, right under the huge banner announcing his arrival, and headed towards the double doors. When he reached the doors, he hesitated before going in. He put his hand in his coat pocket and took out a gun. As he lifted the gun up to shoulder height, a figure jumped over a chair, leapt at his feet and brought him crashing to the ground. The gun fell from his hand and slid under a chair. The woman got to her feet, put her hands on the man's shoulders and pulled him up. 'You're under arrest,' she said, quietly.

Presentation

Prepositions of movement describe the direction of a movement or action. They are always followed by a noun or pronoun. They are often used after verbs. Many prepositions of movement are also used as prepositions of place:

*A figure jumped **over** the chair.* (movement)

*The banner hung **over** the reception area.* (location)

See page 244: Common prepositions and their meanings

The following sections look at groups of prepositions that can sometimes be easily confused.

to, towards, at

Use *to* with the final destination of a movement: *He crashed **to the ground**.*

Use *towards* to say that you are moving nearer someone or something: *He moved **towards the door**.*

Use *at* to show the specific point where the movement is aimed: *She leapt **at the man's legs**.*

Compare the use of *to* and *at* with *throw*.

*She threw the ball **to** me.* (= She wanted me to catch it.)

*She threw the ball **at** me.* (= She wanted the ball to hit me.)

in, into, on, onto

With a verb that shows movement, use either *in* or *into*. There is no change in meaning: *He put his hand **in/into** his coat pocket.*

With a verb that does not necessarily express movement, there is a difference in meaning:

*She danced **in** the hall.* (in = location)

*She danced **into** the hall.* (into = movement from one place to another)

Into can only be used when it is followed by a noun: Say *He went **into the room**.* (don't say *He hesitated before going ~~into~~.*) But you can say *He went in.* (= entered)

The same is true for the prepositions *on* and *on to* (or *onto*):

*He got **on/onto** the plane.*

*She danced **on** the stage.* (location, not movement)

*She danced **onto** the stage.* (movement, not location)

out of, out

Use *out of* when the following noun is the place: *He took a gun **out of** his pocket.*

Use *out* when the following noun is the object (or person) that moves out: *He took **out** a gun.* (don't say *~~He took out of a gun.~~*)

over, across

Both *over* and *across* express the meaning of going from one side of a place or thing to another. They can often be used with the same meaning: *He walked **across/over** the mountains. They drove **across/over** the bridge.*

Over suggests an element of climbing, or going up and then down again. *She jumped **over** the chair.* (don't say *~~She jumped across the chair.~~*)

Over can also describe a movement above something, without touching it: *The plane flew **over** the city.* (don't say *~~The plane flew across the city.~~*)

Across can describe a movement within a space. *He walked **across** the hall.* (don't say *~~He walked over the hall.~~*)

See Unit 49: Prepositions of place 2

Exercises

1 **Complete the sentences with the prepositions given. Use each preposition once only.**

to/towards
1 We got _____ the airport just in time.
2 I moved slowly _____ the open door.

at/to
3 He threw the bag _____ his friend who caught it and ran away.
4 She threw the plate _____ the wall and it broke with a loud crash.

in/into
5 He turned and waved to the crowd before getting _____ the car.
6 The driver opened the door of the car and he climbed _____ .

out/out of
7 She took _____ the photo and looked at it sadly.
8 She looked _____ the window at the falling rain.

across/over
9 The woman walked _____ the snowy field towards the gate.
10 The plane flew _____ the snow-capped mountains.

2 (🔊 2.02) **Complete the text using the prepositions in the box. Then listen and check.**

across around behind out out of past through towards

She walked [1] _____ the revolving doors and marched across the
hall, calling loudly for the manager. The manager came [2] _____
his office and hurried [3] _____ the hall to meet her. He put
out his hand to shake hers, but she stepped [4] _____ him and
walked straight into his office. The manager followed [5] _____
her, looking very worried. He took [6] _____ a handkerchief and
wiped the sweat from his face and his neck as he turned [7] _____
and walked [8] _____ his office.

3 **Add the prepositions in brackets to the sentences.**

1 He stepped out ^of^ the door and walked ^to^ the bus stop. (of, to)

2 He waved to the baker as he walked the shop and stopped the newsagent's to buy a newspaper. (past, at)

3 At the bus stop, he sat down one of the seats and waited. (on)

4 After a few minutes, a bus came the hill. (up)

5 It slowed down as it approached the bus stop, but instead of stopping, it carried on driving the road. (along)

6 The man looked at the bus as it drove away him. (from)

7 He rose slowly his seat and walked back the road his house. (from, down, to)

8 When he got his house, he opened the door, walked, picked up the phone and called a taxi. (to, in)

52 Verbs and dependent prepositions

A: What are you listening to?
B: Here, listen. It's the new Coldplay album.
A: What do you think of it?
B: It's OK, but not as good as the last one.
A: No way! I really don't agree with you. It's really great to listen to … and look at the band – the singer is gorgeous …
B: Yeah, I've got a video of their last concert. Look. I downloaded it from the internet.

Presentation

Some verbs need a preposition to introduce their objects. Many of these verbs are always followed by the same preposition. These prepositions are called dependent prepositions.

*I'm **listening to** the new Coldplay album.*

*What do you **think of** it?*

***Look at** the cover.*

(*Listen, think* and *look* can also be used with other prepositions, but their meanings change. See Units 53 and 54.)

Some verbs have more than one dependent preposition. The preposition changes depending on the nature of the object, but the meaning of the verb stays the same:

*I don't **agree with** you.* (agree with + person)

*I **agree about** the cover.* (agree about + something)

*We **went to** their concert last week.* (go to + place)

*We **went with** Jake and Casi.* (go with + person)

Sometimes you can use both prepositions at the same time:

*I **agree with** you **about** the cover.*

*We **went to** the concert **with** Jake and Casi.*

Prepositions are normally followed by a noun or pronoun:

*Listen to **this**. Look at **the rain**. We were just talking about **you**!*

Many of these verbs can be used without an object. In this case, do not use the dependent preposition.

*Can you be quiet and just **listen?*** (don't say *Can you be quiet and just listen ~~to~~?*)

*Open your eyes and **look**.* (don't say *Open your eyes and look ~~at~~.*)

*I have to **go**.* (don't say *I have to go ~~with/to~~.*)

However, you must include the dependent prepositions:

* at the end of questions with *who, what* or *which*:
  *What are you listening **to**?*
  *What are you talking **about**?*

* in relative clauses: *This is the album that I was talking **about**.* (See Unit 83.)

* with adjectives followed by an infinitive: *This music is very easy to listen **to**.*

Verb + object + dependent preposition

With some verbs, the dependent preposition comes after the direct object:

*I've already downloaded it **from** the internet.* (See Unit 64.)

With verb + object + dependent preposition, you must include the preposition:

* at the end of questions with *who, where, what* or *which*: *Where did you download it **from**?*

* in relative clauses: *The website that I downloaded it **from** no longer exists.*

See page 242: Common verbs and their dependent prepositions

Exercises

1 Match the two halves of the sentences.

1 I totally forgot … _____
2 Has Pete recovered … _____
3 Are you sure you're prepared … _____
4 We usually disagree … _____
5 I know I can depend … _____
6 You really should apologise … _____
7 We're hoping … _____
8 Can you deal … _____

A about most things.
B about Keira's birthday.
C for better weather next weekend.
D for your exams?
E for your mistake.
F from the flu yet?
G on you.
H with this problem please?

2 Add dependent prepositions to the sentences below.

1 I love listening ∧to music when I'm on my bike.

2 Hey! What are you looking? Can I have a look?

3 Look, that's the car I was telling you. It's great, isn't it!

4 So, what did you think the film? I thought it was great!

5 You go on ahead. Don't wait me. I'll join you later.

6 I really think Ronnie worries work too much. She needs to learn to relax more.

7 Here's the report you asked. I finished it last night.

8 He's a difficult person. He really isn't very easy to live.

3 Complete the questions using a verb and an appropriate dependent preposition.

1 A: I've got to study really hard tonight.
  B: What are you ___studying for___ ?

2 A: We laughed so loud, the boss heard us.
  B: What were you _____ ?

3 A: I had a huge argument last night.
  B: Who did you _____ ?

4 A: I've just sent off an application for a job.
  B: What job have you _____ ?

4 Write the words in the correct order to make sentences.

1 their mistake / they / me / for / blamed _____
2 you / a cake / for / I've made _____
3 Beth / the party / have you / to / invited ? _____
4 my hard work / me / he / on / congratulated _____
5 never / him / I'll / forgive / that / be able to / for _____
6 me / she / my homework / with / helped _____
7 the money / they / from / where / steal / did ? _____
8 arrested/ was / for / what / he ? _____

53 Phrasal verbs 1
Two-part verbs

Presentation

A phrasal verb is a verb + a particle (preposition or adverb). The same verb may be used with a number of different particles. The meaning of the verb changes each time:

Look out! (= be careful)

*I've been **looking for** you all morning!* (= trying to find)

*I'll **look** it **up** on the computer.* (= try to find information)

Intransitive phrasal verbs

Intransitive phrasal verbs don't have objects. They can describe actions or states:

Shut up!

I got up late.

He slept on through all the noise.

Separable phrasal verbs

Many phrasal verbs are transitive and they need an object. Transitive verbs can be separable or inseparable.

With separable phrasal verbs, the object can come either before or after the particle:

Look up 'bonsai' on the computer.

Look 'bonsai' up on the computer.

If the object is a pronoun, it must go before the particle:

Look it up on the computer. (don't say *Look up it on the computer.*)

Common separable phrasal verbs include: *bring out, call off, drop off, give up, look up, make up, pass around, pick up, put across, put out.*

With a few separable phrasal verbs, the object can only come between the verb and the particle:

I'll call the customer back later. (don't say *I'll call back the customer later.*)

Other verbs like this include: *bring round, call (someone) over, invite out, talk (someone) round, tell (two or more things) apart.*

Inseparable phrasal verbs

With inseparable phrasal verbs, the object must go after the particle. It cannot go between the verb and the particle.

Common inseparable phrasal verbs include: *call for, come after, count on, get over, go into, look after, look for, look through, make of, run after, side with.* See page 243: Phrasal verbs

Exercises

1 (🔊 **2.03**) **Choose the correct options. Then listen and check.**

A: Have you had a chance to look ¹*through this report / this report through* yet?

B: No, I haven't. Dave dropped ²*it off / off it* on my desk this morning, but I honestly haven't had the chance to pick ³*it up / up it* yet. I've been too busy.

A: Janet wants to know what you make ⁴*it of / of it*. She's asked me to find ⁵*it out / out* what you think. She wants me to call ⁶*her back / back her* as soon as I have.

B: Why's it so urgent?

A: Well, apparently it's calling ⁷*massive cuts for / for massive cuts* in spending – it could even mean some people losing their jobs. Janet wants to fight it if she can, but she needs to know she can count ⁸*everyone's support on / on everyone's support* – and that, of course, includes you.

B: Mmm, I'd better get ⁹*it down / down* to reading it then! Or maybe we should call ¹⁰*the boss over / over the boss* to explain it to us in person.

2 **Write the words in the correct order. In some cases two different orders are possible. Write both possible word orders.**

1 album new bringing They're out a .
They're bringing out a new album. / They're bringing a new album out.

2 wedding called They've the off .

3 the police after knew come him would He .

4 managed away She finally to get .

5 around the world She her job gave to travel up .

6 acting Amy has go decided to into .

7 the road to you'll Keep or lost get .

8 his message put He very across clearly .

3 **Rewrite the sentences substituting a pronoun for the words in bold.**

1 He made up **a story** and everyone believed him.
He made it up and everyone believed him.

2 They passed around **the photos** for everyone to see.
They _____ for everyone to see.

3 We looked after **their three cats** for our neighbours.
We _____ for our neighbours.

4 They quickly put out **the fire**.
They _____ .

5 He ran after **the woman**, but he couldn't catch up with her.
He _____ , but he couldn't catch up with her.

6 My mother always sided with **my brother**, no matter what he'd done.
My mother _____ , no matter what he'd done.

Presentation

Some phrasal verbs have three parts – a verb and two particles:

*We just want to **get on with** our work.*

***Stand up for** your rights!*

*We're **looking forward to** using the new road.*

*We won't **put up with** the noise.*

Three-part phrasal verbs with one object

All three-part phrasal verbs are transitive, i.e. they have an object. When the verb has only one object, the object comes after the second particle:

*They soon got **on with their work**.*

*I think you stood **up to him** very well.*

Other verbs that follow this pattern include: *come up with, come down with, face up to, get away with, get down to, go through with, live up to, look up to.*

Three-part phrasal verbs with two objects

A few three-part phrasal verbs have two objects. The first object comes after the verb and the second object comes after the two particles:

*She played **one boy** off against **the other**.*

*I've decided to take **you** up on **your offer**.*

Other verbs that follow this pattern include: *put (something) down to (something), put (somebody) up to (something), talk (somebody) round to (something).*

Two-part phrasal verbs + dependent preposition

Some phrasal verbs can be both intransitive (i.e. have no object) and transitive (i.e. have an object).

Intransitive: *We **get on**.*

Transitive: *I don't **get on** with my brother.*

When there is no object, they have two parts:

*He says he's going to **drop out**.* (*drop + out* = leave school or college without finishing your course of studies)

When there is an object, you need to add a dependent preposition (*drop + out + of*).

*He says he's going to **drop out of** school.*

Other verbs that follow this pattern include: *catch up (on/with), go out (with), keep up (with), move out (of), run out (of).*

See Unit 52: Verbs and dependent prepositions

See page 243: Phrasal verbs

Exercises

1 (♪ 2.04) **Put the lines in the correct order. Then listen and check.**

_1_   The authorities seem to think they can talk us round

     through our village. We're ready to stand up

     to accepting the situation. We don't seem to be able to get it through

     with their plans to ruin our countryside and run a road straight

     to them and fight for our rights. They're certainly not going to get away

     to them that we are not going to put up

_7_   with it that easily!

2 **Write the words in italics in the correct order.**

1   Hey! I've just come _a brilliant idea with up_ for the end-of-term party!   up with a brilliant idea

2   I think I'm going to take _on you up_ your invitation to stay the night.

3   I really need to catch _up some work on_ tonight.

4   Have you got any idea who might have put _up to him_ this?

5   Jamie's come _the flu with down_ again I'm afraid.

6   I really used to look _to my maths teacher up_.

7   How do you get _with Fiona on?_

8   It was Steff who brought _in up his name_ the conversation, not me.

3 **Add the preposition in brackets to the sentences.**

1   I'm really not sure if I can go through ∧ this. (with)   [with]

2   He's going to have to learn to face up his responsibilities. (to)

3   I put their success to hard work and good organisation. (down)

4   Have you heard? Will's dropped of university. (out)

5   Is that the girl you went out last night? (with)

6   She's really going to find it hard to live to their expectations. (up)

7   It's not going to be an easy situation to put up. (with)

8   He very cleverly played them off each other. (against)

4 **Complete these sentences so that they are true for you.**

1   I get on really well with ....

2   I've always looked up to ....

3   I'm really looking forward to ....

55 Review of units 51 to 54

Grammar

1 Choose the correct options.

1 He reached *out / out of* and gently touched her hair.

2 I love lying in bed listening *at / to* the rain.

3 She started walking slowly *to / towards* him, then stopped and turned away.

4 I often think *about / in* the times we spent together.

5 Could you come and pick *up me / me up* after work?

6 What about your dogs? Who's going to look *after them / them after*?

7 Please remember to knock on the door before coming *in / into*.

8 We rarely disagree *about / with* anything.

9 What have you been talking *about / about it*?

10 The plane flew *across / over* the city before it descended towards the airport.

2 Cross out the one unnecessary preposition in each sentence.

1 He took out of his phone and looked at the time.

2 Everybody gets on really well with in the office.

3 He made up of an excuse for being late.

4 We really must get together soon to have a coffee and catch up on.

5 Look at! Isn't that your swimming instructor getting into that car?

6 If you listen to carefully, you'll hear the waves breaking on the shore.

7 Please don't walk so fast – I can't keep up with!

8 She looked down at and saw a small child sitting at her feet.

3 Complete the questions using a word from the box.

about	after	from	of	on	to	up	with

1 Where did you come _____ ?

2 Is that the man you were telling me _____ ?

3 How much more nonsense do I have to put up _____ ?

4 How many dogs do you usually look _____ at the one time?

5 Who was that person you were talking _____ just then? He looked interesting.

6 Is this the house you grew _____ in?

7 Which door did he come out _____ ?

8 Do you really think he's someone you can depend _____ ?

4 Use the same word to complete all three sentences in each group.

Group 1

1 Have you finished looking _____ the newspaper?

2 He walked _____ the door and out into the street.

3 I've been trying to talk to him all day, but I just couldn't get _____ to him on the phone.

Group 2

1 The bus drove slowly _____ the bridge.

2 It took her a long time to get _____ the shock.

3 He handed the money _____ to the cashier.

Group 3

1 We're really looking forward _____ seeing you at the weekend.

2 Hey! Throw the keys down _____ me, will you?

3 He walked down _____ the end of the road.

Group 4

1 Kevin dropped _____ of school when he was 15.

2 I moved _____ of my parents' home when I got married.

3 Oh dear! We seem to have run _____ of fuel!

Grammar in context

5 Complete the article using the words in the box.

> across cleaning down get off out through (x2) to tore

7 _____

Tornado sweeps ¹_____ coastal town

■ Early this morning, a tornado hit the small tourist resort of Newport. It brought ²_____ trees and street lamps and left more than 3,000 homes without electricity.

Bins and other heavy objects were blown ³_____ roads and a small wooden structure was blown ⁴_____ a roof-top terrace onto the road below. Luckily no one was hurt.

The tornado ⁵_____ down more than 100 trees, and residents have reported damage to cars, gardens and properties. One seafront restaurant lost 50 chairs and 15 tables when a wave carried them ⁶_____ to sea.

Several pleasure boats were damaged as the tornado passed ⁷_____ the marina, leaving destruction and mayhem in its wake.

Officials are assessing the damage today as the town starts a massive clear-up operation. 'The tourist season starts in three weeks. We all need to ⁸_____ down to work now if we're going to have any chance of ⁹_____ up this mess before the tourists arrive,' said the mayor, talking ¹⁰_____ journalists at the town hall.

Pronunciation: stress patterns for separable phrasal verbs

6 ⊘**2.05** Read and listen to the two sentences below and notice where the main stress falls. Notice that when the object of the separable phrasal verb is a noun, the stress falls on the noun (*light*). When the object is a pronoun, it falls on the particle (*off*).

Can you turn the <u>light</u> off, please?

Can you turn it <u>off</u>, please?

7 ⊘**2.06** Look at the sentences below and decide where the main stress falls on the phrasal verbs (in italics). Then listen and check.

1 Can you *pick the kids up* from school, please?
2 Can't you do it? I *picked them up* yesterday.
3 Can you *switch on the TV*, please?
4 Can't you *switch it on*? You're much nearer.
5 Do you want me to *look that address up* for you?
6 No, it's OK, thanks. I've already *looked it up*.

Listen again and repeat the sentences.

Listen again

8 ⊘**2.07** Listen to two colleagues discussing a report. Answer the questions using the words in brackets.

1 When did the man get the report? (drop off)

....

2 Has he read it yet? (pick up)

....

3 Why is it so urgent? (call for)

....

4 Why does Janet want to know what the man thinks of the report? (count on)

....

56 Future verb forms review
Present simple, present continuous, future simple, *going to*

A: Ah! So you've got two kids now. I didn't know! How old's your youngest?

B: She's two. She'll be three on Sunday. We're going to have a party. There'll be fun and games for the kids, and food and drink for the adults.

A: Where are you having it?

B: At the café in the park. There's plenty of room for the kids to run around, and we're going to get a clown to come and do a little show.

A: Sounds like it'll be great fun!

B: Fancy coming? The show starts at five.

A: Er, no thanks. Maybe I'll join you for ten minutes to say hello. I'm not really that good with kids!

Presentation

Present simple

Use the present simple for timetabled or scheduled events in the future:

*The show **starts** at five.*

Present continuous and *going to*

You can use both the present continuous and *going to* to talk about plans and arrangements in the future. They can often be used with the same meaning:

*We're **going to** have a party.*

*Where **are you having** it?*

*We're **having** it in the park.*

Use the present continuous (and not *going to*) when a formal arrangement has been made:

*I'm **having** a party tomorrow.*

*We're **flying** to Barcelona tomorrow. We booked the tickets last week.*

Use *going to* (and not present continuous) to talk about personal intentions when there is no clear time reference or expression:

*I'm **going to study** hard for my exams.* (= I intend to study hard in the future.)

*I'm **studying** hard for my exams.* (= I'm studying hard NOW.)

TIP You normally use the verbs *go* and *come* in the present continuous, not with *going to*.

Say *Are you going to the party?* (don't say *Are you going to go to the party?*)

going to and *will*

You can use both *going to* and *will*:

* to talk about future facts and inevitable events:
  *She'll **be** / She's **going to be** three next birthday.*

* to make predictions about the future: *It'll **be** great fun. / It's **going to be** great fun.*

Use *going to* when you make a prediction based on information in the present situation:

*Look at those clouds! Get in the car, it's **going to** rain!*

You often use *will* with verbs like *think, expect, imagine*:

*I **think** it'll be OK. I **expect** he'll be here on time. I **imagine** he'll call later today.*

To talk about decisions, *I'm going to …* and *I'll …* are both used.

Use *going to* to talk about a decision that has been made before the moment of speaking:

*I'm **going to** get a bus.*

Use *will* to talk about a decision that is made at the moment of speaking:

*Oh no! It's really late. I'll **call** a taxi!*

See page 236: Summary of future forms

Exercises

1 Match 1–8 with A–H.

1 There's been a change of plan. _H_
2 We'll need to leave here at about 7.30. ____
3 I didn't do very well in my exams. ____
4 You'd better bring some sun cream. ____
5 I forgot that it's Amy's birthday today! ____
6 Oh no! Look at the traffic. ____
7 Tomorrow is the last day of term. ____
8 Sorry, I can't come to the cinema tomorrow evening. ____

A We're going to be late!
B The doors open at 8 o'clock.
C I'm babysitting for my neighbour.
D But I'm going to study much harder this year.
E It's going to be really hot today.
F All classes will finish at 1 p.m.
G I'll send her a text message.
H We're meeting at 12 instead of 1.30.

2 ⓑ2.08 Choose the best options. Then listen and check.

A: ¹*We're going / We'll go* to the theatre on Saturday.

B: What ²*are you going to / will* you see?

A: It's a Cuban dance group. They're great. Do you want to come, too?

B: What time does the show start?

A: At 9.30. ³*We're going to meet up / We will meet up* for something to eat at the Thai Dragon beforehand. ⁴*There's / There'll* be me, Rob, Teresa and Stefano. ⁵*It's being / It'll be* fun.

B: I'd love to come too. Have you got the tickets yet?

A: No, I think ⁶*I buy / I'm going to buy* them online later today. Do you want me to get one for you?

B: Could you get two? Jane ⁷*is staying / will stay* with me this weekend.

A: Sure, ⁸*I'm doing / I'll do* that this morning – as soon as I've finished my breakfast!

B: Thanks a lot! Let me know how much it is and ⁹*I'm paying / I'll pay* you on Saturday.

A: OK. Speak soon!

3 Rewrite the sentences with a similar meaning using the words in bold.

1 What are your plans for tomorrow?
   doing   What are you doing tomorrow?

2 Who do you think will win the competition?
   think/going ____

3 Don't worry, it isn't going to rain tomorrow.
   will ____

4 I've arranged to take the day off tomorrow.
   taking ____

5 The flight will leave Naples at 18.30 and arrive in London at 20.25.
   leaves ____

6 Do you intend to sell your bike at the end of the summer?
   going ____

7 It's going to be really difficult to get there by nine.
   will ____

8 The exam will start at 9.00 and the doors to the exam room will close at 8.50.
   starts ____

57 Future continuous, future perfect, future perfect continuous

Presentation

Future continuous

Use *will be + ing* to talk about an action that you know or think will be in progress at a certain point in time, or during a certain period of time, in the future.

This time tonight, I'll be celebrating with my friends! (= point in time)

Next week, I'll be lying in the sun. (= period of time)

Future perfect simple

Use *will have + past participle* to talk about an action that is going to be completed at or before a given time in the future.

Just two more hours to go and, I'll have finished the last exam of my whole life!

TIP You often use the future perfect simple with expressions using *by*:

I'll have finished all my exams by the end of the week.

I'll have finished work by five o'clock.

Future perfect continuous

Use *will have been + -ing* to talk about an action that is going to be in progress at some time *before and/or until* a given time in the future. It emphasises the fact that the action will take place over *an extended period of time.*

At the end of this month, I'll have been working here for 35 years!

By ten o'clock tomorrow, we'll have been travelling for 24 hours.

See page 236: Summary of future forms

Future continuous	Future perfect	Future perfect continuous
I'll be studying for my exams all weekend.	We'll have finished the exam by 12 p.m.	We'll have been doing exams all week.
I won't be going out at all.	We won't have finished until 12 p.m.	We won't have been doing exams all week.
What will you be studying?	Will you have finished by 12 p.m.?	Will you have been doing exams all week?

Exercises

1a 🔊 **2.09** **Complete the text using the future continuous form of the verb in brackets. Then listen and check.**

1   Good morning Ladies and Gentlemen. This is flight LH344 from Berlin to New York's John F Kennedy airport. We ¹_____ (take) off shortly so please fasten your seatbelts.

2   We ²_____ (fly) at a speed of 885 kilometres per hour and at a height of over 10,000 metres. We ³_____ (land) in New York in about ten hours, so sit back and enjoy the flight.

3   In a few minutes, our staff ⁴_____ (serve) a hot lunch. After lunch, we ⁵_____ (start) our duty-free service when we ⁶_____ (sell) perfumes and other gift items.

1b 🔊 **2.10** **Complete the text using the future perfect simple form of the verbs in brackets.**

By this time next week, we ¹_____ (cross) the whole of Australia. We ²_____ (drive) more than 2,000 miles, we ³_____ (sleep) under the stars, we ⁴_____ (see) the sun set over Uluru, we ⁵_____ (visit) the famous town of Alice Springs, and we ⁶_____ (arrive) at our final destination – Darwin – on the tropical north coast.

1c 🔊 **2.11** **Complete the dialogue using the future perfect continuous form of the verbs in brackets.**

A: When we've finished our exams, we'll be exhausted. We ¹_____ (work) really hard for weeks. We ²_____ (not/get) enough sleep, we ³_____ (not/eat) properly …

B: Yes, but just think how you'll be feeling afterwards. You'll be a new person!

2   Choose the correct form of the verb.

1   A: Will you be in the office tomorrow?

   B: I'll *be travelling / have travelled* all day, but you can call me on my mobile.

2   A: I promise you we'll *be finishing / have finished* it by midday tomorrow.

   B: I should hope so. You'll *be working / have been working* on it for over a week!

3   A: How long have you been here? A year and a half?

   B: No, longer. We'll *be living / have been living* here for three years in May.

4   A: Will you *be seeing / have seen* Patricia this afternoon?

   B: No, sorry. I won't *be going / have gone* to the sports centre this afternoon.

3   Complete these sentences so that they are true for you.

1   This time tomorrow, I'll be _____ .

2   By this time next week, I'll have _____ .

3   By the end of the weekend, I'll be feeling _____ because I'll have been _____ .

58 Present verb forms in future time clauses
if, when, once, until, as soon as, before, after

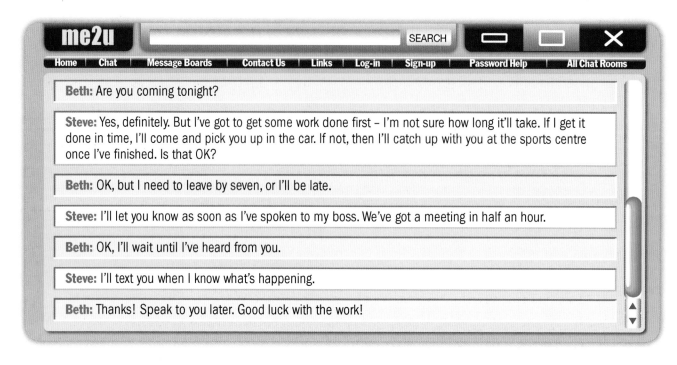

Beth: Are you coming tonight?

Steve: Yes, definitely. But I've got to get some work done first – I'm not sure how long it'll take. If I get it done in time, I'll come and pick you up in the car. If not, then I'll catch up with you at the sports centre once I've finished. Is that OK?

Beth: OK, but I need to leave by seven, or I'll be late.

Steve: I'll let you know as soon as I've spoken to my boss. We've got a meeting in half an hour.

Beth: OK, I'll wait until I've heard from you.

Steve: I'll text you when I know what's happening.

Beth: Thanks! Speak to you later. Good luck with the work!

Presentation

A future time clause explains when the action described in the main clause is going to happen.

main clause	future time clause

*I'll let you know **as soon as I've spoken to my boss.***

To form future time clauses, use conjunctions like *before, when* or *once* followed by a verb in the present simple, present continuous or present perfect:

*I'll call you **when I know** what's happening.*

*I'll call you **once I've finished.***

*I'll call you **when I'm leaving** the office.*

Notice that the verb in the main clause is in a future form (*will, going to*, etc.). The time clause may come before or after the main clause:

***Once I've finished**, I'll call you.*
*I'll call you **once I've finished.***

We use the present perfect to show that the action will be completed:

*… once **I've finished** this work …*

*… as soon as **I've spoken** to my boss …*

Conjunctions we commonly use in future time clauses include *after, as soon as, before, by the time, next time, once, until, when.*

TIP We don't use **will** in future time clauses:
   I'll call you before ~~I'll buy~~ the tickets.

if or *when*?

Use *when* to talk about things that you think are certain to happen:

*I'll text you **when I know what's happening.** (= I'm sure I will know what's happening at some point in the future, but I don't know exactly when that will be.)

Use *if* when you are not sure that the action is going to happen:

***If I don't finish in time**, I'll meet you at the sports centre.* (= It's possible that I will finish my work in time; it's also possible that I won't finish in time.)

See Unit 86: *if* clauses 1: present verb forms

See Unit 87: *if* clauses 2: past simple

See page 236: Summary of future forms

Exercises

1 Write the words in the correct order to make sentences.

1 home when I'll get you I call.

   I'll call you when I get home.

2 my work I until won't finished I've come out.

3 Sue I'll next time her I speak to see.

4 the dinner you cooked I'll get home have by the time.

5 text the station us they they'll get to before.

6 I a chance as soon as get I'll to the boss speak.

7 the dishes do the football I'll after finished has.

8 be once I the exams won't finish so busy.

2 ⓟ2.12 Choose the correct form of the verbs. Then listen and check.

A: Have you spoken to Tim yet?

B: No, sorry, I forgot. I ¹call / 'll call him as soon as I ²'ve finished / 'll have finished this email.

A: No, don't worry. I ³see / 'll see him this afternoon when he ⁴comes / 'll come to get his stuff.

A: Come, on! The shops ⁵are / 'll be closed by the time we ⁶get / 'll get there if you ⁷don't / won't hurry up a bit!

B: OK, I'm coming. Don't panic, we ⁸'re / 'll be there in plenty of time.

A: I ⁹get / 'll get your dinner ready for you for when you ¹⁰arrive / 'll arrive.

B: No thanks, Mum. We ¹¹'ve had / 'll have had something to eat before we ¹²leave / 'll leave.

3 Complete the sentences using *if* or *when*. In two sentences, both answers are possible.

1 We won't go to the beach this afternoon _____ it rains.

2 We'll tell you all about it _____ we see you.

3 _____ you get there before me, you'll have to ask the neighbour for the key.

4 What are we going to do _____ the train's late?

5 It's been a long day. We're going to be exhausted _____ we get home.

6 _____ you don't get a good night's sleep, you'll be exhausted in the morning.

7 _____ you've finished your dinner, you can watch some TV.

8 What are you going to do _____ you grow up?

4 Complete these sentences so that they are true for you.

1 When I finish this exercise, I'm going to _____.

2 If I've got enough time later today, I'll _____.

3 I'll _____ when I've finished _____.

4 I won't _____ until I _____.

5 I'll be happy with my English when _____.

59 Future phrases and future in the past
about to, bound to, likely to, unlikely to, was/were going to

You are about to enter the Twilight Zone – a place where strange things are sure to happen. A new world will open before your eyes. It's likely to change the way you think and feel. It's an experience you're unlikely to forget. And one you're bound to want to repeat!

The Twilight Zone

Wow! That was amazing! I thought I was going to die!

Presentation

about to

Use *be about to* + infinitive to say that something is going to happen in the immediate future:

*You **are about to enter** the Twilight Zone.*

bound to

Use *be bound to* + infinitive to say that you believe something is sure to happen:

*You're **bound to want** to do it again.* (= We're sure you'll want to do it again.)

likely to

Use *be likely to* + infinitive to say that you think it is probable that something will happen:

*It's **likely to change** the way you think.*

unlikely to

Use *be unlikely to* + infinitive to say that you don't think that something will happen:

*It's an experience you're **unlikely to forget**.*

future in the past

You can use all the expressions above to talk about the future in the past:

*I **was about to leave** the house when the phone rang.*

*He **was bound to find** out in the end.*

*We had no idea when he **was likely to arrive**.*

*It **was unlikely to rain**, so we didn't take an umbrella.*

was / were going to

You can also use *was/were going to* to talk about the future in the past. Use *was/were going to*:

- to make a prediction which may or may not have been fulfilled: *It **was going to** be a great experience.*

- to talk about an intention which may or may not have been fulfilled: *I **was going to** work all night, but then a friend called and persuaded me to go out.*
  *I **was going to** work all night, even if it meant I was exhausted the next day.*

- to talk about a plan or arrangement which then changed: *We **were going to** go to the party, but then we changed our minds.*

- to report a thought: *I knew I **was going to** fall, but I could do nothing to stop myself.*

- in reported speech: *I told you it **was going to** be the best ride ever!*

See Unit 56: Future verb forms review

See Unit 71: Reported speech

128

Exercises

1 **⊘2.13** **Choose the correct options to complete the sentences. Then listen and check.**

1 A: Where's John?

   B: He's *about / bound* to be late. He always is.

2 A: Do you think I should remind Tina about her mum's birthday?

   B: No, I don't think it's necessary. She's *bound / unlikely* to forget.

3 A: Sorry, are you *about / likely* to go out? Have you got a minute?

   B: Sure, how can I help you?

4 A: We'd better say goodbye now, as we're *about / unlikely* to see you later.

   B: Yes, it was great meeting you. Have a good trip.

5 A: Oh no! That was Sue's favourite glass! What are we going to do?

   B: There's no point hiding it. She's *likely / bound* to find out sooner or later.

2 **Complete the second sentence using the words in bold.**

1 It'll probably rain this weekend.

   likely   It _____ rain this weekend.

2 I was sure he'd come back again soon.

   bound   He _____ come back again soon.

3 I was getting ready to leave the office when the boss walked in.

   about   I _____ leave the office when the boss walked in.

4 I didn't think he was going to find out about the plan.

   unlikely   I thought he _____ find out about the plan.

5 Ssh, it's almost time for the film to start.

   about   Ssh! The film _____ start.

6 It doesn't look as if he's going to get the job.

   unlikely   He _____ get the job.

3 **Match 1–6 with A–F to make sentences.**

1 I wasn't going to call you, _____

2 He wasn't going to have a holiday that summer _____

3 They were going to leave for the airport at 5 a.m., _____

4 They weren't going to take their dog with them _____

5 She was going to study fashion and design at university, _____

6 You weren't going to leave _____

A because it hated travelling.

B but she failed her exams.

C but then Jen said you'd appreciate it if I did.

D so they had to get to bed early.

E until his father offered to pay for him.

F without saying goodbye, were you?

4 **Answer these questions using *was/were going to*.**

1 When you were a child, what did you want to be as an adult? _____

2 What were your holiday plans last year? Did everything go to plan? _____

3 Have you ever had to change a plan? Why? _____

60 Review of units 56 to 59

Grammar

1 Match 1–6 with A–F.

1 What time are you arriving? _____
2 When do the doors open? _____
3 Do you think it's going to rain? _____
4 Are you going to the park this afternoon? _____
5 Do you think you'll be ready in time? _____
6 Did you tell John about the letter? _____

A It says 6.30 on the programme. I'm meeting Phil outside at 6.20.
B I'm not sure. I'll let you know when I get to the station.
C No, the forecast says it'll be warm and sunny all day.
D I was going to, but Sue had already shown it to him.
E Yes, if it doesn't rain.
F Yes, I'll have finished well before it's time to go.

2 Find and correct the mistakes in the sentences below.

1 It's really cold outside. I think it's ~~snowing~~ *going to snow* later tonight.

2 I know you already have your ticket, but when exactly will you go to Spain? It's quite soon, isn't it?

3 I'll have been finishing the book by the end of the week.

4 I'll call you as soon as I'll get home.

5 I promise I'll tidy my room if I get home from school.

6 Come in, come in. I'm just bound to make a cup of coffee. Would you like one?

7 When I saw the smile on his face, I knew everything is going to turn out all right in the end.

3 Choose the best answer.

1 I'm really sorry. I broke the handle on the door.
   A That's OK. I'm fixing it later. _____
   B That's OK. I'll fix it later. _____

2 Do you think they'll have finished by this time next week?
   A Yes, they have. _____
   B I hope so! _____

3 What will you be doing this time next week?
   A I'll have done my last exam and I'll have been starting my holidays. _____
   B I'll have done my last exam and I'll have started my holidays. _____

4 When are you coming home?
   A When I've finished work. _____
   B When I'll have finished work. _____

5 Is Janie going to the party tonight?
   A Yes, if she's feeling better. _____
   B Yes, when she's feeling better. _____

6 Do you think Ben will win the election?
   A Yes, he was going to. _____
   B Yes, he's bound to. _____

4 Choose the correct options. Sometimes both options are possible.

A: Where [1]*are you going / will you go*?

B: To the shops. I [2]*'m not going to be / won't be* long. Do you want me to get anything for you?

A: Will you [3]*be going / have gone* past the post office?

B: Yes, probably. Why? Do you need to post something?

A: Yes, I was [4]*bound / going to go* myself, but if you're going that way …

B: Sure, no problem. I [5]*'m doing / 'll do* it on my way back.

A: Thanks, I'll [6]*have gone / have been going* to work by the time you get back – I'll leave some lunch in the microwave if you [7]*want / 'll want*.

B: Don't bother, thanks. I [8]*'m getting / 'll get* something when [9]*I'm / I'll be* out.

Grammar in context

5 **Read the three emails and choose the best options to complete the text.**

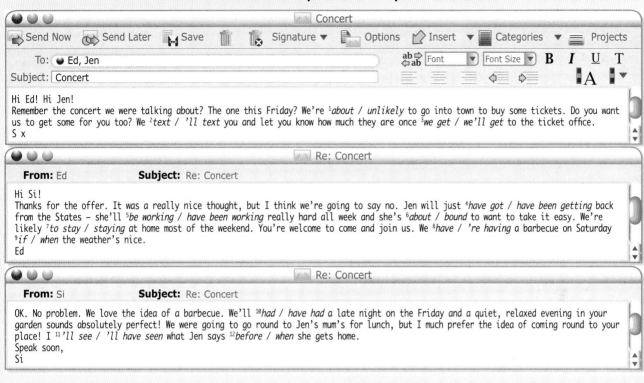

Concert

Send Now Send Later Save Signature ▼ Options Insert ▼ Categories ▼ Projects

To: Ed, Jen
Subject: Concert

Hi Ed! Hi Jen!
Remember the concert we were talking about? The one this Friday? We're ¹*about / unlikely* to go into town to buy some tickets. Do you want us to get some for you too? We ²*text / 'll text* you and let you know how much they are once ³*we get / we'll get* to the ticket office.
S x

Re: Concert

From: Ed   **Subject:** Re: Concert

Hi Si!
Thanks for the offer. It was a really nice thought, but I think we're going to say no. Jen will just ⁴*have got / have been getting* back from the States – she'll ⁵*be working / have been working* really hard all week and she's ⁶*about / bound* to want to take it easy. We're likely ⁷*to stay / staying* at home most of the weekend. You're welcome to come and join us. We ⁸*have / 're having* a barbecue on Saturday ⁹*if / when* the weather's nice.
Ed

Re: Concert

From: Si   **Subject:** Re: Concert

OK. No problem. We love the idea of a barbecue. We'll ¹⁰*had / have had* a late night on the Friday and a quiet, relaxed evening in your garden sounds absolutely perfect! We were going to go round to Jen's mum's for lunch, but I much prefer the idea of coming round to your place! I ¹¹*'ll see / 'll have seen* what Jen says ¹²*before / when* she gets home.
Speak soon,
Si

Pronunciation: 'll

6 **2.14** **The contracted form of *will* is *'ll*. Listen to the pronunciation in these two sentences.**

1 I'll be ready at four.
2 He'll have arrived by then.

Now listen to these sentences. Write the numbers 1 and 2 in the order you hear them.

1 **A** They arrive at nine. ___2___
   B They'll arrive at nine. ___1___

2 **A** I have finished all my work. _____
   B I'll have finished all my work. _____

3 **A** I leave the key under the mat. _____
   B I'll leave the key under the mat. _____

4 **A** I have loved every minute of my holiday. _____
   B I'll have loved every minute of my holiday. _____

5 **A** We call you on your mobile. _____
   B We'll call you on your mobile. _____

Listen again and repeat the sentences.

Listen again

7 **2.15** **Listen to the three recordings and answer the questions.**

Recording 1:

Where are they going? ....

When will they be landing? ....

2.16 **Recording 2:**

Where will they be by the end of the week? ....

How far will they have travelled? ....

2.17 **Recording 3:**

What will they have done before their exams have finished? ....

How will she be feeling? ....

61 Verb + infinitive

Presentation

to infinitive

Some verbs can be followed by another verb in the *to* infinitive form:

*I want **to go** home!*

*We seem **to be** lost.*

Verbs followed by the *to* infinitive include: *afford, agree, aim, appear, arrange, attempt, can't bear, choose, decide, demand, expect, hope, intend, learn, manage, need, offer, plan, prepare, pretend, promise, refuse, seem, want, wish.*

- The *to* infinitive can have a continuous form: *to be + -ing.* It has the same meaning or use as the present or past continuous (to talk about an action in progress in or around the time), but it tends to be more formal:

  *You appear **to be reading** the map upside down.*

  *He seemed **to be leaving**.*

- The *to* infinitive can also have a perfect form: *to have + past participle.* Use the perfect infinitive to talk about an action that is (or will be) completed before a given point in time. Using the perfect infinitive is more formal than using a perfect tense.

  *We **seem to have lost** our way.* (= It seems that we've lost our way.)

  *I **expect to have finished** by midnight.* (= more formal)
  *I **expect I'll have finished** by midnight.* (= less formal)

- To make the sentence negative, you can either make the main verb negative or make the *to* infinitive

negative. Form the negative infinitive with *not to*:

*We **don't** seem **to be** in the right place.* ✓

*We seem **not to be** in the right place.* ✓ (don't say *We seem to not be in the right place.*)

simple	continuous	perfect	negative
We seem to be lost.	We seem to be going the wrong way.	We seem to have lost our way.	We don't seem to be in the right place.

verb + object + *to* infinitive

Some verbs are followed by an object and the *to* infinitive:

*Call **someone to rescue** us.*

*Remind **everyone to come** to my party.*

*He wants **Mary to call** him.*

*I'd like **the team to win**.*

Verbs followed by object + *to* infinitive include: *ask, expect, force, help, invite, need, remind, teach, tell, want, would like.*

Note that some verbs including *afford, agree, appear, decide, hope, learn, manage* and *wish* cannot be followed by an object:

I learned ~~them~~ to speak English. ✗

I taught them to speak English. ✓

Exercises

1 **Write the words in the correct order to make sentences.**

1 I can't to go afford out.
   I_____.

2 We soon to see expect you.
   We_____.

3 The police chasing appear be to someone.
   The police_____.

4 They love be falling in seem to.
   They_____.

5 We have to by finished aim Tuesday.
   We_____.

6 They hope have agreed to by morning.
   They_____.

7 Rachel to not come decided.
   Rachel_____.

8 They the expected not to pass exam.
   They_____.

9 Ask at your Malcolm sing party to.
   Ask_____.

10 We to everyone 'd help like us.
   We_____.

2 **Write the verb in brackets in the correct infinitive form.**

1 Let's arrange _____ (meet) again next week.

2 Are you prepared _____ (risk) your life for this?

3 The aim is _____ (not/win), but to enjoy yourself!

4 Prices always seem _____ (go up).

5 At the moment, we seem _____ (work) very long hours!

6 Since we saw him last, he appears _____ (become) much more responsible.

7 He always pretends _____ (not/understand), but he does.

8 Give a man a fish and he'll eat for a day. Teach a man _____ (fish) and he'll eat for a lifetime.

3 **Correct the mistake in each sentence.**

1 I can't bear watch this horror film any more.

2 You seem to breaking the speed limit! Slow down!

3 Sam was sad to have lose the race.

4 I want everyone to gives their opinion.

5 They chose did not to come.

6 Force all our customers pay by next week.

4 **Join the two sentences to make one sentence using an infinitive.**

1 I woke you up. I'm sorry.
   I'm sorry to have woken you up.

2 We have a meeting at nine. We arranged it yesterday.
   Yesterday, we arranged _____ at nine.

3 Why aren't you concentrating on the road! You need to!
   You need _____ on the road!

4 Jack should help us move these books. Tell him.
   _____ us move these books.

5 Your grandmother didn't see you. She was sad.
   Your grandmother was sad _____ you.

6 I'm leaving school at last! I'm so happy.
   I'm so happy _____ at last!

62 Verb + *-ing* or infinitive 1

Presentation

Verb + *-ing*

Certain verbs are always followed by a verb in the *-ing* form (NOT the infinitive):

*I **enjoy listening** to the radio.* ✓

I enjoy ~~to listen~~ to the radio. ✗

These verbs include: *avoid, can't help, consider, dislike, enjoy, fancy, finish, imagine, involve, keep, mention, mind, don't mind, miss, postpone, practise, report, risk, stand, can't stand, suggest.*

Verb + preposition + *-ing*

When a preposition follows the first verb, the next verb is in the *-ing* form:

*I **learn by doing.***

*I **apologise for cheating.***

See also Unit 52: Verbs and dependent prepositions

Verb + object + *-ing*

Some verbs can be followed by an object and a verb in the *-ing* form:

*I don't **like other people helping** me.*

*This fence **prevents the animals running** away.*

These verbs include: *imagine, hate, like, dislike, keep, love, prevent, remember, risk, see, stop, mind.*

Infinitive or *-ing*?

Some verbs can be followed by either form, with very little or no change in meaning. These verbs include: *hate, like, love, prefer.*

You can use *-ing* after these verbs to describe the action (or activities) in general:

*I **like reading** science fiction novels. / I **like to read** science fiction novels.*

*I **love singing.** / I **love to sing.***

You can also use the *to* infinitive after these verbs to describe an action in certain circumstances or on specific occasions:

*I **like to read** the instructions first when I buy something new.*

*I **love to sing** when I'm on my own.*

You can use *-ing* or the *to* infinitive after some verbs with no change in meaning. These verbs include: *begin, start, continue, can't bear.*

*I always aim to finish the job when I **start to work** on something.* ✓

*I always aim to finish the job when I **start working** on something.* ✓

See also Unit 63 for changes in meaning with infinitive and *-ing.*

Exercises

1 **Complete the sentences with the pairs of verbs. Change the form of the verbs where necessary.**

> apologise + be   can't help + think   enjoy + play   mind + stay
> prevent + break   start + work   worry + cook

1 My family always _____ _____ board games.

2 When did you _____ _____ for this company?

3 We _____ for _____ late, but we've been stuck in traffic.

4 Don't _____ about _____ dinner for me.

5 This lock will _____ burglars _____ into your house.

6 My parents don't _____ you _____ at our house.

7 I _____ _____ that he lied to us.

2 ⊘2.18 **Complete the conversation. Write the word in brackets in the *-ing* form or as an infinitive. Then listen and check.**

A: Did you enjoy [1] _____taking_____ (take) the quiz?

B: Yes, it was interesting. I discovered that I'm good at [2] _____ (do) creative things.

A: So you're right-brain dominant?

B: Yes, I am. I don't appear [3] _____ (be) as good with details. What about you?

A: I was a mixture. On the whole I learn by [4] _____ (study) the rules first, and afterwards I attempt [5] _____ (answer) questions one by one. That's left-brain dominant. But I also risk [6] _____ (make) mistakes from time to time, which is more right brain.

B: Have you asked anyone else in the class [7] _____ (try) the quiz?

A: Not yet. I was thinking of [8] _____ (ask) Pietro.

B: Good idea. I'd expect the test [9] _____ (show) that he's left-brain dominant.

A: Me too. But you never know!

3 **Underline the correct options in italics. In some sentences both options are possible.**

1 I love *reading* / *to read* poetry.

2 Getting a driving licence involves *taking* / *to take* a test.

3 Pretend *liking* / *to like* her cooking or she'll be upset.

4 When did you begin *collecting* / *to collect* stamps?

5 He hates *asking* / *to ask* for help.

6 I demand *seeing* / *to see* the manager!

7 Remind the children *tidying* / *to tidy* their rooms.

8 Even after the police have caught them, some people continue *breaking* / *to break* the law.

9 Why do you always keep people *waiting* / *to wait*?

10 Some people prefer *studying* / *to study* online instead of learning in a classroom.

4 **Complete these sentences so that they are true for you. Use a verb in the *-ing* form or as an infinitive.**

1 Recently, I've started _____.

2 In my spare time, I love _____.

3 I can't bear people _____.

4 When choosing a film, I always prefer _____.

63 Verb + *-ing* or infinitive 2
remember, forget, go on, mean, regret, stop, try

A profile of Andrea Bocelli

World-famous singer Andrea Bocelli lost his sight at the age of 12. He remembers taking huge comfort from his music during this difficult period of his life. He started to play the piano at the age of six and he went on to learn the flute, saxophone, trumpet, trombone, harp, guitar and drums.

When he left home, Bocelli studied law at university. He never meant to become a professional singer but, as a student, he tried to earn extra money by singing in bars at night.

In 1992, he won a singing competition and, since then, he hasn't stopped performing to huge audiences around the world and recording number-one albums. Looking back on his career, Bocelli sometimes regrets doing 'things that were profitable' instead of 'more artistically satisfying work', but it's a regret most of us can only dream of.

Presentation

Some verbs can be followed by either the *to* infinitive or the *-ing* form but the meaning changes. These verbs include: *remember, forget, go on, mean, regret, stop* and *try*.

	+ *-ing*	+ *to* infinitive
remember / forget	To talk about your memories: *He remembers taking comfort from his music during this difficult period of his life. He'll never forget hearing music for the first time.*	To talk about actions which are necessary: *I must remember to send that letter. Don't forget to practise the piano.* To say whether or not the action took place: *Did you remember to post the letter? Sorry, I forgot to send it.*
go on	To talk about a continuing action already in progress: *He went on performing for the rest of his life.*	To talk about a change of situation or sequence of events: *He learnt to play the piano and went on to learn other musical instruments.*
mean	To talk about the result of an action: *Success as a singer meant changing his career plans.*	To talk about something you intend to do: *He always meant to become a lawyer.*
regret	To say you are sorry for something that you did: *I regret doing things for money.*	To say you are sorry for something that you are about to say. This is a polite way to introduce bad news: *I regret to tell you that you have not won.*
stop	To talk about an action which has ended: *He stopped performing to audiences in 2001.*	To talk about the reason for stopping: *He stopped to talk to his fans.*
try	To talk about an experiment to see if something is successful: *He tried working as a lawyer but he didn't like it.*	To talk about an attempt to do something: *He tried to earn extra money.*

136

Exercises

1 Complete the pairs of sentences. Write the words in brackets as an infinitive or in the *-ing* form.

1 A I remember _____ (leave) my wallet on the table, but now it isn't there.

   B Did you remember _____ (do) your homework?

2 A Don't forget _____ (take) the books with you when you leave.

   B I'll never forget _____ (fall) off my bicycle for the first time.

3 A After a bad start, the team went on _____ (win) the tournament.

   B Mike told us a ghost story and then we all went on _____ (tell) each other scary stories.

4 A Leaving university meant _____ (give up) his dreams of becoming a doctor.

   B I'm sorry. I didn't mean _____ (be) rude.

5 A I don't regret _____ (hit) him at all! He deserved it.

   B We regret _____ (inform) you that we are unable to reimburse the full amount.

6 A You're so selfish. Do you ever stop _____ (think) how other people might feel?

   B Stop _____ (bother) your brother. He needs to finish his homework.

7 A Try _____ (press) that key again and see if the program stops this time.

   B I'm trying _____ (learn) Arabic at the moment, but it isn't easy!

2 🔊2.19 Correct six more mistakes in these conversations. Then listen and check.

Conversation 1

Shelley: Did you remember ^to^ buy more paint, Diego?

Diego: Yes, I did. But I forgot bringing it with me. I can go back and get it now.

Shelley: It's OK. I think Marie is on her way here, so she can stop getting some.

Conversation 2

Shelley: Hi Marie. It's Shelley. Are you on your way?

Marie: No, not yet. I meant leaving ages ago, but my ex-boyfriend called round.

Shelley: Really? What did he want?

Marie: To say how much he regretted to leave me. He went on say how sorry he was for over an hour!

Shelley: What happened?

Marie: Well, I tried be nice at first but it didn't help, so in the end I told him to go.

3 Rewrite the first sentence using the word in bold followed by a verb as an infinitive or in the *-ing* form.

1 After he joined the army, he became a general.

   went on After he joined the army, he _went on to become_ a general.

2 Don't worry so much!

   stop _____ it so much!

3 As the window is stuck from the inside, see if you can open it from the outside.

   try As the window is stuck from the inside, _____ it from the outside.

4 I'm sorry that I lied to you.

   regret I _____ to you.

5 The security guard was sure he had checked the lock before he went home.

   remembered The security guard _____ the lock before he went home.

6 I had less money to spend because I lost my job.

   meant Losing my job _____ less money to spend.

64 Verb + two objects

+ + + NOTICE TO CUSTOMERS + + + NOTICE TO CUSTOMERS + + +

Now MoreMart pays customers money!

The new MoreMart loyalty card gives you big discounts. It's so simple. With every purchase, we'll award you points and these save you money.

So speak to one of our staff today. They'll be happy to explain **ALL** the benefits to you so you can start saving **NOW!**

Presentation

Some verbs can have two objects: a direct object and an indirect object.

*The new loyalty card gives **customers big discounts**.*

direct object – *big discounts*

indirect object – *customers* (= The person or thing that receives the direct object.)

Here is a list of common verbs that can have two objects. Notice that these verbs often describe some kind of transaction (giving or receiving) between two people: *allow, ask, bring, buy, cost, find, forgive, get, give, leave, lend, make, offer, order, owe, pass, pay, play, promise, read, refuse, reserve, save, send, serve, show, sing, take, teach, tell, throw, wish, write.*

The indirect object usually comes before the direct object:

	indirect object	direct object
We give	customers	big discounts.
He bought	me	a present.
He asked	each person	a question.

The indirect object can also come after the direct object. When this happens you need to add a preposition (*to* or *for*).

	direct object	indirect object
We give	big discounts	to customers.
He bought	a present	for me.
He asked	a question	to each person.

Common verbs + *to*: *lend, pass, promise, read, refuse, send, serve, show, sing, teach, tell.*

Common verbs + *for*: *buy, forgive, make, order, play, save.*

Some verbs can be followed by either *to* or *for*. There is often a change in meaning.

*He **wrote** a letter **to** me.* (= He wrote the letter and I received it.)

*He **wrote** a letter **for** me.* (= I couldn't write the letter, so he wrote it in my place.)

*I **owe** some money **to** Rob.* (= the person who lent me the money)

*I **owe** some money **for** last night's meal.* (= the thing I bought with the money)

Other common verbs + *to/for*: *bring, get, leave, offer, pay, take, wish.*

(Use a good dictionary to find out how the meaning changes according to the preposition used.)

With the verbs *describe, explain, say* and *suggest*, the direct object must always come before the indirect object.

*They'll explain the benefits to **you**.* (not *They'll explain you the benefits.*)

Say something to me. (not *Say me something.*)

See page 242: Common verbs and their dependent prepositions

Exercises

1 Write these words in the correct order to make sentences.

1 sweets don't them give.
   Don't give them sweets.

2 please some money me lend.

3 a seat me can you reserve?

4 to can send Michael the email you?

5 us served the waiter soup.

6 they're for you this playing song.

7 their to house describe me.

8 suggest to eat something nice can you?

2 Rewrite these sentences without *to* or *for*.

1 Leave some water for the dogs.
   Leave the dogs some water.

2 I'll give this to you.

3 You owe £1,000 to your brother.

4 Order a drink for me, please.

5 Please tell the truth to us.

6 Every year, he buys a present for his wife.

3 ⓐ 2.20 Complete these conversations. Use the indirect objects on the left of the box and the direct objects on the right. Then listen and check.

me us him	a tip the menu the bill

1 A: Do we have a table?
   B: Yes, I've reserved [1]_____ this one.
   A: Great! By the window.
   B: I'll just ask the waiter to bring us [2]_____.

2 A: Can you describe the *penne arrabiata* for [3]_____?
   B: Yes, it's an Italian dish. It's pasta with a hot tomato sauce. They serve it with garlic bread I think.

3 C: How was your food?
   B: Very good thanks. Can you bring us [4]_____, please?
   C: Certainly.

4 A: Do you normally leave [5]_____ for the waiter?
   B: Yes, I'll give [6]_____ about ten per cent.

65 Review of units 61 to 64

Grammar

1 Match 1–6 with A–G.

1 I forgot _____
2 I remember _____
3 I was always bad at _____
4 We heard a crowd of people _____
5 Sing the tune _____
6 Sing me _____
7 He pretended not to _____

A singing this tune as a child.
B to me.
C to bring the music with me.
D singing, but I enjoy listening to music.
E be able to sing, but he could.
F the tune, please.
G singing outside our door.

2 The word _to_ is missing in six more sentences. Write it in.

1 I can't bear ^to^ lose a game!
2 I enjoy playing games. ✓
3 They seem not be friends anymore.
4 Teach them cook their own breakfast.
5 He'll never forget meeting her for the first time.
6 I don't think I remembered switch the cooker off.
7 We regret inform you we no longer offer this service.
8 After appearing on the stage, Virginia went on become famous in Hollywood.
9 Why don't you suggest the idea her?
10 Her parents lent her some money.

3 Underline the correct words in italics. In some sentences, both options are possible.

1 The class continued _to talk / talking_ even after the bell rang.
2 After studying the geography of Peru, the class went on _to talk / talking_ about the country's history.
3 Explain the homework _me / to me_, please.
4 It _doesn't appear / appears not_ to be snowing at the moment.
5 I can't imagine anyone _to like / liking_ this music.
6 We all regret _to say / saying_ things that have hurt someone.
7 Don't keep me _to wait / waiting_!
8 When did you begin _to study / studying_ physics?
9 Everyone here risks _to lose / losing_ their job because of this strike.
10 Don't you hate _to watch / watching_ other people playing a computer game?

4 Rewrite the sentences using the words in bold.

1 I don't like watching sport.

hate _I hate watching_ sport.

2 I wanted to learn French, but I never did.

meant _____ but I never did.

3 She'll always remember meeting him for the first time.

forget She'll _____ for the first time.

4 Your teacher doesn't appear to know the answer.

appears Your teacher _____ the answer.

5 The band was leaving the hotel, but talked to the waiting fans.

stopped The band was leaving the hotel, but _____ the waiting fans.

6 Tell us about your journey.

describe _____

Grammar in context

5 Complete the quotations with the pairs of words in the box. Change the verb form where necessary to the *to* infinitive or *-ing* form. There are two possible answers in some questions.

> dream + become   learn + walk   ~~not mind + live~~   ~~owe + a lot~~   pay + $1,000   try + find   want + be
> want + grow

FAMOUS QUOTATIONS OF MARILYN MONROE

1 I __don't__ __mind__ __living__ in a man's world, as long as I can be a woman in it.

2 I don't know who invented high heels, but all women __owe__ him __a__ __lot__.

3 I'm not interested in money. I just _____ _____ wonderful.

4 I _____ _____ as a baby and I haven't had a lesson since.

5 There are thousands of girls who _____ of _____ a movie star. But I'm not going to worry about them. I'm dreaming the hardest.

6 I _____ _____ old without facelifts.

7 Hollywood is a place where they _____ you _____ for a kiss and 50 cents for your soul.

8 I'm _____ _____ myself as a person. Sometimes that's not easy to do.

Pronunciation: /tə/ and /fə/

6 ⏺ **2.21** Listen to the sentences below. Notice how *to* or *for* are not stressed and are pronounced /tə/ or /fə/.

1 I want to go home.
2 They promised not to be late.
3 Don't forget to write.
4 I regret doing things for money.
5 Leave something for the waiter.

Listen again and repeat the sentences.

Listen again

7 ⏺ **2.22** Listen to two conversations. Are these sentences true or false? Circle the correct answer.

1 Diego didn't remember to buy the paint. True / False
2 He forgot to bring it with him. True / False
3 Marie has stopped buying paint. True / False
4 Marie has left her house. True / False
5 Marie's ex-boyfriend left her. True / False
6 Marie told her ex-boyfriend to go. True / False

66 Ability
can, could, be able to, manage to, succeed in

Scientists close to invisibility

■ Scientists have succeeded in creating a new device which can bend light and make solid objects invisible. The team of scientists couldn't say when the device would be ready for production, but once they have managed to perfect the device, they are hoping to be able to use it for a range of different uses, both civilian and military.

Presentation

You can use *can, could* and *be able to* to talk about ability:

*The new device **can** bend light.*

*They will **be able to** use the device for a range of uses.*

*They **couldn't** say when the device would be ready.*

can / could

Use *can/can't (cannot)* to talk about ability in the present and the future. If you want to talk about ability in the past, use *could/couldn't*.

*It **can** bend light.* (= present)

*We **can't** show you until next week.* (= future)

*They **couldn't** say anymore.* (= past)

See also Units 67–69 and 86–89.

be able to

There is no infinitive or participle form (*-ed* or *-ing* form) of *can* or *could*. When we need an infinitive or participle form, we use *be/been/being able to*.

*We'll soon **be able to** put the device into production.*

*They haven't **been able to** find a sponsor.*

***Being able to** speak Japanese is very important.*

could and was / were able to

You can use both *could* and *was/were able to* to talk about general abilities in the past:

*He was the best person for the job. He **could** speak Japanese and he had experience of working in the arts.*

*I was the only one in my class who **wasn't able to** / **couldn't** swim.*

We use *was/were able to* (not *could*) to talk about success in a particular task or activity:

*She **was able to** find a substitute for Tim.* (not *She ~~could~~ find a substitute for Tim.*)

You can use both *couldn't* and *wasn't/weren't able to* to talk about not succeeding in a particular task or activity:

*She **couldn't/wasn't able to** help him.*

manage to and succeed in

You can also use *manage to* (+ infinitive) and *succeed in* (+ *-ing*) to talk about success (or lack of success) in a particular task or activity, but not to talk about general abilities:

*Once the team **manage to perfect** their device, they will be able to put it on the market.*

*Scientists have **succeeded in creating** a new device.*

Exercises

1 Underline the correct options.

1 He loved the water and _could / couldn't / wasn't able to_ swim when he was three.

2 I'd love to _can / could / be able to_ swim like him.

3 She teaches French and she _can't / could / is able to_ speak Chinese as well.

4 He's lost his driving licence. He _can't / couldn't / hasn't been able to_ drive for the last two years.

5 We're a bit worried about Jake. He's six years old, but he still _can / can't / couldn't_ read.

6 You used to _could / be able to / was able to_ see the sea from here, before they built that block of flats.

7 He was heartbroken, but he _can / could / couldn't_ understand why she'd left him.

8 I'm having laser treatment on my eyes, so I'll _can / could / be able to_ read without glasses.

2 Complete the sentences with the verbs in brackets. Use negative forms where necessary.

1 I'm really sorry we .... to the party last night. (able/come)

2 She finally .... a job as a waitress. (manage/find)

3 My father's going to give me some money so I .... my first car. (able/buy)

4 We were only at home for a few days and unfortunately we .... all the people we'd wanted to see. (not succeed/visit)

5 She did as well as she could, but on this particular occasion she just .... the exam on time. (able/finish)

6 The cup fell off the table, but luckily he .... it before it hit the floor. (manage/catch)

3 Complete the sentences using _can, could_ or _was able to_. Use negative forms where necessary. Sometimes more than one form is possible.

1 A: [1] .... you speak Dutch?

   B: No, not really. I [2] .... speak it when I was a child, but then my family left the Netherlands and I lost touch with the language.

2 A: Did you go to the concert last night?

   B: No, I [3] .... get a ticket.

3 A: Do you know if Sarah [4] .... get home alright last night?

   B: Yes, she caught the last train with just minutes to spare!

4 A: How's the snow?

   B: Amazing! Another ten inches fell two nights ago. I [5] .... get to the office yesterday morning!

5 A: I'm sorry I [6] .... come to the meeting this afternoon. Something's come up.

   B: OK. Don't worry. I'll take notes for you.

4 Write sentences about yourself.

1 I can ...., but I can't ....

2 I'd love to be able to ....

3 When I was .... I could ....

4 I couldn't .... until I ....

5 I was really pleased when I succeeded in .... for the first time.

6 I'll never forget the time I managed to ....

67 Permission, obligation, prohibition and no necessity

can, could, must, need to, have to, had to, let, allow, make

> IT'S NOT FAIR! I HAVE TO STAY IN TO LOOK AFTER MY LITTLE SISTER AND MY PARENTS WON'T EVEN LET ME INVITE MY FRIENDS ROUND!

> COUNT YOURSELF LUCKY! WHEN I WAS YOUR AGE, I HAD TO GET UP AT FIVE IN THE MORNING TO MILK THE COWS! I WAS NEVER ALLOWED TO GO OUT WITH MY FRIENDS – MY PARENTS ALWAYS MADE ME STAY AT HOME AND GO TO BED EARLY!

Presentation

Use *can, could, must, need to, have to* and *be allowed to* to talk about permission, obligation, prohibition and necessity.

	present	past
permission	can, is/are allowed to	could, was/were allowed to
obligation/ necessity	must, have to, need to	had to, needed to
prohibition	mustn't, can't	couldn't, wasn't/ weren't allowed to
no necessity	don't have to, needn't/ don't need to	didn't have to, needn't have/didn't need to

Notice that there is no past form of *must* and *mustn't*. Use *had to, couldn't* or *was/weren't allowed to*.

must, have to, need to

Use *must, have to* and *need to* to say that it is obligatory or very important to do something. There is very little difference between the three verbs in the affirmative:

Must can be used to show that the person who is speaking has the authority to insist that something is done: *You must stay in tonight.* (= parent speaking to child)

Have to can be used to show that an obligation is being imposed by someone else: *I have to stay in tonight.* (= My parents said so.)

Need to can be used to explain that an action is necessary rather than obligatory: *I need to stay in tonight to look after my little sister.*

mustn't, don't have to, don't need to

Use *mustn't* to say that it is important not to do something: *You mustn't forget your homework.* (= It's important that you don't forget.)

Use *don't have to* and *don't need to* to show that …

* something is not important or essential: *I don't have to get up early at the weekend.*

* you can choose not to do something if you want: *You don't need to do your homework now. You can do it later.*

needn't / don't need to

You can use *needn't* or *don't need to* with the same meaning:

You needn't stay at home tonight. You don't need to stay at home tonight.

Do not use *to* before the infinitive with *needn't: You needn't get up early today.* (don't say *You needn't to get up early today.*)

needn't have / didn't need to

Use *needn't have* with a past participle to say that a past action was not necessary. Use *didn't need to* with an infinitive to say that an action wasn't necessary and therefore wasn't performed.

You needn't have bought me a present! (= You did it, but it wasn't necessary.)

We didn't need to pay. (= It wasn't necessary and we didn't do it.)

let, allow, make

Use *let* and *allow* + object + infinitive to talk about permission and prohibition. Use the *to* infinitive with *allow*. *Allow* is slightly more formal than *let*.

They never let me go out with my friends.

They don't even let me talk to them on the phone!

They allowed me to stay up late.

Use *make* + *object* + *infinitive* to talk about an obligation. *They made me get up at five o'clock.* (= I had no choice.)

Exercises

1 **Look at the signs and complete the sentences using the words in brackets.**

WELCOME TO LAKEVIEW CAMPSITE
Please respect your fellow campers and these simple rules:

Please help yourselves to the free bicycles at reception – but remember to sign them in and out!

1 You _____ (can) bring dogs to the campsite.

2 You _____ (must) light a fire.

3 You _____ (must) be quiet after 10 p.m.

4 You _____ (have to) leave your car in the car park.

5 You _____ (allowed to) ride bicycles on the campsite.

6 You _____ (have to) pay to hire a bike.

2 **2.23 Complete the conversation using the past form of *allow, can* or *have to*. Use no more than two words in each gap. *Weren't* or *didn't* count as one word. Then listen and check.**

A: How was your camping weekend?

B: It was OK. They had a no-pets rule, so we ¹ _____had to_____ leave the dogs at home and we ² _____ be really quiet. We ³ _____ to play music or make any noise after 10 p.m. But at six o'clock in the morning, you ⁴ _____ make as much noise as you wanted! There was a no-fires rule, so we ⁵ _____ have barbecues. But luckily, there was a great café. We ate there the whole time and we ⁶ _____ to do any cooking at all.

3 **Circle the correct options.**

1 We *need / needn't* to get up at 6.30 tomorrow to catch the early train.

2 I *don't need / needn't* go to work today. I've got the day off.

3 You *didn't need / needn't* have brought a towel you know. There are plenty here.

4 He *didn't need / needn't* to take the car. He went on the bus.

4 **Complete the sentences using *let, allow* and *make*. You may need to make changes to the verb.**

My parents are really strict. They don't ¹ _____ us to watch TV during the week. They always ² _____ us get up early on Saturday mornings to do our homework – even in the holidays! But if we do it quickly and well, they ³ _____ us go out with our friends in the afternoon.

Your boss ⁴ _____ you take time off work, doesn't he? I asked my boss for a day off last week. He was really angry with me for asking and ⁵ _____ me stay late to finish off some extra work!

68 Certainty, speculation and deduction
can't, could, may, might, must

> He must have gone for a coffee. He can't have gone far. He could be in the coffee shop round the corner.

> Or he may be visiting a client. Shall we wait?

> No. It looks as if it could rain. Let's go to the coffee shop. You never know, he might be there, and if not, we can just come back later.

> OK.

Presentation

You can use the modal verbs *can, could, may, might* and *must* to speculate about the past, present or future, and to say how certain you are that something is true or not.

must	→	you feel certain that something is true
may, might, could	→	it is possible that something is true
may not, might not	→	it is possible that something is not true
can't, couldn't	→	you feel certain that something is not true

Use *can't, could, may, might* and *must* with the infinitive (no *to*) …

* to make predictions about future events:

  It looks as if it could rain.

  It might rain later.

* to speculate about present events using stative verbs:

  He can't be in the coffee shop. (= I don't think he is in the coffee shop because …)

  He could be in the coffee shop.

  He must be at work by now!

Use *can't, could, may, might* and *must* with *be + -ing*:

* to speculate about events in progress at the moment:

  He may be visiting a client.

  He could be having his car washed.

* to speculate and make predictions about future plans and intentions:

  They might not be coming to visit us next week after all.

  They must be planning to come back tomorrow.

Use *can't, could, may, might* and *must* with *have* + past participle …

* to speculate about past events:

  He can't have gone far.

  He might have broken down.

* to make deductions about past events based on present evidence:

  His coat is on the back of the chair. He must be here somewhere.

See page 240: Modal verbs

Exercises

1 *2.24* **Choose the correct options. Then listen and check.**

A: Where can she be? She's late.

B: Well, that's no surprise. She must ¹*be forgetting / have forgotten*.

A: No, she wouldn't forget. She must ²*be / have been* stuck in traffic somewhere.

B: You always give her the benefit of the doubt. I reckon she might ³*sleep / have slept* late, that's all. Or she could ⁴*get distracted / have got distracted* on the way – you know what she's like! She might even ⁵*be doing / do* some shopping.

A: Oh, come on. That's not fair! I think she must just ⁶*look / be looking* for somewhere to park her car. Look! There she is now, coming round the corner.

B: At last!

2 *2.25* **Correct the mistakes in the conversations. Use modal verbs in your answers. Then listen and check.**

1 A: Is that your brother over there?

    B: No, it ~~mustn't~~ can't be him. He's away on business.

2 A: Are you going cycling this weekend?

    B: No, the weather forecast says it can rain.

3 A: I heard that Jeff had left the company.

    B: That may be right! Look, he's sitting at his desk.

4 A: Do you think we're going the right way?

    B: It might be right. It says so on the map.

5 A: Do you know where the car keys are?

    B: I think they can't be on the kitchen table.

6 A: So, are you coming for a swim?

    B: You may be joking! The water's freezing!

3 **Complete the sentences using *can, must* or *might*. Use negative forms where necessary.**

1 It _____ have been him. I refuse to believe it.

2 I'm not sure you can do that. You _____ need to ask the boss first.

3 I _____ be able to go to the meeting tomorrow. I'll let you know in the morning.

4 I can't understand this message. It _____ be written in code.

5 A: Hey, guess what! It's snowing!

    B: It _____ be! It's far too warm!

6 A: Steve told me you were going to stand for election. Is that true?

    B: I _____ be. I haven't decided yet.

4 **Look at the picture. Complete the sentences using a variety of modal verbs.**

1 She _____ (try) to climb in.

2 Or she _____ (climb) out.

3 She _____ (be) a thief.

4 Or it _____ (be) her van.

5 She _____ (forget) her keys.

6 She _____ (be) very comfortable.

7 She _____ (feel) very embarrassed.

69 Requests, suggestions, offers, advice and opinions
can, could, may, would, will, shall, let's, should, ought to, had better, mind

Presentation

Formality in requests

Could, would and *may* are more polite than *can* or *will*. Use *possibly* or *Do you think you could possibly …?* to make requests with *could* even more polite:

Could I possibly *have a glass of water, please?*

Do you think you could possibly *move your bags?*

You can also use *Would you mind …?* or *Do you mind …?* to make polite requests. Use *if* to ask for permission to do something. With *Do you …*, use the present simple after *if*. With *Would you …*, use the past simple:

*Do you mind **if I sit** here? Would you mind **if I sat** here?* (= I want to sit here.)

Use *-ing* to ask another person to do something:

*Would you mind **opening the window**?* (= I want you to open the window.)

TIP The normal positive response to a request with *Would you mind …?* or *Do you mind …?* is *No* or *No, not at all*. This shows that you are happy to do something.

Suggestions and offers

Use *let's* and *shall* to make suggestions:

Let's *get a coffee on the train.*

Shall *we get a coffee on the train?*

Use *will* and *shall* to offer to do something. Use *shall* in questions with *I* or *we*. Use *will* in the affirmative only. Don't use *will* in questions to make an offer.

Say *I'**ll** move my bag. / **Shall** I move my bag?* (don't say ~~Will I~~ *move my bag?*)

Giving advice and expressing opinions

Use *should* and *ought to* to give advice, express opinions and talk about what you think is the right thing to do. *Ought to* is less common than *should*, especially in questions and negatives.

*We **should/ought to** do this more often!* (= I think it's a good idea.)

*Passengers **should not** leave their bags unattended.* (= This is not a good idea.)

Use *had ('d) better* to give advice in specific situations:

Affirmative: *You'd better hurry up or you'll be late.*

Negative: *You'd better not forget.* (not ~~You hadn't better forget.~~)

Question: **Had** *you better leave it until tomorrow?*

Negative question: **Hadn't** *you better leave it until tomorrow?* (= I think it would be better to leave it until tomorrow.)

TIP The negative form of the question is more common than the affirmative question in everyday speech.

148

Exercises

1 **Make the requests more polite using the words in brackets.**

1   Can I ask a personal question? (may, please)

2   Will you lend me some money? (think, possibly)

3   Can you hold the door open for me? (would, mind)

4   Can I smoke? (do, mind)

5   Will you help me with my homework? (could, please)

6   Can I leave the room for a short while? (would, mind)

2 **Match the requests you wrote in exercise 1 with the responses below.**

1   No, not at all. But please don't be too long.

2   I'm sorry, but I haven't got my wallet with me.

3   I'm sorry, but you can't – not inside the building.

4   No, not at all. It's a pleasure.

5   Yes, sure. Just wait a minute. I'll be with you shortly.

6   Well, I don't know. It depends what it is.

3 **⊘ 2.26 Complete the dialogues using the words in the boxes.**

> better   ought   let's   shall

1   A: I'm getting tired. ¹_____ take a break. We could go out for lunch.

     B: OK. ²_____ we try that new sandwich bar?

     A: Yes, fine. We'd ³_____ be quick, though. We really ⁴_____ to try and finish this work today.

> better   could   shall

2   A: ⁵_____ you tell me the best way to get to the station?

     B: Well, you could get a number 27 bus. It leaves from the stop on the corner. When does your train leave?

     A: At 10.30. That's in 20 minutes.

     B: Hadn't you ⁶_____ get a taxi then? You don't want to miss it. ⁷_____ I call one for you?

> let's   ought   should   would

3   A: What do you think I ⁸_____ do?

     B: I really don't know. It's a difficult situation. I think you really ⁹_____ to talk to your boss about it. I mean she needs to know if someone's stealing from the company, doesn't she?

     A: ¹⁰_____ you mind coming with me? It'd make things easier.

     B: OK. ¹¹_____ do it now then. No time like the present!

70 Review of units 66 to 69

Grammar

1 Match the sentences and questions 1–8 with the responses A–H.

1 Do you mind if I bring a friend? ....
2 Did you manage to get there OK? ....
3 Could you do that last question? ....
4 My parents let me watch TV after dinner. ....
5 Do you think John will get the job? ....
6 Did Hans take the car out last night? ....
7 Do you think I ought to take the job? ....
8 Let's stay in tonight and watch a film. ....

A I suppose he could have done.
B I suppose he might.
C OK. We could get a pizza, too.
D No! It was really difficult. I left it out.
E No, not all. Please do.
F Yes, I think you should.
G Yes, I was able to find it quite easily.
H You lucky thing! I had to do my homework!

2 Choose the correct options.

1 Luckily, the firefighters *could finally / were finally able to* put out the flames.
2 I'm sorry I didn't *manage / succeed* to make it to the party last night.
3 A: What does that sign mean?
   B: It means you *don't have to / mustn't* play ball games on the beach.
4 You *didn't need to / needn't have* got a taxi. I could have come to pick you up!
5 Everything was free. We *didn't need to pay / we needn't have paid* for anything.
6 I don't really like our maths teacher – she always *lets us / makes us* do so much homework!
7 It could rain tomorrow, but then again it *could / might* not.
8 That's the third time he's failed his driving test. He *can / must* be really disappointed!
9 You'd *better not / hadn't better* forget Sarah's birthday. She'll be furious!

3 Complete the second sentence using the words in bold so that it has a similar meaning to the first.

1 He was able to find a cheap flight at the last minute.
   succeed He ....
   at the last minute.
2 She couldn't find her keys anywhere.
   able to She ....
   anywhere.
3 It's obligatory to wear a helmet when you're riding a motorbike.
   must You ....
   when you're riding a motorbike.
4 Our parents said we could stay up late last night.
   let Our parents ....
   last night.
5 Nobody had to bring food with them. It was all provided by the organisers.
   need We ....
   It was all provided by the organisers
6 They don't allow us to bring our mobile phones to class.
   can We .... to
   class.
7 It's possible that the train will be late because of the snow.
   might The train ....
   because of the snow.
8 He definitely didn't write this letter. It isn't his handwriting.
   can He ....
   It isn't his handwriting.
9 It's possible that they're waiting for us at the entrance.
   might They ....
   at the entrance.
10 Would you mind paying for the taxi, please?
   think Do ....
   possibly pay for the taxi?

Grammar in context

4 Choose the correct options to complete the text.

Culinary disaster!

Q I had wanted to move out of my parents' house for a long time, but I hadn't ¹*been able / succeeded* to find a nice flat. I thought I might have to give up on the idea when finally, last week, I ²*managed to / could* find something really nice. A friend at work was looking for someone to share her two-bedroom flat and I moved in last Saturday. I thought it ³*might be / must be* a bit difficult to start with, but it's mostly fine and we get on really well. There's only one problem. My new flatmate loves cooking. She insists on preparing all our meals and she won't ⁴*let me / make me* go anywhere near the kitchen. The thing is she just ⁵*can't / mustn't* cook! Everything she makes is disgusting and I haven't the heart to tell her! What ⁶*better had / should* I do?

A I really think you'd ⁷*better / ought to* say something. She ⁸*can / must* have some idea of how you feel. Who knows, you might be able to help her improve. But you ⁹*are able to / have to* be tactful and sensitive. You'd ¹⁰*better not / not better* tell her exactly how you feel or you may find yourself looking for a new flat! Maybe you ¹¹*ought / should* make a few gentle suggestions or buy her a recipe book as a thank-you present for ¹²*allowing you / letting you* share the flat with her.

Pronunciation: weak form of *have*

5 **2.27** Listen to the sentences below. Notice the pronunciation of *have*.

1 He can't have meant what he said, surely?
2 They must have gone out somewhere.
3 You needn't have bought her a present.
4 We might have left it at home.
5 She may have left on an earlier train.

Listen again and repeat the sentences.

Listen again

6 **2.28** Listen to three short dialogues. In which dialogue, 1, 2 or 3, does someone …

1 ask for advice about a difficult problem? ....
2 ask someone to do something? ....
3 give advice about how to get somewhere? ....
4 offer to do something? ....
5 suggest going somewhere? ....

71 Reported speech
Tense, *say*, *tell*, pronouns, place and time

Presentation

Reported speech

Use reported speech to report someone's words or thoughts. The reporting verb can be followed by the conjunction *that*, although it is not necessary:

'I'm working from home.' → *She said (that) she was working from home.*

When you are reporting something that someone said or thought in the past, the verb in the direct speech often moves backwards in time:

*'We **aren't** well.'* → *They said they **weren't** well.*

*'I **work** from home.'* → *He said he **worked** from home.*

See Unit 72 for more about changing the tense in reported speech.

say and tell

The reporting verbs *say/said* and *tell/told* are commonly used for reporting statements.

Use *say/said* to:

- report someone's words: *She **said** she was working from home.* (don't say *She told she was working from home.*)
- report **who** you said something **to** using the preposition *to*: *She **said to me** she was working from home.* (don't say *She told to me she was working from home.*)
- Use *tell/told* to report **who** someone is talking to (don't use *to*): *The boss **told her** she was fired.* (don't say *The boss said her she was fired.*)

(don't say: *She told she was working from home.* / *She told to me was working from home.* / *The boss said her she was fired.*)

Changes to pronouns, place and time

When you use reported speech to refer to words spoken at a different time or place from where you are now, you might need to change the pronoun, possessive adjective or any other words referring to time and place.

Change the pronoun and possessive adjective

'I'm ill.' → *She said **she** was ill.*

*'**My** children are ill.'* → *She said **her** children were ill.*

Common changes: *I* → *he/she*, *we* → *they*, *my* → *his/her*, *our* → *their*.

Change the place

*'I'm staying **here**.'* → *She said she was staying **there**.*

Change the time

*'I'm feeling ill **today**.'* → *She said she was feeling ill **that day**.*

Common changes: *now* → *then*, *today* → *that day*, *tomorrow* → *the next day*, *yesterday* → *the day before*, *last night* → *the night before*.

See page 238: Summary of tense changes backwards in reported speech

Exercises

1 Write *said* or *told*.

1 She ....*said*........ she was leaving.

2 My teacher .... me to do it again.

3 My teacher .... something to me, but I couldn't hear.

4 Who .... they didn't understand?

5 She .... 'yes' to him, so they're getting married in the summer.

6 Who .... him the answer?

2 Read the first sentence in direct speech. Add the missing words in the second sentence in reported speech.

1 'We're really tired.'

They said that .... were really tired.

2 'That's my cat.'

The woman downstairs said that it was .... cat.

3 'We're only here for a day.'

They said that they were only .... for a day.

4 'I forgot to do my homework last night.'

He said that he'd forgotten to do .... homework the ....
....

5 'I'll call you back tomorrow.'

I'm sure she said that .... 'd call us back the ....
....

3 Rewrite the first sentence using direct speech or reported speech.

1 'I'm hungry.'

Rose said that *she was hungry.*

2 'We're riding our bikes to work today.'

They said that they ....

3 He said that he was leaving his job.

He said, 'I ....'

4 They all thought they were going to be famous.

They all thought, 'We ....'

5 Martin told me, 'I don't live here anymore.'

Martin told me that ....

6 My father said he started his new job that day.

My father said, 'I ....'

4 Think of three things you said or other people said to you today. Write them down using reported speech.

1 ....

2 ....

3 ....

72 Reported statements
Change or no change to the verb

I will not raise taxes.

Here's some breaking news.
The President says he won't
raise taxes.

Good evening and here is
the news. This morning, the
President said he wouldn't raise
taxes.

Presentation

Verb changes in reported speech

When you report what someone said, you often move
the tense of the verb backwards in time, like this:

present simple → past simple: *I want change.* → *He said
he wanted change.*

present continuous → past continuous: *We're lowering
taxes.* → *He said his government was lowering taxes.*

present perfect → past perfect: *He's cut taxes.* → *He said
he had cut taxes.*

past simple → past perfect: *We lowered taxes last year.*
→ *They said they'd lowered taxes last year.*

You also change the modal verbs *will, can* and *must*:

I will cut taxes by five per cent. → *The President said he
would cut taxes by five per cent.*

We can spend more on healthcare. → *He said they could
spend more on healthcare.*

You must create more jobs. → *The public said the
government had to create more jobs.*

No change to the verb

You do not change the verb when:

- the tense is the past perfect simple or past perfect
  continuous:

  They hadn't cut taxes for three years. → *She said they
  hadn't cut taxes for three years.*

- you use the modal verbs *could, might, should, would*:

  I couldn't finish my supper. → *She said she couldn't
  finish her supper.*

You should see a doctor. → *He said I should see a doctor.*

We would love to come! → *They said they would love
to come.*

- the reporting verb is in the present tense (e.g. *says/
  tells* not *said/told*):

  'I agree.' → *He says he agrees.*

  'She's leaving.' → *They tell me she's leaving.*

Change or no change?

You can change the verb, or leave it as it is, with no
change in meaning when:

- the verb in the reported statement refers to a fact or
  ongoing state:

  'We have three children.' → *She said they had three
  children. / She said they have three children.*

- the information in the reported statement is still
  happening, very recent or true:

  'I will not raise taxes.' → *This morning, the President
  said he would not raise taxes. / This morning, the
  President said he will not raise taxes.*

- the verb follows a conjunction such as *when, after,
  as soon as,* etc.:

  'I'll cut taxes as soon as I become President.' →
  *He said he would cut taxes as soon as he became
  President. / He said he will cut taxes as soon as he
  becomes President.*

  See page 238: Summary of tense changes backwards
  in reported speech

Exercises

1 **②2.29** **Read the dialogues. Move the tense of the verb in bold 'backwards' and use it to rewrite the second sentence. Then listen and check.**

1 A: Bye. I'm **going** to be home at eight.

   B: But you said you ____were going____ to be home at seven.

2 A: Brian **isn't coming**.

   B: I know. He told me _____ because of work commitments.

3 A: Susie **works** in Sales.

   B: Really? I thought she _____ in Accounts.

4 A: You **can help** me later.

   B: But you said I _____ you now.

5 A: Sorry, no one **wanted** any cake.

   B: But I made it especially because everyone said they _____ some cake.

6 A: When you drive in this country you **must drive** on the right.

   B: Really? I thought I _____ on the left.

2 **Read the direct speech. Then underline the correct words in italics in the reported speech. In some sentences both options are possible.**

1 'I couldn't finish this book.'

   She said that she *can't / couldn't* finish that book.

2 'My family has always lived here.'

   He told me that his family *has always / had always* lived there.

3 'We totally disagree.'

   They say they totally *disagree / disagreed*.

4 'We'll eat after they get home.'

   She said they*'ll / 'd* eat after they *get / got* home.

5 'There's someone at the door.'

   You said there *is / was* someone at the door, but I didn't see anyone.

6 'I hadn't seen my brother for 50 years until yesterday.'

   My grandfather said he *hasn't seen / hadn't seen* his brother for 50 years until that day.

7 'I saw the new film with Hugh Grant. You'd love it.'

   Mum said she *saw / 'd seen* the new film with Hugh Grant and that I *will / would* love it.

8 'I can't watch this horror film – it's too scary!'

   My little brother said he *can't / couldn't* watch this film because it was too scary.

3 **Four sentences have a mistake. Correct them.**

1 Nowadays, many scientists say that the world was getting warmer.

2 A week ago, my boss said he was leaving, but he still hasn't.

3 The teachers at my school always used to say we have to sit still and never speak.

4 Bill told me yesterday he'll help to set up the website, but he never came.

5 We've played this song to lots of people and they all say we should record our music.

6 Everyone thinks it's a good idea.

7 He said the computer crashes when you clicked here.

73 Reported questions, requests, instructions and orders

Presentation

Reported questions

When you report questions, the verbs in the reported questions are often given in the past. Do not use a question mark in the reported question.

'*Why **are you** opening the window?*' → *She asked me why I **was** opening the window.*

When you report questions which need *Yes* or *No* as the answer, use *if* or *whether* and do not use the auxiliary verb *Do/Did*:

'***Did** you open it?*' → *She asked me **if** I'd opened it.* (not *She asked me ~~did I open it?~~*)

The word order in a reported question is the same as for an affirmative statement:

'*Where are you going?*' → *He asked me where I was going.* (not *He asked me where ~~was I~~ going.*)

Reported requests, instructions and orders

When you report requests, instructions or orders, you often use the reporting verbs *ask* and *tell*.

Requests

Use *ask* + object + *to* infinitive to report a request:

'*Could you open the window?*' → *She **asked me to open** it.*

You can also use *ask* + indirect object + *for* + direct object:

'*Could you pass me a pen?*' → *She **asked me for** a pen.*

Instructions and orders

Use *tell* + indirect object + *to* infinitive to report instructions and orders:

'*Keep the window closed.*' → *He **told me to keep** the window closed.*

'*Type your password in.*' → *He **told me to type** my password in.*

Exercises

1 **Write the words in the correct order to make reported questions, requests, instructions and orders.**

1 She asked / my job / what / me / was .
    She asked me what my job was.

2 some change / asked people / to give / A man in the street / him .

3 The customs officer / what / in my bag / I / asked me / was carrying .

4 I'd gone / after school / where / My parents / wanted to know .

5 our music down / to turn / asked / The neighbours / us .

6 if / I asked / to come over / they / to my house / 'd like .

7 Jack / had to / why / asked me / he / study Maths .

8 told / The parking attendant / him / to move / his car .

2 ⏺**2.30** **Write the original questions for 1–8 in exercise 1. Then listen and check.**

1 *What's your job?*
2 *Could you give me some change?*
3
4
5
6
7
8

3 **Read the top ten questions at a job interview. Then imagine you have been asked all ten and report them.**

September issue

Top ten questions asked at job interviews

1 Tell me about yourself.	*1* to tell him about myself.
2 What have you been doing since university?	*2*
3 Why did you leave your last job?	*3*
4 What are your greatest strengths?	*4*
5 Do you work well with other people?	*5*
6 How would other people describe you?	*6*
7 Are you willing to travel?	*7*
8 Give me one reason why I should choose you.	*8*
9 What will you do if you don't get this position?	*9*
10 What's your current salary?	*10*

The interviewer asked me...

Presentation

Say, tell, think and *ask* are the most common reporting verbs, but you can also use other reporting verbs to summarise or express the sentiment of the original statement:

'*Why don't we celebrate the town's 500th anniversary with a large party?*' → The chairperson **suggested** *celebrating the anniversary with a large party.*

'*Would you like me to investigate the cost?*' → Mrs Holden **offered** *to investigate the cost.*

TIP When deciding which reporting verb to use, think about the function or purpose of the speaker's words. For example: *Why don't you ...?* = suggesting; *Would you like me to ...?* = offering.

Reporting verbs are followed by different verb patterns:

Verb + *that*

*Everyone agreed **that** it was a good idea.*

Reporting verbs with this pattern include: *admit, agree, explain, deny, say, warn.*

Verb + someone + *that*

*Mr Lloyd **warned everyone that** spending more money was a bad idea.*

Reporting verbs with this pattern include: *advise, persuade, tell, warn.*

Verb + *to* infinitive

*Mrs Holden offered **to investigate** the costs.*

Reporting verbs with this pattern include: *agree, offer, promise, refuse, threaten.*

Verb + someone + *to* infinitive

*The advertisement **encouraged customers to buy** the product.*

Reporting verbs with this pattern include: *advise, ask, convince, encourage, invite, persuade, remind, tell, warn.*

Verb + *-ing*

*The chairperson **suggested celebrating** the anniversary with a large party.*

Reporting verbs with this pattern include: *advise, admit, deny, mention, propose, recommend, suggest.*

Verb + preposition + *-ing*

*The employee **apologised for being** late.*

Reporting verbs with this pattern include: *apologise (+ for), insist (+ on).*

Verb + someone + preposition + *-ing*

*Their teacher **warned all of them about copying** in the exam.*

Reporting verbs with this pattern include: *accuse (+ of), blame (+ for), congratulate (+ on), thank (+ for), warn (+ about).*

See Units 61 and 62 for more on verb patterns with *to* infinitive and verb + *-ing.*

Exercises

1 Complete the reported speech with a verb in the box.

accused   admitted   apologised   encouraged   recommended   refused   ~~suggested~~   warned

1 'Why don't you see a doctor?'   She _suggested_ seeing a doctor.

2 'Be careful going up that ladder.'   He _____ me about going up the ladder.

3 'Sorry. I broke your vase.'   I _____ for breaking her vase.

4 'It's true. I stole the car.'   The thief _____ stealing the car.

5 'No, we won't work late.'   The employees _____ to work late.

6 'This book is brilliant. You have to read it.'   She _____ reading the book.

7 'I think you're telling me lies!'   His mum _____ him of telling lies.

8 'Well done. Keep going. I know you can do it!'   The coach _____ the athlete.

2 Match the two halves of the sentences.

1 One person warned everyone that _____   A everyone for coming.

2 Mrs White promised to _____   B building a new park would be expensive.

3 Mr Jones proposed _____   C on reaching a final decision at the meeting.

4 The chairperson insisted _____   D find out the exact costs for the next meeting.

5 The chairperson thanked _____   E asking for more prices from different builders.

3 ⓐ2.31 Read the conversation. Complete the report (1–8) of this conversation using words from the conversation. Change the verb form where necessary. With some verbs there is more than one possible answer. Then listen and check.

Baldesi: I'd like to propose that we introduce regular English lessons for everyone in the office.

Song: I agree. English lessons will be very useful for all those telephone calls from abroad.

Webb: Sorry, but I don't think staff need help with English. Most of our clients are Spanish speakers.

Song: Yes, actually you are probably right about the clients being Spanish. But some use English, so what about offering lessons in both languages?

Baldesi: But have you considered the cost of such a plan?

Webb: I have an idea. I could find out which language people think they need most.

Baldesi: Sorry, I don't understand.

Webb: They would choose between English or Spanish lessons.

1 Mr Baldesi proposed _introducing_ regular English lessons for everyone in the office.

2 Ms Song agreed that _____ very useful for all those telephone calls from abroad.

3 However, Mr Webb disagreed _____ with English, because most of their clients are Spanish speakers.

4 Ms Song admitted _____ probably right.

5 She suggested _____ lessons in both languages.

6 Mr Baldesi asked them _____ the cost of such a plan.

7 Mr Webb offered _____ which language people thought they needed most.

8 He explained that _____ between English or Spanish lessons.

75 Review of units 71 to 74

Grammar

1 **Each sentence has one mistake. Correct it. Note that one sentence has incorrect punctuation.**

   1 The waiter ~~told~~ *said*, 'He was in here earlier but he's gone now.'

   2 He asked me for my number?

   3 Everyone says you give a great performance last night.

   4 He said me to talk to you about my complaint.

   5 My manager asked her when she plans to take her holiday.

   6 She told to me that something was wrong.

   7 My father ordered me come home immediately.

   8 The customer asked how much this ring costs.

   9 You haven't convinced that we should buy a new car.

  10 They blamed me for make this mess, but I was out all day.

2 **Complete the sentences with the pairs of verbs, changing the form where necessary.**

> advise + run   promise + be
> ask + see   suggest + look
> know + build   tell + lock
> ~~offer + lend~~

   1 They _____ *offered* _____ to _____ *lend* _____ me some money if I needed some.

   2 She _____ him to _____ the door when he left.

   3 Your maths teacher _____ if I _____ you at all today. I said I hadn't.

   4 My fitness instructor always _____ me to _____ three kilometres a day before breakfast.

   5 I _____ he _____ it up online, but he ignored me.

   6 The tourists wanted to _____ when they _____ this castle.

   7 We _____ to _____ home by ten so we'd better go.

3 **Complete the exact words spoken for sentences 1–7 in exercise 2.**

   1 'We _____ *'ll lend* _____ you some money if you need some.'

   2 'Remember to _____ when _____ .'

   3 ' _____ Michael at all today?'

   4 ' _____ should _____ before breakfast.'

   5 'Why don't _____ online?'

   6 'When _____ this castle?'

   7 'We'll _____ by ten.'

4 **Write *that* in four more sentences where possible.**

   1 But you said *that* he was coming, too.

   2 Why did Bryan tell me he loved me when he didn't?

   3 The person at the bank wanted to know if I wanted a loan.

   4 The university told me to repeat the class because I failed the exam.

   5 You said to Sarah she couldn't ride your bike.

   6 Police are warning drivers the roads are icy.

   7 How did you persuade the bank to lend you the money?

   8 How did you persuade the bank they should lend you the money?

   9 My boyfriend asked me to marry him!

Grammar in context

5 A journalist interviewed some people and wrote down what they said. Then he wrote the news article. Use his notes to help you write the missing words in the article.

THE LOCAL

Note:
'We have been discussing proposals to raise the retirement age from 65 to 70 over the next ten years.'
'We have not come to a final decision.'
'People must expect a change.'
'I am 99 percent certain that it will happen.'
'When exactly is any change going to happen? How will it affect our pensions?'
'It has to happen sooner or later.'
'If the working population is growing smaller, but older people are living longer, then I can't see an alternative.'

Government to raise age

Last night, the government finally admitted that it ¹ _had_ _been_ _discussing_ proposals to raise the retirement age from 65 to 70. However, it denied that it ² _____ _____ to a final decision. Many politicians have been warning people ³ _____ _____ a change and one minister even told reporters that he was 99 per cent certain that it ⁴ _____ _____.

The news immediately attracted a reaction from some older people who wanted to know exactly when any change ⁵ _____ _____ _____ and also how ⁶ _____ _____ affect ⁷ _____ pensions. The majority of younger people thought it ⁸ _____ to happen sooner or later. One young woman in her twenties said that if the working population ⁹ _____ _____ smaller, but older people ¹⁰ _____ _____ longer, then ¹¹ _____ _____ see an alternative.

Pronunciation: contrastive stress

6 ⏵2.32 Listen to four conversations. Underline the word with the main stress in B's responses.

1   A: Bye. I'm going.
      B: Why? You said you were <u>staying</u>.

2   A: Jane works in a factory.
      B: Really? I thought she worked in a shop.

3   A: Let's look at the answers tomorrow.
      B: But you said we'd look at them today.

4   A: They're driving over now.
      B: Driving? I thought they were walking.

Listen again and repeat B's responses.

Listen again

7 ⏵2.33 Listen to a report and answer questions 1–5.

1   What are the reasons for introducing English lessons?

2   Why does Mr Webb disagree with the plan?

3   How does Ms Song think they might solve the problem?

4   What is Mr Baldesi's argument against this?

5   What is Mr Webb's final solution?

The Hadron Collider

▶ The Hadron Collider is the largest machine in the world. It was planned by over 10,000 scientists in 100 different countries. The science of the Hadron Collider is so complex that its purpose still isn't fully understood by most of the general public. The machine's purpose is to fire sub-atomic particles at each other. Scientists think that by doing this, the origins of the universe might be discovered. However, since it was completed in 2008, it has suffered a number of technical setbacks. One theory for these has been that the problems are being caused by future time – that's one theory that even most of the scientists don't understand!

Presentation

Use the passive form when you want to focus on the person or thing affected by the action of the verb. The subject of the passive verb is the object of the active verb:

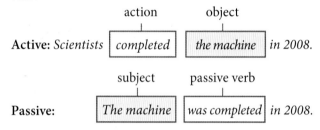

Active: *Scientists* | *completed* | *the machine* | *in 2008.*

Passive: | *The machine* | *was completed* | *in 2008.*

The passive is often used when *the agent* (who or what did the action) …

* is unknown: *It was built in 1990 ~~by someone~~.*

* is obvious or has already been mentioned: *Scientists fire atoms so that the origins of the universe might be discovered ~~by scientists~~.*

* is not important: *The machine has been fixed ~~by someone~~.*

* refers to people in general: *More information about the Hadron Collider can be found ~~by you~~ at www.lhc.ac.uk.*

* doesn't want to be known, in order to avoid criticism or embarrassment: *I'm afraid the machine has been broken ~~by me~~.* (= The speaker either did this or is protecting the person responsible.)

See also Unit 77 for when to include the agent after the passive.

Tenses and modal verbs

To form the passive, use *to be + past participle*:

present / past simple	*Scientists **test/tested** the machine.* → *The machine **is/was** tested.*
present / past continuous	*Scientists **are/were developing** a new machine.* → *A new machine **is/was being developed**.*
present / past perfect	*Scientists **have/had made** a new discovery.* → *A new discovery **has/had been made**.*
present, future and past modals	*Scientists **may discover** the origins of the universe.* → *The origins of the universe **may be discovered**.* *Scientists **will be testing** the theory.* → *The theory **will be being** tested.* *Scientists **might have discovered** the origins of the universe.* → *The origins of the universe **might have been discovered**.*

*Note that perfect continuous forms in the passive are rarely used.

You cannot use the passive form with intransitive verbs (e.g. *arrive, die, go, sit*) because they have no direct object: *The tests went well.* (not *~~The tests are gone well.~~*)

See page 236: Summary of active to passive verb forms

Exercises

1 ⓟ**2.34** Complete the first half of an article by writing the verb in brackets in the correct tense and passive form. Then listen and check.

SCIENCE NEWS

◇ The International Space Station (ISS) [1] *is currently being run* (currently / run) as a joint project between five space agencies. The main structure [2] .... (complete) in 1998, but the idea for cooperation in space began at the end of the Cold War. An agreement for a joint space programme between the USA and Russia [3] .... (not / reach) until 1992, and final plans for a new space station [4] .... (announce) a year later. Unlike previous spaceships and satellites, the ISS [5] .... (build) in space while in orbit. In fact, components [6] .... (still / add) today.

2 ⓟ**2.35** Complete the second half of the article by underlining the active or passive form. Then listen and check.

SCIENCE NEWS

◇ The ISS [7]*has become / has been become* the biggest space station ever. It [8]*can even see / can even be seen* from earth with the naked eye. The space agencies [9]*carry out / are carried out* daily experiments on the ISS. For example, new spacecraft systems [10]*regularly test / are regularly tested* here. It [11]*has continuously staffed / has been continuously staffed* since 2000, so it [12]*is using / is being used* as a research centre to assess the long-term effects of zero gravity on the human body. The results [13]*will affect / will be affected* the preparations for long-term space colonisation.

3 Rewrite the sentences in the passive where possible. Mark the sentence that cannot be written in the passive with an ✗.

1 We are currently discussing your situation.
Your situation is currently being discussed .

2 The class had answered every question.
....

3 I'm afraid they've already gone.
....

4 The doctor should prescribe some medicine.
....

5 We might have sold all those dresses.
....

6 The council is going to make the final decision at the next council meeting.
....

77 The passive 2: the agent, verbs with two objects
by, for, with

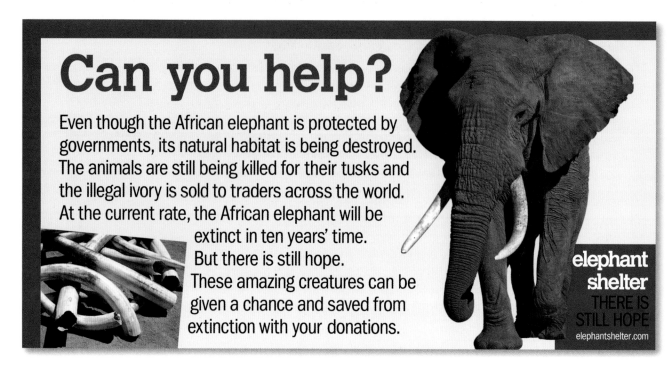

Presentation

Passive with *by + agent*

In the passive, the subject of the active form becomes the agent of the passive verb. The agent is introduced by *by*:

subject · active verb

| Governments | | protect | the African elephant.

passive verb · agent

The African elephant | is protected | *by* | governments.

You include the agent if the information is important or especially relevant:

These elephants can still be saved ~~by organisations~~. (= The name of the organisations are unknown or not important.)

*The elephants can still be saved **by organisations such as the World Wildlife Fund**.* (= The extra information about the organisations is important.)

See Unit 76 for more information on omission of *by* + agent.

Passive with *for / with*

In sentences without the agent, we often give extra information using *for* and *with*.

Use *for* to describe the purpose: *The animals are still being killed **for their tusks**.*

Use *with* to describe the method: *These amazing creatures can be saved from extinction **with your donations**.*

Verbs with two objects

With verbs followed by two objects (see Unit 64), there are two ways to form the passive sentence:

- put the indirect object of the active sentence first: ***Traders** are sold the ivory.*

- put the direct object first and use a preposition with the indirect object: *The ivory is sold **to** traders.*

Verbs commonly used in the passive with two objects include: *give, leave, lend, pay, promise, sell, send, show, teach, tell.*

Exercises

1 **Read the two possible options in sentences 1–6. Delete the agent you would omit.**

1 The bank robber was arrested after he was recognised by ~~a man~~ / *a security guard* from the bank.

2 Do you like that new song at number one by *Beyoncé* / *a singer*?

3 Many art historians think this painting could have been painted by *Michelangelo* / *an artist*.

4 Have you read *Hamlet* by *a playwright* / *Shakespeare*?

5 These socks were made especially for me by *a clothes manufacturer* / *my grandmother*.

6 Last week, I was flown on a plane by *a pilot* / *someone I was at school with*.

2 **Rewrite the active sentences in the passive with the agent.**

1 A woman on our street found a thousand euros.
A thousand euros ....

2 Da Vinci probably painted this portrait.
This portrait ....

3 This dog saved a child from drowning.
A child ....

4 My aunt encouraged me to learn to play the piano.
I ....

3 **Complete these sentences with *by, for* or *with*.**

1 Mammoths were hunted .... early humans.

2 They were hunted .... spears.

3 They were hunted .... their meat and hide.

4 The meat was eaten .... the whole tribe.

5 Their hides were used .... clothing.

6 Nowadays, their fossilised remains are still found .... palaeontologists.

4 **Rewrite the active sentence starting with the words given.**

1 My grandfather left me this painting.
I was left this painting by my grandfather .

2 The bank lent Joe enough money to buy a car.
Joe .... for a car.

3 Why haven't you sent us the results yet?
Why haven't the results .... yet?

4 The company pays its employees their wages on the last Friday of the month.
Wages .... on the last Friday of the month.

5 The teacher is telling the children a scary story.
The children ....

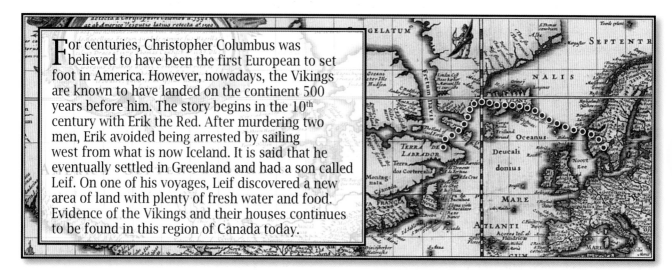

For centuries, Christopher Columbus was believed to have been the first European to set foot in America. However, nowadays, the Vikings are known to have landed on the continent 500 years before him. The story begins in the 10th century with Erik the Red. After murdering two men, Erik avoided being arrested by sailing west from what is now Iceland. It is said that he eventually settled in Greenland and had a son called Leif. On one of his voyages, Leif discovered a new area of land with plenty of fresh water and food. Evidence of the Vikings and their houses continues to be found in this region of Canada today.

Presentation

Passive infinitive and passive -ing form

You form the passive infinitive with *to be* + past participle:

*Evidence continues **to be found** in the region today.*

You can use the passive infinitive with verbs that are followed by the *to* infinitive, e.g. *agree, demand, want* (see also Unit 61):

*The Prime Minister **agreed to be interviewed**.*

*The shopkeeper **demanded to be paid**.*

You form the passive -ing form with *being* + past participle:

*Erik avoided **being arrested** for murder.*

The passive -ing can be used with verbs that are followed by verb + -ing (e.g. *enjoy, hate*) or after a preposition (*bored with, learn by*):

*The children **enjoy being taken** to the zoo.*

*I'm **bored with being taught** history.*

See also Units 62 and 63.

Passive reporting structures (*it is said …*)

Use passive reporting structures with reporting verbs such as *said, thought, believed, claimed, reported, suggested.*

See also Unit 74.

It is said that he lived in Greenland.

*Christopher Columbus **was believed** to be the first European to set foot in America.*

*Vikings **are known** to have landed on the continent.*

Passive reporting structures are formed like this:

- *It + be +* past participle of reporting verb + (*that*) clause: ***It is known that*** *he lived in Iceland.*

- *It/He/She/They + be +* past participle of reporting verb + *to* infinitive: ***She is said to be*** *unhappy here.*

- *It/He/She/They + be +* past participle of reporting verb + *to + have +* past participle: ***They are believed to have lived*** *on the island.*

The speaker in passive reporting structures is often unknown or unimportant:

It has been reported that *there is a delay.*

He is believed to have stolen *over a million pounds.*

Passive reporting structures are also used when someone wishes to remain anonymous:

*A: **It has been reported that** you were not at your desk.*

B: That isn't true! Who told you that?

Exercises

1 Underline the correct option. In two sentences, both answers are possible.

1 All the students hope <u>*to be put*</u> / *being put* into Mr Brown's class.

2 He can't stand *to be proved* / *being proved* wrong in an argument.

3 Are you prepared *to be asked* / *being asked* some difficult questions?

4 Anyone who is late for the bus risks *to be left* / *being left* behind!

5 Your aunt appeared *to be shocked* / *being shocked* by the film. What were you watching?

6 We knew he was missing school because he kept *to be seen* / *being seen* around town during the day.

7 I'm worried about *not to be chosen* / *not being chosen* for the team.

8 No one likes *to be delayed* / *being delaying* at airports.

9 The winning team stopped in their home town *to be cheered* / *being cheered* by their fans after they won the cup.

2 Match 1–6 with A–F.

1 In the past, it was believed that _____   A review their education policy.

2 It is commonly known that _____   B most students are in debt.

3 It has been claimed that there are _____   C the world was flat.

4 A serious car crash is reported _____   D to have happened on the motorway this morning.

5 Native American Indians are thought _____   E other life forms in the universe.

6 The government has agreed to _____   F to have crossed over originally from Asia.

3 ⏺2.36 Rewrite the reporter's sentences starting with the words in 1–5. Then listen and check.

Robbery notes:

1 We know the robbery happened at three in the morning.
2 We think the robbers dug a tunnel underneath the road.
3 Some people claim it goes right into the bank vault.
4 Someone says they saw a blue van.
5 We heard a rumour that they stole up to a million pounds, but that's unconfirmed.

1 It is known that the robbery happened at three in the morning .

2 It is _____ .

3 It is _____ .

4 A blue van is said to have _____ .

5 The robbers are _____ .

4 Complete the text with the words in brackets, using reporting passive structures.

When Columbus proposed a plan to reach the East by sailing west, [1]_____ (it / criticise) by many people including his own King of Portugal. [2]_____ (it / claim) that Columbus had underestimated the actual circumference of the Earth. Eventually, Columbus is [3]_____ (know / convince) the King and Queen of Spain who [4]_____ (expect / reward) him with new lands. After some weeks at sea, his crew were growing angry and Columbus only [5]_____ (avoid / kill) by the desperate men when an island was finally sighted. The island [6]_____ (believe / be) part of what is now the Bahamas.

79 *get, have, need* with passive meaning

My car needed fixing.

I had it towed away.

I got the garage to fix it.

My car got hit as I was leaving!

I hit the other driver!

I got arrested.

Presentation

Passive with *get*

You can replace the passive *be* + past participle with *get* + past participle when you are speaking informally. *Get* is only used with dynamic verbs (not with stative verbs) to talk about something that happened to you. The event or action is often unwelcome or unexpected:

*I **was** arrested.* → *I **got** arrested.*

*He **was** stopped for speeding.* → *He **got** stopped for speeding.*

You cannot replace *to be* with *get* when the verb is stative:

*My car **is kept** in the garage.* (not *My car ~~got~~ kept in the garage.*)

Sometimes you use *get* to talk about positive events:

*I **was/got** paid.*

*I **was/got** promoted at work.*

get someone to do something / have someone do something

You use *get someone to do something / have someone do something* to explain that you have asked someone to do something for you:

*I **got the mechanic to** repair my car. / I **had the mechanic** repair my car.* (= I asked the mechanic to repair my car.)

Notice that with *get* you use the *to* infinitive. With *have* you use the bare infinitive.

get / have something done (causative)

You use *get/have* + object + past participle to explain that you asked someone else to do something for you, but you don't say who:

*I **got** my car fixed.* (= *I **had** my car fixed.*)

This use is called 'causative' because you caused it to happen:

*I **got/had** my car fixed at the garage.* (= I arranged it.)

get / have something done (non causative)

You can also use *get/have something done* to talk about something that happened to you, although you did not ask for it to happen. You usually use this structure in this way to talk about something unexpected and generally unwelcome:

*I **got/had** my car stolen.*

This use is non causative because you did *not* cause it to happen.

need + *-ing*

You use *need* + *-ing* to say that something needs to be done (by someone), but you don't say who:

*The car **needs** fixing.*

*Your hair **needs** cutting.*

*The engine **needs** checking.*

Exercises

1 Write the verb in brackets in the correct form.

YOU KNOW YOU ARE RICH WHEN...

1 ... you get your stylist _____ (choose) your outfits for the day.
2 ... you have your personal assistant _____ (fetch) the morning newspaper.
3 ... you have your make-up and hair _____ (do) before you go out.
4 ... you get your personal trainer _____ (come) to the house.
5 ... you get your dogs _____ (walk).
6 ... you have your post _____ (bring) to your room on a silver tray.
7 ... you get your pilot _____ (fly) you to Paris for breakfast.
8 ... you have your security guard _____ (remove) the paparazzi from outside your window.

2 Replace the verb *be* with the correct form of *get* when possible.

1 My wallet ~~was~~ *got* stolen.

2 I was given a new job.

3 The goalkeeper was replaced by a substitute.

4 In the good old days, life was lived at a slower pace.

5 Only the lights on my car were damaged.

6 The temperature is kept below zero degrees.

3 Look at the four pictures. What needs doing?

1 (cut) The boy's hair needs cutting.

2 (mend) _____

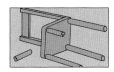

3 (fix) _____

4 (pay) _____

4 ⓟ 2.37 Complete the conversation with the pairs of verbs. Change the form of the verbs where necessary. Then listen and check.

got + drop	have + look at	have + send	~~need + fix~~	need + replace

A: Hello again. My watch ¹needs fixing _____ .

B: But you only ² _____ it _____ a month ago.

A: Yes, but that was because the battery ³ _____ . Now both hands have stopped.

B: I see. Well, unfortunately madam, the inside of the watch is completely broken. It looks like it
⁴ _____ .

A: I don't know when that happened. Oh dear.

B: I can't fix it here. You'll have to ⁵ _____ the whole thing _____ back to the manufacturer, I'm afraid.

80 Review of units 76 to 79

Grammar

1 Correct the mistake in each sentence.

1 Construction of the new tower has been complete.

2 New discoveries in spacc are been made all the time.

3 Your flowers are going to being delivered before midday.

4 The earth's climate may have be changed forever by human activity.

5 All ten questions should to be answered within five minutes.

6 Stocks are sold with traders on the stock market.

7 Students will be awarded to prizes on the last day of term.

8 The area continues searching by local police.

2 Rewrite the sentences in the passive form. Only include the agent if you think it is necessary.

1 My mother sang this to me when I was a child.

This song _____ when I was a child.

2 Someone is delivering an urgent package before noon.

An urgent package _____ .

3 The famous writer, Charles Dickens, lived in this house at one time.

This house _____ at one time.

4 The engineer fixed my heating.

I got _____ .

5 A real magician taught me this trick.

This trick _____ .

6 A shark can attack most living things in the water, including humans.

Most living things in the water, including humans, _____ .

7 The weather report said 50 centimetres of snow fell last night.

Fifty centimetres of snow was said _____ .

3 Complete the dialogue using got, had, by, for or to.

Detective: So you [1] got _____ burgled last night, Lady Smithers. Is that right?

Lady Smithers: Yes, that's right. And I [2] _____ my diamond necklace stolen. It was given [3] _____ me [4] _____ my late husband, Lord Smithers.

Detective: And you have no idea who it was stolen [5] _____ ?

Lady Smithers: Absolutely none. I'd been wearing the necklace all evening and then left it by my bedside.

Detective: So last night, a thief could have broken in and taken the necklace, and by this morning, it could have been sold [6] _____ a customer [7] _____ cash.

Lady Smithers: It's possible, but unlikely. The house was full of guests last night and we [8] _____ no windows broken.

Detective: So that leaves the bedroom door which was locked and could only have been opened [9] _____ a key. Who had a key, Lady Smithers?

Lade Smithers: Only the maid. One was given [10] _____ her [11] _____ cleaning.

Detective: Cleaning?

Lady Smithers: The room is cleaned [12] _____ my maid once a day.

Detective: I'd like to talk to this maid.

Lady Smithers: But you can't suspect her. She's been employed [13] _____ our family for over 20 years …

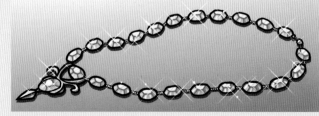

Grammar in context

4 **Complete the text by writing the words in brackets in the correct form.**

How to get promoted

It ¹_____ (believe) by most people that if you excel in your new job, it won't be long before you ²_____ (approach) with more job offers. It's partly true, but some things ³_____ (can / still / do) to accelerate that promotion. Here is some good advice to ⁴_____ (follow) by anyone with career ambitions:

- Relations with the boss: promotion ⁵_____ (mainly / influence) by one person – your boss. Build good relations with this person.
- Have your skills ⁶_____ (update): attend training courses and keep up to date with new trends in your area.
- Be ⁷_____ (see / be) enthusiastic: volunteer for tasks and ask for more responsibility.
- Get yourself ⁸_____ (know): modesty ⁹_____ (often / think) to be preferable to self-promotion, but there's nothing wrong with having your accomplishments and achievements ¹⁰_____ (promote) around the office. If you don't do it, who will?
- Be a team player: show you can work with others and be supportive. Make sure praise for successes ¹¹_____ (give / to) the whole team and criticism for failure ¹²_____ (share).

Pronunciation: intonation in passive reporting

5 **🔊 2.38 Listen to these sentences. Write [↗] where the intonation rises.**

       [↗]
1 It's said that the machine is the largest in the world.

2 It's thought that it'll be completed next year.

3 It was believed that it would be finished by now.

4 It's known that they've had some problems with it.

5 It's been reported that they've made a new discovery.

Listen again and repeat the sentences.

Listen again

6 **🔊 2.39 Listen and make notes about the International Space Station for each year. Use the passive form in your notes.**

1 1998: The main structure was completed.

2 1992: ....

3 1993: ....

4 Today: ....

81 Relative clauses 1
Defining relative clauses, *who, which, that*

Woman:	That's him.
Police Officer:	Who?
Woman:	That's the man who I saw!
Police Officer:	Can you be more precise?
Woman:	The one that's wearing a blue T-shirt stole my handbag.
Police Officer:	Which T-shirt?
Woman:	It's the T-shirt which has a rip.

Presentation

Relative clauses

You use a relative clause to give more information about a noun in the main clause of the sentence. The relative clause always follows the noun it is referring to:

*That's the man **who I saw**!*

*The one **that's wearing a blue T-shirt** stole my handbag.*

Defining relative clauses

When the extra information in the relative clause is essential, it is called a defining relative clause. Without the defining relative clause, the meaning of the main clause can be unclear or need further explanation. In this dialogue, the Police Officer needs more information so the woman uses a defining relative clause:

Woman: *That's him.*

Police Officer: *Who?*

Woman: *That's the man **who I saw**!*

who, which, that

Who, *which* and *that* are relative pronouns and you use them at the beginning of the relative clause.

- Use *who* for people: *That's the woman **who** identified the thief.*
- Use *which* for objects or things: *That's the handbag **which** was stolen.*

You can replace both *who* or *which* with the relative pronoun *that* in defining relative clauses:

*That's the woman **that** identified the thief.*

*That's the handbag **that** was stolen.*

Subject or object of the relative clause

The relative pronoun (*who, which, that*) in the relative clause can be …

- the subject of the clause:

  It's the T-shirt which has a rip.
  The T-shirt has a rip.

- the object of the clause (with a noun or pronoun following it):

  That's the man who I saw.
  I saw that man.

Do not use another object in the relative clause when the relative pronoun is the object:

That's the man. I saw him . → That's the man who I saw ~~him~~.

Verb agreement

When the relative pronoun is the subject, the verb agrees with the subject of the main clause:

*This is **the shop** that **sells** T-shirts.*

Omitting the relative pronoun

In defining relative clauses, you always need a relative pronoun when it is the subject of the defining relative clause (i.e. when it is immediately followed by a verb).

Say *That's the man **who** stole my handbag.* (don't say *~~That's the man stole my handbag.~~*)

However, you don't have to use a relative pronoun when it is the object of the relative clause (i.e. when it is followed by a subject + verb):

That's the man I saw. = That's the man who/that I saw.

Exercises

1 Join the two sentences using a relative clause and *who* or *which*.

1 My neighbour is the person. He called the police.
   My neighbour is the person who called the police.

2 These are the books. They are for my course.

3 This is the car. It's for sale.

4 Those are the same boys. They smashed our window.

5 That's the actor. I saw him in a film last week.

2a Look at your sentences in exercise 1. Is the relative pronoun in each sentence the subject or the object of the relative clause? Write *S* or *O*.

1   S   2   3   4   5

2b Look at your sentences in exercise 1 again. From which of the sentences can you omit the relative pronoun?

1   ✗   2   3   4   5

3 (2.40) Look at the family photograph. Complete the conversations in your own words using defining relative clauses. Then listen and check.

1 A: Which man is your dad?
   B: The man who 's wearing a red and white jumper .

2 A: Who are the two women?
   B: Well, the woman _____ is my mother and the other woman is my aunt.

3 B: They're my twin brothers. That's Ryan.
   A: Which one?
   B: Ryan is wearing the green T-shirt _____ .

4 A: Are these your pets?
   B: Max is mine and Spike is the twins'. Max is the one _____ .

4 Find a photograph with a group of people (e.g. family, friends, your class). Write three sentences to describe and define some of them using relative clauses.

> # HANDBAG THIEF CAUGHT AT LAST!
>
> ■ A thief who has stolen over 100 handbags has finally been arrested. Roger Slack was identified last night as the 'handbag thief' by an elderly lady. The witness, who police have not named, was also a victim of Slack, but she had seen his face before he ran away with her handbag. At midnight, the police entered Slack's flat, which was full of handbags. Strangely, all the handbags in the flat, which also included the main witness's bag, still contained all their owners' original money and possessions.

Presentation

Defining and non-defining relative clauses

Defining and non-defining relative clauses both give extra information about the noun in the main clause.

Defining: *A thief who has stolen over 100 handbags has finally been arrested.*

Non-defining: *The witness, who police have not named, was also a victim of Slack.*

The extra information in a non-defining clause is not essential. The meaning of the main clause is still clear without the non-defining relative clause.

The police entered Slack's flat. + The flat was full of handbags. = The police entered Slack's flat, which was full of handbags.

Non-defining clauses are also different from defining relative clauses because …

- you cannot replace *who* or *which* with *that*:

  The witness, ~~that~~ police have not named, had her handbag stolen.

  The handbags, ~~that~~ also included the woman's, contained all the original money.

- you cannot omit the relative pronoun:

  Say *The witness, who police have not named, also had her handbag stolen.* (don't say *The witness, ~~police have not named~~, also had her handbag stolen.*)

In written English, the non-defining relative clause is separated from the main clause by commas (there are no commas in a defining relative clause):

The witness, who police have not named, had her handbag stolen. ✓

The witness who police have not named had her handbag stolen. ✗

TIP In spoken English, the speaker usually pauses slightly before and after the non-defining clause: *Mr Slack, [pause] who is still in police custody, [pause] lives at 28 Haversham Gardens.*

	defining	non-defining
adds extra information	✓	✓
adds essential information	✓	✗
can use *that* instead of *who* and *which*	✓	✗
can omit the subject relative pronoun	✗	✗
can omit the object relative pronoun	✓	✗
uses commas	✗	✓

Exercises

1 Underline six more relative clauses in this article. Then decide if they are defining or non-defining. Write *D* or *N-D*.

Robbery attempt put on ice!

A THIEF, <u>who broke into an office block</u>, was seen by the security guard, but he escaped before the police arrived. However, the 38-year-old man, who had taken two laptop computers, was also recorded on security cameras and the police were able to identify him as Adam Mader. When police entered his flat, which was only five minutes from the office block, they found no sign of him. But just as the police officers were leaving, they heard a sneeze that came from the inside of the fridge. When they opened the door of the fridge, which was only a metre high, they found Mader curled up inside and shivering. Mader, who had been in the fridge for over two hours, had a cold and was given a blanket and a packet of tissues before the police took him away. The two laptops which had been stolen were returned to the office after they had been defrosted!

1 _D_   2 _____   3 _____   4 _____   5 _____   6 _____   7 _____

2 Combine the three pieces of information into one sentence using a non-defining relative clause.

1   Burj Khalifa / was completed in 2010 / the tallest building in the world.
    Burj Khalifa, which was completed in 2010, is the tallest building in the world.

2   Coca-Cola® / also called Coke® / sold in over 200 countries.

3   Barack Obama / born in Hawaii / the 44th President of the USA.

4   The moon / has water under its surface / might be a future home for humans.

3a Replace *who* or *which* with *that* where possible.

1   Are you the person ~~who~~ *that* told the teacher about me?

2   My aunt, who has now retired, was a teacher for over 30 years.

3   The internet, which we take for granted nowadays, never even existed when I was a child.

4   She's someone who I've known for years.

3b Delete *who, which* or *that* where possible.

1   These shoes ~~which~~ I bought are too small.

2   These shoes, which are too small, need to be returned.

3   Joe's Café, which has only been open since June, is closing.

4   The bank robbers who the police caught will only go to prison for a month.

5   The owner of this restaurant, who is a friend of mine, lives in Bermuda.

6   That group that you like so much are playing live at a local club.

83 Formality and prepositions in relative clauses
whose, when, where, why, who(m)

t's hard to explain why the legend of King Arthur has become such an important part of British mythology. Arthur, about whom very little is known, is the subject of many biographies. If he existed at all, it was probably around the 5th century, when Britain was a collection of much smaller kingdoms. Arthur, whose kingdom would have covered parts of southwest England and Wales, is portrayed in art and literature as a noble leader and heroic warrior. Further stories have been added to this image over the centuries. For example,

there is the legend of the castle of Camelot in which he lived, but which no historian has successfully located. And no story of Arthur is complete without the stories of his loyal knights and the round table at which they all sat as equal men.

Presentation

whose, when, where, why

- Use *whose* to refer to possession: *Arthur, **whose** kingdom would have covered parts of southwest England and Wales, is portrayed as a noble leader.*

- Use *when* to refer to a time: *He lived in the 5th century, **when** Britain was a collection of much smaller kingdoms.*

- Use *where* to refer to a place: *There was the castle of Camelot **where** he lived.*

- Use *why* to refer to a reason: *It's hard to explain **why** the legend of King Arthur is such an important part of British mythology.*

Formality in relative clauses

More formal use of relative clauses is common in written English such as academic texts, and in formal speaking such as presentations or lectures.

who or whom?

When *who* is the object of the relative clause, it is possible to use *whom* instead of *who*.

*Arthur is a king **whom** many historians have studied.* (= more formal)

*Arthur is a king **who** many historians have studied.* (= less formal/everyday speech)

Prepositions in relative clauses

In everyday and less formal English, you leave the preposition at the end of the relative clause:

*This is the house (which) I used to live **in**.*

In more formal English, when the relative pronoun is the object of the relative clause, you put the preposition before the relative pronoun:

*This is the round table which the knights sat **at**.* (= less formal)

*This is the round table **at** which the knights sat.* (= more formal)

Do not use *who* or *that* after a preposition. Use preposition + *whom* instead of *who*:

*Arthur, **about whom** very little is known, is the subject of many biographies.* ✓

Arthur, about ~~who~~ very little is known, is the subject of many biographies. ✗

Use preposition + *which* instead of *that*:

*There was the castle of Camelot **that** (or **which**) he lived **in**.*

*There was the castle of Camelot **in which** he lived.* (not *in ~~that~~ he lived*)

You cannot use prepositions with *where, when* or *why*:

This is the palace where the Queen lives ~~in~~.

This is the time when we normally leave ~~at~~.

The university is the reason why Oxford is famous ~~for~~.

You can make these more formal by using the preposition + *which*:

*This is the palace **in which** the Queen lives.*

*This is the time **at which** we normally leave.*

*The university is the reason **for which** Oxford is famous.*

Exercises

1 Match 1–5 with A–E.

1 My old teacher is someone _____
2 Dan Brown is an author _____
3 The beach is a place _____
4 2001 was a year _____
5 My old teacher at school was one of the reasons _____

A I chose to study literature at university.
B whose books I often read.
C when lots of important world events happened.
D who I admire.
E where I often go to relax.

2 (2.41) Write the missing words in this conversation. Then listen and check.

A: Wow! Here's a photograph [1] *which* I haven't seen for years.

B: Who is it?

A: It's my great-grandmother [2] _____ son was my grandfather. This is her with the man [3] _____ asked her to marry him.

B: You mean your great-grandfather?

A: No. Before that, there was someone else [4] _____ asked her to marry him, before the war.

B: What happened?

A: She never told me the reason [5] _____ they didn't get married, but this photo was taken in 1939 [6] _____ the Second World War was just starting, so I assume he never came back. I think this photo was taken at the place [7] _____ they probably said goodbye for the last time.

3a Make these sentences more formal by moving the preposition and changing the relative pronoun where necessary.

1 King Henry VIII is someone who you've probably heard of.
   King Henry VIII is someone *of whom you've probably heard.* .

2 0°C is the temperature which water starts to freeze at.
   0°C is the temperature _____ .

3 Princess Diana is a woman who magazines still publish articles about.
   Princess Diana is a woman _____ .

4 This is a stage which many famous people have performed on.
   This is a stage _____ .

5 He was a man who I had absolute trust in.
   He was a man _____ .

3b Make these sentences more formal by replacing where, when, why or that with a preposition + which.

1 The ancient stone circle is the reason why Stonehenge is well known.
   The ancient stone circle is the reason _____ .

2 The Tower of London is the fortress where many kings, queens and princes were imprisoned.
   The Tower of London is the fortress _____ .

3 Is this really the hill that Arthur built his castle on?
   Is this really the hill _____ ?

84 Reduced relative clauses

Passengers travelling without a valid ticket will receive a fine.

Metro police will remove and destroy any bags left unattended.

Presentation

Relative clauses can sometimes be shortened by omitting the relative pronoun and using a present or past participle.

Relative clause	Reduced relative clause
Passengers **who travel** without a valid ticket will receive a fine.	Passengers **travelling** without a valid ticket will receive a fine.
Metro police will remove and destroy any bags **which are left** unattended.	Metro police will remove and destroy any bags **left** unattended.

If the verb in the relative clause is in the active form, use the present participle (*-ing*).

Active: *The 10:30 train to London, which **leaves** from platform nine, is now ready to depart.* → *The 10:30 train to London, **leaving** from platform nine, is now ready to depart.* ✓

The 10:30 train to London, ~~left~~ from platform nine, is now ready to depart. ✗

If the verb in the relative clause is in the passive form, use the past participle form:

Passive: *Some train services which **have been delayed** by today's severe weather have now been cancelled.* → *Some train services **delayed** by today's severe weather have now been cancelled.* ✓

Some train services ~~delaying~~ by today's severe weather have now been cancelled. ✗

You cannot use a reduced relative clause when the relative pronoun is the object of the relative clause:

The train for London, which I was going to take, has now been cancelled. ✓

~~The train for London taking has been cancelled.~~ ✗

Exercises

1 Complete the sentences using only the verb in brackets in the correct form.

1 Anyone _____ (drive) over the speed limit will be stopped.

2 Any employee _____ (work) hard could receive a bonus this month.

3 Passengers _____ (wait) for trains can use the waiting room on platform two.

4 Letters _____ (send) with a first class stamp arrive the following day.

5 Any items _____ (leave) in the classroom at the end of term will be thrown away.

6 Glass _____ (put) in green bins is recycled.

7 The people _____ (live) in this house have been here for years.

8 Many products _____ (buy) online are much cheaper than in the shops.

9 There is a fine for any library books _____ (return) late.

10 We'll give a reward to anyone _____ (provide) the police with information about the missing jewels.

2 Combine the two sentences with a reduced relative clause.

1 A bag was stolen from my hotel room. It had my passport in it.

The bag ___*stolen*___ from my hotel room ___*had*___ my passport in it.

2 She's the one. She's demanding a pay rise.

She's the one _____ a pay rise.

3 This is a job. It needs someone with plenty of experience.

This is a job _____ someone with plenty of experience.

4 A package was delivered this morning. It's on my desk.

The package _____ this morning is on my desk.

5 It's a university. It specialises in medicine.

It's a university _____ in medicine.

6 That's the baby. She was born only three hours ago.

That's the baby _____ only three hours ago.

3 (2.42) Read these announcements. Reduce the relative clauses where possible. Then listen and check.

>   *travelling*
> 1 All passagers ~~who are travelling~~ to Delhi, please proceed to gate number 31, where your plane is ready for boarding. That's flight AI 511, which departs from gate 31.
>
> 2 Could those passengers who are waiting for their luggage from flight AI 552 please come to the baggage claim desk where we have their suitcases.
>
> 3 Anyone that enters Passport Control should have their passport and boarding card ready for inspection. Any hand luggage which is carried with you must conform to size restrictions.
>
> 4 This is a no-smoking flight. Any passenger who is caught smoking will be detained by airport police after landing.
>
> 5 We are about to land. All electronic items which are switched on should now be turned off.

85 Review of units 81 to 84

Grammar

1 Correct the mistake in each sentence. Some of the mistakes are punctuation.

1 That's the woman who I saw ~~her~~.

2 It's a shop which sell everything you need.

3 The new student, who is in my class is Italian.

4 That's the singer from Wales has a great new song.

5 Usain Bolt, that is the fastest man in the world, won three gold medals at the 2008 Olympic Games.

6 The politician, has been in parliament for over 20 years, has finally resigned.

7 People in Britain which is surrounded by water, don't each much fish.

8 Packages sending overseas need a customs form.

9 Eighteen is the age at when you can vote in many countries.

10 This is the car in that I learned to drive.

2 Delete one or two words in each sentence without changing the meaning.

1 The driver who we saw driving too quickly was arrested.

2 There's a new place that we like to eat at.

3 Something which we always like to do at the weekend is go walking in the mountains.

4 Anyone who is caught smoking in school is in big trouble!

5 The paper which is put in the green bin can be recycled.

3 Replace the words in bold with the words in the box.

> in which   that   when   whom   why

1 Computers are the things **which/** _____ changed the modern world.

2 We have also invited Doctor Moore, **who/** _____ I think you already know.

3 They say he wanted to retire but the reason **for which/** _____ he left so suddenly is unknown.

4 Here's the store cupboard **where/** _____ all cleaning materials are kept.

5 Midnight is the time **at which/** _____ most people believe witches come out!

4 Rewrite the first sentence starting with the words in the second sentence.

1 Here's the child who we were informed about.

Here's the child about _____ .

2 This is the great hall where the king and his court used to eat.

This is the great hall in _____ and his court used to eat.

3 The person dealing with your complaint is on another line.

The person who _____ is on another line.

4 Every question answered correctly receives one mark.

Every question which _____ correctly receives one mark.

5 Underline the correct words in italics. In some cases, both options are possible.

Have you seen our dinosaur?

A remote-controlled dinosaur robot [1]*which is valued/ valued* at £60,000 has gone missing. The monster was taken from a theatre [2]*where it was appearing/ appearing* in a show called 'Walking with Dinosaurs'. People [3]*who are involved/ involved* in the show expressed their amazement that the dinosaur, [4]*which/ that* is over two metres high, could have disappeared. Furthermore, no one can explain [5]*why/which* the thief (or thieves) would be interested in an object [6]*which/that* would be extremely hard to sell.

A spokesperson for the show, [7]*which has been seen/ seen* by over four million people worldwide, asked for anyone [8]*who/that* has knowledge of the dinosaur's whereabouts to contact the show immediately.

Staff discovered that the robot-dinosaur was missing last Friday, [9]*when/where* the show opened in Guadalajara. The exhibit was the least expensive of all, so it could have been much worse for the show's producers, [10]*of whom/ whose* dinosaurs can measure up to 13 metres high and cost as much as £600,000.

Grammar in context

6 Complete this biography of Leonardo da Vinci with the missing clauses below. Afterwards, add commas where necessary.

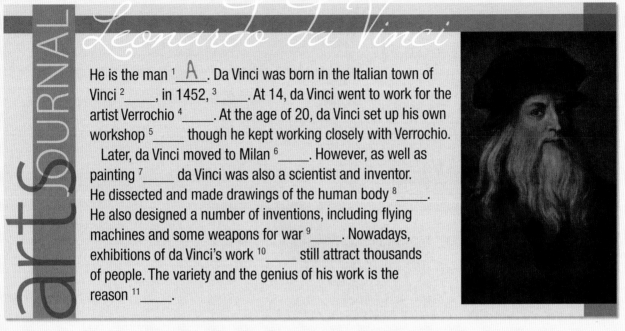

Leonardo da Vinci

He is the man ¹_A_. Da Vinci was born in the Italian town of Vinci ²_____, in 1452, ³_____. At 14, da Vinci went to work for the artist Verrochio ⁴_____. At the age of 20, da Vinci set up his own workshop ⁵_____ though he kept working closely with Verrochio.
   Later, da Vinci moved to Milan ⁶_____. However, as well as painting ⁷_____ da Vinci was also a scientist and inventor. He dissected and made drawings of the human body ⁸_____. He also designed a number of inventions, including flying machines and some weapons for war ⁹_____. Nowadays, exhibitions of da Vinci's work ¹⁰_____ still attract thousands of people. The variety and the genius of his work is the reason ¹¹_____.

A who is often called the greatest artist of all time

B of which many still survive today

C for which he is probably most famous

D why so much of his work is still admired by so many

E where he painted one of his most famous paintings, *The Last Supper*.

F which, in some cases, were made and used to defend cities

G which was paid for by his father

H which is near the city of Florence

I when many artists and architects worked for rich patrons

J whose workshop was known as one of the finest in Florence

K which are shown around the world

Pronunciation: pausing

7 ⏺**2.43** The commas are missing in these sentences. Listen and decide where the speaker pauses. Mark each pause with a comma.

1 Johnny Depp who is probably my favourite actor has another film coming out.
2 Your assistant who I also mentioned last week is always rude on the phone.
3 The Nestlé company which is a multinational is based in Switzerland.
4 I'll try the strawberry ice cream which looks delicious.

Listen again and repeat the sentences.

Listen again

8 ⏺**2.44** Listen to a conversation. Complete the sentences with relative clauses.

1 It's a photograph which *she hasn't seen for years* .
2 It's the mother's great-grandmother whose
_____ .
3 The photograph is of her with the man who
_____ .
4 She never gave the reason why
_____ .
5 It was taken in 1939 when
_____ .
6 The photograph was taken at a place where
_____ .

86 *if* clauses 1: present verb forms
Real situations in the present and future

Presentation

You use an *if* clause to describe a situation, and the main clause to describe the consequences:

If clause: situation   main clause: consequence

If you go,   *I'll go.*

The *if* clause can come before or after the main clause.

When it is at the beginning of the sentence, use a comma to separate it from the main clause:

I'll go if you pay.   *If you pay⊙ I'll go.*

To describe present and future situations that are real or likely to happen, use the verb forms below:

	If clause	Main clause
Situations that are generally true, habits and repeated actions (often called zero conditional)	*If* + present simple *If / When* the temperature drops,*	Present simple, imperative, modal verbs such as *can, must, should* or *might* … *there's a ghost nearby.* … *get ready to see a ghost!* … *there may be a ghost nearby.*
Other present situations, rules and regulations	*If* + present verb form *If you're looking for excitement,* *If you've always been interested in ghosts,* *If you are under 14,*	Present simple, imperative, modal verbs such as *can, must, should* or *might* *this is the tour for you!* *come along and find out more!* *you must be with an adult.*
Future situations (often called first conditional)	*If* + present verb form or *be going to*. Do not use ~~will~~. Say *If I go.* (don't say *If I'll go.*) *If you go,* *If you're going to go,* *If you're looking for me later,*	Future verb forms (see unit 56), imperative, modal verbs such as *can, must, should* or *might* *I'm going too.* *can you take Nick with you?* *I'll be in the bar.*

*if or *when*?

Either *if* or *when*: when you are talking about predictable, repeated actions, you can use either *if* or *when*: *If/When the temperature drops below 1°, it snows.*

when but not *if*: if you know something is going to happen, use *when*: *We'll come to the café **when** the tour finishes.*

if but not *when*: if you're not sure that something is true or will happen, use *if*: *If the tour finishes before the café closes, we'll join you for a coffee.*

See page 238: Summary of conditionals

Exercises

1 **Match 1–6 with A–G.**

1 If you like ghost stories, _E_
2 Please arrive on time. If you're late, _____
3 If you can't go to the match tonight, _____
4 If you're going to be here tomorrow, _____
5 If you're planning a birthday party, _____
6 If we don't see you tomorrow, _____
7 If you've finished with that newspaper, _____

A we won't wait for you.
B ask about our special group prices.
C can I have it?
D have a great holiday!
E you'll love this new tour.
F you can join us for our 10th anniversary.
G can I have your ticket?

2 **Choose the correct options.**

1 If you*'re going/ will go* to the match tomorrow, *can / will* I come with you in your car?
2 If you *don't / won't* get the tickets today, there *aren't / won't* be any left!
3 If you*'ll see / 're seeing* Tom later this afternoon, *can / do* you give him a message, please?
4 If *you'll want / you want* to get fit quick, follow these simple rules.
5 You know he *doesn't / won't* come tomorrow if you *don't / won't* ask him in person.
6 If *you need / you'll need* any help, just let me know.

3 **Replace *if* with *when* where possible.**

1 Blue litmus paper turns red if you place it in acid.

2 Children only. You cannot go beyond this point if you are over 14.

3 If you like chocolate, why not try our special triple chocolate treat?

4 We sometimes have our class out in the garden if the weather's nice.

5 The oven switches itself off if it gets too hot.

6 If you keep going straight on down this road, you'll see the station at the end.

4 **Complete these sentences so they are true for you.**

1 If it's raining tomorrow, I _____ .
2 I _____ this weekend, if I've got enough time.
3 I really enjoy _____ if _____ .
4 If I finish this exercise in time, I can _____ .

87 *if* clauses 2: past simple
Imaginary situations in the present and future, *would, could, might*

Presentation

Use *if* + past simple to talk about imaginary or hypothetical situations in the present or future.
Use *would* in the main clause to talk about the consequences.

If I knew where he was, I certainly **wouldn't** tell the police.

If I were him, I'd leave the country.

What **would** you do **if the bank gave** you a million dollars?

If clause	Main clause
Use *if* + past simple to talk about: 1 a present situation that is the opposite of the real situation. 2 a future situation that you think is not likely to happen.	Use *would* to talk about the consequences of the imaginary situation. Use *would* + *be* + *-ing* to talk about an action in progress:
If I knew where he was, (but I don't) *If I had a million dollars,* (but I haven't) *If the bank gave you a million pounds,* (you don't think it's likely to happen) ⟶	⟶ *I* **wouldn't tell** the police. *I'd be lying* on a beach in the Bahamas. what **would you do**?
Note: this is often referred to as the second conditional.	Note: the contracted form of *would* is *'d*. The contracted form of *would not* is *wouldn't*.

was / were

You can use *was* or *were* with *I, he, she* and *it*. *Were* is considered to be more formal.

*If I **was/were** him, I'd give the money to charity.*

You often use *If I were you* … to give advice:
If I were you, I'd hand myself in to the police.

could, might

Use *could* to talk about abilities in the imaginary situation:

*If I had a million dollars, I **could** pay off all my debts.*
(= I'd be able to pay.)

Use *might* to talk about one of two or more possible consequences:

*If he handed himself in to the police, they **might** arrest him for theft.*

TIP *could* can be used in both clauses. In the *if* clause, *could* is the past simple of *can*: *If I could sing* …. In the main clause, *could = would be able to*: … *I could join your band.*

Real or imaginary?

When a present or future situation is real or likely, use a present verb form with *if*:

If you know where this man is, please contact the police.
(= It is possible that someone knows where the man is.)

When the situation is imaginary or unlikely, use the past simple with *if*:

If I knew where he was, I wouldn't tell the police.
(= I don't know where he is.)

See page 238: Summary of conditionals

Exercises

1 Choose the correct options. In one sentence, both answers are possible.

1 If they invited me, I *might / would* go I suppose, but I'm not sure.
2 I *couldn't / wouldn't* worry if I were you.
3 If there were too many people staying at Bill's, you *could / would* stay at ours.
4 I *mightn't / couldn't* accept a job from him, even if he offered me a million dollars!
5 Even if they doubled my salary, I still *couldn't / wouldn't* be able to afford to buy a house.
6 Honestly, I *might / would* help you if I could.
7 If I *was / were* you, I'd tell your parents the whole truth.
8 If someone *gives / gave* me too much change by mistake, I wouldn't say anything!

2 Correct the mistakes in the sentences below. There is one mistake in each sentence.

1 If the bank gave me all that money by mistake, I gave it all away to charity.

2 I'd fire the person who made the mistake if I'd be the bank manager.

3 If I were the customer, I leave the country and take on a new identity.

4 The bank might let the customer keep some of the money if he would give himself up.

5 I didn't recognise him if I saw him in the street.

6 If I were given a million dollars, I tried to spend it all as soon as I possibly could.

3 ⊙ **2.45 Write the correct form of the verbs in brackets. Use the past simple or *would*. Use contracted forms where possible. Then listen and check.**

1 A: If you are coming tonight, can you bring your car?
   B: Sorry, if I ¹_____ (have) it, I ²_____ (bring) it, but I've lent it to Zara.
2 A: What ³_____ (you/do), if you ⁴_____ (be) me?
   B: I think I ⁵_____ (accept) the job, but only if they ⁶_____ (offer) to give me a pay rise!
3 A: If you know where he is, please tell me.
   B: But I don't know! Honestly, if I ⁷_____ (know) where he ⁸_____ (be), you ⁹_____ (be) the first person I'd tell.

4 Complete these sentences so they are true for you.

1 If I have time tonight, I _____ .
2 If I didn't have to _____ tomorrow, I _____ .
3 I don't usually _____ if I don't have to.
4 I would never _____ even if I _____ .

88 *if* clauses 3: past perfect

Talking about things that did not happen, *would have, could have, should have*

They really shouldn't have let it go.

Oh no! Did you just see that! It could have got killed!

If the driver hadn't seen the dog in time, he'd have hit it.

Presentation

Use *if* + past perfect to talk about situations that did not happen in the past. The situation described is often the opposite of what really happened. Use *would have* + past participle to talk about the hypothetical past consequences of the imagined past situation:

imagined past situation	imagined past result
if + past perfect **If the driver hadn't seen** the dog in time,	*would have* + past participle **he'd have hit** it.

Note: this is often referred to as the third conditional.

The contracted form for both *had* and *would* is *'d*:
*If **I'd** told you, **you'd** have told the police.*

Don't confuse the two forms. *Had* is followed by a past participle: *If I'd told you, … = If I **had** told you, …*

Would is followed by *have* + past participle: *You'd have told the police. = You **would** have told the police.*

would have, could have, might have

Use *would have* to describe the logical consequence of a hypothetical situation: *He **would** definitely **have** hit the dog (if he hadn't seen it in time).*

Use *could have* or *might have* to speculate on one of two or more possible consequences of a hypothetical past situation: *If the driver hadn't stopped in time, it **could/might have** got killed! (= This is one possible hypothetical consequence.)*

TIP You can use *couldn't have* to talk about a lack of ability in the past. In this case you cannot use *might have*, nor can you use an *if* clause: *The driver couldn't have reacted any quicker.* (= it was physically impossible)

Real or imaginary?

When you want to talk about a real past situation, use *if* + past simple:

If you knew the dog wasn't on the lead, why didn't you warn the driver?

If you knew = you did know.

Compare it with a sentence using *if* + past perfect:

If I'd known the dog wasn't on the lead, I would have warned the driver.

If I'd known = I didn't know.

You often use *if* + a real past situation to express criticism of a past action.

should have, ought to have

Use *should have* and *ought to have* to talk about the correct or morally right thing to do in a past situation. You often use these forms to criticise past actions:

*If they couldn't control the dog, it **shouldn't** (or **ought not to**) have been off the lead.*

*If you knew the dog was loose, you **ought to have** (or **should have**) warned the driver.*

Exercises

1 Choose the correct options.

1 If I'd *arrive / arrived* on time, I'd *have / had* spoken to him before he left.

2 If my phone *hadn't / wouldn't have* run out of battery, I'd *called / have called* you.

3 I *hadn't arrived / wouldn't have arrived* late if my car *hadn't / wouldn't have* broken down.

4 They'd never *found out / have found out*, if he *hadn't / wouldn't have* said something.

5 I think we *could have / had* won, if we'd *try / tried* harder.

6 If you'd really *want / wanted* to come, you'd *found / have found* a way.

2 Complete the sentences about the imagined past situations.

1 The teacher was very angry with him because he hadn't done his homework.
The teacher wouldn't have been _____ so angry with him if he had done his homework.

2 I was very tired this morning because I went to bed late last night.
If I _____ late last night, I _____ so tired this morning.

3 You didn't tell me it was her birthday, so I didn't bring her a present.
If you _____ her birthday, I _____ a present for her.

4 I passed the exam because you helped me.
I _____ the exam if you _____ me.

5 I didn't see you, so I didn't say hello.
I _____ hello if _____ you.

6 I didn't miss my train because it was delayed.
If the train _____ on time, I _____ it.

3 Complete the sentences using the verbs in the boxes.

| might have   would have   should have |

1 That was a very silly thing to do! You really _____ been more careful.

2 If I'd paid more attention, I _____ learnt something new.

3 If she'd won the competition, she _____ been the first woman to do so.

| could have   shouldn't have   wouldn't have |

4 If you'd paid more attention, you _____ got lost.

5 If you didn't know what you were doing, you _____ been on the boat!

6 That was very irresponsible. Someone _____ got hurt.

4 ⓑ2.46 **Write the correct form of the verbs in brackets. Then listen and check.**

A: You missed a good concert last night. You really should have been there.

B: But I was!

A: If you [1] _____ (be) there, why [2] _____ (I/not/see) you?

B: I was in the gallery. If you [3] _____ (look) up, you [4] _____ (see) me. I waved at you, but you didn't wave back.

A: If I [5] _____ (not wave) back, it [6] _____ (be) because I couldn't see you! Why didn't you text me or something? If you [7] _____ (send) a text, we [8] _____ (go) out for a drink or something.

B: I tried, but I didn't have any credit on my phone. And anyway, I had to go home early.

89 *if* clauses 4: past simple and past perfect
Mixed time references

Presentation

In conditional sentences describing unreal situations, the *if* clause and the main clause do not have to refer to the same time.

An imagined situation in the present (*If I didn't have to work late every night*) or the future (*If I didn't have to do an exam next week*) could have had an effect on the past:

- present situation, past consequence: *If you weren't such a good friend, you wouldn't have called me.* (= We are good friends; you did call me.)
- future situation, past consequence: *If I didn't have a meeting later today, I would have gone to that party last night.* (= I didn't go to the party.)

An imagined situation in the past (*If you hadn't called me*) can have an imagined consequence in the present or future:

- past situation, present result: *If you hadn't called me, I'd still be asleep.* (= You called me; I am not asleep.)
- past situation, future result: *If I hadn't lent my car to my brother, I could take you to the airport this afternoon.* (= I lent my car; I can't take you this afternoon.)

Use the following verb forms to describe the situations and their consequences.

	situation	consequence/result
Present or future time	*If* + past simple	*would, could, might* + infinitive or *be* + *-ing*
Past time	*If* + past perfect	*would have, could have, might have* + past participle

Note: sentences of this type that include more than one time reference are often referred to as mixed conditionals.

Exercises

1 Match 1–4 with A–D.

1 If he wasn't so easy going, _____
2 If Don hadn't told me about the exhibition, _____
3 If he wasn't the boss's husband, _____
4 If I'd finished this work last night, _____

A I'd be going to the beach with everyone else.
B I'd have told him exactly what I thought of him!
C I wouldn't be here.
D I think Jeff might have hit him!

2 Choose the correct options.

1 If I didn't have so much work on at the moment, I *would / couldn't* have accepted their invitation to go away for the weekend.

2 If we hadn't had that stupid argument, I suppose we *might / wouldn't* still be together now, but I'm not sure.

3 If he'd explained the situation better, they *wouldn't do / could have done* something to help.

4 I *wouldn't / could* have trusted him if he weren't so arrogant and aggressive.

5 If you hadn't told him about the money, everything *might / couldn't* still be OK.

6 If you knew more about him, you *might / shouldn't* have reacted differently.

3 Read the situations, then complete the sentences using the verbs in brackets and the past simple, past perfect and *would*.

1 John went to a job interview, but he didn't get the job because he was too shy.
   If he _____ (be) so shy, I'm sure he _____ (get) the job.

2 My boss was looking for an assistant who can speak Japanese. I don't speak Japanese, so I didn't apply for the job.
   I _____ (apply) for the job if I _____ (speak) Japanese.

3 My brother needed a lift to the airport, but I don't have a car.
   If I _____ (have) a car, I _____ (give) him a lift to the airport.

4 I passed my exams, so my parents bought me a new computer.
   If I _____ (not pass) my exams, I _____ (still/use) my old computer.

5 You were out late last night. You're feeling very tired this morning.
   If you _____ (go) to bed early, you _____ (not/feel) so tired now.

6 You didn't listen to my advice. Now you're in trouble.
   If you _____ (listen) to my advice, you _____ (not/be) in trouble.

4 Complete these sentences so that they are true for you.

1 If I'd been born ten years earlier, I'd/I wouldn't _____ .
2 If I knew how to _____ , I'd/I wouldn't have _____ .
3 If I hadn't _____ yesterday, I'd/I wouldn't be _____ today.

90 Review of units 86 to 89

Grammar

1a Add *if* to the sentences below. Add commas where necessary.

1 I'd think again I were you.

2 I get home early enough I'll call you.

3 I'd have bought the other one I'd had enough money.

4 You were so sure about the answer why didn't you say something?

5 You want to bring a pet with you please let us know beforehand.

6 Remember to check the oil and tyres you're going on a long car journey.

1b In which sentence above can you replace *if* with *when* without changing the meaning of the sentence? _____

2 Find two main clauses (A–H) to match each of the *if* clauses (1–4) below.

1 If you can't come tomorrow, _E_ / _H_

2 If I didn't have so much work on, _____ / _____

3 If I'd passed the test, _____ / _____

4 If you hadn't been there to catch me, _____ / _____

A I'd have loved to have come to the party last night.

B I'd be driving my own car by now.

C I'd be in hospital right now!

D I'd be more than happy to help you.

E I'll let you know what happened in the meeting.

F I might have broken my back!

G they'd have given me the job.

H you should at least send her a card.

3 Write the correct forms of the verbs in bold.

1 **need**

a If you _____ help last night, why didn't you ask?

b If you _____ anything, just let me know.

c If you _____ help, who would you ask?

d If he _____ help last night, he'd have asked you.

2 **be**

a If I _____ you, I'd think about getting a new car.

b If you _____ planning a holiday, visit our new website.

c If you _____ born 50 years earlier, how would your life have been different?

d If you _____ at the party, you must have met Zack.

3 **win**

a If I _____ a million pounds, I'd throw a huge party.

b If we _____ the match tonight, we'll go into the finals.

c If she _____ the competition, she'd have been on TV.

d If he _____ the last race, he should stand a good chance of winning this one, too.

4 Choose the correct options to complete the conversation.

A: If we [1]*want / wanted* to finish this job in time, we're going to have to work all night!

B: If we [2]*wasted / hadn't wasted* so much time on the photos at the beginning of the week, we [3]*'d have finished / 'll have finished* by now!

A: I know! Do you think if we [4]*asked / 'd ask* for more time, they [5]*'d give / gave* us an extension? Maybe until the end of the weekend?

B: I really don't think so!

A: What, even if we [6]*'d said / said* that we're sure it'd make a big difference to the quality of the final product?

B: Well, you can try if you [7]*want / wanted*. If you [8]*'ll succeed / succeed*, [9]*I buy / I'll buy* a bottle of champagne to celebrate! Mind you, if they [10]*gave / give* us an extension, it'll mean having to work all weekend!

A: I know, but what else can we do?

Grammar in context

5 **⌖2.47** Match the two halves of the sentences in the quiz. Write your answers in the grid. Then listen and check.

1	2	3	4	5	6	7	8	9	10
f									

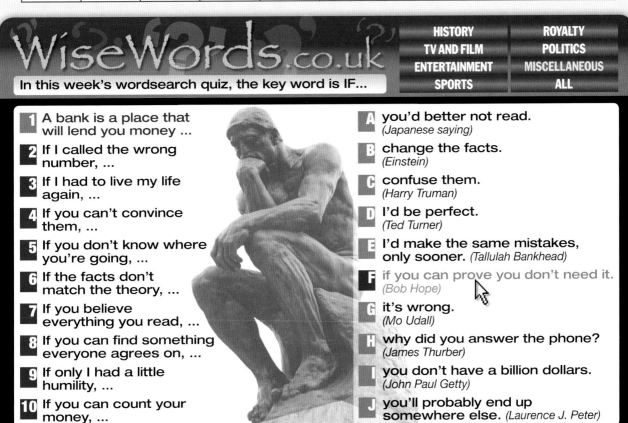

WiseWords.co.uk

HISTORY	ROYALTY
TV AND FILM	POLITICS
ENTERTAINMENT	MISCELLANEOUS
SPORTS	ALL

In this week's wordsearch quiz, the key word is IF...

1 A bank is a place that will lend you money ...

2 If I called the wrong number, ...

3 If I had to live my life again, ...

4 If you can't convince them, ...

5 If you don't know where you're going, ...

6 If the facts don't match the theory, ...

7 If you believe everything you read, ...

8 If you can find something everyone agrees on, ...

9 If only I had a little humility, ...

10 If you can count your money, ...

A you'd better not read.
(Japanese saying)

B change the facts.
(Einstein)

C confuse them.
(Harry Truman)

D I'd be perfect.
(Ted Turner)

E I'd make the same mistakes, only sooner. *(Tallulah Bankhead)*

F if you can prove you don't need it.
(Bob Hope)

G it's wrong.
(Mo Udall)

H why did you answer the phone?
(James Thurber)

I you don't have a billion dollars.
(John Paul Getty)

J you'll probably end up somewhere else. *(Laurence J. Peter)*

Pronunciation: *'d, had* and *would*

6 **⌖2.48** Listen to the sentences below. Circle *had* and *would* if they are contracted to *'d*.

1 If I had more money, I would not need to work so hard.

2 If I (had) known, I would have said something.

3 If he had any sense, he would have apologised to her immediately.

4 If she had really felt that offended, she should have said something.

5 I would have thought twice about accepting the job if it had been me.

Listen again and repeat the sentences.

Listen again

7 **⌖2.49** Listen to two people talking about a concert and answer the questions.

1 Were both people at the same concert?

2 Did they see each other?

3 Why couldn't the man send a text message?

4 Why couldn't he go for a drink afterwards?

91 *wish / if only*

Girlfriend: OK, well, if you're not coming, you can at least wish me good luck!

Boyfriend: If only I could come. I really wish I didn't have this meeting tonight. But you know how it is – I have to go. If only you'd told me about it earlier, I could have asked Bob to go in my place.

Girlfriend: I wish you'd stop lying! I know you hate these things. If only you'd be honest about it for once!

Presentation

Use *wish* and *if only* to talk about regrets and to describe an imaginary situation which is the opposite of the real situation.

Past simple

Use the past simple to talk about present or future situations using a stative verb:

*I wish / If only I **had** more time.* (But I don't have time.)

*I wish / If only I **wasn't / weren't*** so busy.* (But I am very busy.)

*You can use *was* or *were* with *I, he, she* and *it*. *Were* is more formal. (See Unit 87)

could

Use *could* to talk about abilities and possibilities:

*I wish / If only I **could** read.* (but I can't read)

*I wish / If only I **could** come with you.* (but I can't)

would

Use *would* to talk about a desire for someone to do something differently or for a situation to be different. You often use *would* to talk about another person's annoying habits or an annoying situation:

*I wish / If only you **wouldn't** do that.* (but you insist on doing that annoying thing.)

I wish / If only you'd stop worrying. (but you don't stop)

Notice that you cannot use the same subject in both clauses with *would*: *I wish I wouldn't work so hard.* ✗ (say *If only I didn't have to work so hard.*)

*I wish **you wouldn't** work so hard.* ✓

Past continuous

Use the past continuous to talk about . . .

- actions in progress at the present time: *I wish / If only it **wasn't raining**.* (but it is raining)

- future plans and intentions: *I wish / If only I **wasn't working** this evening.* (but I am working this evening)

Past perfect

Use the past perfect to talk about past situations:

*I wish / If only you**'d told** me about it earlier.* (but you didn't tell me)

*I wish / If only I **hadn't done** that.* (but I did)

could have

Use *could have* to talk about lost opportunities in the past:

*I wish / If only I **could have** found someone to cover for me.* (but I couldn't)

*I wish / If only you **could have** been there.* (but you weren't)

Exercises

1 Choose the correct options.

1 I wish I *knew / would know* how to play golf.

2 You speak Russian so beautifully. I wish I *could / would* speak Russian like you.

3 I wish you *came / were coming* to the party this evening.

4 This film is awful! I wish I *stayed / 'd stayed* at home.

5 I wish I *could have met / would have met* your father.

6 A: I'm bored!

   B: I wish you *weren't saying / wouldn't say* that!

2 (2.50) **Look at the pictures and complete the people's thoughts using the verbs in brackets. Then listen and check.**

1 I wish I _____ (read) Japanese.

2 If only I _____ (bring) my umbrella.

3 I wish it _____ (be) so hot!

4 I wish you _____ (bite) your nails all the time!

5 If only I _____ (not/go) home tomorrow.

6 If only I _____ (have) enough money.

3 Complete the sentences so that they are true for you.

1 I wish I were _____.

2 I wish I could _____.

3 If only I wasn't _____ tomorrow.

4 If only I hadn't _____.

193

92 Alternatives for *if*

unless, so/as long as, provided/providing, inversion with *were to* and *had*

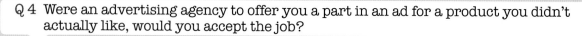

RightorWrong.com | Home | Registration | Sign In | Help | Quizzes | Links | Contact Us

How honest are you? part 3

Q 3 If you were to find a wallet on the street, would you hand it in to the police?

A   Yes, I would, unless it had a lot of money in it!
B   Yes, provided there was something that showed who the owner was, like a bank card or a driving licence.
C   No, I'd keep it, so long as no one saw me pick it up.

Q 4 Were an advertising agency to offer you a part in an ad for a product you didn't actually like, would you accept the job?

A   Yes, so long as I thought the product was harmless.
B   No, I would never sell a product unless I really believed in it.
C   Yes, provided the money was good enough!

Presentation

unless

Unless = *if … not* or *except if …*

I would never sell a product **unless** *I really believed in it.*
(= If I didn't believe in it, I wouldn't sell it.)

I won't go **unless** *you go too.* (= I'll only go if you go.)

so / as long as, provided/providing

These expressions mean *only if* or *on condition that.*

I'd keep the wallet **as long as** *no one saw me pick it up.*

Provided/providing are more formal than *as/so long as.*

I would accept the job **provided** *the money was good enough.* (= only if the money was good enough)

If I were to …, Were I to …, Had I …

In *if* clauses which talk about imaginary future situations, you can replace the past simple with *were + to + infinitive* to emphasise the improbability of the situation.

If I saw him … → *If I were to see him …*

If you won … → *If you were to win …*

It is also possible to drop *if* and invert the order of the subject and *were*:

If I were to see him … → *Were I to see him …*

If you won … → *Were you to win …*

Were I to is far less frequent than *If I were to.*

You cannot use *were … to …* to talk about imaginary present situations.

If I knew how to swim (but I don't) … *Were I to know how to swim …*

However, you can use inversion with the verb *to be* + adjective to talk about imaginary present situations:

Were I rich, I'd live a life of luxury.

In *if* clauses which talk about imaginary past situations, you can drop *if* and reverse the order of *had* and the subject.

If I'd known … → *Had I known …*

TIP The inverted forms are more formal and distant than standard *if* clauses.

Exercises

1 (2.51) **Write *unless* or *as long as* in the gaps. Then listen and check.**

1 A: Would you steal from a member of your own family?

   B: No, not _____ I really, really had to.

2 A: Can I borrow your bike?

   B: Yes, _____ you bring it back before five.

3 A: You know who the winner is, don't you? Go on, you can tell me.

   B: OK, but only _____ you don't tell anyone else. It's supposed to be a secret.

4 A: Would you like to sit by the window?

   B: Yes, please. _____ you want to sit there, of course.

5 A: Are you going out this afternoon?

   B: No, I don't think so, _____ Paul calls me to play football.

6 A: Would you jump from a flying aeroplane?

   B: Yes, _____ I had a parachute!

2 **Rewrite the sentences using the word or words in bold.**

1 I'll get the bus if Glen can't take me in the car.

   unless I'll get the bus unless Glen can take me in the car.

2 Give me £5.00 and I'll clean your car for you.

   provided _____

3 We could go out to eat, or if you prefer, we could stay at home and order a takeaway.

   unless _____

4 You can come in, but you have to leave before my parents get back.

   as long as _____

5 I really didn't want to do it if Simon wasn't going to help me.

   unless _____

3 **Rewrite the *if* clause using *were to* or *had*.**

1 If I'd known you were coming, I'd have made more food.

   Had I known ...

2 If he found out about all your lies, you'd lose your job.

3 If I lost my job, it'd be very hard to find another one in the same town.

4 If we'd got here a little sooner, we'd have seen the start of the match.

5 If I'd never met you, my life would have been very different.

6 If we could start again, things would be so much better.

93 Connectors 1: contrast
although, though, even though, despite, in spite of

Mountain marathon goes ahead despite worst July weather in ten years.

In spite of repeated warnings of bad weather, the annual mountain marathon went ahead as planned. And although more than half of the runners failed to complete the course due to the wet conditions, the winner, Matthew Goldy of Bethesda, managed to set a new record, running the race in a little over two hours and 40 minutes.

Presentation

Use *although*, *despite* and *in spite of* to contrast two situations and to say that something is surprising or unexpected:

They had the worst July weather in ten years. The race went ahead as planned. →

***Despite** the worst July weather in ten years, the race went ahead as planned.* (It is surprising that the race took place, considering the weather conditions.)

although, though, even though

Although, *though* and *even though* are conjunctions. You use them to join two sentences. They can be used at the beginning of the sentence, in which case the clause is followed by a comma, or in the middle of a sentence, in which case no comma is needed.

***Although** they knew it was going to rain⊙ the race went ahead as planned.*

*The race went ahead **even though** they knew it was going to rain.*

Though is slightly less formal than *although*. You use it in the same way as *although*, with the same meaning:

***Though** they knew it was going to rain, the race still took place.*

You can also use it at the end of a sentence. This use is more frequent in informal speech.

*They knew it was going to rain. The race still took place, **though**.*

When you use *though* at the end of the sentence, use a comma before it to separate it from the rest of the clause.

Use *even* to strengthen and emphasise *though* (but not *although*): ***Even though** they knew it was going to rain, that didn't stop the race.*

*They didn't take any dry clothes **even though** they knew it was going to rain.*

You cannot use *although* or *even though* at the end of a sentence.

despite, in spite of

Despite and *in spite of* are prepositions. They are followed by a noun, pronoun or the *-ing* form of the verb: ***Despite** the weather, the winner set a new record.*

*The winner set a new record **in spite of** the weather.*

***Despite/In spite of** running the whole race in a storm, the winner set a new record.*

***Despite/In spite of** this, the winner set a new record.*

You can also use *despite* and *in spite of* with *the fact that* + clause: ***Despite/In spite of the fact that** it rained heavily throughout the race, the winner set a new record.*

When *despite* or *in spite of* comes at the beginning of the sentence, the clause is followed by a comma. In the middle of a sentence, no comma is needed.

Exercises

1 **Complete the sentences with the words in brackets. Add commas where necessary.**

1   *Although*
   ∧He fell once or twice before reaching the finishing line, he still completed the race. (although)

2   We really enjoyed our holidays the awful weather. (despite)

3   I felt really tired the next morning I'd had a good night's sleep. (even though)

4   The fact that more than half of the runners didn't actually complete the race it was still a huge success. (in spite of)

5   The job's well paid it's not particularly challenging. (although)

6   All the talk of reform and modernisation nothing has really changed. (despite)

2 (2.52) **Choose the correct connector. Then listen and check.**

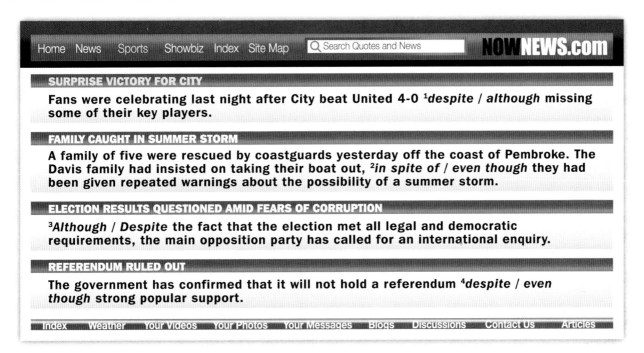

Home   News   Sports   Showbiz   Index   Site Map   🔍 Search Quotes and News   **NOW NEWS.com**

SURPRISE VICTORY FOR CITY
Fans were celebrating last night after City beat United 4-0 ¹*despite / although* missing some of their key players.

FAMILY CAUGHT IN SUMMER STORM
A family of five were rescued by coastguards yesterday off the coast of Pembroke. The Davis family had insisted on taking their boat out, ²*in spite of / even though* they had been given repeated warnings about the possibility of a summer storm.

ELECTION RESULTS QUESTIONED AMID FEARS OF CORRUPTION
³*Although / Despite* the fact that the election met all legal and democratic requirements, the main opposition party has called for an international enquiry.

REFERENDUM RULED OUT
The government has confirmed that it will not hold a referendum ⁴*despite / even though* strong popular support.

Index   Weather   Your Videos   Your Photos   Your Messages   Blogs   Discussions   Contact Us   Articles

3 **Join the two sentences using the word or words in bold.**

1   We have worked together for more than five years. I don't really know him that well.
   despite   *Despite having worked together for more than five years, I don't really know him that well.*

2   We hardly ever go to the beach. We live near the coast.
   although

3   They have had a lot of problems. He still loves her.
   in spite of

4   The concert was cancelled. We had a great time last night.
   even though

5   He failed all his exams. He worked really hard.
   despite

94 Connectors 2: reasons and purposes
as, since, because, because of, due to, in order to/that, so as to, so that

Since Nik was a boy, he's been afraid of lifts. And since he lives in a flat on the 21st floor, this means he has to climb 21 flights of stairs in order to get home every day. He also has to walk down 21 flights so that he can get to work or to the shops.

When he first moved into his flat, just under a year ago, it took him 20 minutes to climb the stairs. But because of his daily stair-climbing workouts, he soon became very fit. He now runs from the ground floor to his front door in just under three minutes.

As 21 floors are no longer a challenge, Nik has signed up for his first international tower running race. He will be running up 10,000 steps in the company of professional athletes, so that he can put his new-found stair-running fitness to the test!

Presentation

as, since

The conjunctions *as* and *since* can be used as:

- conjunctions of time:

  as = while, at the same time

  *He often listens to podcasts **as** he runs up the 21 flights to his flat.*

  since = starting from a certain event or point in time

  ***Since** Nik was a boy, he's afraid of lifts.*

- conjunctions that introduce an explanation of why someone does something or why a certain situation exists:

  ***As / Since** he's afraid of lifts, he has to go up the stairs.*

because, because of, due to

You can also use *because*, *because of* and *due to* to introduce an explanation of why someone does something or why something happens. *Because* is a conjunction and is followed by a clause. *Because of* and *due to* are both prepositions and are followed by a noun or *-ing* form of the verb.

because + clause: *Nik climbs the stairs **because** he's afraid of lifts.*

because of / due to + noun: *Nik has to climb the stairs **because of / due to** his fear of lifts.*

because of / due to + *-ing* form: *Nik is fit **because of / due to** climbing so many stairs.*

in order to, in order that, so as to, so that

Use these expressions to introduce the intended purpose of an action.

Use *in order to* and *so as to* + infinitive: *He has to climb 21 flights of stairs in **order to** / **so as to** get home every day.*

To form the negative, use *in order not to* + infinitive: *He has to be very careful **in order not to** fall.*

Use *in order that* and *so that* + clause: *He has signed up for a tower running race **in order that** / **so that** he can test his fitness.*

In informal speech and writing, it is possible to omit *that* after *so*: *He's running the race **so** he can see how fit he is.*

Exercises

1 Choose the best position, a or b, for the words in bold.

1 **because** (a) _Because_ our flat is on the first floor on a busy street, (b) _____ it can get very noisy.

2 **as** (a) _____ there are three bars on our street, (b) _____ it gets particularly noisy at night.

3 **due to** (a) _____ it's also noisy (b) _____ the buses and taxis that drive by at all hours.

4 **in order to** (a) _____ I have to wear ear plugs (b) _____ get to sleep at night.

5 **so** (a) _____ my wife sometimes takes sleeping pills (b) _____ she can sleep through the noise.

6 **so that** (a) _____ our children sleep in the back room (b) _____ the noise doesn't disturb them.

7 **since** (a) _____ early mornings are the only quiet time (b) _____ the bars are shut and there's very little traffic.

8 **as** (a) _____ I like to sleep late when I can, (b) _____ the mornings are so quiet.

2 Choose the correct options.

1 They closed the road to traffic *in order to / in order that* let the procession through.

2 The shop remained closed for four days *so that / so as to* they could redecorate.

3 She opened the window *because / because of* it was hot in the car.

4 We could hardly see the road ahead of us *because / because of* the fog.

5 All classes were cancelled that week due to *the staff were ill / sickness among the staff.*

3 Join the two sentences using the connector in brackets.

1 I signed up for an intensive course. I wanted to learn to speak Chinese. (in order to)
In order to learn to speak Chinese, I signed up for an intensive course.

2 I didn't go out last night. I was feeling really tired. (as)

3 There was heavy rain last night. Some roads are closed to traffic. (due to)

4 He wanted to show her he still loved her. He bought her some flowers. (so as to)

5 You don't really like football. I didn't buy you a ticket for the match. (since)

6 A new law has been passed. Many small businesses will close. (because of)

7 One hundred new schools have been built. More children have access to education. (in order that)

8 We can go out tonight. My brother has offered to babysit. (so)

95 Review of units 91 to 94

Grammar

1 Match 1–8 with A–H.

1 I wish it would stop raining   A

2 If only we'd known about the problem sooner, _____

3 There's no way you're going to get a place on the course _____

4 You are free to use the university parking facilities _____

5 We had a great holiday _____

6 In spite of all the problems, _____

7 Tom had to get a second job _____

8 We're leaving at 6.30 _____

A   because I want to go out for a walk.

B   even though the weather was really awful.

C   in order to pay off his debts.

D   provided you pay a monthly fee.

E   so that we get to the airport in plenty of time.

F   unless you're a personal friend of the director.

G   we could have done something about it.

H   we still managed to have a good time.

2 Correct one mistake in each sentence.

1 If only I ~~have~~ ^{had} more time!

2 I wish I weren't going to that party last night.

3 Were you win the lottery, what would you do with the money?

4 I won't go to the meeting unless you don't come too.

5 No one will ever find out about it so long as you'll keep quiet!

6 The garden party went ahead as planned despite of the rain.

7 My father lent me some money so as I could buy a car.

8 Your flight has been delayed due to there's a staffing problem.

3 Complete the dialogues using the words in the box.

> as long as   despite   if only   in order to
> unless   wish

1 A: Why did they sell their car?

   B: _____ buy a new one.

2 A: I'm sorry, we've just sold the last ticket.

   B: Oh no, _____ I'd got here sooner!

3 A: So that's it then? We're closing down the business?

   B: Yes, _____ you've got a better idea.

4 A: So we can have the party in the flat? Are you sure?

   B: Yes, _____ you don't make too much of a mess.

5 A: They didn't win in the end.

   B: I know, _____ all that hard work.

6 A: Oh, I'm so sorry to hear that. I _____ I could do something to help.

   B: There isn't really anything anyone can do. But thanks for the offer.

4 Complete the second sentence so that it has a similar meaning to the first. Use no more than four words.

1 I would really like to go to the concert tonight, but I can't.

I wish _____ to the concert tonight.

2 It's a pity I forgot to phone my mother.

If _____ to phone my mother.

3 Even though we had lovely weather, we didn't spend much time on the beach.

Despite _____, we didn't spend much time on the beach.

4 Remember that you may not find a hotel room if you don't book well in advance.

Remember that you may not find a hotel room unless _____ well in advance.

5 The planes couldn't take off because of the strong wind.

The planes couldn't take off since _____ so strong.

Grammar in context

5 **Choose the correct options to complete the text.**

here'sHow
Got a question? Here's the answer!

HOME | FACT FINDER | PROFILE | DISCUSS | CONTACT US I ABOUT US I HELP | SEARCH

How to get over failing an exam

Like it or not, exams are part of life and, ¹*although / because* nobody actually enjoys doing them, we all have to take them. And most of us will probably, ²*despite / in spite* our best efforts, fail one at some point in our lives. So, ³*you were to / were you to* fail that all-important exam, here are some words of advice from people who've been there before and survived!

Step 1 Don't waste time saying 'I wish I ⁴*studied / 'd studied* more' or 'If only ⁵*I'd / I hadn't* paid more attention in class'. This will only make you feel worse.

Step 2 Talk to other students who failed the same exam. ⁶*Even though / Provided* it won't change the result, it might make you feel better.

Step 3 If you can, get a copy of the exam and study the mistakes you made ⁷*in order not to / in order that* repeat them in the next exam.

Step 4 Above all, be positive! You need to believe in yourself ⁸*since / so that* you go into the next exam focused and full of confidence.

Related articles:
Here's how… to study for an exam
Here's how… to apply for a course

Pronunciation: linking

6 (2.53) **Listen to the sentences below. Look at the phrases in bold. Notice how the words that end in a consonant sound link with the following word when it starts with a vowel.**

1   You can come **with us**, **as long as** you behave.
2   We couldn't go out **because of** the snow.
3   We managed to **arrive on** time **in spite of** the delays.
4   I **bought a** bike **in order to** cycle to work.
5   **If only** I hadn't had that last chocolate!

Listen again and repeat the sentences.

Listen again

7 (2.54) **Listen to four short news stories. Decide whether the sentences are true or false. Correct the ones that are false.**

1   Key City players did not play in last night's match.

2   The Davis family did not know about the storm.

3   The opposition party is not happy with the election results.

4   A referendum is going to be held.

96 Emphasis 1: *do, does, did*

Presentation

do, does, did for emphasis

You can add emphasis to affirmative sentences by adding:

- *do / does* before the main verb in the present simple:

  You look beautiful. → *You **do** look beautiful.*

  She looks beautiful. → *She **does** look beautiful.*

  Notice that the main verb is in the infinitive after *do / does*. (don't say *She ~~does looks~~ beautiful.*)

- *did* before the main verb in the past simple:

  I told you she'd be late. → *I **did tell** you she'd be late.*
  Notice that the main verb is in the infinitive after *did*. (don't say *~~I did told~~ you she'd be late.*)

For negative sentences using *don't, doesn't, didn't*, you add emphasis by using the full form *do not, does not, did not* and stressing *not*:

We don't need to hurry. → *We do **not** need to hurry!*

He didn't have to wait too long. → *He did **not** have to wait too long.*

Do not use *do / does / did* for emphasis with the verb *to be* and with continuous or perfect tenses. Add emphasis to these forms by using the full form (affirmative and negative). Do not use the contracted form:

We're late. → *We **are** late!*

We aren't late. → *We are **not** late!*

Everyone's waiting. → *Everyone **is** waiting.*

I've remembered the ring. → *I **have** remembered the ring.*

do with imperatives

You can add emphasis to an imperative sentence with *do*. It is often used to express anger or annoyance:

Hurry up! → ***Do** hurry up!*

Clean up your mess! → ***Do** clean up your mess!*

Exercises

1 *2.55* **Make each conversation more emphatic in two places. Use the two forms of *do* in brackets and change the main verb where necessary. Then listen and check.**

Conversation 1: (~~does~~ / did)

           does look

A: That cake ~~looks~~ delicious. Can I try some?

B: No, it's for later.

A: But you made it for my birthday.

B: Yes, but everyone's coming later. So wait!

Conversation 2: (do / do)

A: Why are Gretel and Colin smiling?

B: I don't know, but they seem very happy.

A: Maybe they have some good news for us.

B: Oh! I hope you're right.

2 **Make the sentences as short, direct and emphatic as possible. Start with the emphatic *Do ....***

1   Would you mind tidying up your bedroom.

   Do tidy up your bedroom _____ !

3   I'm asking you for the last time to slow down.

   Do _____ !

2   I wish you'd look where you're going.

   Do _____ !

4   Can you turn the TV down?

   Do _____ !

3 *2.56* **In each dialogue, speaker B contradicts speaker A using *do* or *did* for emphasis. Write B's response in 2–6. Then listen and check.**

1 A: If he was behind me, why didn't you say something?

    B: I did say something _____ !

2 A: You don't love me anymore, do you?

    B: I _____ you.

3 A: If I remember correctly, he doesn't eat meat.

    B: He _____ meat, but he doesn't eat fish.

4 A: Why hasn't Marjorie tried to call us?

    B: Well, maybe _____ to call. Check your voicemail.

5 A: I keep pressing the red button, but the TV doesn't work.

    B: The TV _____ . You have to switch it on at the wall as well!

6 A: I didn't realise it's Tuesday! I've got a lecture at ten. Why didn't you remind me?

    B: I _____ you, and anyway, you should have it in your diary.

97 Emphasis 2: cleft sentences

A: Hello. What would you like today?

B: Actually, what happened was that I was walking past your window when I saw your advert for part-time staff.

A: Right. It's the manager you need to see about that, but she isn't here at the moment. Basically, what you have to do is fill in this application form and she'll call you.

B: Thanks. So what's the job like?

A: Well the hours are long but the thing I like is the free lunch …

Presentation

A cleft sentence is a sentence which is divided (*cleft* means *divided*) into two parts. The introductory part of the sentence often uses the words *what, it* or *the thing* + the verb *be*:

I like the free lunch. → **What** *I like is the free lunch.*

The free lunch is **what** *I like.*

It's the free lunch I like.

The thing *I like is the free lunch.*

Cleft sentences with *what*

Use *what … be / … be what* to emphasise the noun:

What I like **is / are*** *the free lunches.*

The free lunches **is / are*** *what I like.*

* Notice that both *is* and *are* are possible when the noun is plural.

Use *what … do / did + be* to emphasise the verb:

Fill in this application form. → **What you do is** *fill in this application form.*

He applied for a new job. → **What he did was*** *apply for a new job.*

* Notice that when the verb in the *what* clause is in the past, the verb *to be* is also in the past.

• Use *what happened + be* to emphasise the rest of the sentence:

I was walking past when I saw your advert in the window. → **What happened was (that)** *I was walking past your window when I saw your advert for part-time staff.*

Cleft sentences with *it*

Use *it + is/was + emphasised language + relative clause:

You need to see the manager. → **It's the manager (who)** *you need to see.*

You sign your name on this line. → **It's on this line (that)** *you sign your name.* (= not the one above/below it)

You don't normally include the pronoun (*who, that*) in these cleft sentences.

See also Units 81 and 82: Relative clauses

Cleft sentences with *the thing*

Cleft sentences with *the thing … is/was* can emphasise:

• the noun: *I like the holidays.* → **The thing** *I like is the holidays.*

• the verb: *Talk to the manager.* → **The best thing to do is** *talk to the manager.*

Cleft sentences with *place, person, reason* or *way*

You can make other cleft sentences that introduce and emphasise information about place, person, reason or how something was done. The construction is the same as for cleft sentences with *the thing*.

The place *(where) he works is a fast food restaurant.*

The person *(who) you need to see is the manager.*

The reason *(why) I'm here is because I saw the advert in your window.*

The way *to do this is by filling in this form.*

Exercises

1 Match 1–5 with A–E.

1 What I like ....   A I like.
2 What he did was ....   B is the long holidays.
3 It's the long holidays ....   C I like is the long holidays.
4 What you need is ....   D a long holiday.
5 The thing ....   E take a long holiday.

2 Rewrite the first sentence as a cleft sentence.

1 I love the French fries in this restaurant.
   What I love about this restaurant _is the French fries_ .

2 Sign your name here and here.
   What you .... and here.

3 My brother has to wear a uniform and check everyone's identity.
   What my brother has .... and check everyone's identity.

4 There was a sudden crash and all the lights went out.
   What happened .... and all the lights went out.

5 They need to tell their teacher not me.
   It .... , not me.

6 I want to hear the facts, not everyone's opinion!
   It .... , not everyone's opinion.

7 I like the special effects in this movie.
   The thing I like .... the special effects.

8 You need to see the manager about your complaint.
   The person you need to see about your complaint ....

9 I'm waiting because I'd like to get tickets for the concert.
   The reason I'm waiting .... tickets for the concerts.

3 ⓑ2.57 Read the dialogues. Speaker B corrects speaker A using cleft sentences. Write B's sentences using the words in brackets. Then listen and check.

1 A: Doesn't Martin build model cars?
    B: No. _What Martin builds are aeroplanes._ (What / builds / aeroplanes)

2 A: Do I put this is in the oven now?
    B: No. .... (What / do / in the fridge)

3 A: Did they take the wrong train?
    B: No. .... (What happened / the wrong bus)

4 A: We need to call an electrician.
    B: No. .... (It / plumber / call)

5 A: We can't afford to go to the museums in London. It'll be so expensive.
    B: No. .... (The good thing about museums in London / they / free)

6 A: The car's broken down. Call the police!
    B: No. .... (The person / need to call / a mechanic)

98 Emphasis 3: negative and limiting adverbials

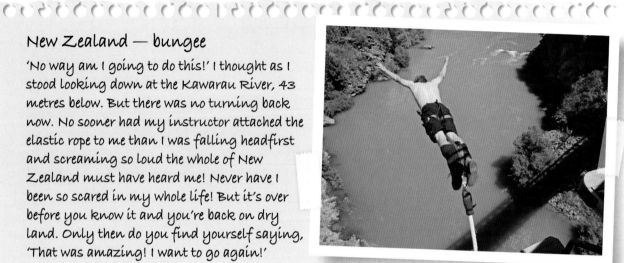

New Zealand — bungee

'No way am I going to do this!' I thought as I stood looking down at the Kawarau River, 43 metres below. But there was no turning back now. No sooner had my instructor attached the elastic rope to me than I was falling headfirst and screaming so loud the whole of New Zealand must have heard me! Never have I been so scared in my whole life! But it's over before you know it and you're back on dry land. Only then do you find yourself saying, 'That was amazing! I want to go again!'

Presentation

Negative and limiting adverbials

You can put negative and limiting adverbs or adverbials at the beginning of a sentence to add emphasis:

Never have I been so scared in all my life.

Only then do you find yourself saying, 'That was amazing!'

This is more common in formal written English but you will also hear the structure in spoken English, for example:

No way am I going to do that!

Negative adverbials are expressions with the word *no*, *not* or *never*. They include *never before, at no time, no sooner … than, no way, not since* and *not until*.

Limiting (or restrictive) adverbials include *hardly … when, rarely, seldom* and expressions with *only* such as *only when, only after* and *not only*.

Seldom have I been so scared!

no sooner … than / hardly … when

These adverbials are followed by *than* and *when*:

*No sooner had he attached the elastic rope to me **than** I was falling …*

*Hardly had I reached the top **when** I was falling to the bottom …*

Inversion

After the adverbial, you must change the order of the subject and verb (this is called inversion).

With sentences with auxiliary verbs, use adverbial + auxiliary verb + subject:

*I've **never** been so scared in all my life. → **Never have I** been so scared in all my life.*

*We **haven't been** bungee-jumping **since we were in New Zealand**. → **Not since we were in New Zealand** have we been bungee-jumping.*

(Don't say ~~Never I have~~ been so scared … or *Not since we were in New Zealand* ~~we have~~ been bungee-jumping.)

TIP Remember that an adverbial starting with *Not since …* needs information about the time: *Not since we were in New Zealand …*

For sentences with the verb *to be*, you only invert the subject and the verb with no other changes:

*Never **was I** so happy to stand on solid ground.*

With verbs in the simple form, use adverbial + *do / does / did* + subject + main verb:

She rarely gets scared. → Rarely does she get scared.

Exercises

1 **Complete sentences 1–8 using the words in the box.**

| never   no (x2)   not (x2)   only   rarely   when |

1 Only _____ the exam had finally ended could I relax.

2 _____ do they reply to our letters any more. We hear from them about once a year.

3 _____ since the 19th century has anyone lived in that castle. The last family left in 1891.

4 _____ way are you going to convince me to climb that mountain!

5 Not _____ did he pass the test, but he also got the highest mark in his class.

6 _____ will I do that again. It was a terrifying experience.

7 _____ sooner had the fire started than the fire brigade arrived.

8 _____ once did they offer to clean up or cook during the whole six months they were here!

2 **Complete sentences 1–6 with the words in the correct order.**

1 was / I / going to / way
No way was I going to _____ let him win.

2 anything / had / they / seen /
Never _____ quite as beautiful.

3 had / they split up / sooner / than
No _____ they were back together again.

4 we / set off / had
Hardly _____ when someone in the group needed a rest.

5 win / did / only / she
Not _____, but she also broke a world record.

6 did / after years of hard work / Rachel / qualify
Only _____ as a doctor.

3 **Rewrite the first sentence starting with the adverb or adverbial.**

1 I have rarely tasted anything so disgusting!
Rarely _____ .

2 We had hardly started class when the fire alarm rang.
Hardly _____ .

3 It seldom rains at this time of year.
Seldom _____ .

4 My parents never want to go on a cruise again.
Never _____ .

5 You don't often see Michaela work that hard.
Not often _____ .

6 There's no way we're going to work for less money!
No way _____ .

7 There hasn't been an Olympic Gold medallist from our country since 1988.
Not since 1988 _____ .

4 **Complete these sentences so that they are true for you.**

1 Not once have I ever wanted to _____ .

2 Never have I been so scared as the time when I _____ .

3 Seldom do I _____ any more.

4 No way am I going to _____

99 Emphasis 4: *so, such, neither, nor*

> **ACROSS COURT**
>
> # Can this man be beaten?
>
> ▶ So predictable is the world of men's tennis nowadays that no one ever expects Ray Frederick to lose – even a set. And such is his confidence at present that he plays as if he doesn't believe he can be beaten, and neither do many of his opponents …

Presentation

so, such

You can place *so* or *such* at the beginning of a sentence to add emphasis:

So predictable is the world of men's tennis nowadays …

Such is his confidence that he plays as if he doesn't believe he can be beaten.

When you use *so* and *such* for emphasis, you must invert the verb and subject afterwards. This structure is normally used in formal writing more than speech.

Use *so* + adjective + inversion + *that* to emphasise the adjective:

*The victory was **so easy** that …* → ***So easy** was the victory that …*

*His serve is **so fast** that no one can return it.* → ***So fast** is his serve that no one can return it.*

> **TIP** *So* + adjective is often followed by a *that* clause. You can also replace *that* with a comma: *So fast is his serve that no one can return it. / So fast is his serve, no one can return it.*

Use *such* + *be* + noun to emphasise the noun:

He was so confident as he walked out on the court … → ***Such was his confidence** as he walked out on the court …*

His backhand is so powerful … → ***Such is the power of his backhand** …*

See also Unit 39 for more information on *so* and *such*.

neither, nor

After a negative sentence or clause, use *neither* or *nor* to add and emphasise more negative information. Invert the verb and the subject:

*I don't know who won the match and **neither do I care**.*

*You've never seen him play tennis and **neither have I ever seen him play golf**.*

*We couldn't afford the tickets and **nor could we watch it on TV**.*

You do not have to include the main verb after *neither / nor* when you are repeating the verb from the main clause:

*He never looked like losing the match and **nor did he** (lose the match).*

You can use *neither* or *nor*, but *neither* is more common in everyday speech.

See also Unit 27 for more information on *neither*.

> **TIP** You also use inversion with the short answers *So do I, So does he, Neither do I, Nor does he*, etc.

See Unit 19 for more information on short answers.

Exercises

1 Complete the text using the words in the box.

> nor   so   such

| News | Matches | Groups | Teams | Ticketing | Hospitality | Photos | **Yesterday's round up** | More ▾ |

Comfortable victory for Brazil

Early on in this World Cup final, Brazil were one goal down, but ¹_____ is the skill of this team that we never believed they would lose and ²_____ did any of their fans. By midway through the second half, they were four goals ahead. ³_____ comfortable was their lead that it was all over with fifteen minutes to spare.

2 Match 1–5 with A–E.

1 So loud _____

2 Such is _____

3 Rainer and Illona couldn't get tickets and _____

4 They promised not to disappoint the crowd _____

5 I didn't like the concert venue, _____

A   their popularity, tickets for their concerts sell out within hours.

B   and nor did they.

C   are concerts nowadays that it's damaging young people's hearing.

D   nor did I enjoy the music.

E   neither could I.

3 Rewrite the words in the correct order to make sentences.

1 the rollercoaster / they went on it again / that / ~~so enjoyable~~ / was
   So enjoyable _____ .

2 his generosity / ~~such~~ / that he gives / is / to many charities
   Such _____ .

3 and / him at backgammon / ~~you couldn't~~ / neither / could you beat / beat him at chess
   You couldn't _____ .

4 nor / she / ~~he didn't~~ / and / did / pay to get in
   He didn't _____ .

4 Rewrite the sentences using the words in bold.

1 Such is the power of his serve, no one can return the ball.
   so _____ his serve, no one can return the ball.

2 They didn't like the show and I didn't either.
   neither   They didn't like the show and _____ .

3 So skilled was the winning team that the other teams played for second place.
   such _____ that the other teams played for second place.

4 Neither of us wanted to go.
   nor   You didn't want to go and _____ .

100 Review of units 96 to 99

Grammar

1 **Underline the correct options in these emphatic sentences. In two sentences, both options are possible.**

1 I *do / did* tell you, but as usual you weren't listening!

2 Martha *does / did* love reading. She always has a book in her hand.

3 *What / It*'s good about this film is the scenery.

4 *What / The thing* you need to do is delete the software and reinstall it.

5 *Not / No* sooner had I put my coat on, than my boss asked me to stay and work late.

6 Rarely *have I / I have* met someone who's so difficult to talk to.

7 No one in the house saw the burglar climb in and *neither / nor* did any of the neighbours.

8 *So / Such* is the height of this mountain that every mountaineer wants to climb it.

2 **Correct the mistake in each sentence without removing the emphasis.**

1 Your mother does ~~looks~~ young in this photograph.
    look

2 I did said this film was very long.

3 Not only you were late but you were rude as well!

4 Not way am I jumping off that diving board.

5 Such strong is his desire to win, I think he'll do it.

6 Your car won't start and neither mine will!

3 **Write the words in brackets in the correct form.**

1 She _____ (do/know) where he's hiding but she won't say.

2 Such is their _____ (kind), they'll help anyone in need.

3 So _____ (taste) was the soup, I asked for another bowl.

4 She didn't enjoy family meals nor _____ (she/enjoy) family holidays.

5 Seldom _____ (Sandra/smile) since she lost her cat.

6 The best way _____ (learn) is by doing.

7 No way _____ (I/be going to) miss the final episode on TV tonight.

4 **Add emphasis to the sentences using the word(s) in brackets.**

1 The boy tried harder at school. (did)

2 I enjoy the excitement of sport. (It)

3 Log in using your username and password. (thing to do)

4 They go hang-gliding for the thrill. (reason)

5 I didn't get the job and he didn't either. (neither)

6 It really annoys me when people don't tell the truth. (what)

7 They are not going to pay £100 for a ticket. (no way)

8 Antonia works hard when she puts her mind to it. (does)

Grammar in context

5 Complete the article with the correct answer from 1–8.

gameON

New game release brings mixed reviews

→ Reviewed: **StreetBattle II**

¹_____ was the anticipation for the release of *StreetBattle II* that fans queued outside computer stores through the night. Not since *StreetBattle I* – the fastest-selling computer game of all time – ²_____ anything like it. 'We ³_____ expect it to be popular,' said Mike Bryan, a store manager, 'but we hadn't expected this.' ⁴_____ had he opened the doors than crowds of fans rushed in to be the first. 'We sold every copy within an hour.' One lucky fan, calling himself *Warhead* (after one of the characters in the game), explained, 'The places that you visit ⁵_____ so real. You really ⁶_____ feel like you're living inside them.' But not everyone is so happy about this kind of reality. ⁷_____ violent are some of the images that the game has come under criticism from parents and school teachers. Jean Cottrell is one parent who won't let her twelve-year-old son buy the game. '⁸_____ really object to is the way the makers of these games target children with horrifying images,' she said.

1	**A** So	**B** Such	**C** It
2	**A** have store owners seen	**B** store owners have seen	**C** store owners did see
3	**A** do	**B** did	**C** did not
4	**A** Not only	**B** No way	**C** No sooner
5	**A** is	**B** are	**C** do
6	**A** do	**B** so	**C** did
7	**A** So	**B** Such	**C** Nor
8	**A** It's	**B** The thing is	**C** What I

Pronunciation: emphatic sentence stress

6 🎧 **2.58** **Listen to these emphatic sentences. Underline the word with the most stress.**

1 You do look ill.
2 The whole story did happen.
3 I did not take your pen.
4 Such was the noise that we called the police.
5 We are not late.
6 Never have I been so scared.

Listen again and repeat the sentences.

Listen again

7 🎧 **2.59** **Listen to two conversations and correct the auxiliary *do* in sentences 1–4 where necessary.**

1 The cake doesn't look delicious.
2 The woman didn't make it for the birthday.
3 Gretel and Colin don't seem very happy.
4 The woman doesn't hope they have some good news.

1 Progress test (units 1 to 10)

1 Jamal's house _____ almost 200 years old.
   a is being   b is   c are

2 The Uyuni Salt Flats in Bolivia _____ incredibly valuable deposits of lithium.
   a contains   b are containing   c contain

3 Hyun Tae _____ the international news online every morning.
   a is reading   b read   c reads

4 I absolutely _____ to help you with your homework again!
   a refuses   b am refusing   c refuse

5 So, then the policeman _____ over the wall, shouting at the thief!
   a is jumping   b jumps   c jump

6 In the last chapter, the hero's wife _____ him for the soldier.
   a leaves   b is leaving   c leave

7 The sales representatives often _____ in the Chalgrove Hotel on the corner.
   a are staying   b stays   c stay

8 At the moment, Carol _____ six cats, I think!
   a is having   b has   c have

9 The pills sometimes _____ dizziness.
   a cause   b causes   c are causing

10 The government's _____ to control rising crime.
   a tries   b trying   c try

11 Where _____ ? It's after midnight!
   a do you go   b you goes   c are you going

12 Alfredo _____ studying Astrophysics this term.
   a does   b is   c are

13 The shops in the town centre _____ open later and later these days.
   a stays   b are staying   c stay

14 Sarah's brother _____ her DVDs without asking her.
   a always is borrowing   b borrows always
   c is always borrowing

15 Don't leave yet. The rain _____ down outside.
   a is pouring   b are pouring   c pours

16 It _____ a pity that the party has to be cancelled. We've invited so many people!
   a seems   b is seeming   c seem

17 Not everyone _____ that the winner deserved the cup.
   a agrees   b is agreeing   c does agree

18 _____ everything politicians tell you?
   a Are you believing   b Do you believe
   c Believe you

19 We _____ enough time to finish the exercise before lunch.
   a haven't got   b aren't having   c has not

20 Helen and Gary _____ to the chess club in the leisure centre.
   a are belonging   b doesn't belong   c belong

21 _____ milk in his tea, or lemon?
   a Is Ivan preferring   b Is Ivan prefers
   c Does Ivan prefer

22 The fire alarm _____ for almost half an hour now.
   a has been ringing   b is ringing   c rings

23 Who _____ the last piece of cheesecake?
   a takes   b has taken   c has been taking

24 Mr and Mrs Rossi _____ the café since 1987.
   a have been owning   b have owned   c own

25 _____ my keys? I can't find them anywhere.
   a Have you been seeing   b Do you see
   c Have you seen

26 The employment agency _____ its offices to Holborn.
   a moved recently   b has recently moved
   c has been recently moving

27 No, we _____ lunch yet. We're starving!
   a didn't have   b hadn't   c haven't had

28 Where _____ when you were in Paris?
a did you stay **b** have you stayed **c** do you stay

29 _____ the new Dan Brown novel yet?
a Have you read **b** did you read
c did you reading

30 So far, the weather this summer _____ really good.
a was **b** is **c** has been

31 Liam and I _____ our holiday back in December.
a have booked **b** booked **c** were booking

32 The surgeon _____ the operation to Mrs Dakers.
a already explained **b** has already explained
c already explains

33 She _____ in hospital before.
a has never been **b** was never
c was never being

34 How many times _____ you in London?
a does your mother visit **b** has your mother visited
c has your mother been visiting

35 Keith _____ at least 20 emails this morning.
a has been writing **b** was writing
c has written

36 'Where is Adrian?'
'He _____ to Paris for the weekend'.
a has gone **b** has been **c** has been going

37 I can't pay for the meal because someone _____ my wallet!
a stole **b** has been stealing **c** has stolen

38 News flash! The Prime Minister _____ to resign.
a has decided **b** decided
c has been deciding

39 How much money _____ in the January sales this week?
a did you spend **b** have you spent
c have you been spending

40 Before Hamid _____ to Cambridge, he had never seen snow.
a came **b** had come **c** comes

41 When news of the company closure was released, the employees _____ on strike for several days.
a were **b** had been **c** were being

42 Sarah _____ for the school for two years when Elena joined the staff.
a had been working **b** was working
c worked

43 Tanya is off work today. She _____ well for a few days now.
a isn't feeling **b** wasn't feeling
c hasn't been feeling

44 Before I went to Australia last summer, I _____ Europe!
a never left **b** had never been leaving
c had never left

45 The police _____ the area for two hours and they still hadn't found any clues.
a were searching **b** searched
c had been searching

46 Paul _____ Wanda and he knew he was going to marry her one day.
a has only just met **b** had only just met
c had only just been meeting

47 I'm sorry. I _____ ten tickets because you said you didn't want to come.
a had only been buying **b** have only bought
c had only bought

48 The band _____ long when there was a power cut and they had to stop.
a hasn't played **b** hadn't been playing
c wasn't playing

49 I _____ for almost an hour before I saw the outskirts of the town.
a walked **b** had been walking **c** had walked

50 I don't think she _____ the soup before she served it. It was so salty!
a had tried **b** had been trying **c** tried

2 Progress test (units 11 to 20)

1 .... the doors were opened, a lot of people had started queuing for tickets.
   a Before b While c Once

2 The train was almost empty .... it arrived at the last station.
   a after b while c by the time

3 Give me your empty plate .... you have finished. I'll do the washing-up.
   a as b when c while

4 The teacher collected in the homework .... the lesson had ended.
   a since b while c as soon as

5 Karen was first in the race .... the last bend. Then she was overtaken.
   a while b when c until

6 .... the Collins family had reached the coast, the children were really hungry.
   a By the time b While c Until

7 You should never eat or drink anything immediately .... doing a yoga class.
   a until b once c before

8 Daniel sometimes likes to have a glass of port .... dinner.
   a as soon as b once c after

9 We won't find out the exam results .... the end of May.
   a until b by the time c as soon as

10 .... Suzanna got the job in the bank, she had been unemployed for a year.
   a After b While c Before

11 The passengers waited on the platform .... the engineers repaired the train.
   a before b as soon as c while

12 Everyone in the courtroom went quiet .... the judge came in.
   a while b by the time c when

13 .... the glue on the handles is dry, you can paint the door.
   a When b Until c While

14 There .... be a cinema on the corner of Grafton Street when I was a child.
   a would b was c used to

15 Did May always .... feed the horses, or did you do it sometimes?
   a would b used to c use to

16 Jan .... never tell us why she left her job in the bank.
   a would b used to c wouldn't

17 Sarah just .... working so hard. The new job was a shock!
   a didn't use to b wasn't used to
   c didn't get used to

18 If you come here every day, you'll quickly .... the routine.
   a are used to b would be used to c get used to

19 We were just .... the new timetable when they decided to change it again.
   a getting used to b used c got used to

20 Mandy's dogs are .... going for a walk first thing in the morning.
   a used to b get used to c being used to

21 People .... use the tennis courts more at the weekend than during the week.
   a use to b get used to c used to

22 '........... the new wallpaper in her bedroom yet?'
   a Did she use to b Is she being used to
   c Has she got used to

23 'Which wallpaper .... ?'
   'The wallpaper with the orange stripes.'
   a she chooses b did she choose c chose she

24 How many eggs .... for this cake recipe?
   a need you b need c do you need

25 How long .... from New York to Denver?
   a is the flight b does the flight
   c takes the flight

26 .... for dinner tonight or tomorrow?
   a Coming your friends b Your friends are coming
   c Are your friends coming

27 I haven't seen you since the show. _____?
   a Enjoy you   **b** You enjoy it
   c Did you enjoy it

28 _____ enough soup? There's plenty left.
   a Have you   **b** Are you having
   c Have you had

29 You look absolutely awful! What _____?
   a the matter is **b** 's the matter **c** does the matter

30 What is Dan doing here? _____ today?
   a Doesn't he work   **b** Wasn't he working
   c Isn't he working

31 Can you tell me _____ the next train arrives?
   a when   **b** when does   **c** when is

32 Mum was wondering if the kids _____ their bedrooms?
   a have they tidied   **b** tidied they
   c have tidied

33 _____ be quiet? I'm trying to finish my essay.
   a Can you   **b** You can't   **c** Do you

34 Sarah _____ a car? How does she get to work?
   a hasn't got   **b** she's not got **c** hasn't she

35 Do you mind if _____ this seat? Thank you.
   a I will take   **b** I am taking   **c** I take

36 It's almost time for the lecture, _____?
   a isn't it   **b** is it   **c** isn't there

37 There have been too many accidents on the road this year, _____?
   a weren't there **b** aren't there **c** haven't there

38 Graziella doesn't live here any more, _____?
   a does there   **b** does she   **c** doesn't she

39 Let's see if we can beat the last record, _____?
   a shan't we   **b** won't we   **c** shall we

40 The management can't make a decision on that just yet, _____?
   a can they   **b** can it   **c** can't they

41 Pete is going to get a productivity bonus, _____?
   a isn't he   **b** is he   **c** he is

42 His house was sold for a high price, _____?
   a wasn't it   **b** didn't it   **c** is it

43 We really should stop buying chocolate, _____?
   a shouldn't we **b** should we   **c** don't we

44 Don't stand too close to the loudspeaker, _____?
   a won't you   **b** do you   **c** will you

45 'I haven't seen *Avatar* at the cinema.'
   '_____?'
   a So do I   **b** So haven't I
   c Neither have I

46 'I don't really understand what this article is about.'
   '_____!'
   a Neither do I **b** So don't I   **c** Nor I do

47 'My class couldn't find enough information on that topic.'
   '_____.'
   a Neither could we   **b** So couldn't we
   c We too

48 I'd really like to have a go on his motorbike.'
   '_____!'
   a So do I   **b** Neither would I   **c** So would I

49 'My next door neighbours aren't very friendly.'
   '_____ mine.'
   a So aren't   **b** Neither   **c** Neither are

50 'My dog hates the postman.'
   '_____?'
   a Doesn't it   **b** Does it   **c** Is it

3 Progress test (units 21 to 30)

1. I hope the red stripy socks are _____ . I packed them in your case.

   a your   **b** yours   **c** yourselves

2. 'Give me back my CDs!' 'But they aren't _____ !'

   a you   **b** yours   **c** your

3. Don't have another piece of cake. You'll make _____ sick!

   a yours   **b** you   **c** yourself

4. I met Grace at the shopping centre and we bought _____ a present.

   a each other   **b** yourselves   **c** us

5. The oven on this cooker is good because it can clean _____ .

   a it   **b** itself   **c** oneself

6. In some countries, businessmen bow to _____ when they meet.

   a each other   **b** themselves   **c** himself

7. There are lots of copper coins and a few _____ in the box.

   a silver coin   **b** silver ones   **c** silvers

8. Let's watch _____ on TV before dinner.

   a news   **b** a news   **c** the news

9. What on earth is that? It looks like _____ of jellyfish.

   a the kind   **b** a kind   **c** kind

10. It's difficult to get _____ from the call centre.

    a any information   **b** some informations
    c an information

11. They are finding it hard to find good _____ teachers in the Science department.

    a the Physics   **b** Physics   **c** Physical

12. 'What shall we have for supper?'
    'Let's defrost _____ and make some chips.'

    a the fishes   **b** fishes   **c** the fish

13. The law considers _____ to be nine tenths of the law.

    a a possession **b** possession **c** the possessions

14. That was _____ best curry I've ever had!

    a a   **b** the   **c** -

15. _____ are capable of hearing much higher frequencies than us.

    a Dogs   **b** The dogs   **c** A dog

16. Karen's sister learned to play _____ at the Paris Conservatoire.

    a the violin   **b** some violin   **c** a violin

17. Boris has applied to join _____ force.

    a the police   **b** a police   **c** police

18. How long have you lived in Tokyo? Can you speak _____ ?

    a Japanese   **b** a Japanese   **c** the Japanese

19. We need to go by _____ as there is no bus service here.

    a the taxi   **b** a taxi   **c** taxi

20. It's not a good idea to skip _____ breakfast.

    a -   **b** any   **c** the

21. My boss has booked a holiday in _____ Philippines.

    a island   **b** -   **c** the

22. That gold Mercedes parked outside is _____ .

    a the Bertrand's   **b** his Bertrand's
    c Bertrand's

23. The person who invented _____ zipper was Swedish.

    a the   **b** -   **c** a

24. 'Why are you going out again?' 'I forgot, I must get to _____ before it closes.'

    a the bank   **b** bank   **c** a bank

25. _____ is absolutely icy today! Wrap up warm!

    a Wind   **b** The wind   **c** A wind

26. _____ people can't stand the sight of blood.

    a Any   **b** Some   **c** No

27. There _____ biscuits left in the tin. Sorry!

    a aren't some   **b** are none   **c** aren't any

28 There must be a power cut. _____ of the lights are working.

a None   b No   c Not any

29 This cupboard is so full; there's _____ to put the boxes.

a no place   b not any space   c nowhere

30 I thought I heard _____ moving about upstairs!

a some person   b someone   c anybody

31 _____ thinks that James is Scottish, but he's actually Irish.

a Either   b Everybody   c Nobody

32 There's _____ time like the present!

a none   b not any   c no

33 _____ time Emma comes into the room, Joshua blushes!

a All the   b Every   c Each of the

34 We couldn't do _____ question four or question six. They were impossible!

a either   b or   c neither

35 _____ trees in the wood had to be checked for disease.

a All the   b Each   c All of

36 I had two keys for the house, but _____ of them would open the door.

a either   b none   c neither

37 The snow was falling heavily and _____ houses in the village were white.

a all of   b all   c all the

38 The twins shared _____ they owned.

a all   b everything   c each

39 I'd like _____ sugar with that, if that's alright.

a a little   b a bit   c little

40 It's difficult to tell _____ that second-hand car is worth.

a how many   b how much   c the more

41 Although we have used weedkiller, there are still _____ weeds in the lawn.

a a lot   b much   c lots of

42 Although there are a lot of good writers, too _____ of them make a living from writing.

a few   b little   c less

43 There were 400 guests and _____ them were in national costume.

a much of   b most   c many of

44 The meal was good but there wasn't _____ bread for everyone.

a enough of   b plenty of   c enough

45 The children were sleeping even though there was _____ of noise from next door.

a a great deal   b much   c enough

46 It took _____ days for the gloss paint to dry properly.

a plenty   b several   c much

47 That dish can hold a _____ of food. It'll be big enough for us all.

a lots   b plenty   c large amount

48 _____ British houses have a front and a back garden.

a Many of   b Most   c Most of

49 There aren't _____ language teachers in schools these days.

a enough   b enough of   c plenty

50 The results showed that _____ the candidates were of a very high standard.

a many   b little of   c most of

4 Progress test (units 31 to 40)

1 I really like that _____ vase in the shop window.
   a big red Italian   b red Italian big
   c Italian red big

2 Cleo had _____ wardrobe in her bedroom.
   a an old heavy walnut   b a walnut heavy old
   c a heavy old walnut

3 I'm looking on the internet for some _____ blouses.
   a Victorian silk pale blue
   b pale blue Victorian silk
   c silk pale blue Victorian

4 Pauline was bidding for a _____ desk in the auction.
   a French 17th century writing
   b 17th century French writing
   c writing 17th century French

5 A _____ saucer was hovering above the house.
   a strange oval silver   b silver oval strange
   c oval strange silver

6 The little cottage was neat _____ clean.
   a , and tidy, and   b , tidy and   c , tidy,

7 Please remember to put something in the box for _____ on your way out.
   a the poors   b the poor   c the poor ones

8 Whose is that _____ bike?
   a fantastic black Harley Davidson
   b black Harley Davidson fantastic
   c Harley Davidson black fantastic

9 _____ always makes their tea with boiling water.
   a A British person   b British   c A British

10 The tourist leaflets are all really _____ !
   a interested   b interesting   c interest

11 Everyone who is _____ about the new power station, please sign the petition.
   a concerning   b of concern   c concerned

12 Some domestic cleaning products can be _____ to the eyes.
   a irritable   b irritated   c irritating

13 My mother is very _____ pink roses.
   a fond about   b fond of   c fond with

14 What is it that Jason is _____ ? It seems very suspicious!
   a involved in   b involving in   c involving

15 Janice seems very angry _____ her sister at the moment. Do you know what she's done?
   a with   b at   c to

16 Most of the class is _____ studying grammar.
   a tired at   b tiring of   c tired of

17 The yellow jackets are _____ in the dark.
   a easy to see   b easy seeing   c easy for seeing

18 Mr Dunn opened _____ and took out a small box.
   a slow his desk drawer   b his desk drawer slow
   c his desk drawer slowly

19 Oh Selina! I am _____ !
   a truly sorry   b sorry truly   c truely sorry

20 _____ all wearing their seatbelts.
   a Fortunately, they were
   b They were fortunately
   c They fortunately

21 Su Yung _____ in his room.
   a plays often Korean pop loudly
   b often plays Korean pop loudly
   c plays loudly Korean pop often

22 The pretty little brown dog was _____ .
   a aggressive surprisingly
   b surprisingly aggressive
   c aggressively surprising.

23 The police _____ who was sitting on the wall.
   a spoke firmly to the teenager
   b firmly spoke to the teenager
   c spoke to the teenager firmly

24 The older children _____ .
   a watch TV usually in their bedrooms
   b usually watch TV in their bedrooms
   c in their bedrooms watch TV usually

25 Tom and Juanita are living _____ .
   a next door to us at the moment
   b to us next door at the moment
   c at the moment next door to us

26 The bus _____ at that stop.

   a often doesn't stop   **b** doesn't stop often
   c doesn't often stop

27 John _____ . When I phoned him, he was out.

   a wasn't at midday at home
   b at midday wasn't at home
   c wasn't at home at midday

28 Giacinta _____ a bike even though she's tried many times.

   a still can't ride   **b** can't still ride
   c can't ride still

29 Heinrich _____ deserve to pass the exam. He's done no work at all!

   a doesn't definitely   **b** definitely doesn't
   c does definitely not

30 _____ the new hairdryer I bought her.

   a She's already broken   **b** Already she's broken
   c She's broken already

31 My neighbours had _____ . It looks lovely.

   a last week painted their house
   b their house painted last week
   c painted last week their house

32 I'm hoping to _____ to see the Rembrandt exhibition.

   a go tomorrow to London
   b tomorrow go to London
   c go to London tomorrow

33 Tina earns a good salary but _____ rich!

   a certainly she's not
   b she's certainly not
   c she's not certainly

34 I _____ that there is a bird nesting in that tree.

   a have noticed just   **b** have just noticed
   c just have noticed

35 _____ their new house, and it's gorgeous!

   a Already we've seen   **b** We've already seen
   c We've seen already

36 My friend Anton can play the saxophone really _____ .

   a well   **b** goodly   **c** good

37 He worked so hard that he passed the final exam _____ .

   a easy   **b** in an easy way   **c** easily

38 There were _____ enough plates for all the guests.

   a hard   **b** hardly   **c** not hardly

39 Sarah hasn't been feeling very well _____ . I hope she's OK.

   a later   **b** lately   **c** late

40 The picture was _____ good, but not that good!

   a absolutely   **b** a bit   **c** quite

41 When they opened the curtains they saw that it was _____ day.

   a an absolutely fine   **b** absolutely a nice
   c an absolutely beautiful

42 The soup was _____ . It was perfect.

   a too hot   **b** hot enough   **c** enough hot

43 Francesca speaks Swahili _____ .

   a well really   **b** fairly well   **c** real good

44 _____ meat, as well as fish, in the restaurant.

   a They also serve   **b** Also they serve
   c They serve also

45 Although a lot of students did well in the exam, _____ got an A.

   a Franz just   **b** Franz only   **c** Franz alone

46 The food was so bad that _____ to eat it.

   a even the boys refused   **b** the boys even refused
   c even refused the boys

47 'I'm going to have a swim this afternoon.' '_____ ?'

   a Me too   **b** Me as well   **c** As well me

48 That was _____ film! I'd like to see it again.

   a such a wonderful   **b** a such wonderful
   c a so wonderful

49 The weather was _____ that they had to stay indoors all week.

   a such bad   **b** so bad   **c** even bad

50 There are _____ different kinds of ice cream.

   a such many   **b** too much   **c** so many

5 Progress test (units 41 to 50)

1 The second book was _____ the first, I thought.
   a the far best **b** far better as **c** far better than

2 That meeting was _____ I've ever had to face.
   a one of the hardest **b** a hardest
   c one of the harder

3 Gounod wrote _____ ballet music ever written.
   a some better **b** some of the best
   c the best of the

4 I'm afraid learning new dance steps _____ difficult as you get older.
   a gets more **b** more gets **c** gets most

5 The Volvo was _____ car in the race.
   a the fastest second **b** the next fastest
   c the second fastest

6 Some people think the Taj Mahal is the _____ building in the world.
   a most beautifulest **b** more beautiful
   c most beautiful

7 Alan has taken _____ anyone else on the trip. He's got thousands!
   a more photos as **b** the most photos than
   c more photos than

8 Yasmin makes a little _____ than Harriet.
   a less money **b** fewer money
   c not as much money

9 When it comes to jigsaw puzzles, _____ !
   a the harder the more **b** the harder the better
   c the more hard is best

10 Ian usually gives _____ than he can really afford to. He's so generous!
   a more **b** most **c** too much

11 Mrs Grant says that _____ you worry, the less you achieve.
   a more **b** the more **c** the less

12 As the sledge went down the hill it got _____ .
   a fast and fast **b** more fast **c** faster and faster

13 The birthday present _____ was the silver locket from my mum.
   a I appreciated the most **b** the most I appreciated
   c the more I appreciated

14 The staff emptied out the warehouse in _____ time.
   a the fastest **b** the fastest possible
   c the possible fastest

15 This pink rose is _____ fragrant than the white one.
   a slightly more **b** more slightly **c** a little bit

16 There are _____ more people in Paris than in Marseille, in fact twice as many.
   a far **b** a bit **c** much

17 If you drove _____ more carefully, you wouldn't keep on having accidents.
   a fairly **b** rather **c** a bit

18 This suitcase is not _____ that old one.
   a as heavy as **b** so heavy as **c** so heavy like

19 The blue shoes look _____ the red ones with that dress.
   a just as good like **b** as good just as
   c just as good as

20 It's amazing how much your cousin looks _____ you!
   a as **b** like **c** similar

21 The wall at the bottom of his garden is _____ as the fence.
   a nearly not so high **b** not nearly as high
   c not so high nearly

22 Jamal's Audi doesn't accelerate _____ as the BMW.
   a quite as quick **b** quite as quickly
   c so quickly quite

23 Helen's nephew is working _____ lab technician in Toronto at the moment.
   a like **b** as **c** as a

24 What was that? It sounded _____ wolf howling in the forest!
   a as if a **b** like a **c** as a

25 The alarm is set to ring _____ 6.30 sharp!
   a on **b** at **c** in

26 The nurse always brings round cups of tea _____ evening.
   a in the **b** at **c** at the

27 We should leave _____ about half an hour or we'll get stuck in the rush hour.

a for   b at   c in

28 Tom said he was going to move in _____ but I haven't seen him yet.

a on yesterday   b yesterday   c at yesterday

29 'When are you going to phone Adam?'
' I thought I'd phone him _____.'

a the Monday   b on Monday   c in Monday

30 'What day are you _____?'

a returning at   b returning   c returning in

31 _____ of the film, the hero is even more miserable than at the start!

a At the end   b In the start   c At the first

32 One of the first things you learn is to get to business meetings _____.

a in time   b at the time   c on time

33 Ulrike is hoping to find a job in Latvia _____ six months.

a during   b to   c for

34 The doorbell rang some time _____ midnight.

a since   b after   c for

35 The seeds should be planted some time _____ March and May.

a in   b between   c until

36 The film started _____ seven and eight o'clock. I'm not sure exactly when.

a for   b in   c between

37 I think the new library should be completed _____ the end of the year.

a by   b until   c between

38 It's been a long time _____ Sara had a really relaxing weekend.

a for   b until   c since

39 Shall we all meet _____ the theatre? I'll wait beside the entrance.

a into   b at   c to

40 There was a brilliant documentary on molluscs _____ TV yesterday.

a in   b at   c on

41 Stephen is going to live _____ Singapore for a couple of years.

a at   b in   c to

42 The Angel of the North is a statue that can be seen _____ a hill outside Gateshead.

a in   b at   c on

43 Oh no! It's almost nine o'clock. I should be _____ the staff meeting by now!

a at   b in   c on

44 The bank is very _____ the cinema on the High Street.

a close   b near   c next

45 Where are the theatre tickets? I think they're _____ the shelf in the hall.

a on top of   b in   c on

46 Mr Harland lives in that little house just _____ the bridge.

a by   b next   c between

47 Are you _____ a computer at the moment? You could check online.

a below   b near   c over

48 There was a beautiful old mirror hanging _____ the bed.

a over   b on   c above

49 The church stands in a clearing in the woods _____ the town.

a over   b on   c above

50 I spotted Carlo immediately _____ the crowd by the pool.

a among   b between   c on

6 Progress test (units 51 to 60)

1 The avalanche was moving quickly _____ the ski lodge in the valley.
   a to   **b** at   **c** towards

2 When Gordon walked into the garden, the dog lunged _____ him, growling fiercely.
   a to   **b** at   **c** for

3 This meat needs salt. Can you pass it _____ me, please?
   a at   **b** towards   **c** to

4 I think it's best if you turn the car round _____ the car park, not the road.
   a in   **b** into   **c** on

5 The train stopped at Didcot and three Greek tourists got _____ .
   a onto   **b** on   **c** into

6 I know you're in there. Come _____ the house immediately!
   a out of   **b** on   **c** out

7 The horse was not quite big enough to jump _____ the fence.
   a across   **b** away   **c** over

8 Miss Brannagh noticed a small child crawling _____ the room.
   a over   **b** across   **c** out

9 Where does Omar _____ ? He looks Egyptian.
   a come at   **b** come   **c** come from

10 What do you think _____ the new sofa?
    a of   **b** to   **c** for

11 'Where's your coat?'
    'The woman I gave _____ put it on a hanger.'
    a to it   **b** that for   **c** it to

12 The lecturer was talking _____ the Jurassic Age.
    a to   **b** at   **c** about

13 I really hope Jack gets _____ my parents. I want them to like him.
    a up to   **b** on with   **c** into

14 Pat knows Ken isn't right for her but she can't _____ .
    a give up him   **b** him give up   **c** give him up

15 There's smoke everywhere! _____ !
    a Put out the fire   **b** Put it out the fire
    c The fire put out

16 Peter is really behind at school so he really must catch _____ his work.
    a on up   **b** up to   **c** up with

17 If you don't know the right answers, just _____ !
    a make up them   **b** up them make
    c make them up

18 The little dog used to _____ when he went for a bike ride.
    a run him after   **b** after him run
    c run after him

19 Kelly _____ for a meal on his birthday.
    a invited her dad out   **b** invited out her dad
    c her dad invited out

20 Are you _____ your birthday party next week?
    a looking at   **b** looking for
    c looking forward to

21 Tammy and Jess don't _____ each other, unfortunately.
    a get very well on with   **b** get on with very well
    c get on very well with

22 Jamal is pretty depressed. I _____ the weather.
    a put down it to   **b** put it down to
    c put it to down

23 Everyone must _____ the possibility of failure.
    a to face up   **b** face to up   **c** face up to

24 Tara runs so fast it's quite difficult to _____ her.
    a catch up to   **b** catch up her   **c** catch up with

25 Everyone in the house uses milk, so it's easy to _____ it without realising.
    a of run out   **b** run out of   **c** out of run

26 Bill _____ his new car this evening.
    a will collect   **b** is going to collect
    c does collect

27 I think _____ the sea bass with spinach.
    a I'm ordering   **b** I order   **c** I'll order

28 Patrick has been offered a place at King's College. He _____ in the autumn.

a will starts　　b is going to starting
c starts

29 I _____ to class on time all this week!

a 'm going to get　　b am getting
c get

30 Don't worry about spilling your coffee. The waiter _____ you another one.

a brings　　b 'll bring　　c is going to bring

31 If Val asks me out, I _____ the invitation.

a am not accepting　　b won't accept
c don't accept

32 'Shall we meet on Monday afternoon?'
'No, I _____ Physics in the library.'

a 'm studying　　b 'll have studied
c 'll be studying

33 Come at seven. The restaurant will _____ by then.

a have opened　　b be opened
c have been opened

34 'I'm going to Turkey for two weeks.'
'How _____ ?'

a do you travel　　b will you travelling
c will you be travelling

35 You could meet me at the station. I _____ at about eight.

a 'll have been arriving　　b 'll have arrived
c 'll be arriving

36 I hope it _____ raining by the time the film finishes.

a will have stopped　　b will be stopping
c is going to stop

37 In January, Diana _____ there for 25 years.

a has been working　　b will have been working
c is working

38 Yvonne _____ in a luxury room in Acapulco at this time tomorrow.

a is going to sleep　　b will be sleeping
c will have been sleeping

39 Mum gets home at nine tomorrow. I hope you will _____ the house by then.

a have been tidying up　　b be tidying up
c have tidied up

40 Please give me a call as soon as you _____ she's had the baby.

a hear　　b are hearing　　c will hear

41 Harry is going to fly home once his visa _____ out.

a is running　　b runs　　c will run

42 Let's sit here until the café _____ . It's freezing outside!

a is closing　　b has closed　　c closes

43 _____ , we'll go to the cinema.

a When it's closed　　b If it is closed
c When it will close

44 Ella said she will help you if you _____ her to.

a will need　　b need　　c will have needed

45 I thought that the cat _____ into the road.

a is bound to run　　b was going to run
c is running

46 The divers _____ go down to the wreck and bring it up to the surface.

a were likely to　　b were bound to
c were going to

47 The horse was _____ win the Grand National, but we bet on it anyway.

a bound to　　b about to　　c unlikely to

48 Gerard knew he _____ the train home, so he didn't rush.

a was going to miss　　b is going to miss
c will be missing

49 Peter _____ enter the competition, but then he injured his ankle.

a is going to　　b was going to　　c would

50 If Helen comes to the party, John _____ upset.

a is bound to be　　b is likely being
c is about to be

1 When you decide _____ home, I'll give you a lift.
   a on going b to go c going

2 Jason promised _____ Selina the following year.
   a marrying b marry c to marry

3 Giovanna _____ really angry with Carlo.
   a is seeming to be b seems to be getting
   c seems to get

4 The class chose _____ for the exam this term.
   a to not register b not to register
   c to register not

5 Can you manage _____ the lesson again, Simon?
   a not to interrupt b not interrupting
   c to not interrupt

6 We have decided _____ President of the Literary Society.
   a Adnan to be b to elect Adnan as
   c being Adnan

7 Can you imagine _____ for anything? Not a chance!
   a Phil to apologise b apologises Phil
   c Phil apologising

8 It's not worth risking _____ there quicker. Drive slower!
   a to get your life b your life getting
   c your life get

9 Some people prefer _____ and not heard.
   a children to be seeing b children to be seen
   c to be seen children

10 You can all finish the yoga class by _____ down on the floor for ten minutes.
    a to lie b lie c lying

11 Do you remember _____ me that you weren't going to be in this evening?
    a to tell b tell c telling

12 I'm sure you didn't mean _____ Steve while you were playing football.
    a to kick b kicked c kicking

13 After studying medicine for five years, Sarah went on _____ a job as a barmaid.
    a getting b and gets c to get

14 Please don't forget _____ the door when you leave.
    a to lock b lock c locking

15 The article said that we should all stop _____ so much!
    a to worry b worrying c worry

16 The online store was offering _____. It's cheaper to buy online.
    a new customers discounts
    b discounts new customers
    c to new customers discounts

17 Read _____, Daddy! I can't go to sleep.
    a story me b me a story c to me a story

18 Tom said he would order _____, but he forgot!
    a the food for the party b for the party the food
    c to the party the food

19 I offered _____, but he refused to take one.
    a him a sandwich b a sandwich him
    c a sandwich to him

20 Don't send _____ as my computer's crashed.
    a to me any emails b any emails to me
    c to me emails

21 You all owe _____ the meal last night.
    a me some money for b some money me to
    c for me some money to

22 Tina's uncle leant over and said _____. She laughed.
    a to her something b her something
    c something to her

23 Pay _____, if you don't mind. I'll get some money from the cash machine.
    a the waiter the meal
    b for the meal to the waiter
    c the waiter for the meal

24 Dita has been teaching _____ all this week.
    a the elementary class the past simple
    b the past simple the elementary class
    c the past simple to the elementary class

25 A servant had to serve _____ when the King was playing tennis, as he was too fat to raise his arms!

a the ball for Henry VIII
b Henry VIII the ball
c to the ball Henry VIII

26 Gary's got a car so he _____ drive down to see his girlfriend at the weekend.

a can   b could have   c manage to

27 Don't be silly – I know you _____ do it if you try.

a able to   b can   c could

28 Dina tried to repair her dishwasher by herself but she _____.

a wasn't able to   b can't   c could

29 _____ this car run on electricity as well as petrol?

a Is able to   b Manages   c Can

30 Do you think Jake _____ beating his personal 400m record?

a managed to   b could
c has succeeded in

31 To _____ keep calm in a crisis is a very valuable ability.

a succeed in   b can   c be able to

32 I hope we _____ park in the road behind the club.

a need   b can   c must

33 It's OK. You _____ cook the onions before you add them to the soup.

a don't need to   b mustn't   c aren't allowed to

34 You really _____ bring me a birthday present, but thanks anyway!

a couldn't   b didn't need to   c mustn't

35 The coach _____ the team do 50 press-ups at the beginning of the session.

a made   b let   c had to

36 Students are not _____ to eat or drink anything in the classroom.

a let   b made   c allowed

37 The hikers _____ left the gate open. The cows have got into the road.

a might have   b must have   c could have

38 'Where is Kevin?'
'I don't know. He _____ still be in bed.'

a mightn't   b could   c doesn't have to be

39 David _____ win the first prize, but he will probably come second.

a couldn't   b might   c mustn't

40 It _____ be six o'clock already! We haven't finished the chapter yet.

a can't   b mustn't   c might not

41 Wearing high heels in the snow _____ be dangerous.

a can   b must   c couldn't

42 Carina looks as if she _____ fall asleep at any moment!

a must   b couldn't   c might

43 Isn't that Lorenzo's car? He _____ be visiting Harriet this evening.

a can   b couldn't   c must

44 Excuse me, but _____ moving your coat off this seat?

a are you   b would you mind   c could you

45 Would you mind _____ your pencil a moment?

a borrowing   b if I borrowed   c me to borrow

46 _____ tell Jane her husband's arrived?

a Shall we   b Let's   c Do we

47 When the weather is stormy, the ferry _____ be running.

a shall not   b shouldn't   c ought not

48 It's getting dark. _____ stop weeding and come in from the garden?

a Had better you   b Should you
c Hadn't you better

49 _____ I possibly interrupt you for a minute? Sorry.

a Would   b Can't   c Could

50 It's freezing this evening. You _____ take a taxi to the station.

a had better   b shall   c would better

8 Progress test (units 71 to 80)

1 I saw Helena this morning and she said _____ to see you this evening.

   a she is wanting   **b** will want
   c she wanted

2 The doctor told _____ have to have an operation.

   a to Sarah she will   **b** Sarah she would
   c Sarah she

3 'What did Liam say?'
   'He said _____ to class today.'

   a he couldn't come   **b** me he can't come
   c to me he can't coming

4 My aunt said she couldn't chat because she was moving house _____ .

   a this day   **b** that day   **c** today

5 Sheila promised that she _____ me back as soon as she had saved enough money.

   a will pay   **b** would pay   **c** is paying

6 The police reported that they still _____ the murderer.

   a couldn't find   **b** won't find   **c** don't find

7 Did you just ask Tom _____ you his car?

   a to lend   **b** lending   **c** have lent

8 Samantha wanted to know where _____ .

   a was Tom   **b** had been Tom
   c Tom had been

9 The front door was closed. Graham asked the policeman _____ .

   a opening it   **b** to open it   **c** opens

10 Charlie asked us if we _____ the film before.

   a did see   **b** saw   **c** had seen

11 The teacher told the class _____ their course books.

   a take out   **b** to take out   **c** taken out

12 The secretary asked us why _____ to see Mr Kennington.

   a we want   **b** we wanted   **c** did we want

13 Ulli wanted to know whether our rooms _____ warm enough.

   a felt   **b** feel   **c** did feel

14 The class agreed _____ be great to start writing a blog.

   a that it would   **b** it that would   **c** it to

15 Lisa offered _____ one of her famous coffee cakes to the office.

   a bringing   **b** to bring   **c** will bring

16 I hope he will apologise _____ so rude to me yesterday!

   a to be   **b** to have been   **c** for being

17 Don't blame me _____ your scarf! I didn't touch it.

   a for losing   **b** to have lost   **c** losing

18 The manager insists _____ on time in the morning.

   a to everyone to arrive   **b** on everyone to arrive
   c on everyone arriving

19 I got a letter inviting _____ to a cheese-tasting evening.

   a to me to come   **b** me coming
   c me to come

20 I'd really like to congratulate _____ your fabulous performance.

   a you on   **b** you for   **c** to you for

21 I'm sure this towel _____ before. It isn't clean.

   a has been used   **b** was using
   c uses

22 The rules of the game _____ on the back of the box.

   a are finding   **b** find themselves
   c can be found

23 Sorry, I can't come tomorrow afternoon.
   I _____ my hair cut then.

   a 'll have   **b** 'm going having
   c 'll be having

24 I think the car in the lead _____ by Alonso.

   a is driving   **b** is being driven   **c** drives

25 The garden _____ a landscape architect in the 18th century.

   a designs with   **b** is designed to
   c was designed by

26 It's possible the race _____ if he had tried harder.
   a could have been won   b we could win
   c could winning

27 The guests _____ to arrive by 7.30 p.m.
   a has been asked   b had been asked
   c is asked

28 Oh no! All the sandwiches _____ already!
   I thought there would be plenty.
   a have been sold   b were sold to people
   c are sold by people

29 The food parcels _____ the soldiers.
   a were distributed to   b have distributed
   c distribute for

30 A bar of soap _____ each prisoner.
   a has given for   b gives   c is given to

31 Parcels _____ by airmail or by train.
   a can be sending   b can be sent
   c can send

32 The model planes can _____ varnish or paint.
   a paint by   b have painted   c be painted with

33 Mr X's true identity _____ at midnight.
   a will be revealed   b will reveal
   c will revealing

34 Gary agreed _____ about his dramatic escape.
   a to be interviewed   b being interviewed
   c to interview

35 The Picts _____ in Scotland before the Romans
   invaded.
   a were believed living   b believe to be living
   c are believed to have lived

36 It _____ that the Prime Minister is going
   to resign.
   a is reported   b reports   c 's been reported

37 The children _____ indoors through the winter.
   a are bored with staying b are boring to stay
   c are bored to stay

38 Queen Elizabeth I _____ in this house.
   a says to have stayed   b is said to staying
   c is said to have stayed

39 There _____ about 50 survivors of the plane crash.
   a are said to be   b are saying to be
   c say being

40 Adam demanded _____ by his kidnappers.
   a being released   b to be released
   c releasing

41 I'm afraid your cat _____ by a car. I've taken her
   to the vet.
   a was hitting   b is been hit   c has been hit

42 The olive oil _____ in the top cupboard.
   a keeps itself   b is kept   c is keeping

43 The script had to _____ the entire cast by Monday.
   a be learning by   b learning for
   c be learnt by

44 You really should avoid _____ outside after the
   curfew.
   a to be caught   b catching   c being caught

45 I need to get _____ . The rain is coming in!
   a my roof repairing   b my roof repaired
   c repaired my roof.

46 Robin got the taxi driver _____ him right to the
   front door.
   a taking   b took   c to take

47 That lock on the front door really _____ .
   a needs fixing   b is needing fixing
   c needs to fix

48 I think we need to have the gas man _____ to look
   at the hot water boiler.
   a coming   b come   c to come

49 That front lawn really _____ . I'll ask my sister to
   do it.
   a needs to cut   b is needing cutting
   c needs cutting

50 My cousin's wedding ring _____ the day after her
   wedding!
   a gets lost   b is losing   c got lost

9 Progress test (units 81 to 90)

1 That's the woman _____ sold me the fake designer handbag.
   a which   **b** who   **c** what

2 What's that noise? It's the kitten _____ your sister brought home today.
   a that   **b** who   **c** where

3 This is the car _____ on the internet! It's cool, isn't it?
   a which I bought   **b** who I bought
   c where I bought

4 I'm sure that was the person _____ in the alley last night.
   a what I saw   **b** who I saw   **c** seeing

5 I believe that's the ring _____ her last night.
   a I gave   **b** that I gave it to
   c who I gave to

6 It's the music _____ a party go well.
   a really makes   **b** who really makes
   c which really makes

7 Can you see the tall blond man at the table over there? He's the actor _____ Tina loves!
   a who   **b** which   **c** where

8 My aunt _____ in Zimbabwe, is a doctor.
   a lives   **b** , who lives   **c** , living

9 The people _____ waiting at the bus stop are all freezing cold.
   a are   **b** which   **c** who are

10 The house _____ to belong to Sting, has been sold for £2 million.
   a used   **b** , who used   **c** , which used

11 Sarah Jakes, _____ a children's TV show, was arrested today.
   a presents   **b** which presents
   c who presents

12 Her car, _____ been badly damaged, was towed away.
   a that had   **b** which had   **c** had

13 The singer, _____ fans had chased from the theatre, jumped into the waiting car.
   a who   **b** which   **c** whose

14 The _____ still full of bank notes, was later found in a lay-by.
   a van, which was   **b** van was
   c van that was

15 The book was written at a time _____ women were not allowed any property.
   a that   **b** which   **c** when

16 Can you see the house at the end of the row? That's the house _____ .
   a where my dad was born in
   b which my dad was born
   c where my dad was born

17 Does anyone know the reason _____ we have to sign this form?
   a for which   **b** why   **c** that

18 I can give the correspondent the address _____ the parcel was sent.
   a at which   **b** that   **c** to which

19 The police officer wouldn't tell us the reason _____ we had been arrested.
   a that   **b** for which   **c** why

20 Charles arrived at 4.00 a.m. _____ most of the family were fast asleep.
   a when   **b** at which   **c** that

21 I'd like to talk to the person _____ car is parked across the entrance.
   a the which   **b** who   **c** whose

22 This is the college _____ you can study to become a vet.
   a for which   **b** at which   **c** in which

23 Those clothes _____ on your bedroom floor must be picked up immediately!
   a lie   **b** to lie   **c** lying

24 Have you ever met that man _____ over there by the door?
   a that stands   **b** standing   **c** to stand

25 The bag _____ by the pickpocket was recovered later in a waste bin.
   a stolen   **b** stealing   **c** was stolen

26 The left luggage office has a sale in which all the items _____ on the trains are sold.

a leaving   b left   c which leave

27 There is a lovely little shop _____ in organic cosmetics.

a specialising   b specialises   c specialised

28 If Sarah takes the train, Gerard _____ her up from the station.

a can pick   b is picking   c picks

29 The floors _____ wet if they don't repair the leaking pipe soon.

a are   b are going to be   c would

30 When the streets _____ really crowded, I hate going shopping.

a will be   b were   c are

31 If you _____ know the right answer, don't say anything.

a won't   b aren't going to   c don't

32 Let's take the bus home _____ the film finishes.

a when   b if   c as

33 If the weather is hot, _____ remember to take a bottle of water.

a you will   b you must   c can

34 If the sun is directly overhead, _____ midday.

a it's going to be   b it is   c be

35 If you are wearing a short skirt, _____ allowed in.

a you won't be   b you can't be   c not

36 Tina says she'll come and see you when she _____ in Florence.

a will be   b is   c is going to be

37 If this café was a bit closer to my house, I _____ here every afternoon!

a would come   b am coming   c will come

38 You could join our band if you _____ play an instrument or sing.

a can   b could   c will

39 If the bomb had fallen a little further to the south, it _____ destroyed the palace too.

a had   b has   c would have

40 What would you say if Toni _____ your wedding anniversary?

a forget   b has forgotten   c had forgotten

41 If Chung had known how much caviar cost, he _____ it in the restaurant.

a wouldn't order   b won't order
c wouldn't have ordered

42 The store manager _____ the customer a refund for the dress if it was torn.

a should have offered   b should offer
c must offer

43 Why did they turn off the heating if they _____ the temperature was so low in the classrooms?

a know   b had known   c knew

44 If Libor _____ passed his FCE exam, he could have taken CAE this year.

a might have   b would have   c had

45 If the lecture _____ so boring, I would be able to remember what it was about.

a isn't   b weren't   c hadn't been

46 We _____ the party tonight if you hadn't forgotten to send out the invitations.

a would be having   b wouldn't have
c have

47 Keith would still be a member of the committee if he _____ the president.

a doesn't annoy   b hadn't annoyed
c wasn't annoying

48 If it wasn't for the bad weather, we _____ to the beach this afternoon.

a could go   b could have gone   c had gone

49 The team would _____ now if their plane hadn't been delayed.

a have competed   b compete
c be competing

50 I _____ you my copy of the magazine if I hadn't already given it to Laura.

a could have lent   b had lent   c will lend

10 Progress test (units 91 to 100)

1. I really wish the exams _____ held in August. I won't be able to have a holiday.

   a isn't **b** not being **c** weren't

2. If only we _____ better friends, I could be more helpful at this difficult time.

   a are **b** were **c** had been

3. If only I _____ ski! I'd love to come to Switzerland with you.

   a can **b** am able to **c** could

4. I really wish reporters _____ only focus on bad news!

   a wouldn't **b** can't **c** won't

5. There isn't really enough food for all of you. If only you _____ me you were coming.

   a told **b** had told **c** tell

6. David is a complete liar! If only I _____ that sooner!

   a could see **b** can see **c** could have seen

7. I really wish I _____ entered the race. I'm useless.

   a didn't **b** hadn't **c** didn't have

8. The students won't be entered for the exam _____ they are well prepared.

   a if **b** providing **c** unless

9. The play starts on Friday, _____ they sell some tickets.

   a providing **b** unless **c** when

10. _____ bump into Graham, you would be amazed. He's shaved his head!

    a If you **b** Did you **c** If you were to

11. If the board of directors _____, we could have opened a new branch.

    a were to agree **b** agreed **c** had agreed

12. _____ the Queen of England, I would make you a Lord!

    a Were I **b** Was I **c** Being

13. Julia went on holiday _____ having a really bad cold.

    a although **b** in spite **c** in spite of

14. _____ her aggressive behaviour, they promoted her to deputy head.

    a In spite **b** Although **c** Despite

15. People continue to buy cheap vegetables _____ they are not as tasty as organic ones.

    a in spite of **b** although **c** despite

16. That soup wasn't very good. It warmed us up, _____ .

    a although **b** even though **c** though

17. We decided to buy a meal in the restaurant _____ we didn't have much money left.

    a although **b** in spite **c** despite

18. Liam was happy to be offered a job in Dublin _____ his family still lived there.

    a due to **b** since **c** in order to

19. _____ property is a bit cheaper now, Jake and Lana have bought a bigger flat.

    a As **b** In order that **c** Because of

20. The value of the car is much less _____ the scratches on the paintwork.

    a since **b** due to **c** because

21. This plant is very popular with gardeners _____ its beautiful foliage.

    a since **b** because of **c** as

22. You need to wear special glasses _____ appreciate 3D films.

    a because of **b** so that **c** in order to

23. Linda is going to India _____ experience the culture first hand.

    a in order that **b** because **c** so as to

24. Tim bought a webcam _____ his mother could chat with him and see him as well.

    a since **b** because of **c** so that

25. _____ his children should have the best in life, Ali went to work in America.

    a So that **b** Due to **c** Because

26. I really hate that noise. _____ stop fiddling with the coins in your pocket!

    a Do **b** Do you **c** Must

27 That's crazy! I _____ want to pay extra for first-class seats.

a not   **b** do not   **c** am not

28 I'm trying to write an email. _____ me any more questions!

a Not ask   **b** Do not ask   **c** Am not asking

29 It's quite tiring, but _____ the variety I like about the job.

a the thing is   **b** what it is   **c** it's

30 _____ you remember most about Sardinia is the beautiful, clean seawater.

a It's what   **b** The thing   **c** That

31 Oliver didn't get the job. _____ turn up late for the interview.

a What he did was   **b** The thing was to
c It was

32 It's my sister _____ the successful one in my family.

a is   **b** who is   **c** is being

33 Don't blame the team. _____ to blame for the relegation.

a Who is the manager   **b** That's the manager
c It's the manager who is

34 She didn't want a necklace. _____ she wanted from him!

a That was a ring that   **b** It's a ring
c The thing was a ring

35 The film lasts for three hours, and _____ can you relax and breathe again.

a after that   **b** only after   **c** only then

36 It was an awesome experience. _____ I seen so many people so excited before.

a Never have   **b** When have   **c** Only then have

37 No sooner was the engine repaired _____ they resumed the journey.

a that   **b** when   **c** than

38 The children were so hungry that, hardly had they sat down at the table _____ the food disappeared.

a when   **b** but   **c** than

39 I really didn't enjoy the concert. _____ been so bored, if I'm honest!

a Never I have   **b** Not have I   **c** Never have I

40 _____ their honeymoon had they spent so much time together.

a Since only   **b** Only since   **c** Not since

41 We were absolutely exhausted. _____ so happy to lie down and sleep.

a Never have I been   **b** I was never
c Never since I was

42 I don't eat very much. _____ finish a plateful of food.

a Rarely I   **b** Rarely do   **c** Rarely do I

43 My cousin is a carpenter. _____ is his skill that he can charge a fortune for a table or chair.

a So   **b** Such   **c** So much

44 Hyun Tae lives in a tower block. _____ is his apartment that he can see the sea in the distance.

a So high   **b** Such is high   **c** So highly

45 _____ the general's reputation that the enemy surrendered to him.

a So it was   **b** So does   **c** Such was

46 You must be punished. _____ the law!

a So is   **b** Such is   **c** So does

47 Neither _____ been to Cyprus nor Malta.

a have I   **b** I have   **c** I haven't

48 'I didn't enjoy the flight very much.'
'_____.'

a Nor did I   **b** Neither I did   **c** Nor I

49 'We go to the cinema at least once a week.'
'_____.'

a And we too   **b** Do we too   **c** So do we

50 The Democrats didn't look like winning the election but _____ .

a nor the Republicans did
b the Republicans didn't neither
c nor did the Republicans

Appendix 1 Punctuation

Capital letters

Use a capital letter for:

- the first letter of a sentence. *He climbed up the mountain.*
- the names of people and places: *Benjamin Franklin, Hedy Lamarr, Marilyn Monroe, Machu Piccu, Oxford University.*
- the names of countries, nationalities and languages: *China/Chinese, France/French, Australia/Austra~~li~~, England/E~~nglish~~*
- days ~~seaso~~
- scho~~ol~~
- peopl~~e~~ Obam~~a~~
- the pr~~~~
- the na~~mes~~ Jaws, T~~~~
- initials J Peter.
- the nam~~es~~ Eve, Th~~~~
- abbrevia~~~~
- the names of institutions and organisations: *Scripps Institution of Oceanography, World Wide Fund for Nature.*

End of a sentence

Normally, we end a sentence with a full stop (British English) or period (American English): *I live in London.*

Question mark

- Put ? at the end of a question (not a full stop): *Where do you live?*
- Do not put a ? at the end of a question if you are asking it indirectly: *I was wondering if you'd seen my glasses.*

Exclamation mark

- Put ! at the end of a sentence exclaiming something (not a full stop): *That's amazing!*
- At the end of a negative question form used as an exclamation: *Don't you look amazing!*

Commas

Use commas …

- for lists of nouns: *I bought a pen, a book and a bag.*
- after *Yes* or *No* in short answers: *Yes, it is.*
- to separate a question tag from the main sentence: *You're John, aren't you?*
- between a reporting verb and direct speech: *Mr Connor said, 'The decision will be made tomorrow.'*
- to separate a time clause from a main clause when it is at the beginning of a sentence: *As soon as I'd finished lunch, I went for a walk.*
- to separate a comment adverb from the rest of the sentence: *Thankfully, the test wasn't too difficult.*
- instead of *that* following *so* + adjective: *The train was so crowded, I was unable to get a seat.*
- to separate a non-defining relative clause from the main clause: *The house, which was beautifully decorated, belonged to his grandfather.*
- to separate two clauses when the first starts with *if* or *when*: *If the weather is good, we'll take a picnic.*

  to separate two clauses when the first starts with *although* or *though*: *Although the house was dirty, we had to stay there.*
- in large numbers: *7,210,000, £5,400.*
- for lists of qualitative adjectives: *It's a large, heavy suitcase.* (Note: you do not need commas to separate classifying adjectives: *The large white rhino lives in Africa.*

Apostrophe

Use an apostrophe for …

- contracted verb forms: *I'm, doesn't, he'd*
- possessive 's: *a Valentine's card, Phil's best friend, the scientists' theory*

Quotation marks

Use quotation marks …

- around words which are spoken or thought:

  'But does that mean I'm next?' he thought to himself.

  'Well, gentlemen,' Mr Fogg said. 'I'm off.'
- to draw attention to the use of a particular word or term: *Somehow, the animals 'felt' the tsunami before it hit.*

Appendix 2   Spelling rules

Plural nouns

- We usually form plural nouns by adding -s or -es.

road → road**s**	hippo → hippo**s**
Monday → Monday**s**	bus → bus**es**

- Add -es to nouns ending in -ch, -s, -ss, -sh and -x.

sandwich → sandwich**es**	dish → dish**es**
bus → bus**es**	box → box**es**
class → class**es**	

- Change nouns ending in -y (after a consonant) to -i.

country → countries
story → stories
city → cities
family → families

Don't change the -y to -i after a vowel: *holidays, keys.*

- Some nouns are irregular. For example:

man → men	person → people
woman → women	potato → potatoes
child → children	foot → feet

Note also:

loaf → loaves
roof → roofs

Present simple third person (he/she/it) verbs

- Add -s to most verbs in the present simple third person form.

live → live**s**
start → start**s**
work → work**s**

- Add -es to verbs ending in -ch, -o, -s, -ss, -sh and -x.

watch → watch**es**	finish → finish**es**
do → do**es**	relax → relax**es**
pass → pass**es**	

- Change verbs ending in consonant + -y to -i.

study → studies
fly → flies

Do not change the -y to -i after a vowel: *buys, plays.*

- A few verbs have irregular forms.

be → is
have → has

Comparative and superlative adjectives

- Add -er to short adjectives to form the comparative. Add -est to short adjectives to form the superlative.

young → young**er** → young**est**
cheap → cheap**er** → cheap**est**

- When the adjective ends in -e, add -r/st.

large → large**r** → large**st**
late → late**r** → late**st**

- Change adjective endings in -y (after a consonant) to -i.

happy → happ**i**er → happ**i**est
angry → angr**i**er → angr**i**est

- Double the final consonant on adjectives ending with consonant + vowel + consonant.

hotter → ho**tt**er → ho**tt**est
big → bi**gg**er → bi**gg**est
fat → fa**tt**er → fa**tt**est

- Don't double the consonant with adjectives ending in -w or -y.

slow → slower → slowest
scary → scarier → scariest

- Some adjectives and adverbs are irregular. Irregular adjectives:

good → better → best
bad → worse → worst
far → further/farther → furthest/farthest

Irregular adverbs:

well → better → best
badly → worse → worst
far → further/farther → furthest/farthest

Adverbs ending in *-ly*

- We often add *-ly* to an adjective to form an adverb.

quick → quick**ly**
slow → slow**ly**

Sometimes you have to make small changes to the spelling:

Adjectives ending in *-l*: beautiful → beautifu**lly** (not beautifu**l**y)
Adjectives ending in *-y*: happy → happ**ily**
Adjectives ending in *-ble*: terrible → terrib**ly**
Adjectives ending in *-e*: true → tru**ly**
Adjectives ending in *-ll*: full → full**y**
Some adjectives ending in *-ic*: realistic → realistic**ally**

Past simple regular verbs (*-ed* endings)

- Add *-ed* to verbs ending in a consonant.

watch → watch**ed**

- Add *-d* to verbs ending in *-e*.

arrive → arriv**ed**

- With verbs ending in *-y* (after a consonant), change the *-y* to *-i*.

apply → app**lied**

- Don't change the *-y* to *-i* after a vowel.

play → played

- Double the final consonant on most verbs ending with consonant + vowel + consonant.

stop → sto**pp**ed

Present participles (*-ing* endings)

- With most verbs, add *-ing* to the verb.

wait → wait**ing**
learn → learn**ing**

- With verbs ending in *-e*, delete the *-e* before adding *-ing*.

live → liv**ing**
have → hav**ing**

- Double the final consonant on most verbs ending with a vowel and a consonant.

stop → sto**pp**ing
run → ru**nn**ing

- Sometimes you have to make small changes to the spelling.

die → d**y**ing
lie → l**y**ing

British and American spelling

There are a few differences between British and American spelling.

- Words ending in *-re* often end in *-er*:

centre (Br Eng) → center (Am Eng)
metre (Br Eng) → meter (Am Eng)

- Words with *-our* often omit the *u*:

colour (Br Eng) → color (Am Eng)
favourite (Br Eng) → favorite (Am Eng)

- Verbs ending with *-ise* or *-ize* are always *-ize*:

memorise (Br Eng) → memorize (Am Eng)
organise (Br Eng) → organize (Am Eng)

Appendix 3   Summary of main verb forms

Summary of present tenses

Present simple

I/You/We/They **live** in Ireland.
He/She/It **lives** in Ireland.

We **don't live** in Ireland.
She **doesn't live** in Ireland.

Where **do** they **live**?
Where **does** he **live**?

Present continuous

I**'m watching** television at the moment.
You/We/They**'re watching** television at the moment.
He/She**'s watching** television at the moment.

I**'m not watching** television at the moment.
He **isn't watching** television at the moment.
We **aren't watching** television at the moment.

What **are** you **doing**?
Where **is** she **watching** television?

Present perfect simple

I/You/We/They**'ve gone** to the supermarket.
He/She**'s gone** to the supermarket.

We **haven't gone** to the supermarket.
He **hasn't gone** to the supermarket.

Where **have** they **gone**?
Where **has** she **gone**?

Present perfect continuous

I/You/We/They**'ve been chatting** for hours.
He/She**'s been chatting** for hours.

We **haven't been chatting** for hours.
He **hasn't been chatting** for hours.

Where **have** they **been chatting**?
Where **has** she **been chatting**?

been and gone

- Use *been* to say that someone went somewhere and came back:
  He's been to the Arctic Circle three times.
- Use *gone* to say that someone went somewhere and they're still there:
  He's gone on another trip to the North Pole.

Summary of past tenses

Past simple

I/You/He/She/It/We/They **arrived** yesterday.

I/You/He/She/It/We/They **didn't arrive** yesterday.

Did I/you/he/she/it/we/they **arrive** yesterday?

Past continuous

I/He/She/It **was sitting** in the park.
You/We/They **were sitting** in the park.

I **wasn't sitting** in the park.
We **weren't sitting** in the park.

Was he **sitting** in the park?
Were you **sitting** in the park?

Past perfect simple

I/He/She/It/You/We/They **had eaten** before the plane landed.

I/He/She/It/You/We/They **hadn't eaten** before the plane landed.

Had you/he/she/they **eaten** before the plane landed?

Past perfect continuous

I/He/She/It/You/We/They **had been reading** the newspaper.

I/He/She/It/You/We/They **hadn't been reading** the newspaper.

Had I/he/she/it/you/we/they **been reading** the newspaper?

used to

I/He/She/It/You/We/They **used to** visit us twice a year.

I/He/She/It/You/We/They **didn't use to** visit us twice a year.

Did I/he/she/it/you/we/they **use to** visit us twice a year?

be used to

I/He/She/It/We **was used to living** overseas.

Were you/we/they **used to living** overseas?

Was he/she **used to living** overseas?

You/We/They **weren't used to living** overseas.

Summary of future forms

I'**ll meet** you at 6.30.
We'**re going to fly** to Paris.
We **depart** at ten o'clock.
We'**re meeting** Alison at the airport.

Future continuous

I/He/She/We/You/They **will be travelling** business class.

I/He/She/We/You/They **won't be travelling** business class.

Will I/he/she/we/you/they **be travelling** business class?

Future perfect

I/You/He/She/You/We/They'**ll have arrived** by six-thirty tomorrow morning.

I/He/She/We/You/They **won't have arrived** by six-thirty tomorrow morning.

Will I/he/she/we/you/they **have arrived** by six-thirty tomorrow morning?

Future perfect continuous

I/He/She/We/You/They **will have been travelling** for eleven hours.

I/He/She/We/You/They **won't have been travelling** for eleven hours.

Will I/he/she/we/you/they **have been travelling** for eleven hours?

Future in the past

She **was unlikely to be able** to keep the party a secret.
He **was certain to discover** the arrangements.
It **was going to be** a lovely surprise for him.
His father **was going to fly** over from Australia.

Future time clauses

I'll confirm the details **when I've spoken to Oliver**.
As soon as I've spoken to Oliver, I'll confirm the details.
If Sonny can get to the station, I'll collect him from there.
I'll be waiting at the station **when Sonny arrives**.
I'll text you **once I've met him**.

Summary of active to passive verb forms

Present simple: *He tests a theory. → A theory is tested.*

Present continuous: *He is testing a theory. → The theory is being tested.*

Present perfect: *He has tested the theory. → The theory has been tested.*

Past simple: *He tested the theory. → The theory was tested.*

Past continuous: *He was testing the theory. → The theory was being tested.*

Past perfect: *He had tested the theory. → The theory had been tested.*

Future (will): *He will test the theory. → The theory will be tested.*

Future (be going to): *He is going to test the theory. → The theory is going to be tested.*

Must: *He must test the theory. → The theory must be tested.*

Can: *He can't test the theory. → The theory can't be tested.*

Might: *He might test the theory. → The theory might be tested.*

Get: *Someone tested the theory. → He got the theory tested.*

Summary of statements, questions, short answers and short responses

question word	auxiliary verb	subject	main verb
What	*did*	*the journalists*	*ask?*
What	*will*	*the minister*	*do?*
Where	*does*	*the chancellor*	*live?*
When	*are*	*the results*	*announced?*
Why	*will*	*the system*	*change?*
How	*does*	*the system*	*work?*

	affirmative	negative
Are you …?	*Yes, I am.*	*No, I'm not.*
Was it …?	*Yes, it was.*	*No, it wasn't.*
Have you …?	*Yes, I have.*	*No, I haven't.*
Do you …?	*Yes, I do.*	*No, I don't.*
Did we …?	*Yes, we did.*	*No, we didn't.*
Will they …?	*Yes, they will.*	*No, they won't.*
Would you …?	*Yes, I would.*	*No, I wouldn't.*

+	+
I'm interested in politics. *She's got a new job.* *She gets a car and a mobile.* *They love that restaurant.*	*So am I.* *So has he.* *So does he.* *So do we.*
−	−
I'm not interested in politics. *She hasn't got a new job.* *She didn't get a car or a mobile.* *We won't be going to the dinner this year.*	*Neither am I.* *Neither has he.* *Neither did he.* *Neither will we.*

+	+
It's midnight. *They were going to get married.* *We've cooked you something special for dinner.* *I love a plate of chips now and then.*	*Is it?* *Were they?* *Have you?* *Do you?*
−	−
That package didn't arrive this morning. *She won't talk to journalists.* *He can't afford to pay the money back.*	*Didn't it?* *Won't she?* *Can't he?*

Summary of tense changes backwards in reported speech

present simple → past simple:

'We sometimes go to the theatre.' → He said they sometimes went to the theatre.

present continuous → past continuous:

'We're going to the theatre.' → They said they were going to the theatre.

present perfect → past perfect:

We've booked tickets for the theatre. → They said they had booked tickets for the theatre.

past simple → past perfect:

'We booked the tickets last month.' → They said they had booked the tickets last month.

will → would:

'I will book the tickets tomorrow.' → He said he would book the tickets tomorrow.

can → could

'I can book the tickets online.' → He said he could book the tickets online.

must → had to

'I must pay for the tickets when I book them.' → He said he had to pay for the tickets when he booked them.

Summary of conditionals

Real conditionals

- Generally true (zero conditional)

When/If it rains, we usually stay indoors.

If guests are bringing a pet, there's a £20 surcharge.

- Possible future situations (first conditional)

If it rains, we'll entertain the children inside.

If you're going to arrive after 8 p.m., please telephone us beforehand.

If you're looking for a relaxing holiday, this is the place for you.

Unreal conditionals

- Impossible or improbable present and future situations (second conditional)

If petrol wasn't so expensive, I'd be able to visit more often.

If the airlines lowered their fares, I'd be able to fly over to see you.

- imagined past situations (third conditional)

If she hadn't sent that e-mail, she wouldn't have lost her job.

If she hadn't sent that e-mail, she might have got the promotion.

Mixed conditionals

If we went to Cornwall, the journey wouldn't be so long.

If we drove to Normandy, we would have the use of the car.

If we had driven, the children would have been really bored.

If we had flown, we could be enjoying the sunshine by now.

Appendix 4 Verbs

Common irregular verbs

infinitive	past simple	past participle	infinitive	past simple	past participle
be	was/were	been	learn	learnt	learnt
become	became	become	leave	left	left
begin	began	begun	lend	lent	lent
bite	bit	bitten	lose	lost	lost
blow	blew	blown	make	made	made
break	broke	broken	mean	meant	meant
bring	brought	brought	meet	met	met
build	built	built	pay	paid	paid
burn	burnt	burnt	put	put	put
buy	bought	bought	read /riːd/	read /red/	read /red/
catch	caught	caught	ride	rode	ridden
choose	chose	chosen	ring	rang	rung
come	came	come	rise	rose	risen
cost	cost	cost	run	ran	run
do	did	done	say	said	said
draw	drew	drawn	see	saw	seen
drink	drank	drunk	sell	sold	sold
drive	drove	driven	send	sent	sent
eat	ate	eaten	shine	shone	shone
fall	fell	fallen	show	showed	shown
feel	felt	felt	shut	shut	shut
fight	fought	fought	sing	sang	sung
find	found	found	sit	sat	sat
fly	flew	flown	sleep	slept	slept
forget	forgot	forgotten	speak	spoke	spoken
get	got	got	spend	spent	spent
give	gave	given	stand	stood	stood
go	went	gone/been	steal	stole	stolen
grow	grew	grown	swim	swam	swum
hang	hung	hung	take	took	taken
have	had	had	teach	taught	taught
hear	heard	heard	tear	tore	torn
hide	hid	hidden	tell	told	told
hit	hit	hit	think	thought	thought
hold	held	held	throw	threw	thrown
hurt	hurt	hurt	wear	wore	worn
keep	kept	kept	win	won	won
know	knew	known	write	wrote	written

Modal verbs

Use **will** for …

- talking about the future:
  I'll be in the café at six.
  She won't be here tonight.
- predictions, certainty and possibility:
  I think she'll pass her exams.
  I'm sure they'll get married.
- offers, promises and requests:
  I'll pick you up at the station.
  I'll be there in ten minutes.
- instant decisions:
  I think I'll have the fish, please.
  Don't worry. I'll go and get her.

Use **shall** for …

- asking what to do:
  Shall I answer it?
  Shall we stand here?
- suggesting:
  Shall I tell her?
  Shall we go out later?
- offering:
  Shall I pick you up?
  Shall we help?

Use **can** for …

- ability
  I can speak Spanish.
  I can't play the guitar.
- offers and requests:
  Can I help you?
  Can I have a drink?
- permission
  You can go after nine.
  You can't go tonight.
- possibility:
  Sorry, I can't come tomorrow.

Use **could** for …

- past ability:
  Franklin could speak many languages.
  She could sing, dance and act.
- possibility (in the past):
  How could it have disappeared?
  Why couldn't he use the lift?
- polite requests:
  Could I speak to the manager, please?
  Could you open the window?

Use **would** for …

- talking about the results or consequences of an imagined situation:
  A: *What would you do if you won the lottery?*
  B: *I'd buy a yacht.*
- past habits and tendencies:
  He would often go off for the weekend without her.

Use **would like** for …

- requests and offers:
  I'd like some water.
  Would you like a drink?

Use **would you like to** for …

- requests and offers:
  Would you like to help me?
  Would you like me to help you?

Use **must** for …

- obligation:
  You must be home by eleven.
  You mustn't be late.
- prohibition:
  You mustn't park on a yellow line.
  You mustn't stay later than six o'clock.

Use **should** for …

- advice and suggesting:
  You should buy that dress.
  He shouldn't go with them.

Dynamic / Stative verbs

Some verbs can be both stative and dynamic:

Verb	Stative	Dynamic
have	*I have a shower.* = I own a shower.	*I'm having a shower.* = I'm taking a shower at the moment. *I have a shower every morning.* = I take a shower every morning.
come	*They come from Scotland.* = They were born there.	*They're coming from Scotland.* = They're travelling from there. *It's quicker if you come from Scotland by train.* = It's quicker to travel by train.
love	*I love you.* = I'll always love you.	*I'm loving my new job.* = My new job is great at the moment.
appear	*Nicole appears confident.* = Nicole seems to be confident.	*Nicole is appearing in a new film.* = You can see Nicole in a new film.
see	*I see your point.* = I understand your point.	*I'm seeing friends for dinner.* = I'm meeting friends.
weigh	*How much does it weigh?* = What is the weight of the object?	*What's he weighing?* = What is the object?
be	*Sandy is kind.* = Sandy is a kind person (this is her nature).	*Sandy is being kind.* = Sandy is behaving in a kind way at the moment.
think	*I think he's five.* = I believe he's five years old (this is my opinion).	*We're thinking about moving.* = We're considering the idea of moving house.
taste	*It tastes wonderful!* = I like it. It has a good flavour.	*Are you tasting the wine?* = Are you trying the wine to see if it's good?
smell	*It smells awful!* = It doesn't have a nice aroma.	*She's in the garden, smelling the roses.* = She is breathing in the aroma of the roses.
look	*That dress looks gorgeous!* = It's a gorgeous dress (this is a description of its appearance).	*He's looking at the TV listings.* = He's reading the TV guide.
mean	*It means nothing.* = It has no meaning.	*I've been meaning to write, but didn't have time.* = I intended to write.

Common verbs and their dependent prepositions

agree about/on/with = *He didn't agree with the director.*

aim at/for = *They aimed at the middle of the target.*

apologise for = *He apologised for his behaviour.*

apply to/for = *I'd really like to apply for that job.*

ask for = *Shirley asked for a payrise.*

belong to = *The family had belonged to the club for over 30 years.*

beware of = *Beware of the dog!*

boast about = *Simon boasted about his good grades.*

comment on = *The director commented on the quality of the new product.*

deal with = *The manager dealt with the angry customer.*

decide about/on = *Linda couldn't decide on the colour scheme for her new bathroom.*

depend on = *The results depend on the time of day the test is taken.*

disagree about/on/with = *Simon disagreed with his lawyers about the best way forward.*

discriminate against = *It is illegal for employers to discriminate against any sector of society.*

distinguish from = *It was hard to distinguish the original from the copy.*

download from = *It is illegal to download music from unlicensed sites.*

dream of/about = *I have always dreamt about living in the South of France.*

escape from = *The zebra managed to escape from the crocodile.*

forget about = *It was impossible to forget about Xavier.*

go to/with/on etc. = *I went to the cinema with the kids.*

hide from = *Georgia hid from her mother.*

hope for = *They had been hoping for a better result.*

insist on = *Ben insisted on wearing a suit.*

joke about = *The Dawsons joked about the incident for years.*

laugh at = *The audience laughed at the jokes.*

look at = *What are you looking at?*

listen to = *Can I listen to your CD?*

long for = *Hilda longs for the day when her son will return from Australia.*

object to = *I object to this mess on my desk.*

participate in = *It's good for children to participate in team events.*

pay for = *Duncan offered to pay for the flights.*

persist in = *They were determined to persist with their original plan.*

prepare for = *Let's prepare for the hike next weekend.*

protest about = *I must really protest about all this noise.*

recover from = *Sandra is recovering well from her operation.*

refer to = *Please refer to page 101.*

rely on = *I relied on Sandy to produce a great design.*

respond to = *Peter responded to the letter yesterday.*

side with = *Neil sided with his sister for once.*

smile at = *Smile at the camera!*

stare at = *Don't stare at Mrs Wheeler.*

succeed in = *Yvonne succeeded in getting the contract signed.*

suffer from = *Mum suffers from hay fever.*

think about/of = *Well, that's given them something to think about!*

vote for = *The people voted for a change of government.*

wait for = *Could you wait for me at the station, please?*

worry about = *Don't worry about a thing!*

Phrasal verbs

Two-part phrasal verbs

Intransitive (= have no object)

end up: *He ended up in jail.*

get up: *They get up really early.*

Examples include: *end up, get up, look out, shut up, sleep on, wake up*

Transitive (= have an object)

a) inseparable (= object must always follow the particle)

call for: *They called for a full investigation.* (not *They called a full investigation for.*)

look through: *I'll look through the report before the meeting.* (not *I'll look the report through before the meeting.*)

Examples include: *call for, come after, count on, get over, go into, look after, look for, look through, make of, take after*

b) separable (= object can come either before or after the particle, when it is a pronoun it must come between the verb and the particle)

bring out: *He brings out the best in me. / He brings the best out in me.*

bring round: *He brought round some friends from university for dinner. / He brought some friends from university round for dinner.*

Examples include: *bring out, bring round, call off, drop off, get up, give up, look up, make up, pass around, pick up, put across, put out*

c) always separable (= object must always come between the verb and the particle)

call back: *Can you call Jane back?* (not *Can you call back Jane?*)

invite out: *He invited all the staff out to dinner.* (not *He invited out all the staff to dinner.*)

Examples include: *call back, call over, invite out, talk round, tell apart*

Three-part phrasal verbs

All three part phrasal verbs are transitive. Some have two objects.

a) three part phrasal verbs with one object – the object always follows the particles (vppn)

come down with: *Alex has come down with chicken pox.*

face up to: *He's going to have to face up to the fact that she's left him.*

Other examples include: *come up with, face up to, get away with, get down to, get on with, get through to, go through with, live up to, look forward to, look up to, put up with, stand up for*

b) examples of three part phrasal verbs with two objects – the first object follows the verb, the second object follows the particles (vnppn)

bring up in: *I thought I asked you not to bring that up in the conversation!*

put down to: *I put it all down to lack of experience.*

Other examples include: *play off against, put down to, put up with, put up to, take up on, talk round to*

Appendix 5 Common prepositions and their meanings

Prepositions of time

for

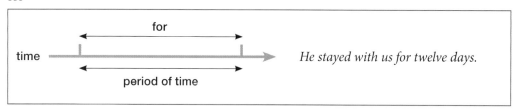

He stayed with us for twelve days.

in / during

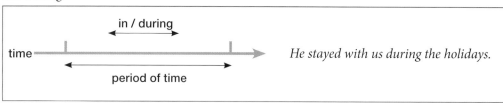

He stayed with us during the holidays.

from ... to ... / between

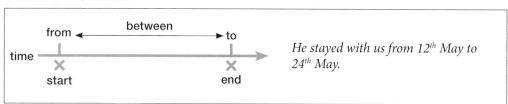

He stayed with us from 12th May to 24th May.

Prepositions of place

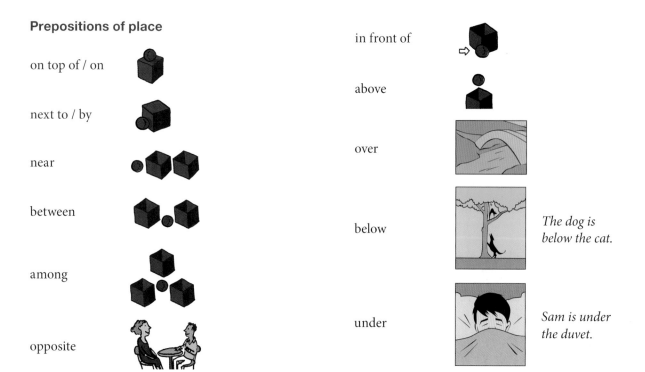

on top of / on

next to / by

near

between

among

opposite

in front of

above

over

below

The dog is below the cat.

under

Sam is under the duvet.

Prepositions of movement

to, towards, at

*The car sped **towards** the wall.*

in

*The driver was **in** the car.*

into

*The car crashed **into** the wall.*

out of

*The man came **out of** his house.*

out

*The man took **out** his phone.*

over / across

*The man went **across** the road to phone the police.*

*Gemma and Fido walked **along** the path.*

*The cat ran **down** the other side.*

*They walked **past** a tree.*

*Gemma lifted Fido **from** the tree.*

*Fido chased a cat **up** a tree.*

Answer key (and tapescript)

Unit 1

1   **1** makes   **2** watches   **3** has   **4** carries   **5** spends
    6 brushes   **7** eats   **8** loves

2   **1** 's   **2** goes
    3 asks   **4** does everyone call
    5 looks   **6** replies
    7 don't believe   **8** doesn't look
    9 isn't   **10** studies
    11 serves   **12** celebrate
    13 Do you have   **14** don't cut
    15 don't need   **16** slices

3   **1** I take a long holiday once a year.
    2 Why are you always late?
    3 It isn't always sunny here.
    4 He practices the piano three times a week.
    5 Do they go canoeing every weekend?
    6 Robert rarely misses a day from work.

4   **1** Students' own answers

Unit 2

1   **1** are looking for   **2** 's studying for
    3 isn't always going up   **4** 're always working

2   **1** are you watching   **2** 's working   **3** discovers
    4 Is it   **5** are playing   **6** 're always watching
    7 never watch   **8** enjoy   **9** I don't watch

3   **1** They are currently developing
    2 The postman delivers our letters
    3 You always talk
    4 This room is always cold
    5 Why are my course fees going up
    6 It's night time and the wind is blowing

Unit 3

1   **1** B   **2** A   **3** A   **4** B   **5** B   **6** A   **7** B   **8** A   **9** A   **10** B

2   **1** ~~I'm not knowing~~/I don't know
    2 ~~I'm not understanding~~/I don't understand
    3 ~~I'm not speaking~~/I don't speak
    4 ~~Are you meaning~~/Do you mean
    5 ~~I'm not believing~~/I don't believe
    6 ~~I'm being in England~~/I'm in England

3   **1** I believe   **2** belongs   **3** love   **4** don't agree
    5 owns   **6** see   **7** is seeing   **8** have

4   Students' own answers

Unit 4

1   **1** They have been in this traffic jam for hours.
    2 I've had toothache for three hours.
    3 They've been married since 1957.
    4 We've supported this team since we were children.

2   **1** 've been living in France for a month
    2 has been smoking since he was a child
    3 've been watching it for three hours
    4 've been driving since nine this morning
    5 has been practising the same piece since
        yesterday/has been practising the same piece of
        music for two days

3   **1** 've been working   **2** haven't seen
    3 have you been   **4** have you been waiting
    5 've been staying   **6** has wanted
    7 's been talking   **8** 've always spent

Unit 5

1   **1** B   **2** B   **3** A   **4** A   **5** A   **6** B   **7** A   **8** A   **9** B   **10** A

2   **1** Have you always worked   **2** Do you always work
    3 Has he been waiting   **4** Are you thinking
    5 do you think   **6** Does Leila eat seafood
    7 is she weighing   **8** does he weigh

3   **1** always   **2** at the moment   **3** all week   **4** always
    5 three times a day   **6** for a few years   **7** nowadays

4   **1** agrees   **2** always changing
    3 are appearing   **4** have been using
    5 for   **6** believe
    7 thinks   **8** have been
    9 since   **10** has been comparing
    11 have been saying   **12** has also been studying
    13 don't often change   **14** evolve

5   **1** I do not believe you!
    2 He doesn't live here any more.
    3 Wait! Caroline's coming, too.
    4 The trains are not stopping here.
    5 I am not going and that is final!
    6 You've been studying for hours.
    7 No, I have not.

6 1 A 2 B 3 A

7 the present simple

Track 🔊 1.06

Announcer:	Comedy show
Comedian:	There's this man and he goes to his doctor and asks: 'Doctor, Doctor. Why does everyone call me a liar?' The doctor looks at him and replies: 'I don't believe you.'
Announcer:	Sports programme
	It doesn't look good for the opponents of the two Williams sisters. Surely, it isn't possible to survive match point against the powerful serve of Venus. She studies the ball and then she serves. It's all over! The two sisters celebrate an easy victory.
Announcer:	Cookery show
Voiceover:	Do you have problems with your kitchen knives? Perhaps they don't cut the way you want. Well now you don't need to worry. The new 'Goliath' slices through any type of meat every time.

Unit 6

1 1 have won   2 has made
    3 has travelled   4 circled
    5 did   6 has visited
    7 has also been 8 has ever visited
    9 developed   10 drove

2 1 Has / ever won   2 did / follow
    3 has / visited   4 has – visited
    5 did / develop

3 1 have ever done 2 've done 3 climbed
    4 've climbed 5 reached 6 wanted 7 was
    8 caught 9 have never felt 10 haven't visited
    11 never been 12 never seen

4 1 Has John arrived yet?
    2 Have you ever been on a cruise?
    3 No, I've already cooked dinner.
    4 I haven't read it yet.
    5 I've seen this film twice already./I've already seen this film twice!

Unit 7

1 1 They have been playing in the garden.
    2 She's been chopping onions.
    3 What have you been doing?
    4 Have you been hitting your sister?

2 1 broken   2 been looking
    3 been cooking   4 baked
    5 been helping   6 finished

3 1 ✓ 2 I've written 3 ✓ 4 They've won
    5 He's made 6 He's just finished

4 1 Have you heard
    2 has just resigned
    3 hasn't been getting on
    4 have been arguing
    5 have had
    6 has decided
    7 has quit
    8 has already started

Unit 8

1 8 7 3 5 2 4 6 1

2 1 was climbing   2 happened
    3 was coming   4 fell
    5 broke   6 were
    7 had finished   8 got
    9 had stopped   10 were getting
    11 explained   12 had broken
    13 had already put   14 invited
    15 heard   16 ran
    17 was happening   18 had knocked
    19 was eating   20 had fallen

3 1 did / hear   2 happened
    3 was having   4 was playing
    5 broke   6 didn't find out
    7 had already / left 8 did / take

Unit 9

1 1 had been working   2 hadn't been listening
    3 had been crying   4 hadn't been living

2 1 had she been working 2 Had he been listening
    3 had he been doing   4 had she been living

3 1 fallen 2 been going 3 started 4 met
5 been seeing 6 realised 7 seen 8 found

4 1 'd been working 2 'd seen 3 'd noticed
4 'd never spoken 5 'd been doing 6 'd been having
7 had all been talking 8 hadn't noticed
9 had never felt 10 'd just bought 11 'd been spending

Unit 10

1 1 a 2 a 3 b 4 a 5 a 6 a

2 1 was   2 sent
3 have collected   4 has been collecting
5 has built   6 created
7 started   8 didn't have

3 1 had spent   2 wanted/had wanted
3 was walking   4 passed
5 was driving   6 offered
7 stopped   8 had already started
9 drove   10 looked
11 laughed   12 have never felt

4 1 yet   2 never
3 when   4 just
5 all weekend   6 for years and years
7 already   8 last year

5 1 've been thinking   2 've never met
3 was   4 was driving
5 flew   6 looked
7 had disappeared   8 appeared
9 was   10 had fallen
11 been trying   12 Had it saved

6 1 unstressed   2 stressed
3 unstressed   4 unstressed
5 stressed   6 stressed
7 stressed   8 unstressed
9 stressed

7 1 ~~years~~ → months
2 ~~They'd been working on a project~~ → They'd been doing a training course
3 ~~They'd been having lunch~~ → They'd been having a drink
4 ~~easy~~ → difficult
5 ~~in front of~~ → behind
6 ~~She stood on his foot and spilt his drink.~~ → He stepped back and spilt her drink.
7 ~~car~~ → house
8 ~~gardening~~ → painting and decorating

Track ⊘1.13

We'd been working for the same company for a couple of months. I'd seen her in the distance and I'd noticed how attractive she was, but we'd never spoken. Then, while we'd been doing a training course together, we finally got to know each other. We'd been having a drink with the other people on the course at the end of the first day, and we had all been talking about how difficult it was. I hadn't noticed that she was standing just behind me. I laughed at one of the jokes, stepped back, and spilt her drink down her dress! I had never felt so embarrassed in my life. But she was really nice about it. I bought her another drink and we got talking. She told me she had just bought a house on my street and that she had been spending her weekends painting and decorating. I offered to help her. That's how it all started!

Unit 11

1 1 When I got home …
2 I checked my emails before I …
3 Once I'd seen …
4 I waited until the pasta had cooked …
5 As soon as I had finished watching the news …

2 1 We checked the train times carefully before we left for the concert./Before we left for the concert, we checked the train times carefully.
2 By the time our train arrived at the station, it was getting late./It was getting late by the time our train arrived at the station.
3 As soon as we got off the train, we ran to the bus stop./We ran to the bus stop as soon as we got off the train.
4 Once we were on the bus, we texted the others to tell them we were on our way./We texted the others to tell them we were on our way once we were on the bus.
5 When we finally got there, we found out that the concert had been cancelled./We found out that the concert had been cancelled when we finally got there.

3 1 Before leaving the house …
2 -ing form not possible
3 After leaving our bags at the hostel …
4 Before playing an important match …
5 -ing form not possible
6 Before leaving home and moving into her own flat …

4 Students' own answers

Unit 12

1 1 ~~While~~ → When   2 ✓
3 ~~while~~ → when   4 ✓
5 ✓   6 ✓
7 ~~while~~ → when   8 ~~While~~ → When

2 1 ~~While~~   2 all possible
3 ~~While~~   4 ~~While~~
5 ~~as/while~~   6 ~~when~~

3 1 When giving a presentation to a room full of people, always speak slowly and clearly.
2 When crossing the road, remember to look both ways.
3 While waiting for the pasta to cook, you can prepare the sauce.
4 He looked very uncomfortable when answering questions from the press./When answering the questions from the press, he looked very uncomfortable.
5 She looked distractedly through the window at the rain while listening to my questions./ While listening to my questions, she looked distractedly through the window at the rain.
6 Don't use your mobile phone while driving the car./While driving the car, don't use your mobile phone.

Unit 13

1 1 Did you use to live
2 did
3 used to have
4 Did you use to eat
5 used to have to
6 used to take
7 used not to like
8 used to be

2 1 I used to go to belly dancing classes when I was at school.
2 I started my first classes when I was eight.
3 We used to take part in competitions.
4 I used to love performing in front of an audience.
5 I continued dancing for almost six years.
6 Then I lost interest and I took up basketball instead.

7 I used to play in the school team and we used to train every day of the week.
8 We used to be pretty good and we won three local championships.

3 1 – 2 would 3 wouldn't 4 – 5 would 6 would
7 – 8 – 9 would 10 wouldn't

4 Students' own answers

Unit 14

1 1 I'm 2 get 3 I'm slowly getting 4 got 5 get

2 1 was 2 got 3 'll get 4 wasn't 5 was 6 aren't

3 1 did / use to
2 used to
3 used to
4 was used to
5 get used to
6 was used to
7 get used to
8 was not used to
9 getting used to
10 got used to
11 used to

4 Students' own answers

Unit 15

1 1 ~~call~~ → calling
2 ~~used~~ → use
3 ~~while~~ → when
4 ~~use~~ → used
5 ~~would~~ → used to
6 ~~have~~ → having
7 ~~already started~~ → had already started
8 ~~last~~ → a
9 ~~making~~ → make

2 1 What did you do after he left?
2 Are you getting used to your new routine?
3 What did you use to do?
4 What must you remember to do before leaving?
5 What were you doing when she came in?
6 Are you used to working with animals?
7 What did you use to do on those long winter nights?
8 Where did they go after leaving the restaurant?

Answer key (and tapescript)

3 1 6   2 1   3 3   4 4   5 8   6 2   7 7   8 5

4 1 until 2 Did 3 used to 4 didn't even use to
5 get 6 'm 7 before 8 While 9 When
10 by the time

5 1 would 2 when 3 to 4 used 5 when 6 get
7 By 8 would 9 when 10 soon

6 1 A: Did you **use to** enjoy school? /s/
B: No, I didn't! I **used to** hate it! I didn't use
to want to go and I **used to** make all kinds
of excuses to try and stay at home! /s/, /s/, /s/
A: Did you **use** computers in your last
school? /z/
B: Yes, for forms and records and things, but we
never **used** them in class. /z/

2 no

7 1 He used to be a banker.
2 Because his job used to be very stressful.
3 His old job was stressful and the working day
was longer. His new job has shorter working
hours and he has longer holidays now.
4 Yes. He was used to earning more money.
5 He likes working shorter hours and having
longer holidays.

Track 🎧 1.17

A: So, what did you use to do before you became a
teacher?
B: I used to work as a banker in the City, in London.
A: Why did you decide to become a teacher?
B: My working life used to be very stressful. I was
used to working ten or twelve hours a day and
under a lot of pressure. It was very tiring and I
decided it was time for a change.
A: Was it difficult to get used to your new lifestyle?
B: Well, I was used to earning a lot more money, so
it took me a bit of time to get used to living on
a teacher's salary! And I wasn't used to working
with kids, but now I'm slowly getting used to the
role of teacher and I'm loving every minute of it –
well, almost!
A: And what about your new working routine?
B: I got used to the shorter working hours and the
longer holidays very quickly! I only used to take
ten or fifteen days holiday a year when I was
a banker. Now I have six weeks' holiday in the
summer alone. That's great!

Unit 16

1 1 Am 2 Is 3 Has 4 Does 5 Did 6 Had

2 1 met   2 did he meet
3 did he spend   4 did he tell
5 did he return   6 children has he got?
7 made   8 did he give

3 1 for 2 sort 3 like 4 many 5 can 6 –

Unit 17

1 1 Hasn't he done a good job
2 Can't I come with you
3 Won't they take a break soon
4 Don't they know how expensive this is
5 Can you tell me where Phillip is
6 Do you think Marilyn will like our idea
7 I don't know how I made so many mistakes
8 Do you have any idea how many people are coming

2 1 c 2 a 3 f 4 e 5 d 6 b

3 1 haven't you talked to your boss
2 I take the rest
3 today's lesson
4 how much potatoes are
5 aren't coming
6 help me move
7 how long Gabriel has been playing
8 spell his name C-H-U-I, don't you

Unit 18

1 1 haven't we   2 weren't you
3 wasn't it   4 are you
5 isn't it   6 didn't you
7 do you   8 shouldn't I
9 won't you   10 shall we
11 will you

2 1 aren't you   2 isn't it
3 do they   4 doesn't she
5 wasn't there   6 haven't they
7 aren't I   8 could I
9 hadn't he   10 isn't she
11 will you   12 mustn't you
13 shall we   14 hasn't it

3 Students' own answers

Unit 19

1   1 D 2 I 3 H 4 F 5 A 6 J 7 B 8 E 9 G 10 C

2
1 did	2 wasn't
3 is	4 haven't
5 am	6 have
7 was	8 do
9 Won't	10 Will
11 Doesn't	12 Did

3   Students' own answers

Unit 20

1   1 did 2 didn't 3 Is 4 Could/Would 5 haven't
6 Would 7 did 8 shall

2   1 did 2 at 3 not 4 do 5 is (getting) 6 do
7 B: love 8 not

3   1 aren't you 2 you are going 3 you going
4 hasn't she 5 Rachel finished 6 Rachel has finished
7 could you 8 you could help me move
9 you help me move 10 like you, doesn't he
11 look like you, does he 12 he looks like you

4   1 What does he look like?
2 When did it happen?
3 Do you know if it's going to rain this afternoon?
4 You aren't Maria, are you?
5 What type of car do you think she drives?
6 Can't I give you the report tomorrow?
7 My daughter doesn't eat any kind of vegetable.
8 I've bought a new hat.

5   1 Have you brought 2 you haven't 3 you think
4 he is 5 did he die 6 I received 7 Did you
8 aren't you

6   1 up 2 down 3 up 4 up 5 down 6 up 7 down
8 up

Track 1.22
1 Man: We've met before, haven't we?
2 Woman: That was a long time ago, wasn't it?
3 Man: You aren't Michael's colleague, are you?
4 Woman: You don't do any business with us, do you?
5 Man: You will be here later, won't you?
6 Woman: Let's keep in touch about this, shall we?
7 Man: Don't forget to call me, will you?
8 Woman: We weren't at school together, were we?

7   1 False 2 False 3 True 4 False 5 True 6 False

Track 1.23
A: We've met before, haven't we?
B: Sorry, you'll have to remind me.
A: You were on a training course with me in Bristol,
    weren't you?
B: Yes! That was a long time ago, wasn't it? I
    remember now. You aren't Malcolm, are you?
A: That's right. Malcolm Savage.
B: Peter Franks. Nice to meet you again. It's funny
    how you meet people again at these events, isn't it?
A: Well, it's a small world. You worked for Haversham
    Plastics then, didn't you?
B: Yes. I still do. You don't do any business with us,
    do you?
A: No, I'm afraid not. But I have a colleague here who
    works in your industry. In fact he's looking for a
    supplier.
B: I should meet him, shouldn't I?
A: Yes, but I can't see him at the moment. Never
    mind. You'll be here later, won't you?
B: Actually I have to go in a minute.
A: OK. Well, let's keep in touch about this, shall we?
    Here's my card with my phone number. Don't
    forget to call me, will you?
B: No, I won't. Thanks. It was nice meeting you again.

Unit 21

1   1 She doesn't like him.
2 Theirs is easier than ours.
3 Is there any difference between them?
4 They worked with them in Budapest.

2
1 B / myself	2 B / yourself
3 B / themselves	4 B / yourselves
5 A / themselves	

3   1 ones 2 one 3 ones 4 one

4   1 me 2 you 3 us 4 mine 5 hers 6 yourself
7 yourself 8 one

Unit 22

1   1 baggage 2 ✓ 3 snow 4 need 5 times 6 ✓
7 drinks 8 gossip 9 any 10 ✓

2
1 a slice of lemon	2 a tin of soup
3 a loaf of bread	4 a piece of cake
5 a pack of cards	6 a type of insect

3 1 are 2 helps 3 is 4 do 5 cut 6 isn't/aren't
7 haven't

4 1 B 2 A 3 A 4 B 5 A 6 B

Unit 23

1 1 ø 2 an 3 some 4 ø 5 a 6 an

2 1 a 2 the 3 a 4 the 5 an 6 the 7 the 8 a 9 a
10 a 11 a 12 the 13 the 14 the 15 the

3 1A the 1B a 1C ø 2A ø 2B an 2C the 3A ø
3B The 3C a 4A a 4B ø 4C the 5A a 5B the 5C ø

Unit 24

1 1 ø 2 the 3 the 4 ø 5 ø 6 the 7 ø 8 ø 9 ø
10 ø 11 the 12 the 13 ø 14 the 15 the

2 1 the 2 ✓ 3 the 4 the (New York) 5 the (bus)
6 ✓ 7 ✓ 8 the 9 ✓ 10 the 11 ✓

3 Students' own answers

Unit 25

1 1 D 2 I 3 F 4 E 5 B 6 H 7 J 8 C 9 G 10 A

2 1 There's a …
2 … it might be hers
3 Give me …
4 It switches itself off.
5 the President
6 a bit of sugar
7 two apple juices
8 hurt yourself
9 he argues with you

3 1 an 2 one 3 her 4 The 5 some 6 one

4 1 The Gobi desert
2 The Moon
3 Mount Kilimanjaro
4 Lake Balaton
5 The Taj Mahal
6 Dubai

5 1 A 2 A 3 B 4 C 5 B 6 B 7 B 8 A 9 B 10 B

6 /ɪ/ bit, him, his, it
/iː/ she, me, each, piece, we
/aɪ/ mine, I, type, my

7 1 an Austrian
2 one of the
3 a pianist
4 the most beautiful woman
5 London
6 the secret communications system
7 the modern military

Track ⊘ **1.29**

Hedy Lamarr was an Austrian actress born in Vienna who went on to become one of the most famous Hollywood actresses of the 20th century. Her real name was Hedwig Eva Maria Kiesler. Her mother was a pianist and influenced her daughter's artistic skills as she studied ballet and soon became an actress. She became well-known in European films and was called, 'The most beautiful woman in Europe.' In 1933, she married Fritz Mandal, but she left him four years later. She went to London and met Louis B. Mayer, a film producer. He changed her name to Hedy Lamarr and she went to Hollywood. Nowadays, Lamarr is well-known for her many films from the forties and fifties. However, she was also very intelligent and invented the secret communications system in 1942 which could change radio frequencies and protect radio messages. At the time, the technology was too advanced to help the US Army in World War II but since then it has been used by the modern military and the mobile phone industry.

Unit 26

1 1 some 2 no 3 some 4 any 5 some 6 any
7 any 8 none

2 1 ~~some~~ → any
2 ~~any~~ → some
3 ~~no~~ → any
4 ~~none~~ → no
5 ~~Some of~~ → Some
6 ~~no~~ → none/any

3 1 someone   2 anywhere
3 no one   4 anything
5 Something   6 anything

4 Students' own answers

Unit 27

1 1 Every 2 Each/Every 3 Each of the 4 Both
5 Either 6 either

2 1 ✓   2 are → is
3 were → was   4 ✓
5 need → needs   6 ✓
7 ✓   8 ✓

3 1 All   2 Every
3 Each   4 Neither
5 Every   6 either
7 each   8 every
9 Neither

4 Students' own answers

Unit 28

1 1 little 2 a little 3 many 4 much 5 lot 6 lots
7 A lot of 8 Too many 9 few 10 Not much

2 1 A lot of 2 too many/not many 3 Lots 4 too
5 A few 6 too much

3 1 I think there's a little cheese left. Would you like
some?
2 Count how many questions you answered correctly.
3 There are too many people here. I only invited
ten. Who are the other fifteen?
4 A lot of new mobile technology comes out
every week.
5 There are only a few possibilities left to us.
Which should we choose?
6 B: I like a lot of the songs but not all of them.

Unit 29

1 1 B 2 C 3 A 4 F 5 D 6 E

2 1 Most
2 enough
3 plenty
4 A large amount/A great deal of
5 several
6 A large number of
7 most of

3 1 enough 2 not enough 3 plenty 4 most
5 great deal 6 large number

4 Suggested answers:
A large number of / Most
plenty of
A large number of
Several

Unit 30

1 1 A 2 A 3 B 4 A 5 A 6 B 7 B 8 B

2 1 none → no
2 Some of them.
3 are → is
4 nowhere → anywhere
5 All of the products …
6 neither → either
7 … a large number of local people …
8 A few

3 1 There are no new emails in your inbox.
2 Aren't there any left?
3 Some of their products are not very well made.
4 My team won neither match.
5 Every contestant had to run 20 kilometres.
6 We've got plenty of food to share with you.
7 Many people are now concerned about climate
change.
8 There are few parks in our town.
9 Most people don't give much thought to their
future.
10 We haven't got enough time to plan a big party.

4 1 all 2 somewhere 3 lots/a lot 4 Each/Every
5 every 6 any 7 no 8 too much 9 enough
10 A large number 11 little 12 a great deal/plenty
13 lots of 14 few 15 some

5 1 have‿any
2 some‿of
3 chicken‿either
4 large‿amount
5 not‿enough / pay‿for
6 lots‿of
7 take‿a
8 most‿of

6   **1** All football-tennis matches …
    2 Every court …
    3 Neither team …
    4 … either of the teams …
    5 … must score 15 points.
    6 … between every game.
    7 Neither the player's hand …

Track 🎧 1.33

The rules of Football-Tennis.

The court
All football-tennis matches are played on a court. Every court must be the same size as a standard doubles tennis court. The court is divided into two halves by the net.

The teams
Each team has a total of five players with three players on the court. Neither team is allowed to make more than two substitutions per game but they can make more over the whole match.

The match
Every match is decided over three games or when either of the teams has won two games. The winner of each game must score 15 points. There is a three-minute break between every game.

Other rules
A team can pass the ball three times but then has to kick or head it over the net. Neither the player's hand nor arm can touch the ball.

Unit 31

1   **1** a: sleepy   **2** a: main
      b: asleep   b: important
    3 a: good   **4** a: entire
      b: well   b: complete

2   **1** tiny magnetic desktop
    2 amazing new instant
    3 huge warm cotton
    4 delicious home-made Italian/clever little plastic

3   **1** black and white
    2 silly and childish
    3 weird and wonderful
    4 tall, dark and handsome

    5 Asian and Western
    6 strawberry and chocolate

4   **1** the young and the old
    2 a young person
    3 The British
    4 Spanish girl
    5 The Italians
    6 The super rich

5   Students' own answers

Unit 32

1   **1** tired   **2** depressed
    3 exciting   **4** interesting
    5 boring   **6** satisfied
    7 worrying   **8** surprised

2   **1** ~~with~~   **2** ~~with~~
    3 ✓   **4** ✓
    5 ~~with~~   **6** ✓
    7 ✓   **8** ~~about~~

3   **1** ~~about~~ → with   **2** ~~with~~ → about
    3 ~~of~~ → in   **4** ~~on~~ → at
    5 ~~in~~ → to   **6** ~~looking~~ → look

4   Students' own answers

Unit 33

1   **1** critically   **2** truly
    3 horribly   **4** luckily
    5 beautifully   **6** immediately
    7 enthusiastically

2   **1** ✓
    2 I suddenly heard a loud noise from outside./ Suddenly, I heard a loud noise from outside.
    3 ✓
    4 I looked carefully up and down the street./I looked up and down the street, carefully.
    5 Then I stepped out extremely slowly and cautiously. /Then I stepped out slowly and extremely cautiously.
    6 The street outside was completely silent.
    7 ✓/There was apparently nothing or nobody there./ Apparently, there was nothing or nobody there.
    8 So I closed the door quietly and went back to the TV./ So I quietly closed the door and went back to the TV.

3   **1** I can't speak to him honestly.
    2 Personally, I don't think he'll have the courage
       to tell her.
    3 I can't work normally if there's music on.
    4 Happily, he laughed when he heard the joke.
    5 We realised that he couldn't walk quickly.
    6 Incredibly, I said something stupid.

4   **1** b **2** a **3** b **4** b **5** b **6** b

Unit 34

1   **1** He lives at the end of the street.
    2 The children go to school nearby./The children
       go to the nearby school.
    3 My car is parked over there.
    4 Do you live near here?
    5 Both of my parents live locally.
    6 Are there any parks in the area?
    7 She spent ten years working abroad.
    8 I left my shoes outside the door.

2   **1** 2 **2** 2 **3** 1 **4** 2 **5** 1 **6** 2 **7** 1 **8** 1

3   **1** yet **2** just **3** still **4** already **5** soon **6** now
    7 ago **8** already **9** here

4   **1** B **2** B **3** B **4** B **5** A **6** A, B

Unit 35

1   **1** ~~an alone~~ → a lonely
    2 ~~problem main~~ → main problem
    3 ~~white and black~~ → black and white
    4 ~~rich~~ → the rich
    5 ~~exciting~~ → excited
    6 ~~saying~~ → say
    7 ~~tomorrow an appointment~~ → an appointment
       tomorrow
    8 ~~now here~~ → here now

2   **1** That was our chief concern
    2 small red Italian
    3 the old and the sick
    4 terrifying
    5 to see
    6 his head slowly
    7 her food quickly
    8 a truly incredible

    9 remarkably quickly
  10 always worked

3   **1** the baby was asleep
    2 spoke quietly
    3 was alone
    4 apparently wants to
    5 difficult to study
    6 the painting carefully

4   **1** accidentally **2** alone **3** busily **4** quietly
    5 finally **6** whole **7** At the beginning **8** happily
    9 finally **10** that night

5   **1** short, memorable phrase
    2 basic tone or atmosphere
    3 some are totally hilarious
    4 are deadly serious
    5 have successfully become
    6 be afraid, be very afraid
    7 it was safe to go
    8 long time ago
    9 good reasons to stay single

6   two syllables: quickly, really, slowly, truly
    three syllables: beautifully, carefully completely,
    extremely, naturally, normally, recently, terribly
    four syllables: apparently, remarkably

7   **1** ●● <u>quick</u>ly, <u>real</u>ly, <u>slow</u>ly, <u>tru</u>ly
    2 ●●● <u>beau</u>tifully, <u>care</u>fully, <u>na</u>turally, <u>nor</u>mally,
       <u>re</u>cently, <u>ter</u>ribly
    3 ●●● com<u>plete</u>ly, ex<u>treme</u>ly
    4 ●●●● re<u>mark</u>ably, app<u>ar</u>ently

8   **1** tiring **2** depressing **3** excited **4** interesting
    5 bored **6** satisfied **7** worrying **8** surprised

Track 🎧 **1.38**
1	tiring	**5**	bored
2	depressing	**6**	satisfied
3	excited	**7**	worrying
4	interesting	**8**	surprised

Unit 36

1   **1** closely **2** honest **3** easy **4** defiantly **5** terrible
    6 angry **7** quietly **8** tired **9** anxiously
    10 inevitable **11** sadly **12** slowly

2 1 adjective   2 adverb
    3 adverb   4 adjective
    5 adverb   6 adjective
    7 adverb   8 adjective
    9 adjective   10 adjective

3 1 quickly   2 –/–
    3 closely   4 annually

4 1 late   2 lately   3 lately   4 late   5 hard   6 hardly
    7 hard   8 hardly

Unit 37

1 1 too hard
    2 hard enough
    3 very strained
    4 quite a domineering
    5 rather a quiet man
    6 pretty angry

2 1 A: very   B: totally
    2 A: utterly   B: wasn't very
    3 A: rather   B: absolutely
    4 A: completely   B: extremely
    5 A: absolutely   B: pretty

3 1 wasn't walking quickly enough.
    2 was quite a mild day.
    3 had taken them a pretty long time to find a house.
    4 It was too cold to go swimming.
    5 A fairly long time had passed since we last saw them.
    6 She was speaking too softly/quietly.

4 Students' own answers

Unit 38

1 1 only   2 too   3 just   4 also   5 even   6 only

2 1 I also bought …
    2 Even Jeremy …
    3 it's just Richard …
    4 My father thinks it is interesting as well.
    5 to come too, but …
    6 I'm only asking …
    7 Sue alone finished …
    8 I just have to …

3 1 meet the rest of the band, too
    2 alone passed the exam
    3 also like Bollywood movies
    4 only listen to classical music
    5 just want to be left in peace
    6 does most of the housework, even the cooking

Unit 39

1 1 so   2 such   3 so   4 so   5 such   6 such

2 1 such   2 so   3 so   4 such   5 so   6 such

3 1 Why is she driving so slowly?
    2 I don't know why there are so few people.
    3 India is such a beautiful country.
    4 There's so much to do.

4 1 so nice   2 such a difficult   3 such a strange
    4 be so   5 such a handsome   6 so wonderful
    7 such a rude

Unit 40

1 1 He worked hard to finish the job.
    2 Is the coffee strong enough for you?
    3 Have you been on holiday lately?
    4 Would you like to eat something too?
    5 He moved so quietly that nobody heard a sound.
    6 She's much too clever to make that mistake.
    7 He even forgot his mother's birthday.
    8 I've played that game as well.
    9 My hair is such a mess today.
    10 Your work has been so useful.

2 1 Only John   2 you only eat meat
    3 so beautiful   4 such a good idea
    5 got up late   6 quite a good idea

3 1 late   2 just   3 hard   4 as well   5 hardly   6 even
    7 alone   8 only

4 1 His laugh was very loud.
    2 The flat was too small for the four of them.
    3 It was quite a successful party.
    4 I've been going to bed at three o'clock in the morning lately.
    5 We were absolutely starving when we got home.
    6 She was very pleased with her present.
    7 He didn't speak slowly enough.
    8 He smiled (happily) at her (happily).

5 1 late 2 so 3 just 4 also 5 hard 6 so 7 Just 8 such 9 also 10 too

6 1 really 2 so even 3 too 4 such 5 so 6 only 7 alone 8 too

7 1 son 2 son 3 father 4 father 5 father 6 son 7 father

Unit 41

1 1 better   2 worse
       3 most boring   4 longer
       5 worst   6 higher
       7 more slowly   8 faster
       9 more importantly

2 1 less expensive
       2 the most reliable
       3 is less efficient
       4 the least comfortable
       5 less frequently
       6 more successfully

3 1 difficult   2 longer / harder
       3 least / biggest 4 happier
       5 happiest   6 less / less

4 Students' own answers

Unit 42

1 1 more 2 most 3 less 4 least 5 more 6 fewer 7 less 8 most

2 1 more 2 most 3 more 4 less 5 least 6 more 7 most

3 1 less and less 2 less and less 3 They told the fewest people 4 the less I like him 5 the more mistakes I make 6 the least possible effort 7 the fewer options 8 more and more money

4 Students' own answers

Unit 43

1 1 far more quickly / a lot more mistakes
       2 a little more time / a lot less
       3 easily the best / Even better than / much better
       4 a few more people there / a lot more

2 1 slightly 2 far 3 by far 4 far 5 a lot 6 many

3 Suggested answers:
       1 Cádiz is by far the oldest. It's much, much older than both Madrid and Santiago de Compostela.
       2 Madrid is by far the largest city. It's far, far larger than the other two cities.
       3 Cádiz has the best climate. The winter is much less cold and the summer is pleasantly warm.
       4 Madrid is the most popular with tourists. There are far more visitors there each year.
       5 Students' own answers

Unit 44

1 1 quickly 2 fit 3 easy 4 good 5 new

2 1 as difficult as
       2 not as relaxing
       3 not … as dynamic
       4 as many
       5 as good as the other
       6 are not … as many variations

3 1 as / like   2 like / as
       3 like / as   4 as / as / like

4 Students' own answers

Unit 45

1 1 one of the oldest   2 just as old
       3 older than   4 the greatest number
       5 More people   6 Not as many
       7 not as dominant   8 as popular
       9 much less   10 more

2 **1** ~~by far~~ → far
2 ~~than I had~~ → as I had
3 ~~a bit fewer~~ → fewer
4 ~~the fewest time~~ → the least time
5 ~~the easily most~~ → easily the most
6 ~~so I thought~~ → as I thought

3 **1** like / tall
2 a lot / by far
3 hotter and hotter / even
4 worst / a little / just

4 **1** as warm as
2 less money on clothes
3 nearly as happy
4 twice as big as

5 **1** the more
2 the more time
3 less
4 more slowly
5 the fastest
6 as hungry
7 felt like
8 more than enough
9 as slowly

6 **1** good / gold
2 definitely / easy
3 done / can
4 white / snow
5 nearly / good
6 cunning / fox
7 much / time
8 quite / many

Track 🎧 1.48
1 The children were as good as gold.
2 This is definitely not as easy as I thought.
3 A: I'll get it done as soon as I possibly can.
4 B: Her hair was as white as snow.
5 A: The concert wasn't nearly as good as last time.
6 B: Watch out for him! He's as cunning as a fox!
7 A: There's no hurry, take as much time as you want.
8 B: There weren't quite as many people as we'd expected.

7 Suggested answers:
1 It is the most boring job he's ever had. The hours are longer.
2 She's going faster than anyone else on the road, and she can see a police car.

Track 🎧 1.49
A: How's the new job going? Is it any better than the last one?
B: No! It's worse if anything! It's probably the most boring job I've ever had! And the hours are longer than my other job too. Changing jobs was the worst decision I've ever made!
A: Well, if it's so bad, why don't you quit?
B: Because the wages are higher and I need the extra money!
A: I think maybe you should drive a little more slowly.
B: Why? Do you think I'm going too fast?
A: Well you're certainly going faster than anyone else on the road! But more importantly, there's a police car over there, and they're going to stop you for speeding!

Unit 46

1 **1** A: on / B: in
2 A: at / B: in
3 A: on / B: at
4 A: in the night / B: at night
5 A: in time / B: on time
6 A: In the end / B: at the end

2 A: on
B: on
A: –
B: in
A: on
B: on
A: –
B: at
A: at

3 **1** for the job in time
2 meet every Monday
3 In the end
4 within five minutes
5 at night
6 on Friday

Unit 47

1 **1** A **2** B **3** B **4** A **5** B **6** A **7** B **8** A

2 **1** since **2** for **3** During **4** after **5** From **6** between

3 **1** A **2** C **3** B **4** B **5** C **6** A **7** C

Unit 48

1 1 on 2 on 3 at 4 on 5 in 6 in 7 at 8 in

2 1 on the phone 2 in the queue 3 on an island
4 in the newspaper 5 in the photograph
6 at a wedding 7 from home

3a 1 on 2 in 3 in 4 on

3b 1 in 2 at 3 in 4 at 5 in 6 at 7 at

3c 1 at 2 on 3 on 4 at

Unit 49

1 1 on 2 on top of 3 near 4 next to 5 between
6 among 7 in front of 8 opposite

2 1 on/on top of 2 on top of 3 near 4 next to/by
5 next to 6 between 7 among 8 in front of
9 opposite 10 over 11 over 12 above
13 under 14 under 15 below

3 Students' own answers

Unit 50

1 1 in 2 on 3 at 4 on 5 on 6 in 7 in 8 at 9 on
10 at 11 at 12 on

2 1 ✓ 2 ~~in~~ on 3 ~~on~~ at 4 ✓ 5 ~~in~~ on 6 ~~in~~ at 7 ~~on~~
8 ✓ 9 ~~in~~ on (a cruise liner) 10 ~~at~~ in

3 1 for 2 before 3 by 4 above 5 between now and
four o'clock 6 among 7 above 8 under 9 on

4 1 from / to 2 at / in 3 on / over 4 on top of / until
5 In / among 6 In / in 7 opposite / by

5 1 In 2 on 3 in 4 Within 5 at 6 by 7 in 8 in
9 on 10 opposite 11 over/above 12 among
13 on 14 in 15 until 16 at 17 in 18 By 19 on

6 1 it's‿in 2 lives‿on top‿of
3 waiting‿on 4 light‿among
5 Paul‿at 6 stand‿in front‿of
7 were‿over 8 working‿until‿after

7 1 T 2 F 3 T 4 F 5 T

Unit 51

1 1 to 2 towards 3 to 4 at 5 into 6 in 7 out
8 out of 9 across 10 over

2 1 through 2 out of 3 across 4 past 5 behind
6 out 7 around 8 towards

3 1 out of / walked to
2 past the shop / at the newsagent's
3 on one of the seats
4 came up the hill
5 driving along the road

6 drove away from him
7 rose up slowly from his seat / walked back down
  the road to his house.
8 got to his house / walked in

Unit 52

1 1 b 2 f 3 d 4 a 5 g 6 e 7 c 8 h

2 1 listening to
2 looking at
3 telling you about
4 think of
5 wait for
6 worries about work too much
7 you asked for
8 live with

3 1 studying for
2 laughing at
3 argue with
4 applied for

4 1 They blamed me for their mistake
2 I've made a cake for you
3 Have you invited Beth to the party?
4 He congratulated me on my hard work.
5 I'll never be able to forgive him for that.
6 She helped me with my homework.
7 Where did she steal the money from?
8 What was he arrested for?

Unit 53

1 1 through this report yet
2 it off
3 it up
4 of it
5 out
6 her back
7 for massive cuts
8 on everyone's support
9 down to
10 the boss over

2 1 They're bringing out a new album. / They're
  bringing a new album out.
2 They've called the wedding off / called off the
  wedding.
3 He knew the police would come after him.
4 She finally managed to get away.

5 She gave up her job to travel around the world.
6 Amy has decided to go into acting.
7 Keep to the road or you'll get lost.
8 He put his message across very clearly.

3 1 He made it up and everyone believed him.
2 passed them around
3 looked after them
4 quickly put it out
5 ran after her
6 always sided with him

Unit 54

1 1, 3, 6, 4, 2, 5, 7

2 1 up with a brilliant idea
2 you up on
3 up on some work
4 him up to
5 down with the flu
6 up to my maths teacher
7 on with Fiona
8 up his name in

3 1 through with this
2 face up to
3 their success down to
4 dropped out of
5 you went out with
6 to live up to
7 to put up with
8 played them off against each other

4 Students' own answers

Unit 55

1 1 out 2 to 3 towards 4 about 5 me up
  6 after them 7 in 8 about 9 about 10 over

2 1 of 2 with 3 of 4 on 5 at 6 to 7 with 8 at

3 1 from 2 about 3 with 4 after 5 to 6 up
  7 of 8 on

4 Group 1. through   Group 2. over
    Group 3. to   Group 4. out

5 1 through 2 down 3 across 4 off 5 blew 6 out
  7 through 8 get 9 cleaning 10 to

6

Track 2.05

A: Can you turn the <u>light</u> off, please? (short pause)

B: Can you turn it <u>off</u>, please?

7 1 kids 2 up 3 TV 4 on 5 address 6 up

Track 2.06

1 A: Can you pick the <u>kids</u> up from school, please?

2 B Can't you do it? I picked them <u>up</u> yesterday.

3 A: Can you switch on the <u>TV</u>, please?

4 B: Can't you switch it <u>on</u>? You're much nearer.

5 A: Do you want me to look that <u>address</u> up for you?

6 B: No, it's OK, thanks. I've already looked it <u>up</u>.

8 1 It was dropped off this morning.

2 No, he hasn't had the chance to pick it up yet.

3 It calls for massive cuts in spending.

4 She needs to know she can count on everyone's support.

Track 2.07

A: Have you had a chance to look through this report yet?

B: No, I haven't. Dave dropped it off on my desk this morning, but I honestly haven't had the chance to pick it up yet. I've been too busy.

A: Janet wants to know what you make of it. She's asked me to find out what you think. She wants me to call her back as soon as I have.

B: Why's it so urgent?

A: Well, apparently it's calling for massive cuts in spending – it could even mean some people losing their jobs. Janet wants to fight it if she can, but she needs to know she can count on everyone's support – and that, of course, includes you.

B: Mmm, I'd better get down to reading it then! Or maybe we should call the boss over to explain it to us in person.

Unit 56

1 1 H 2 B 3 D 4 E 5 G 6 A 7 F 8 C

2 1 We're going
2 are you going to
3 We're going to

4 There'll be
5 It'll be
6 I'm going to buy
7 is staying
8 I'll do
9 I'll pay

3 1 What are you doing tomorrow?
2 Who do you think is going to win the competition?
3 It will not rain tomorrow.
4 I'm taking the day off.
5 The flight leaves …
6 Are you going to sell …
7 It will be really difficult …
8 The exam starts ….

Unit 57

1a 1 will be taking off
2 will be flying
3 will be landing
4 will be serving
5 will be starting
6 will be selling

1b 1 will have crossed
2 will have driven
3 will have slept
4 will have seen
5 will have visited
6 will have arrived

1c 1 will have been working
2 won't have been getting
3 won't have been eating

2 1 B: I'll be travelling
2 A: have finished / B: have been working
3 B: have been living
4 A: be seeing / B: be going

3 Students' own answers

Unit 58

1 1 I'll call you when I get home.
2 I won't come out until I've finished my work.
3 I'll speak to Sue next time I see her.
4 I'll have cooked the dinner by the time you get home. / I'll have the dinner cooked …
5 They'll text us before they get to the station.
6 I'll speak to the boss as soon as I get a chance.

7 I'll do the dishes after the football has finished.
8 Once the exams finish I won't be so busy.

2 1 'll call 2 've finished 3 'll see 4 comes 5 'll be
6 get 7 don't 8 'll be 9 'll get 10 arrive
11 'll have had 12 leave

3 1 if 2 when/if 3 if 4 if 5 when 6 if 7 when/if
8 when

4 Students' own answers

Unit 59

1 1 bound 2 unlikely 3 about 4 unlikely
5 bound

2 1 's likely to rain
2 was bound to
3 was about to
4 was unlikely to
5 's about to
6 's unlikely to

3 1 C 2 E 3 D 4 A 5 B 6 F

4 Students' own answers

Unit 60

1 1 B 2 A 3 C 4 E 5 F 6 D

2 1 ~~snowing~~ → going to snow
2 ~~will you go~~ → are you going
3 ~~have been finishing~~ → have finished
4 ~~I'll get~~ → I get
5 ~~if~~ → when
6 ~~bound to~~ → about to
7 ~~is~~ → was

3 1 B 2 B 3 B 4 A 5 A 6 B

4 1 are you going
2 won't be
3 be going
4 going to
5 'll do
6 have gone
7 want
8 'll get
9 I'm

5 1 about
2 'll text

3 we get
4 have got
5 have been working
6 bound
7 to stay
8 're having
9 if
10 have had
11 'll see
12 when

6 1 A. 2 B. 1 2 A. 1 B. 2 3 A. 2 B. 1 4 A. 2 B. 1
5 A.1 B.2

Track 🎧 2.14

1 A: I'll be ready at four.
    B: He'll have arrived by then.
2 A: They'll arrive at nine.
    B: They arrive at nine.
3 A: I have finished all my work.
    B: I'll have finished all my work.
4 A: I'll leave the key under the mat.
    B: I leave the key under the mat.
5 A: I'll have loved every minute of my holiday.
    B: I have loved every minute of my holiday.
6 A: We call you on your mobile.
    B: We'll call you on your mobile.

7 Recording 1
1 They're going to New York.
2 They'll be landing in about ten hours.

Track 🎧 2.15

1 FA: Good morning Ladies and Gentlemen. This
    is flight LH344 from Berlin to New York's
    John F Kennedy airport. We'll be taking off
    shortly, so please fasten your seatbelts…
2 FA: We'll be flying at a speed of 885 kilometres
    per hour and at a height of over ten thousand
    metres. We'll be landing in New York in about
    ten hours so sit back and enjoy the flight.
3 FA: In a few minutes our staff will be serving
    a hot lunch. After lunch we'll be starting
    our duty free service when we'll be selling
    perfumes and other gift items.

Recording 2
1 They'll be in Darwin.
2 They'll have travelled more than 2,000 miles.

Unit 61

1
1 can't afford to go out
2 expect to see you soon
3 appear to be chasing someone
4 seem to be falling in love
5 aim to be finished by Tuesday
6 hope to have agreed by morning
7 decided not to come
8 expected not to pass the exam
9 Malcolm to sing at your party
10 'd like everyone to help us

2
1 to meet
2 to risk
3 not to win
4 to go up
5 to be working
6 to have become
7 not to understand
8 to fish

3
1 to watch
2 to be breaking
3 to have lost
4 to give
5 chose not to come
6 to pay

4
1 I'm sorry to have woken you up.
2 to have a meeting
3 to concentrate
4 Tell Jack to help
5 not to see
6 to be leaving school

Unit 62

1
1 enjoys playing
2 start working
3 apologize for being
4 worry about cooking
5 prevent burglars breaking
6 mind you staying
7 can't help thinking

2
1 taking
2 doing
3 to be
4 studying
5 to answer
6 making
7 to try
8 asking
9 to show

3
1 reading / to read
2 taking
3 to like
4 collecting / to collect
5 asking / to ask
6 to see
7 to tidy
8 breaking / to break
9 waiting
10 studying / to study

4   Students' own answers

Unit 63

1
1 A: leaving / B: to do
2 A: to take / B: falling
3 A: to win / B: to tell
4 A: giving up / B: to be
5 A: hitting / B: to inform
6 A: to think / B: bothering
7 A: pressing / B: to learn

2 **Conversation 1**
1 remember to buy
2 forgot to bring
3 stop to get

Conversation 2
4 meant to leave
5 regretted leaving
6 went on to say
7 tried to be nice

3
1 went on to become
2 Stop worrying about
3 try opening
4 regret lying
5 remembered checking
6 meant having

Unit 64

1
1 Don't give them sweets
2 Lend me some money, please. / Please lend me some money.
3 Can you reserve me a seat?
4 Michael can send the email to you.
5 The waiter served us soup.
6 They're playing this song for you.
7 Describe their house to me.
8 Can you suggest something nice to eat?

2
1 Leave the dogs some water.
2 I'll give you this.
3 You owe your brother £1,000.
4 Order me a drink, please.
5 Please tell us the truth.
6 Every year he buys his wife a present.

3 1 us 2 the menu 3 me 4 the bill 5 a tip 6 him

Unit 65

1 1 C 2 A 3 D 4 G 5 B 6 F 7 E

2 1 to lose 2 ✓ 3 not to be 4 to cook 5 ✓ 6 to switch 7 to inform 8 to become 9 to her 10 ✓

3 1 to talk / talking 2 to talk 3 to me 4 doesn't appear / appears not 5 liking 6 saying 7 waiting 8 to study/studying 9 losing 10 to watch / watching

4
1 I hate watching
2 I meant to learn French
3 never forget meeting him
4 appears not to know / does not appear to know
5 stopped to talk to
6 Describe your journey to us.

5
1 don't mind living
2 owe him a lot
3 want to be
4 learnt to walk
5 dream of becoming
6 want to grow
7 pay you a thousand dollars
8 trying to find

6

Track ⊙**2.21**
1 A: I want to go home.
2 B: They promised not to be late.
3 A: Don't forget to write.
4 B: I regret doing things for money.
5 A: Leave something for the waiter.

7 1 False 2 True 3 False 4 False 5 True 6 True

Track ⊙**2.22**

Conversation 1
Shelley: Did you remember to buy more paint, Diego?
Diego: Yes I did. But I forgot to bring it with me. I can go back and get it now.
Shelley: It's OK. I think Marie is on her way here so she can stop to get some.

Conversation 2
Shelley: Hi Marie. It's Shelley. Are you on your way?
Marie: No, not yet. I meant to leave ages ago but my ex-boyfriend called round.
Shelley: Really? What did he want?
Marie: To say how much he regretted leaving me. He went on saying how sorry he was for over an hour!
Shelley: What happened?
Marie: Well I tried to be nice at first but it didn't help, so in the end I told him to go.

Unit 66

1
1 could
2 be able to
3 is able to
4 hasn't been able to
5 can't
6 be able to
7 could
8 be able to

2
1 weren't able to come
2 managed to find
3 will be able to buy
4 didn't succeed in visiting
5 wasn't able to finish
6 managed to catch

3
1 Can 2 could 3 couldn't 4 was able to
5 couldn't 6 can't

4
Students' own answers

Unit 67

1
1 can't 2 mustn't 3 must 4 have to 5 are
6 don't have to

2
1 had to 2 had to 3 weren't allowed
4 were allowed 5 couldn't 6 weren't allowed

3
1 need 2 needn't 3 needn't 4 didn't need

4
1 allow 2 make 3 let 4 lets 5 made

Unit 68

1
1 have forgotten
2 be
3 have slept
4 have got distracted
5 be doing
6 be looking

2
1 ~~mustn't~~ can't
2 ~~can~~ might
3 ~~may~~ can't
4 ~~might~~ must
5 ~~can't~~ might
6 ~~may~~ must

3
1 can't
2 might
3 mightn't
4 must
5 can't
6 might

4
Students' own answers

Unit 69

1
1 May I ask you a personal question, please?
2 Do you think you could possibly lend me some money?
3 Would you mind holding the door open for me?
4 Do you mind if I smoke?
5 Could you help me with my homework, please?
6 Would you mind if I left the room for a short while?

2
1 6 2 2 3 4 4 3 5 5 6 1

3
1 Let's
2 Shall
3 better
4 ought
5 Could
6 better
7 Shall
8 should
9 ought
10 Would
11 Let's

Unit 70

1
1 e 2 g 3 d 4 h 5 b 6 a 7 f 8 c

2
1 were finally able to
2 manage
3 mustn't
4 needn't have
5 didn't need to pay
6 makes us
7 might
8 must be
9 'd better not

3
1 succeeded in finding a cheaper flight
2 wasn't able to find her keys
3 must wear a helmet

4 let us stay up late
5 didn't need to bring food with us
6 can't bring our mobile phones
7 might be late
8 can't have written this letter
9 might be waiting for us
10 you think you could

4 1 been able 2 managed to 3 might be
4 let me 5 can't 6 should 7 ought to
8 must have 9 have to 10 better not
11 should 12 letting you

5

Track ⏺ **2.27**
1 A: He can't have meant what he said, surely?
2 B: They must have gone out somewhere.
3 A: You needn't have bought her a present.
4 B: We might have left it at home.
5 A: She may have left on an earlier train.

6 1 3 2 3 3 2 4 2 5 1

Track ⏺ **2.28**
1 A: I'm getting tired. Let's take a break. We could go out for lunch.
   B: OK. Shall we try that new sandwich bar?
   A: Yes, fine. We'd better be quick, though. We really ought to try and finish this work today.
2 A: Could you tell me the best way to get to the station?
   B: Well, you could get a number 27 bus. It leaves from the stop on the corner. When does your train leave?
   A: At 10.30. That's in 20 minutes.
   B: Hadn't you better get a taxi then? You don't want to miss it. Shall I call one for you?
3 A: What do you think I should do?
   B: I really don't know. It's a difficult situation. I think you really ought to talk to your boss about it. I mean she needs to know if someone's stealing from the company doesn't she?
   A: Would you mind coming with me? It'd make things easier.
   B: OK. Let's do it now then. No time like the present!

Unit 71

1 1 said 2 told 3 said 4 said 5 said 6 told

2 1 they
2 her
3 there
4 his … night before
5 she … next day

3 1 she was hungry
2 were riding their bikes to work that day
3 'm leaving my job
4 are going to be famous
5 he didn't live there any more
6 started my new job today

4 Students' own answers

Unit 72

1 1 were going
2 he wasn't coming
3 worked
4 could help
5 wanted
6 had to drive

2 1 couldn't
2 had always lived
3 disagreed
4 'd eat / got
5 was
6 hadn't seen
7 'd seen / would
8 couldn't

3 1 ~~was~~ → is
2 ✓
3 ~~have to~~ → had to
4 ~~he'll~~ → he'd
5 ✓
6 ✓
7 ~~crashes~~ → crashed

Unit 73

1 1 She asked me what my job was.
2 A man in the street asked people to give him some change.

3 The customs officer asked me what I was carrying in my bag.

4 My parents wanted to know where I had gone after school.

5 The neighbours asked us to turn our music down.

6 I asked if they'd like to come over to my house.

7 Jack asked me why he had to study maths.

8 The parking attendant told him to move his car.

2   1 What's your job?
  2 Will you give me some change, please?
  3 What are you carrying in your bag?
  4 Where did you go after school?
  5 Could you turn down your music, please?
  6 Would you like to come over to my house?
  7 Why do I have to study maths?
  8 Will you move your car, please?

3   1 to tell him about myself.
  2 what I had been doing since university.
  3 why I had left my last job.
  4 what my greatest strengths were.
  5 if I worked well with other people.
  6 how other people would describe me.
  7 if I was willing to travel.
  8 to give him one reason why he should choose me.
  9 what I would do if I did not get this position.
  10 what my current salary was.

Unit 74

1   1 suggested
  2 warned
  3 apologized
  4 admitted
  5 refused
  6 recommended
  7 accused
  8 encouraged

2   1 B 2 D 3 E 4 C 5 A

3   1 introducing
  2 English lessons would be
  3 that staff needed help
  4 that he was
  5 offering
  6 to consider

7 to find out
8 they would choose

Unit 75

1   1 told → said
  2 He asked me for my number.
  3 give → gave
  4 said → asked/told
  5 plans → planned
  6 She told to me
  7 me to come
  8 costs → cost
  9 convinced me
  10 make → making

2   1 offered / lend
  2 told / lock
  3 asked / had seen
  4 advises / run
  5 suggested / look
  6 know / built
  7 promised / be

3   1 'll lend
  2 lock the door / you leave
  3 Have you seen
  4 You ... run three kilometers
  5 you look it up
  6 did they build
  7 be home

4   1 said that
  2 tell me that
  3 –
  4 –
  5 Sarah that
  6 drivers that
  7 –
  8 bank that
  9 –

5   1 had been discussing
  2 had not come
  3 must expect
  4 would happen
  5 was going to happen
  6 it would
  7 their
  8 had

Answer key (and tapescript)

9 was growing
10 were living
11 she couldn't

6 1 staying 2 shop 3 today 4 walking

Track ⊘2.32
1 A: Bye. I'm going.
   B: Why? You said you were <u>staying</u>.
2 A: Jane works in a factory.
   B: Really? I thought she worked in a <u>shop</u>.
3 A: Let's look at the answers tomorrow.
   B: But you said we'd look at them <u>today</u>.
4 A: They're driving over now.
   B: Driving? I thought they were <u>walking</u>.

7 1 They would be useful for telephone calls from abroad
2 Because most of the clients were Spanish speakers.
3 They could offer lessons in both languages.
4 It might cost too much.
5 People could choose between English or Spanish lessons.

Track ⊘2.33
Mr Baldesi proposed introducing regular English lessons for everyone in the office.

Ms Song agreed that English lessons would be very useful for all those telephone calls from abroad. However Mr Webb disagreed that staff needed help with English because most of their clients are Spanish speakers.

Ms Song admitted that he was probably right. She suggested offering lessons in both languages. Mr Baldesi asked them to consider the cost of such a plan.

Mr Webb offered to find out which language people thought they needed most.

He explained that they would choose between English or Spanish lessons.

Unit 76

1 1 is currently being run
2 was completed
3 wasn't reached
4 were announced
5 was built
6 are still being added

2 7 has become
8 can even be seen
9 carry out
10 are regularly tested
11 has been continuously staffed
12 is being used
13 will affect

3 1 Your situation is currently being discussed
2 Every question had been answered by the class
3 ✗
4 Some medicine should be prescribed by the doctor
5 All those dresses might have been sold
6 The final decision will be made by the council at the next meeting

Unit 77

1 1 a man 2 a singer 3 an artist 4 a playwright 5 a clothes manufacturer 6 a pilot

2 1 was found by a woman on our street
2 was probably painted by da Vinci
3 was saved from drowning by this dog
4 was encouraged by my aunt to learn to play the piano

3 1 by 2 with 3 for 4 by 5 for 6 by

4 1 was left this painting by my grandfather
2 was lent enough money
3 been sent to us
4 are paid
5 are being told a scary story by their teacher

Unit 78

1 1 to be put
2 to be proved/ being proved
3 to be asked
4 being left
5 to be shocked
6 being seen
7 not being chosen
8 to be delayed/ being delayed
9 to be cheered

2 1 C 2 B 3 E 4 D 5 F 6 A

3 1 the robbery happened at three in the morning
2 thought that the robbers dug a tunnel underneath the road

3 claimed that it goes right into the bank vault
4 been seen
5 rumoured to have stolen up to a million pounds

4 **1** it was criticised
2 It was claimed
3 known to have convinced
4 were expected to reward
5 avoided being killed
6 is believed to be

Unit 79

1 **1** to choose **2** fetch **3** done **4** to come
5 walked **6** brought **7** to fly **8** remove

2 **1** ~~was~~ → got   **2** ~~was given~~ → got
3 ~~was~~ → got   **4** –
5 ~~were~~ → got   **6** –

3 **1** The boy's hair needs cutting.
2 The bike needs mending.
3 The chair needs fixing.
4 The bills need paying.

4 **1** needs fixing
2 had it looked at
3 got dropped
4 needs replacing
5 have the whole thing sent

Unit 80

1 **1** ~~complete~~ → completed **2** ~~been~~ → being
3 ~~being~~ → be   **4** ~~be~~
5 ~~to~~   **6** ~~with~~ → by
7 ~~to~~ → with
8 ~~searching~~ → to be searched

2 **1** was sung to me by my mother
2 is being delivered before noon
3 was occupied by Charles Dickens, the famous writer,
4 my heating fixed by the engineer
5 was taught to me by a real magician
6 can be attacked by sharks
7 to have fallen last night

3 **1** got **2** had **3** to **4** by **5** by **6** to **7** for
8 had **9** with **10** to **11** for **12** by **13** by

4 **1** is believed
2 are approached
3 can still be done
4 be followed
5 is mainly influenced
6 updated
7 seen to be
8 known
9 is often thought
10 promoted
11 is given to
12 is shared

5 **1** said **2** thought **3** believed **4** known **5** reported

1 A: It's <u>said</u> that the machine is the largest in the world.
2 B: It's <u>thought</u> that it'll be completed next year.
3 A: It was <u>believed</u> that it would be finished by now.
4 B: It's <u>known</u> that they've had some problems with it.
5 A: It's been <u>reported</u> that they've made a new discovery.

6 **1** The main structure was completed.
2 An agreement for a joint space station was reached.
3 Final plans were announced.
4 Components are still being added.

The International Space Station (ISS) is currently being run as a joint project between five space agencies. The main structure was completed in 1998, but the idea for cooperation in space began at the end of the Cold War. An agreement for a joint space programme between the USA and Russia wasn't reached until 1992 and final plans for a new space station were announced a year later. Unlike previous space ships and satellites, the ISS was built in space while in orbit. In fact, components are still being added today.

Unit 81

1 **1** My neighbour is the person who called the police.
2 These are the books which are for my course.
3 This is the car which is for sale.
4 Those are the same boys who smashed our window.
5 That's the actor who I saw in a film last week.

2a 1 S 2 S 3 S 4 S 5 O

2b 1 ✗ 2 ✓ 3 ✓ 4 ✗ 5 ✓

3 1 's wearing a red and white jumper
2 who's got long, dark hair
3 which has a rip
4 that's got a collar

4 Students' own answers

Unit 82

1 1 who broke into an office block D
2 who had taken two laptop computers N-D
3 which was only five minutes from the office block N-D
4 that came from the inside of the fridge D
5 which was only a meter high N-D
6 who had been in the fridge for over two hours N-D
7 which had been stolen D

2 1 Burj Kalifa, which was completed in 2010, is the tallest building in the world.
2 Coca Cola, which is also called Coke, is sold in over 200 countries.
3 Barack Obama, who was born in Hawaii, is the 44th President of the USA.
4 The moon, which has water under its surface, might be a future home for humans.

3a 1 ~~who~~ → that
2 ✓
3 ~~which~~ → that
4 ~~who~~ → that

3b 1 ~~which~~ 2 ✗ 3 ✗ 4 ~~who~~ 5 ✗ 6 ~~that~~

Unit 83

1 1 D 2 B 3 E 4 C 5 A

2 1 which 2 whose 3 who 4 who 5 why 6 when
7 where

3a 1 of whom you've probably heard
2 at which water starts to freeze
3 about whom magazine articles are still published
4 on which many famous people have performed
5 in whom I had absolute trust

3b 1 for which Stonehenge is well known
2 in which many Kings and Queens were imprisoned
3 on which Arthur built his castle

Unit 84

1 1 driving 2 working 3 waiting 4 sent 5 left
6 put 7 living 8 bought 9 returned 10 providing

2 1 stolen had 2 demanding 3 needing
4 delivered 5 specialising 6 born

3 1 ~~who are travelling~~ → travelling
~~which departs from~~ → departing from
2 ~~who are waiting~~ → waiting
3 ~~that enters~~ → entering
~~which is carried~~ → carried
4 ~~who is caught~~ → caught
5 ~~which are switched on~~ → switched on

Unit 85

1 1 ~~her~~
2 ~~sell~~ → sells
3 [remove comma]
4 … singer from Wales who has a …
5 ~~that is~~
6 ~~has been~~ → who has been
7 … Britain, which …
8 ~~sending~~ → sent
9 ~~at when~~ → at which
10 ~~in that~~ → in which

2 1 ~~who~~
2 ~~that~~
3 ~~which~~
4 ~~who is~~
5 ~~which is~~

3 1 that 2 whom 3 why 4 in which 5 when

4 1 whom we were informed
2 which the King
3 is dealing with your complaint
4 is answered

5 1 which is valued/valued
2 where it was appearing
3 who are involved/involved
4 which
5 why

6 which/that
7 which has been seen
8 who
9 when
10 whose

6
1 who is often called the greatest artist of all time
2 , which is near the city of Florence
3 when many artists and architects worked for rich patrons
4 , whose workshop was known as one of the finest in Florence
5 , which was paid for by his father,
6 , where he painted one of his most famous paintings, *The Last Supper*
7 , for which he is probably most famous,
8 , which are shown around the world
9 , which in some cases were made and used to defend cities
10 , of which many still survive today,
11 why so much of his work is still admired by so many

7
1 Johnny Depp, who is probably my favourite actor, has another film coming out.
2 Your assistant, who I also mentioned last week, is always rude on the phone.
3 The Nestlé company, which is a multinational, is based in Switzerland.
4 I'll try the strawberry ice cream, which looks delicious.

Track ⊘2.43
A: Johnny Depp, who is probably my favourite actor, has another film coming out.
B: Your assistant, who I also mentioned last week, is always rude on the phone.
A: The Nestlé company, which is a multinational, is based in Switzerland.
B: I'll try the strawberry ice cream, which looks delicious.

8
1 she hasn't seen for years
2 son was her grandfather
3 asked her to marry him
4 they didn't get married
5 the second world war was just starting
6 they probably said goodbye for the last time

Track ⊘2.44
A: Wow! Here's a photograph which I haven't seen for years.
B: Who is it?
A: It's my great-grandmother whose son was my grandfather.
This is her with the man who asked her to marry him.
B: You mean your great-grandfather.
A: No. Before that, there was someone else that asked her to marry him, before the war.
B: What happened?
A: She never told me the reason why they didn't get married, but this photo was taken in 1939 when the Second World War was just starting so I assume he never came back. I think this photo was taken at the place where they probably said goodbye for the last time.

Unit 86

1 1 E 2 A 3 G 4 F 5 B 6 D 7 C

2
1 're going can
2 don't won't
3 're seeing can
4 you want
5 won't don't
6 you need

3 1 when 2 – 3 – 4 when 5 when 6 –

4 Students' own answers.

Unit 87

1 1 might / would 2 wouldn't 3 could 4 couldn't
5 wouldn't 6 would 7 were 8 gave

2
1 I gave → I'd give
2 I'd be → were
3 I leave → I would leave
4 would give → gave
5 didn't → wouldn't
6 I tried → I'd try

3 1 had it 2 'd bring 3 would you do 4 were
5 'd accept 6 offered 7 knew 8 was 9 'd be

4 Students' own answers

Unit 88

1 1 arrived / have
2 hadn't / have called
3 wouldn't have / hadn't
4 have found out / hadn't
5 could have / tried
6 wanted / have found

2 1 wouldn't have been / if he had done his homework
2 hadn't gone to bed / wouldn't be
3 had told me it was / would have brought
4 wouldn't have passed / you hadn't helped
5 would have said / I had seen
6 had been / would have missed

3 1 should have
2 would have
3 might have
4 wouldn't have
5 shouldn't have
6 could have

4 1 were
2 didn't I see you
3 had looked
4 would have seen
5 didn't wave
6 was
7 had sent
8 could have gone

Unit 89

1 1 D 2 C 3 B 4 A

2 1 would 2 might 3 could have done 4 could
5 might 6 might

3 1 wasn't/weren't / would have got
2 would have applied / could speak
3 had / would have given
4 hadn't passed / would still be using
5 had gone / wouldn't be feeling
6 had listened / wouldn't be

4 Students' own answers

Unit 90

1a 1 , if I were you.
2 If I get home early enough,
3 if I'd had
4 If you were so sure about the answer,
5 If you want to bring a pet with you,
6 if you're going

1b 6

2 1 E/H 2 A/D 3 B/G 4 C/F

3 1 a: needed   b: need
   c: needed   d: had needed
2 a: were   b: are
   c: had been   d: were
3 a: won   b: win
   c: had won   d: won

4 1 want
2 hadn't wasted
3 'd have finished
4 asked
5 'd give
6 said
7 want
8 succeed
9 I'll buy
10 give

5 1 f 2 h 3 e 4 c 5 j 6 b 7 a 8 g 9 d 10 i

6 1 would 2 had would 3 would 4 had 5 would had

Track 2.48
1 A: If I had more money, I wouldn't need to work so hard.
2 B: If I'd known, I'd have said something.
3 A: If he had any sense, he'd have apologised to her immediately.
4 B: If she'd really felt that offended, she should have said something.
5 A: I'd have thought twice about accepting the job if it'd been me.

7 1 Yes
2 No
3 He didn't have any credit on his phone.
4 Because he had to go home early.

A: You missed a good concert last night. You really
   should have been there.
B: But I was!
A: If you were there, why didn't I see you?
B: I was in the gallery. It you had looked up, you
   would have seen me, I waved at you, but you
   didn't wave back.
A: If I didn't wave back, it was because I couldn't see
   you! Why didn't you text me or something? If you
   had sent me a text, we could have gone out for a
   drink or something.
B: I tried, but I didn't have any credit on my phone.
   And anyway, I had to go home early.

Unit 91

1 1 knew 2 could 3 were coming 4 'd stayed
    5 could have 6 wouldn't say

2 1 could read 2 had brought 3 wasn't 4 wouldn't
    bite 5 wasn't going 6 had

3 Students' own answers

Unit 92

1 1 Unless
    2 as long as
    3 as long as
    4 unless
    5 unless
    6 as long as

2 1 I'll get the bus unless Glen can take me in the car.
    2 Provided you give me £5.00 I'll clean your car
      for you.
    3 We could go out to eat unless you prefer to stay
      at home and order a takeaway.
    4 You can come in as long as you leave before my
      parents get back.
    5 I really didn't want to do it unless Simon helped me.

3 1 Had I known…
    2 Were he to…
    3 Were I to lose…
    4 Had we got here…
    5 Had I never met…
    6 Were we to start…

Unit 93

1 1 Although he fell once or twice before reaching
      the finishing line, he still completed the course.
    2 We really enjoyed our holidays despite the awful
      weather.
    3 I felt really tired the next morning even though
      I'd had a good night's sleep.
    4 In spite of the fact that more than half the
      runners didn't actually complete the race, it was
      still a huge success.
    5 Although the job is well paid, it's not
      particularly challenging.
    6 Despite all the talk of reform and
      modernisation, nothing has really changed.

2 1 despite
    2 even though
    3 Despite
    4 despite

3 1 Despite having worked together for more than
      five years, I don't really know him that well.
    2 Although we live near the coast, we hardly ever
      go to the beach.
    3 He still loves her in spite of the fact that they
      have a lot of problems.
    4 We had a great time last night even though the
      concert was cancelled. / Even though the concert
      was cancelled, we had a great time last night.
    5 Despite having worked really hard, he failed all
      his exams.

Unit 94

1 1 a 2 a 3 b 4 b 5 b 6 b 7 b 8 b

2 1 in order to
    2 so that
    3 because
    4 because of
    5 sickness among the staff

3 1 In order to learn to speak Chinese, I signed up
      for an intensive course.
    2 I didn't go out last night as I was feeling really tired.
    3 Due to heavy rain last night, some roads are
      closed to traffic./Some roads are closed to traffic
      due to heavy rain last night.
    4 He bought her some flowers so as to show her
      he still loved her.

5 I didn't buy you a ticket for the match since you don't really like football./Since you don't really like football, I didn't buy you a ticket for the match.
6 Many small businesses will close because of a new law that has been passed./Because of a new law that has been passed, many new businesses will close.
7 In order that more children have access to education, one hundred new schools have been built.
8 My brother has offered to babysit so we can go out tonight.

Unit 95

1 1 A 2 G 3 F 4 D 5 B 6 H 7 C 8 E

2
1 ~~have~~ → had
2 ~~weren't going~~ → hadn't gone
3 ~~win~~ → to win
4 ~~don't come~~ → come
5 ~~you'll~~ → you
6 ~~despite of~~ → despite
7 ~~so as~~ → so
8 ~~there's~~

3
1 In order to
2 if only
3 unless
4 as long as
5 despite
6 wish

4
1 I could go
2 only I hadn't forgotten
3 the lovely weather / having lovely weather
4 you book
5 the wind was

5 1 although 2 despite 3 were you 4 'd studied 5 I'd 6 Even though 7 in order not to 8 so that

6

Track 2.53
1 A: You can come with‿us, as long‿as you behave.
2 B: We couldn't go out because‿of the snow.
3 A: We managed to arrive‿on time in spite‿of the delays.
4 B: I bought‿a bike in‿order to cycle to work.
5 A: If‿only I hadn't had that last chocolate.

7
1 T
2 F. They had been given repeated warnings.
3 T
4 F. The referendum has been ruled out.

Track 2.54
A: Surprise victory for City
Fans were celebrating last night after City beat United 4-0 despite missing some of their key players.
B: Family caught in summer storm
A family of five were rescued by coastguards yesterday off the coast of Pembroke. The Davis family had insisted on taking their boat out, even though they had been given repeated warnings about the possibility of a summer storm.
C: Election results questioned amid fears of corruption
Despite the fact that the election met all legal and democratic requirements, the main opposition party has called for an international enquiry.
D: Referendum ruled out
The government has confirmed that it will not hold a referendum despite strong popular support.

Unit 96

1
1 does look / you did make
2 do seem / do hope

2
1 Do tidy up your bedroom
2 Do look where you're going
3 Do slow down
4 Do turn the TV down

3
1 I did say something
2 I do love
3 He does eat
4 she did try
5 does work
6 did remind you

Unit 97

1 1 B 2 E 3 A 4 D 5 C

2
1 is the French fries
2 do is sign your name here and here

3 to do is to wear a uniform
4 was that there was a sudden crash
5 's their teacher they need to tell,
6 is the facts I want to hear,
7 in this movie is
8 is the manager
9 is because I'd like to get

3   1 What Martin builds are aeroplanes.
    2 What you do is put it in the fridge.
    3 What happened was they took the wrong bus.
    4 It's a plumber we need to call.
    5 The good thing about museums in London is
      that they're free.
    6 The person we need to call is a mechanic.

Unit 98

1   1 when 2 Rarely 3 Not 4 No 5 only 6 Never
    7 No 8 Not

2   1 way was I going to
    2 had they seen anything
    3 sooner had they split up than
    4 had we set off
    5 only did she win
    6 after years of hard work did Rachel qualify

3   1 have I tasted anything so disgusting
    2 had we started class when the fire alarm rang
    3 does it rain at this time of year
    4 do my parents want to go on a cruise again
    5 often do you see Michaela work that hard
    6 are we working for less money
    7 has there been an Olympic gold medallist from
      our country

4   Students' own answers

Unit 99

1   1 such 2 nor 3 So

2   1 C 2 A 3 E 4 B 5 D

3   1 So enjoyable was the roller coaster that they
      went on it again
    2 is his generosity that he gives to many charities
    3 beat him at chess and neither could you beat
      him at backgammon
    4 pay to get in and nor did she

4   1 So powerful is
    2 neither did I
    3 Such skill had the winning team
    4 nor did I

Unit 100

1   1 did 2 does 3 What 4 The thing / What
    5 No sooner 6 have I 7 neither / nor 8 Such

2   1 looks → look
    2 said → say
    3 you were → were you
    4 not → no
    5 such → so
    6 mine will → will mine

3   1 does know
    2 kindness
    3 tasty
    4 did she enjoy
    5 has Sandra smiled
    6 to learn
    7 am I going to

4   1 The boy did try harder at school.
    2 It's the excitement of sport that I enjoy.
    3 The thing to do is to log in using your user
      name and password.
    4 The reason they go hang gliding is for the thrill.
    5 I didn't get the job and neither did he.
    6 What really annoys me is when people don't tell
      the truth.
    7 No way are they going to pay £100 for a ticket.
    8 Antonia does work hard when she puts her
      mind to it.

5   1 B 2 A 3 B 4 C 5 B 6 A 7 A 8 C

6   1 do 2 did 3 not 4 Such 5 not 6 Never

Track 🅟2.58
1   A: You do look ill.
2   B: The whole story did happen.
3   A: I did not take your pen.
4   B: Such was the noise that we called the police.
5   A: We are not late.
6   B: Never have I been so scared.

7 1 does 2 did 3 do 4 does

Track 2.59

Conversation 1
A: That cake does look delicious. Can I try some?
B: No, it's for later.
A: But you did make it for my birthday.
B: Yes, but everyone is coming later. So, wait!

Conversation 2
A: Why are Gretel and Colin smiling?
B: I don't know, but they do seem very happy.
A: Maybe they have some good news for us.
B: Oh! I do hope you're right.

Progress test 1

1 b 2 c 3 c 4 c 5 b 6 a 7 c 8 b 9 a 10 b 11 c
12 b 13 b 14 c 15 a 16 a 17 a 18 b 19 a 20 c
21 c 22 a 23 b 24 b 25 c 26 b 27 c 28 a 29 a
30 c 31 b 32 b 33 a 34 b 35 c 36 a 37 c 38 a
39 b 40 a 41 b 42 a 43 c 44 c 45 c 46 b 47 b
48 b 49 c 50 a

Progress test 2

1 a 2 c 3 b 4 c 5 c 6 a 7 c 8 c 9 a 10 c 11 c
12 c 13 a 14 b 15 c 16 a 17 b 18 c 19 a 20 a 21 c
22 c 23 b 24 c 25 a 26 c 27 c 28 c 29 b 30 c 31 a
32 c 33 a 34 a 35 c 36 a 37 c 38 b 39 c 40 a 41 a
42 a 43 a 44 c 45 c 46 a 47 a 48 c 49 c 50 b

Progress test 3

1 b 2 b 3 c 4 a 5 b 6 a 7 b 8 c 9 b 10 a 11 b 12 c
13 b 14 b 15 a 16 a 17 a 18 a 19 c 20 a 21 c 22 c
23 a 24 a 25 b 26 b 27 c 28 a 29 b 30 b 31 b
32 c 33 b 34 a 35 a 36 c 37 c 38 b 39 a 40 b 41 c
42 a 43 c 44 c 45 a 46 b 47 c 48 b 49 a 50 c

Progress test 4

1 a 2 c 3 b 4 b 5 a 6 b 7 b 8 a 9 a 10 b 11 c
12 c 13 b 14 a 15 a 16 c 17 a 18 c 19 a 20 a 21 b
22 b 23 a 24 b 25 a 26 c 27 c 28 a 29 b 30 a
31 b 32 c 33 b 34 b 35 b 36 a 37 c 38 b 39 b
40 c 41 c 42 b 43 b 44 a 45 c 46 a 47 a 48 a
49 b 50 c

Progress test 5

1 c 2 a 3 b 4 a 5 c 6 c 7 c 8 a 9 b 10 a 11 b 12 c
13 a 14 b 15 a 16 a 17 c 18 a 19 c 20 b 21 b 22 b
23 c 24 b 25 b 26 a 27 c 28 b 29 b 30 b 31 a
32 c 33 c 34 b 35 b 36 c 37 a 38 c 39 b 40 c
41 b 42 c 43 a 44 b 45 c 46 a 47 b 48 c 49 c
50 a

Progress test 6

1 c 2 b 3 c 4 a 5 b 6 a 7 c 8 b 9 c 10 a 11 c
12 c 13 b 14 c 15 a 16 c 17 c 18 c 19 a 20 c 21 c
22 b 23 c 24 c 25 b 26 b 27 c 28 c 29 a 30 b
31 b 32 c 33 a 34 c 35 c 36 a 37 b 38 b 39 c
40 a 41 b 42 c 43 c 44 b 45 b 46 c 47 c 48 a
49 b 50 a

Progress test 7

1 b 2 c 3 b 4 b 5 a 6 b 7 c 8 b 9 b 10 c 11 c
12 a 13 c 14 a 15 b 16 a 17 b 18 a 19 a 20 b 21 a
22 c 23 c 24 c 25 a 26 a 27 b 28 a 29 c 30 c 31 c
32 b 33 b 34 b 35 a 36 c 37 b 38 b 39 a 40 a
41 a 42 c 43 c 44 b 45 b 46 a 47 b 48 c 49 c 50 a

Progress test 8

1 c 2 b 3 a 4 b 5 b 6 a 7 a 8 c 9 b 10 c 11 b
12 b 13 a 14 a 15 b 16 c 17 a 18 c 19 c 20 a 21 a
22 c 23 c 24 c 25 c 26 a 27 a 28 a 29 a 30 c 31 b
32 c 33 a 34 a 35 c 36 c 37 a 38 c 39 a 40 b 41 c
42 b 43 c 44 c 45 b 46 c 47 a 48 b 49 c 50 c

Progress test 9

1 b 2 a 3 a 4 b 5 a 6 c 7 a 8 b 9 c 10 c 11 c
12 b 13 c 14 a 15 c 16 c 17 b 18 c 19 c 20 a 21 c
22 c 23 c 24 b 25 a 26 b 27 a 28 a 29 b 30 c
31 c 32 a 33 b 34 b 35 a 36 b 37 a 38 a 39 c
40 c 41 c 42 a 43 c 44 c 45 c 46 a 47 b 48 b
49 c 50 a

Progress test 10

1 c 2 b 3 c 4 a 5 b 6 c 7 b 8 c 9 a 10 c 11 c
12 a 13 c 14 c 15 b 16 c 17 a 18 b 19 a 20 b 21 c
22 c 23 c 24 c 25 a 26 a 27 b 28 b 29 c 30 b 31 a
32 b 33 c 34 b 35 a 36 a 37 c 38 a 39 c 40 c
41 a 42 c 43 b 44 a 45 c 46 b 47 a 48 a 49 c 50 c

Index

Note: The numbers in this index are page numbers. Key vocabulary is in *italic*.

Index

Index

Index

Notes

Notes

Text credits

pp 51 *The man with the twisted lip,* Sir Arthur Conan Doyle/Penguin Books, 1995; 56 © The J.R.R. Tolkien Copyright Trust 1937, 1951, 1966, 1978, 1995; 57 © Henrik Ibsen, *A Doll's House* and Methuen Drama, an imprint of A&C Black Publishers Ltd.; 66 Aliette Frank/National Geographic News, May 1, 2001; 101 "Health tip of the week" © *The Week* Issue 741, 14th November 2009/ Dennis Publishing Ltd.; 111 *Around the World in Eighty Days,* Jules Verne/Penguin Books, 1973

Photo credits

The publishers would like to thank the following sources for permission to reproduce their copyright protected photographs:

Cover image: Shutterstock Inc.

pp 22 (Shutterstock.com/Armin Rose), 23 (Simon Reeve), 32 (blickwinkel/Alamy), 42 (istockphoto.com), 46 (Simon Jarratt/Corbis), 50 (Mary Evans Picture Library), 54 (Shutterstock.com), 57 (Sean Gladwell/Shutterstock.com), 58 (North Wind Picture Archives/Alamy), 59 (Pictorial Press Ltd/Alamy), 60a (Tatiana Grozetskaya/Shutterstock.com), 60b (Lena Grottling/Shutterstock.com), 60c (Graeme Shannon/Shutterstock.com), 60d (ErikN/Shutterstock.com), 60e (hainaultphoto/shutterstock.com), 60f (Shutterstock.com), 64 (Ray Tang/Rex Features), 65 (John Todd/internationalsportsimages.com/Corbis), 66 (Shutterstock.com), 68 (Johner Images/Alamy), 70 (Peter Clark/Shutterstock.com), 72a (Elfired/Shutterstock.com), 72b (John Montana/Getty Images), 74, 75a, 75b (CSA Images/Snapstock), 81a,b,c,d (Ronald Grant Archive), 87 (aldegonde/Shutterstock.com), 88 (Krishna.Wu/Shutterstock.com), 91 (olly/Shutterstock.com), 95 (Getty Images), 96 (Yenyu Shih/Shutterstock.com), 97a (Shutterstock.com), 97b (Dainis Derics/Shutterstock.com), 97c (S.Borisov/Shutterstock.com), 98 (Hugh Threlfall/Alamy), 101 (Blend Images/Alamy), 102 (Monkey Business/Shutterstock.com), 105 (Shutterstock.com), 106 (Alamy), 109, (Sarah Quill/Alamy), 114 (Chris Lewington/Alamy), 123 (Getty Images), 125 (Boris Karpinski/Alamy), 136 (Wire Image/Getty), 141 (Keystone/Getty) 142 (Lazyfruit/Alamy), 145 (Yobidaba/Shutterstock.com), 151 (Masterfile), 154a (picsfive/Shutterstock.com), 154b (withGod/Shutterstock.com), 154c (Alamy), 161 (Cultura/Alamy), 162 (Rex Features), 163 (Rex Features), 164 (Peter Betts/Shutterstock.com), 167a (Horizon International Images Limited/Alamy), 167b (Getty Images), 171 (Paul Hardy/Corbis), 180 (Getty Images), 181 (Hulton Archive), 183 (sciencephotos/Alamy), 191 (S1001/Shutterstock.com), 196 (Adrian Muttitt/Alamy), 198 (Getty Images), 206 (LOOK Die Bildagentur der Fotografen GmbH/Alamy), 211 (Bernhard Classen/Alamy)

Illustrations by artists at KJA-artists.com:

Adrian@KJA-artists.com: pp 12, 14 ,28, 38, 77, 84, 116, 118, 119, 122, 156, 173, 202; John@KJA-artists.com: 24, 27, 34, 56b, 76, 82, 83, 94, 95, 101, 111, 115, 124, 134, 139, 148, 168, 178c, 182, 184, 185, 208, 209, Kath@KJA-artists.com: 26, 36a-b, 39a-c, 78, 146, 149, 172, 192; Sean@KJA-artists.com: 15a-f, 19a-d, 25a-f, 29a-f, 55a-f, 67a-f, 73a-d, 89a-h, 108b,c,d, 108a-c, 169a-d

Illustrations by Kate Charlesworth: pp 31, 35, 44a-c, 52, 62, 86, 99, 113, 144, 147, 158, 175, 188, 204

Illustrations by Jorge Santillan: pp 16, 21, 48, 70b, 83a-d, 104, 112, 113, 117, 128, 138, 165a-d, 169, 170, 176, 186, 193a-f, 203a-d

Illustrations by Mark Draisey: pp 132, 151, 201

Illustrations by Nigel Jones: pp 13, 18, 30, 31, 32, 34, 41, 43, 44, 50, 56a, 58, 59, 61, 64, 65, 66, 68, 70, 72, 74, 75, 76, 81, 87, 88, 89, 91, 92, 94, 96, 98, 100, 101, 102, 104, 105, 106, 108, 111, 121, 126, 131, 134, 136, 138, 141, 142, 145, 151, 157, 161a-b, 162, 163, 164, 166, 167a-b, 169, 174, 175, 176, 178, 181a-b, 191, 194, 197, 201, 206, 208, 209, 211

CD Track List

CD 1

Unit and Exercise	Track	Unit and Exercise	Track	Unit and Exercise	Track
Unit 1, Ex 2	1.02	Unit 19, Ex 2	1.20	Unit 35, Review, Ex 8	1.38
Unit 2, Ex 2	1.03	Unit 20, Review, Ex 5	1.21	Unit 36, Ex 1	1.39
Unit 3, Ex 2	1.04	Unit 20, Review, Ex 6	1.22	Unit 37, Ex 2	1.40
Unit 5, Review, Ex 5	1.05	Unit 20, Review, Ex 7	1.23	Unit 39, Ex 2	1.41
Unit 5, Review, Ex 6	1.06	Unit 21, Ex 3	1.24	Unit 40, Review Ex 6	1.42
Unit 6, Ex 3	1.07	Unit 23, Ex 2	1.25	Unit 40, Review Ex 7	1.43
Unit 6, Ex 4	1.08	Unit 24, Ex 1	1.26	Unit 41, Ex 1	1.44
Unit 7, Ex 4	1.09	Unit 25, Review, Ex 5	1.27	Unit 42, Ex 1	1.45
Unit 8, Ex 3	1.10	Unit 25, Review, Ex 6	1.28	Unit 43, Ex 1	1.46
Unit 9, Ex 4	1.11	Unit 25, Review, Ex 7	1.29	Unit 44, Ex 1	1.47
Unit 10, Review, Ex 6	1.12	Unit 26, Ex 1	1.30	Unit 45, Review, Ex 6	1.48
Unit 10, Review, Ex 7	1.13	Unit 27, Ex 3	1.31	Unit 45, Review, Ex 7	1.49
Unit 13, Ex 3	1.14	Unit 30, Review, Ex 5	1.32	Unit 46, Ex 2	1.50
Unit 14, Ex 3	1.15	Unit 30, Review, Ex 6	1.33	Unit 47, Ex 3	1.51
Unit 15, Review, Ex 6	1.16	Unit 31, Ex 2	1.34	Unit 50, Review, Ex 5	1.52
Unit 15, Review, Ex 7	1.17	Unit 32, Ex 1	1.35	Unit 50, Review, Ex 6	1.53
Unit 16, Ex 3	1.18	Unit 34, Ex 3	1.36	Unit 50, Review, Ex 7	1.54
Unit 18, Ex 1	1.19	Unit 35, Review, Ex 7	1.37		

CD 2

Unit and Exercise	Track	Unit and Exercise	Track	Unit and Exercise	Track
Unit 51, Ex 2	2.02	Unit 65, Review, Ex 7	2.22	Unit 84, Ex 3	2.42
Unit 53, Ex 1	2.03	Unit 67, Ex 2	2.23	Unit 85, Review, Ex 7	2.43
Unit 54, Ex 1	2.04	Unit 68, Ex 1	2.24	Unit 85, Review, Ex 8	2.44
Unit 55, Review, Ex 6	2.05	Unit 68, Ex 2	2.25	Unit 87, Ex 3	2.45
Unit 55, Review, Ex 7	2.06	Unit 69, Ex 3	2.26	Unit 88, Ex 4	2.46
Unit 55, Review, Ex 8	2.07	Unit 70, Review, Ex 5	2.27	Unit 90, Review, Ex 5	2.47
Unit 56, Ex 2	2.08	Unit 70, Review, Ex 6	2.28	Unit 90, Review, Ex 6	2.48
Unit 57, Ex 1a	2.09	Unit 72, Ex 1	2.29	Unit 90, Review, Ex 7	2.49
Unit 57, Ex 1b	2.10	Unit 73, Ex 2	2.30	Unit 91, Ex 2	2.50
Unit 57, Ex 1c	2.11	Unit 74, Ex 3	2.31	Unit 92, Ex 1	2.51
Unit 58, Ex 2	2.12	Unit 75, Review, Ex 6	2.32	Unit 93, Ex 2	2.52
Unit 59, Ex 1	2.13	Unit 75, Review, Ex 7	2.33	Unit 95, Review, Ex 6	2.53
Unit 60, Review, Ex 6	2.14	Unit 76, Ex 1	2.34	Unit 95, Review, Ex 7	2.54
Unit 60, Review, Ex 7 (1)	2.15	Unit 76, Ex 2	2.35	Unit 96, Ex 1	2.55
Unit 60, Review, Ex 7 (2)	2.16	Unit 78, Ex 3	2.36	Unit 96, Ex 3	2.56
Unit 60, Review, Ex 7 (3)	2.17	Unit 79, Ex 4	2.37	Unit 97, Ex 3	2.57
Unit 62, Ex 2	2.18	Unit 80, Review, Ex 5	2.38	Unit 100, Review, Ex 6	2.58
Unit 63, Ex 2	2.19	Unit 80, Review, Ex 6	2.39	Unit 100, Review, Ex 7	2.59
Unit 64, Ex 3	2.20	Unit 81, Ex 3	2.40		
Unit 65, Review, Ex 6	2.21	Unit 83, Ex 2	2.41		